U0085029

序 言

剛升上高三的同學，正踏入最混亂的時期。首先要面對的，就是暑假結束後，緊接而來的「學科能力測驗」模擬考。這對高三生來說，是非常重要的轉捩點，因為模擬考便是仿照實際「大學入學學科能力測驗」命題，為了要讓同學提早了解並適應實際的學科能力測驗。

高三生活分秒必爭，目標就是要在「學科能力測驗」和「指定科目考試」中拿高分。在這麼重要的時刻，要用最有效率的方式來規劃時間。首先，要把高三新課程學好；第二，要把握每一次的模擬考試，模擬考試可以讓你知道自己目前的程度在哪裡，是很好的參考標準。

練習愈多，分數愈高

即使時間很緊迫，模擬考前也一定要有所準備，絕不能隨便應考。考前雖然沒有時間複習每一冊課本，一定要把「學測英文模擬試題」拿出來練習做，做題目能讓你馬上知道自己不會的地方。你一定要先做題目，再對答案，然後仔細研究詳解，把不會的地方確實弄懂。考試最忌諱兩件事，一是沒準備，二是一錯再錯。只要你能善用這本書，你就會考高分。

「學測英文模擬試題」中所有的考題，都是萬中選一，都是最有練習價值的題目，而且出題方式完全仿照「大學入學學科能力測驗」，讓同學一邊練習，一邊複習，一邊習慣學測的題型，一舉三得。本書在編審及校對的每一階段，均力求完善，但恐有疏漏之處，誠盼各界先進不吝批評指正。

編者 謹識

CONTENTS

大學入學學科能力測驗英文模擬試題 ①

第壹部分：單選題 (佔 72 分)

一、詞彙 (佔 15 分)

說明：第 1 題至第 15 題，每題 4 個選項，其中只有一個是最適當的答案，請畫記在答案卡之「選擇題答案區」。各題答對者，得 1 分；答錯、未作答或畫記多於一個選項者，該題以零分計算。

1. During the flood, people from the nearby villages rushed to the _____. But the fast flowing water prevented them from reaching the victims.
   (A) content   (B) creed   (C) rescue   (D) summit

2. If you stretched out all the toilet paper used in Europe in one year, it would _____ around the world 12,000 times.
   (A) fascinate   (B) travel   (C) shield   (D) splash

3. If you exercise outside in cold weather, dress to stay warm. How you dress can make the _____ between a comfortable workout and misery.
   (A) sorrow   (B) difference   (C) impression   (D) communism

4. Americans use more than 21 million tons of paper every year. If half of this were recycled paper, a forest larger than the state of Florida could be _____.
   (A) erased   (B) dedicated   (C) saved   (D) resolved

5. According to a recent study, the average cyclist _____ a risk on the sidewalk 1.8 times as great as his risk on the roadway.
   (A) imitates   (B) intimates   (C) injures   (D) incurs

6. Breathing deeply through your nose lets the tension drain from your muscles. Deep breathing, even for a minute, can relax you _____.
   (A) inaccurately   (B) intellectually   (C) passively   (D) significantly

7. Teta Beach is preferred by many Panamanian _____ enthusiasts for its excellent waves.

(A) diving   (B) surfing   (C) skiing   (D) cycling

8. Taking notes in class makes the student an active participant in the learning process rather than a(n) _____ listener or daydreamer.

(A) passive   (B) restorative   (C) informative   (D) protective

9. Although it is expensive, the food at the restaurant is so delicious that the _____ do not mind parting with their money.

(A) patrons   (B) candidates   (C) benefactors   (D) economists

10. Students should be encouraged to do their best, but not _____ to set goals too high or schedule too many activities.

(A) obtained   (B) inquired   (C) abolished   (D) pressured

11. Three _____ made by the Japanese government found several new marine species, including shrimp-like animals with claws longer than their bodies.

(A) apprentices   (B) expeditions   (C) meetings   (D) acquaintances

12. Shoveling snow is an excellent whole body workout. It is _____ for your health, especially if you are tired of staying indoors in cold weather.

(A) defensive   (B) embarrassing   (C) beneficial   (D) inferior

13. After heavy rains, a _____ broke and the city was flooded. Thousands of homes were washed away, leaving some 150,000 homeless.

(A) dam   (B) dim   (C) dumb   (D) dome

14. Helen decided to break up with her boyfriend because she thought he was too flirty. She felt very _____.

(A) unsanitary   (B) insecure   (C) unconscious   (D) insufficient

15. No one knows how come a clever man like him could _____
    such an obvious scam. The swindlers were just trying to cheat him
    out of his money.
    (A) fall for   (B) make for   (C) call for   (D) stand for

二、綜合測驗（佔 15 分）

說明： 第 16 題至第 30 題，每題一個空格，請依文意選出最適當的一個答案，
       請畫記在答案卡之「選擇題答案區」。各題答對者，得 1 分；答錯、未
       作答或畫記多於一個選項者，該題以零分計算。

第 16 至 20 題為題組

     Exercise is any type of physical exertion we perform in an effort to
improve our health, shape our bodies and boost performance. Obviously
that ___16___ a broad range of activities and, luckily, there are plenty to
___17___ whether you want to lose weight, get healthy or train for a sport.

     ___18___ the benefits of exercise, I could go on and on about all the
things exercise can do for you, both physically and mentally. The great
thing about it is that even just a few minutes a day can improve your
health and help you lose weight, sleep better, reduce stress, boost your
mood, improve your quality of life and relieve symptoms of depression
and anxiety.

     The hardest part of exercise is getting started. But you can constantly
remind yourself ___19___ your weight loss goals, imagine how relaxed you
will feel after a workout, promise yourself a reward for completing your
workout, and think of all the diseases and illnesses your workout could
protect you from. If you have multiple reasons to exercise, you will always
have something to get you moving, even when motivation is ___20___.

16. (A) extends   (B) associates   (C) covers   (D) adjusts
17. (A) go around   (B) go by   (C) go over   (D) go out
18. (A) Because   (B) As for   (C) Ever since   (D) In spite of
19. (A) of   (B) with   (C) for   (D) in
20. (A) soft   (B) swollen   (C) sour   (D) short

第 21 至 25 題為題組

A toy exhibit, with the theme "Not Sold in Stores," recently opened at United Nations Headquarters in New York. ___21___ together by the Christian Children's Fund (CCF), the exhibit displays over 100 toys made by children from discarded materials and trash in some of the poorest countries of the world. ___22___ part of an assistance program, the CCF encouraged children in Africa, Asia and Latin America to collect every conceivable scrap to make the toys.

The imagination and inventiveness of children ___23___ through these toys show the spirit of childhood and the role of play in childhood development. On display in the exhibit ___24___ trucks made out of pesticide cans; toy cars, motorbikes and airplanes made from wood scraps and discarded wire from construction sites; dolls made from scraps of cloth and ___25___ items; musical instruments out of oil cans and bottle caps; and soccer balls and baseballs from dried fruit and plastic bags.

21. (A) To put　　(B) Put　　(C) Putting　　(D) To be put
22. (A) With　　(B) As　　(C) For　　(D) On
23. (A) reveal　　(B) revealing　　(C) to reveal　　(D) revealed
24. (A) has　　(B) have　　(C) are　　(D) is
25. (A) household　　(B) sympathetic　　(C) academic　　(D) fundamental

第 26 至 30 題為題組

Psychology is the scientific study of behavior and the mind. The term ___26___ two Greek words: psyche, which means "soul," and logos, "the study of." These root words were first combined in the 16th century, ___27___ the human soul, spirit, or mind was seen as distinct from the body.

Many people think of psychologists as individuals who dispense advice, analyze personality, and help those who are mentally ill. But psychology is ___28___ the treatment of personal problems. With its broad scope, psychology investigates an enormous range of phenomena.

Psychologists examine them from a variety of complementary perspectives. Some conduct detailed biological studies of the brain, others explore how we process information; others analyze the role of evolution, and ___29___ study the influence of culture and society. Their goal is to understand the mysteries of human nature. Their discoveries can help people understand themselves, ___30___ better to others, and solve the problems that confront them.

26. (A) consist in   (B) calls for   (C) comes from   (D) relies on
27. (A) which   (B) unless   (C) until   (D) when
28. (A) in turn   (B) without doubt   (C) more than   (D) on average
29. (A) still others   (B) other   (C) the others   (D) another
30. (A) detect   (B) resist   (C) accuse   (D) relate

三、文意選填（佔 10 分）

說明： 第 31 題至第 40 題，每題一個空格，請依文意在文章後所提供的 (A) 到 (J) 選項中分別選出最適當者，並將其英文字母代號畫記在答案卡之「選擇題答案區」。各題答對者，得 1 分；答錯、未作答或畫記多於一個選項者，該題以零分計算。

第 31 至 40 題為題組

A punt is a narrow flat-bottomed boat that somewhat ___31___ a Venetian gondola with the curve removed. Punts generally ___32___ up to four adults while a fifth person stands at the rear and ___33___ the boat with a long pole.

The design was developed in the medieval period to ___34___ easy navigation in areas with shallow water. Until recently punts were used by commercial fishermen working the fens of East Anglia, but today they are almost ___35___ used for recreation.

Poling along the river looks effortless and easy; a relaxing way to enjoy a quiet summer afternoon. Looks can be ___36___, however, as steering a punt is neither as easy nor effortless as it looks. For one thing, the pole can get stuck in the mud of the river bottom, and steering from the rear of a punt ___37___ skill and dexterity.

Unless you are remarkably well-coordinated, your first few attempts to direct a punt in a straight line will provide some entertainment for ___38___ along the banks. Don't worry, it doesn't take long to get the ___39___ of things, and it really is a great deal of fun!

Punting along the River Cam is one of the traditional delights of visiting Cambridge, and something that should be tried—at least once—by everyone! Punts can be ___40___ at Silver Street Bridge, Mill Lane, Magdalene Bridge, Jesus Green, Trinity College, or Grantchester.

(A) hang   (B) seat   (C) allow for   (D) exclusively
(E) resembles   (F) takes   (G) propels   (H) hired
(I) deceiving   (J) onlookers

四、閱讀測驗（佔 32 分）

說明： 第 41 題至第 56 題，每題請分別根據各篇文章之文意選出最適當的一個選項，請畫記在答案卡之「選擇題答案區」。請畫記在答案卡之「選擇題答案區」。各題答對者，得 2 分；答錯、未作答或畫記多於一個選項者，該題以零分計算。

第 41 至 44 題為題組

If you don't have an iPad, should you make the new iPad 3 your first? If you already have an original iPad or iPad 2, is it worth **upgrading** to the new iPad? How about if you're using a BlackBerry, Android tablet, or a Windows netbook? To buy, to upgrade, or to skip and wait for the next one (or something else) is the bottom line for all of us. Is the new iPad just a minor update or a must have, and for whom?

Here's what to consider. If you're in the market for a tablet, there are smaller options, cheaper options, and options that even do one or two very specific things better than the iPad 3. As a complete device, however, no one else is giving away this much technology in this easy-to-use package at this good a price. Not even close.

If price is an issue, consider the $399 iPad 2. You'll miss out on some fantastic specs, but its ease of use and supporting operating system are second to only one—the iPad 3. If price and size are an issue, consider a $199 BlackBerry PlayBook or Amazon Kindle Fire. You'll miss out on Apple's iOS but get a lot of bang for your buck.

If you really need a certain feature the iPad lacks, like a more desktop-style interface, consider one of the many Android tablets or wait for Windows 8 slates. Less ease of use, smaller hard drive, but typically more flexible and configurable. But seriously, if you're considering your first tablet, get the new iPad.

41. This passage is most likely taken from a(n) _____.
    (A) newspaper headline
    (B) instruction manual
    (C) online consumer report
    (D) science and medical journal

42. Which of the following best explains the word "upgrading" in the first paragraph?
    (A) To replace something with a newer version.
    (B) To remodel an existing structure.
    (C) To make something more attractive.
    (D) To give a better score on a consumer survey.

43. How much does the iPad 3 cost?
    (A) $199.   (B) $299.
    (C) $399.   (D) It is impossible to say.

44. What does the author suggest to people who are buying their first tablet?
    (A) Wait for the iPad 4.
    (B) Buy the iPad 3.
    (C) Buy the iPad 2.
    (D) Buy the Blackberry Playbook.

第 45 至 48 題爲題組

Nonverbal communication is important. Most people worry about what they are saying, yet 93 percent of their effectiveness is not related to content. We clearly need to pay attention to nonverbal communication because it plays such a tremendously large role.

A UCLA research study revealed that what we say accounts for only 7 percent of what the other person believes. It also found that the way we say it accounts for 38 percent of what is believed and that the visual message accounts for 55 percent of what is believed. The visual message, of course, includes what the other person sees. These are the three major elements involved in the effectiveness of communication

People express their emotions, desires and attitudes more clearly through their facial expressions and body movements than they do verbally—and often more graphically. Charlie Chaplin created an unforgettable character who conveyed a wide range of emotions without saying a single word. A message delivered with enthusiasm will be more effective than a brilliantly structured message delivered in a **monotone** with eyes focused on the floor and no body movement. There are nonverbal gestures that have universal meaning, such as raising hands above the head to indicate surrender, saluting, shaking hands, and shrugging shoulders. Although there is debate about how precisely you can interpret body positions or movements, there is no doubt that nonverbal communication is a very strong element in any face-to-face exchange.

45. The passage did NOT mention that ＿＿＿＿＿ plays a part in effective communication.
    (A) what we say (B) the way we say something
    (C) where we say something (D) what the other person sees

46. According to the passage, the visual message accounts for ＿＿＿ percent of what the other person believes.
    (A) 93 (B) 7 (C) 38 (D) 55

47. The word **monotone** can be best replaced by _____.
    (A) weird appearance   (B) funny fashion
    (C) interesting way   (D) dull manner

48. Charlie Chaplin conveyed his message _____.
    (A) without using verbal language
    (B) with restless energy
    (C) by debating about movements
    (D) by using universal language

第 49 至 52 題爲題組

    Get the sweaters and long-sleeved shirts ready—autumn officially arrives today at 8:44 a.m. But you probably will not need those fall clothes just yet. Weather conditions will continue to feel like summer this week.

    Today's forecast calls for a high of 91, with sunny skies and a west-southwesterly wind of around 8 mph, becoming northerly, according to the National Weather Service. The weather tonight will be a little more fall-like, with temperatures dipping down to 67 degrees, with an easterly wind of 7 mph, switching over to the west-northwest. The rest of week will be somewhat similar, with highs in the 90s and lows in the high 60s and low 70s.

    Today's expected high of 91 is just shy of the normal high for today of 92 degrees. The record high for today is 104 degrees, set in 1949. Today's morning low was 72 degrees. The normal low for today is 67 degrees. The record low of 51 was set in 1944.

    The autumnal equinox occurs at 8:44 a.m. today, when the sun is directly over the earth's equator. During an equinox, nights and days are approximately the same length. After today, nights will be getting longer and days will get shorter until the winter solstice, which occurs this year on Dec. 21. Then days will gradually get longer again.

49. What is the main idea of this passage?
    (A) The winter solstice brings about weird weather again.
    (B) The weather service has posted its first warning on its website.
    (C) Autumn arrives, but summer-like temperatures remain.
    (D) Autumn weather may be just around the corner.

50. The author of this passage is most likely to be a(n) _____.
    (A) weatherman   (B) anchorperson
    (C) engineer   (D) news correspondent

51. According to the passage, the record high for the day of report is
    _____ degrees.
    (A) 51   (B) 72   (C) 91   (D) 104

52. The autumnal equinox occurs _____.
    (A) when the sun has a northerly motion
    (B) when the sun is at its southernmost point
    (C) when the sun is at its greatest distance from the earth's equator
    (D) when the sun is directly over the earth's equator

第 53 至 56 題為題組

According to a recent study, middle school children who have a television or computer in their room sleep less during the school year. They watch more TV, play more computer games and surf the Net more than their peers who don't have a TV or computer. The study examined 444 middle school pupils with an average age of 14, asking them about their sleep habits, their computer and television use, and their eating habits while watching TV or using the computer.

The study participants reported an average bedtime of 11:04 P.M. and wake-up time of 6:45 A.M. On the weekends, the average bedtime was somewhat later—at 1:45 A.M. and wake-up much later—at 11:30 A.M. Those children with TVs or computers in their room went to sleep half an hour later on average but woke up at the same time.

Middle school pupils watch a daily average of two hours and 40 minutes of TV and use their computer for three hours and 45 minutes. On weekends, they watch half an hour more TV than during the rest of the week and use their computers for four hours a day. Children with a TV in their room watch an hour more than those without and those with their own computer use it an hour more than their peers.

A fifth of pupils said they ate in front of the TV set on a regular basis, while 70 percent said they did so only occasionally. Only 10% reported never eating in front of the TV. Computers were considered to be a less attractive eating place, with only 10% eating in front of the computer on a regular basis, 40% occasionally, and half never eating there.

According to the study, there is a direct connection between exposure to the media and eating in front of the TV or computer. The more a child watches television or uses the computer, the greater the chance he will eat in front of the screen.

53. According to the passage, children with TVs or computers in their room _____.
   (A) covet more online games (B) sleep less
   (C) are better at surfing the Net (D) eat more

54. The study did NOT ask the participants about _____.
   (A) their eating habits
   (B) their computer and television use
   (C) their school performance
   (D) their sleep habits

55. The author of this passage is most likely to be a(n) _____.
   (A) human resources manager
   (B) devoted environmentalist
   (C) human rights activist
   (D) educational psychologist

56. According to the study, which of the following is NOT true?
   (A) Participants spent a daily average of three hours and 45 minutes on a computer during the week.
   (B) Participants reported an average bedtime of 11:04 P.M.
   (C) Participants with a TV in their room reported an average wake-up time of 11:30 A.M. on the weekends.
   (D) Participants with a computer in their room used it for 4 hours on Saturdays.

第貳部分：非選擇題（佔 28 分）

一、中譯英（佔 8 分）

說明： 1. 請將以下中文句子譯成正確、通順、達意的英文，並將答案寫在「答案卷」上。
    2. 請依序作答，並標明題號。每題 4 分，共 8 分。

1. 河的兩岸有許多柳樹，長長的枝條在風中優雅地擺動著。

2. 這項特色著實令人讚嘆，也使我的故鄉成為著名的觀光景點。

二、英文作文（佔 20 分）

說明： 1. 依提示在「答案卷」上寫一篇英文作文。
    2. 文長至少 120 個單詞（words）。

提示：你看到麥當勞（McDonald's）的徵人啓事，有意想應徵一職。你（英文名字必須假設為 David Young 或 Judy Young）要寫一封應徵工作的信，說明你想應徵的職位，以及你為何適任此工作。

請注意：必須使用上述的 David Young 或 Judy Young 在信末署名，<u>**不得使用自己的真實中文或英文名字**</u>。

大學入學學科能力測驗英文模擬試題 ① 詳解

第壹部分：單選題

一、詞彙：

1. (**C**) 洪水發生時，附近村莊的人趕去<u>救援</u>，但快速流動的水使他們無法接觸到受害者。

    (A) content〔'kɑntɛnt〕*n.* 內容；含量
    〔kən'tɛnt〕*adj.* 滿足的（ = *satisfied* ）
    (B) creed〔krid〕*n.* 教條；信條　　soldier's creed 軍人的信條
    (C) ***rescue***〔'rɛskju〕*n. v.* 救援；解救　　rescuer *n.* 解救者
    (D) summit〔'sʌmɪt〕*n.* 山頂；巔峰　*adj.* 高階層的
      a summit conference 高峰會議
    * flood〔flʌd〕*n.* 洪水　　nearby〔'nɪr,baɪ〕*adj.* 附近的
    rush〔rʌʃ〕*v.* 趕去　　flowing〔'floɪŋ〕*adj.* 流動的
    prevent sb. ***from doing*** sth. 防止某人做某事
    reach〔ritʃ〕*v.* 接觸　　victim〔'vɪktɪm〕*n.* 受害者

2. (**B**) 如果你把歐洲一年所使用的衛生紙拉長，它可以繞<u>行</u>世界一萬兩千次。

    (A) fascinate〔'fæsn̩,et〕*v.* 使著迷　　fascinating *adj.* 迷人的
    (B) ***travel***〔'trævl̩〕*v.* 移動；行進
    (C) shield〔ʃild〕*v.* 遮蔽；保護（ = *protect* ）　*n.* 盾；保護物
    (D) splash〔splæʃ〕*v. n.*（水、泥等）飛濺
    * stretch〔strɛtʃ〕*v.* 拉長；延長 < *out* >
    toilet〔'tɔɪlɪt〕*n.* 廁所　　***toilet paper*** 衛生紙
    time〔taɪm〕*n.* 次數

3. (**B**) 如果你在天冷時出外運動，要穿好衣服保暖。你怎麼穿的<u>差別</u>在於你會有舒適的運動，還是會很慘。

    (A) sorrow〔'sɑro〕*n.* 悲傷（ = *grief* ）
    (B) ***difference***〔'dɪfrəns〕*n.* 差異　　make a difference 有差異
    (C) impression〔ɪm'prɛʃən〕*n.* 印象　　impress *v.* 使印象深刻
    (D) communism〔'kɑmju,nɪzəm〕*n.* 共產主義
    * stay〔ste〕*v.* 保持　　workout〔'wɝk,aʊt〕*n.* 運動；健身
    misery〔'mɪzərɪ〕*n.* 悲慘；不幸

4. (**C**) 美國人每年用掉超過兩千一百萬噸的紙。如果這些紙半數是再生紙，就可以<u>拯救</u>比佛羅里達州還要大的森林。

(A) erase〔ɪ'res〕v. 擦掉；刪除；抹去（記憶）

(B) dedicate〔'dɛdə,ket〕v. 致力於；獻身於 < to > (= devote)

(C) **save**〔sev〕v. 拯救；節省　savings n. pl. 存款；積蓄

(D) resolve〔rɪ'zɑlv〕v. 決心；解決

* ton〔tʌn〕n. 噸　recycled〔ri'saɪk!d〕adj. 回收的
recycled paper 再生紙　state〔stet〕n. 州
Florida〔'flɔrədə〕n. 佛羅里達州【美國東南部的一州】

5. (**D**) 根據最近的一項調查，一般騎自行車的人，在人行道上<u>招致</u>的危險，是在馬路上的一點八倍。

(A) imitate〔'ɪmə,tet〕v. 模仿

(B) intimate〔'ɪntəmɪt〕adj. 親密的

(C) injure〔'ɪndʒɚ〕v. 使受傷；傷害 (= harm)　injury n.

(D) **incur**〔ɪn'kɝ〕v. 招致（危險、不愉快等）；負（債）
incur sb's displeasure 惹某人不快　incur debts 負債

* average〔'ævərɪdʒ〕adj. 一般的；平均的
cyclist〔'saɪk!ɪst〕n. 自行車者　risk〔rɪsk〕n. 危險；風險
sidewalk〔'saɪd,wɔk〕n. 人行道　time〔taɪm〕n. 倍
roadway〔'rod,we〕n. 馬路；快車道

6. (**D**) 透過你的鼻子深呼吸，會排除肌肉的緊張狀態。就算只有一分鐘的深呼吸，也可以讓你<u>顯著地</u>放鬆。

(A) inaccurately〔ɪn'ækjərɪtlɪ〕adv. 不正確地 (↔ accurately)

(B) intellectually〔,ɪnt!'ɛktʃuəlɪ〕adv. 智力上　intellectual adj.

(C) passively〔'pæsɪvlɪ〕adv. 消極地 (↔ actively)

(D) **significantly**〔sɪg'nɪfəkəntlɪ〕adv. 顯著地；相當地
significant adj.　significance n.

* breathe〔brið〕v. 呼吸　tension〔'tɛnʃən〕n. 緊張
drain〔dren〕v. 排水；逐漸消失
muscle〔'mʌs!〕n. 肌肉　relax〔rɪ'læks〕v. 放鬆

7. (**B**) 許多巴拿馬的<u>衝浪</u>迷比較喜歡戴塔海灘，因為那裡的浪況極佳。

(A) diving〔'daɪvɪŋ〕n. 潛水；跳水　dive n. 俯衝

(B) *surfing* (ˋsɝfɪŋ) *n.* 衝浪　　　surf *v.* 衝浪；上(網)

(C) skiing (ˋskiɪŋ) *n.* 滑雪　　　ski *v. n.*

(D) cycling (ˋsaɪkḷɪŋ) *n.* 騎腳踏車　　cycle *v.* 騎腳踏車　　*n.* 循環

* prefer (prɪˋfɝ) *v.* 偏愛　　Panamanian (ˌpænəˋmenɪən) *adj.* 巴拿馬的

enthusiast (ɪnˋθjuzɪˌæst) *n.* 狂熱者；迷

excellent (ˋɛksḷənt) *adj.* 極佳的　　wave (wev) *n.* 波浪

8. (**A**) 在課堂上作筆記，會讓學生在學習的過程中，成為積極的參與者，
　　而不是一位<u>消極的</u>聽衆，或神遊發呆的人。

(A) *passive* (ˋpæsɪv) *adj.* 消極的

(B) restorative (rɪˋstorətɪv) *adj.* (藥、食物) 能恢復精力的
　　restore *v.* 恢復；歸還

(C) informative (ɪnˋfɔrmətɪv) *adj.* 提供知識的　　information *n.*

(D) protective (prəˋtɛktɪv) *adj.* 保護的　　protect *v.*

* *take notes* 作筆記　　active (ˋæktɪv) *adj.* 積極的；主動的

participant (pɚˋtɪsəpənt) *n.* 參與者

process (ˋprɑsɛs) *n.* 過程　　*rather than* 而不是

daydreamer (ˋdeˌdrimɚ) *n.* 做白日夢者

9. (**A**) 雖然價格昂貴，但這家餐廳的食物如此美味，使得<u>常客</u>不介意花錢。

(A) *patron* (ˋpetrən) *n.* 常客；贊助人；顧客 (= *customer*)

(B) candidate (ˋkændəˌdet) *n.* 候選人

(C) benefactor (ˋbɛnəˌfæktɚ) *n.* 捐助者；恩人

(D) economist (ɪˋkɑnəmɪst) *n.* 經濟學家　　economics *n.* 經濟學

* mind (maɪnd) *v.* 介意　　*part with* 放棄；和~分開

10. (**D**) 學生應該被鼓勵全力以赴，而不是被<u>強迫</u>去設定過高的目標，或安排
　　太多活動。

(A) obtain (əbˋten) *v.* 獲得 (= *acquire*)

(B) inquire (ɪnˋkwaɪr) *v.* 詢問　　inquiring *adj.* 好問的
　　inquire *sb.* of *sth.* 詢問某人某事

(C) abolish (əˋbɑlɪʃ) *v.* 廢除 (= *do away with*)

(D) *pressure* (ˋprɛʃɚ) *v.* 壓迫；強迫　　*n.* 壓力 (= *stress*)

* *do one's best* 盡全力　　set (sɛt) *v.* 設定

goal (gol) *n.* 目標　　schedule (ˋskɛdʒul) *v.* 排定；安排

11. (**B**) 在日本政府進行的三次<u>遠征探險</u>中，發現了數種新的海洋物種，其中包括一種鉗長超過身長，很像蝦子的動物。

    (A) apprentice〔ə'prɛntɪs〕*n.* 學徒

    (B) *expedition*〔ˏɛkspɪ'dɪʃən〕*n.* 探險（隊）；遠征（隊）

    (C) meeting〔'mitɪŋ〕*n.* 會議

    (D) acquaintance〔ə'kwentəns〕*n.* 認識的人

    * marine〔mə'rin〕*adj.* 海洋的

      species〔'spiʃɪz〕*n.* 種類【單複數同型】

      shrimp〔ʃrɪmp〕*n.* 蝦子　　claw〔klɔ〕*n.* 爪；鉗

12. (**C**) 鏟雪是絕佳的全身運動。它對你的健康<u>有益</u>，尤其是如果你對天氣冷時待在室內感到厭倦的時候。

    (A) defensive〔dɪ'fɛnsɪv〕*adj.* 防禦的

      defend *v.* 保衛；辯護

    (B) embarrassing〔ɪm'bærəsɪŋ〕*adj.* 令人困窘的

      embarrassed *adj.* 感到困窘的

    (C) *beneficial*〔ˏbɛnə'fɪʃəl〕*adj.* 有益的；有利的

      benefit *n.* 利益；津貼　　medical benefit 醫療津貼

    (D) inferior〔ɪn'fɪrɪə〕*adj.* 較低的；差的 < to > *n.* 下屬；下級

      inferiority *n.* 低劣　　feelings of inferiority 自卑感

    * shovel〔'ʃʌvḷ〕*v.* 鏟起；鏟去　　*be tired of* 對…感到厭倦

      indoors〔'ɪn'dorz〕*adv.* 在室內

13. (**A**) 大雨過後，一座<u>水壩</u>破裂，使城市被水淹沒。數千個住宅被水沖走，使大約十五萬人無家可歸。

    (A) *dam*〔dæm〕*n.* 水壩

    (B) dim〔dɪm〕*adj.* 昏暗的；模糊的　　a dim light 昏暗的燈光

    (C) dumb〔dʌm〕*adj.* 啞的（= *mute*）；愚蠢的（= *stupid*）

    (D) dome〔dom〕*n.* 圓屋頂　　the dome of the sky 蒼穹；天頂

    * *heavy rain* 大雨　　*wash away* 沖走

      flood〔flʌd〕*v.* 淹沒；使氾濫　　leave〔liv〕*v.* 使處於（某種狀態）

      some〔sʌm〕*adv.* 大約　　homeless〔'homlɪs〕*adj.* 無家可歸的

14. (**B**) 海倫決定和她男朋友分手，因為她覺得他太花心。她感到很<u>不安</u>。

    (A) unsanitary〔ʌn'sænəˏtɛrɪ〕*adj.* 不衛生的（↔ sanitary）

(B) *insecure* 〔͵ɪnsɪˋkjʊr〕*adj.* 感到不安的　　insecurity *n.*
a sense of insecurity　不安全感

(C) unconscious〔ʌnˋkɑnʃəs〕*adj.* 無意識的；未察覺的（= *unaware*）

(D) insufficient〔͵ɪnsəˋfɪʃənt〕*adj.* 不足的（= *deficient*）

* *break up* 分手　　flirty〔ˋflɝtɪ〕*adj.* 愛調情的；愛拈花惹草的

15. (**A**) 沒人知道為何像他這樣聰明的人，會上如此明顯的騙局的當。這些騙子只想把他的錢騙走。

(A) *fall for* 上當；中計；迷戀（= *fall in love with*）

(B) make for 有助於；走向

(C) call for 需要

(D) stand for 代表；支持；忍受

* *how come* 為何　　clever〔ˋklɛvɚ〕*adj.* 聰明的
obvious〔ˋɑbvɪəs〕*adj.* 明顯的　　scam〔skæm〕*n.* 騙局；詐騙
swindler〔ˋswɪndlɚ〕*n.* 騙徒
cheat sb. out of sth. 從某人身上騙取某物

二、綜合測驗：

第 16 至 20 題為題組

運動是一種體能的耗費，我們努力做運動，以增進健康、雕塑體態，和提高體能。顯然地，運動<u>涵蓋</u>的活動種類很多，而幸運的是，不論你是想減輕體
　　　　16
重、讓身體健康，或是做運動訓練，都有很多種運動可以<u>滿足大家的需要</u>。
　　　　　　　　　　　　　　　　　　　　　　　　　17

* physical〔ˋfɪzɪkl̩〕*adj.* 身體的　　exertion〔ɪgˋzɝʃən〕*n.* 努力；費力
perform〔pɚˋfɔrm〕*v.* 做；執行　　*in an effort to V.* 努力去～
shape〔ʃep〕*v.* 塑造；雕塑　　boost〔bust〕*v.* 提高
performance〔pɚˋfɔrməns〕*n.* 表現；體能
obviously〔ˋɑbvɪəslɪ〕*adv.* 顯然　　range〔rendʒ〕*n.* 範圍
plenty〔ˋplɛntɪ〕*pron.* 大量之物；充份　　*lose weight* 減重

16. (**C**) (A) extend〔ɪkˋstɛnd〕*v.* 擴大；延伸
(B) associate〔əˋsoʃɪ͵et〕*v.* 聯想
(C) *cover*〔ˋkʌvɚ〕*v.* (範圍) 包含
(D) adjust〔əˋdʒʌst〕*v.* 調整

17. (**A**) 依句意，選 (A) *go around*「滿足人人的需要；人人能分到」。而
     (B) go by「經過」，(C) go over「(費用)超過；檢查」，
     (D) go out「出去」，則不合句意。

    <u>至於</u>運動的好處，我可以滔滔不絕地說出，運動在身體上和精神上，能為
       18
    你做到的所有事情。運動最棒的，就是一天只要幾分鐘，就能增進你的健康、
    幫助你減輕體重、讓你睡得更好、減輕壓力、提振你的心情、改善你的生活品
    質，並且減輕憂鬱和焦慮的症狀。

    * benefit〔'bɛnəfɪt〕*n.* 利益；好處   ***on and on*** 連續不斷地；不停地
      mentally〔'mɛntḷɪ〕*adv.* 精神上   reduce〔rɪ'djus〕*v.* 減少
      stress〔strɛs〕*n.* 壓力   mood〔mud〕*n.* 心情
      quality〔'kwɑlətɪ〕*n.* 品質   relieve〔rɪ'liv〕*v.* 減輕
      symptom〔'sɪmptəm〕*n.* 症狀   depression〔dɪ'prɛʃən〕*n.* 憂鬱
      anxiety〔æŋ'zaɪətɪ〕*n.* 焦慮

18. (**B**) 依句意，選 (B) *As for*「至於」。而 (A) because「因為」，後要接子句，
     (C) ever since「自從」，(D) in spite of「儘管」，則不合句意。

    運動最困難的部分就是開始。但你可以不斷提醒自己你<u>的</u>減重目標，想像
                                                              19
    運動完你會覺得多麼輕鬆，給自己一個做完運動的獎賞，並想著運動可以保護
    你免於疾病。如果你運動的原因有好幾個，那麼就算是<u>欠缺動機</u>的時候，也永
    遠會有某件事能讓你動起來。   20   20

    * constantly〔'kɑnstəntlɪ〕*adv.* 不斷地；常常
      remind〔rɪ'maɪnd〕*v.* 使想起；提醒   imagine〔ɪ'mædʒɪn〕*v.* 想像
      relaxed〔rɪ'lækst〕*adj.* 輕鬆的；舒暢的   workout〔'wɜk,aut〕*n.* 運動
      reward〔rɪ'wɔrd〕*n.* 獎賞   complete〔kəm'plit〕*v.* 完成
      think of 想想   ***protect sb. from sth.*** 保護某人免於某事
      multiple〔'mʌltəpḷ〕*adj.* 多數的；多重的
      motivation〔,motə'veʃən〕*n.* 動機

19. (**A**) ***remind sb. of sth.*** 提醒某人某事

20. (**D**) (A) soft〔sɔft〕*adj.* 柔軟的   (B) swollen〔'swolən〕*adj.* 腫脹的
     (C) sour〔saur〕*adj.* 酸的   (D) ***short***〔ʃɔrt〕*adj.* 短的；缺乏的

<u>第 21 至 25 題爲題組</u>

　　以「市面未販售」爲主題的玩具展覽會，最近在紐約的聯合國總部開幕。這個展覽由「基督敎兒福基金會」（CCF）<u>所集結</u>，展示了世界上最貧窮的一些
　　　　　　　　　　　　　　　　　　　　　　　21
國家的兒童，用廢棄物和垃圾，所製作出來的一百多件玩具。「基督敎兒福基金會」鼓勵非洲、亞洲，與拉丁美洲的兒童，收集每樣他們想得到的廢物，來做成玩具，以<u>作爲</u>協助計畫的一部分。
　　　　　　22

* exhibit〔ɪg'zɪbɪt〕*n.* 展覽會；展覽品　　theme〔θim〕*n.* 主題
  united〔ju'naɪtɪd〕*adj.* 聯合的　　***United Nations*** 聯合國
  headquarters〔'hɛd'kwɔrtəz〕*n. pl.* 總部
  Christian〔'krɪstʃən〕*adj.* 基督敎的　　fund〔fʌnd〕*n.* 基金（會）
  Christian Children's Fund 基督敎兒福基金會
  display〔dɪ'sple〕*v. n.* 展示　　discard〔dɪs'kɑrd〕*v.* 丟棄
  material〔mə'tɪrɪəl〕*n.* 材料　　assistance〔ə'sɪstəns〕*n.* 協助
  program〔'progræm〕*n.* 計畫　　collect〔kə'lɛkt〕*v.* 收集
  conceivable〔kən'sivəbl〕*adj.* 可想到的
  scrap〔skræp〕*n.* 廢物；碎屑；破爛東西

21. (**B**)　本句是由對等子句簡化而來的分詞構句，原句爲：***The exhibit is put***
　　　together by...*, **and** displays over 100 toys made...*，而分詞構句可代替
　　　第一個對等子句，但必須放在主詞前面，改成：***Being put*** together...,
　　　the exhibit displays over 100 toys made...，又 Being 可省略，故選
　　　(B) ***Put***。

22. (**B**)　依句意，「作爲」協助計畫的一部分，介系詞用 ***As***，選 (B)。

　　透過這些玩具所<u>展現</u>出來的兒童想像力及創造力，表現出童年的精神，與
　　　　　　　　23
遊戲在童年發展中的角色。

* imagination〔ɪ,mædʒə'neʃən〕*n.* 想像力
  inventiveness〔ɪn'vɛntɪvnɪs〕*n.* 發明才能；創作力
  spirit〔'spɪrɪt〕*n.* 精神　　childhood〔'tʃaɪld,hud〕*n.* 童年時期
  play〔ple〕*n.* 遊戲　　development〔dɪ'vɛləpmənt〕*n.* 發展

23. (**D**)　空格前省略了關係代名詞 which 以及 be 動詞 are，故選被動態的
　　　(D) ***revealed***。　　reveal〔rɪ'vil〕*v.* 顯示

展覽中所展示的<u>有殺蟲劑罐子</u>製成的卡車；由木頭碎片和建築工地找來的廢棄
　　　　　　　24

鐵絲，所製成的玩具車、玩具機車，與玩具飛機；由衣物碎布和<u>家庭</u>用品製成
　　　　　　　　　　　　　　　　　　　　　　　　　　　25

的玩偶；用油罐和瓶蓋做成的樂器；以及用乾燥水果和塑膠袋，所做成的足球
與棒球。

　　　* *on display* 展示中　　　*make* A *out of* B 以 B 製作 A
　　　　pesticide〔'pɛstɪˌsaɪd〕*n.* 殺蟲劑　　can〔kæn〕*n.* 罐子
　　　　motorbike〔'motəˌbaɪk〕*n.* 輕型機車　　airplane〔'ɛrˌplen〕*n.* 飛機
　　　　be made from 以～製成　　wire〔waɪr〕*n.* 鐵絲；電線
　　　　construction〔kən'strʌkʃən〕*n.* 建築　　site〔saɪt〕*n.* 用地；地點
　　　　item〔'aɪtəm〕*n.* 物品　　musical〔'mjuzɪkl̩〕*adj.* 音樂的
　　　　instrument〔'ɪnstrəmənt〕*n.* 器具　　bottle〔'batl̩〕*n.* 瓶子
　　　　cap〔kæp〕*n.* 蓋子　　soccer〔'sakə〕*n.* 足球
　　　　dried〔draɪd〕*adj.* 乾燥的　　plastic〔'plæstɪk〕*adj.* 塑膠的

24. (**C**)　「地方副詞（片語）+ be 動詞」，表「…有～」，又 trucks 為複數名詞，
　　　　　　故選 (C) *are*。

25. (**A**)　(A) *household*〔'haʊsˌhold〕*adj.* 家庭的
　　　　　　(B) sympathetic〔ˌsɪmpə'θɛtɪk〕*adj.* 同情的
　　　　　　(C) academic〔ˌækə'dɛmɪk〕*adj.* 學術的
　　　　　　(D) fundamental〔ˌfʌndə'mɛntl̩〕*adj.* 基本的

<u>第 26 至 30 題為題組</u>

　　心理學是對行為與心智所做的科學研究。這個名詞語<u>源自</u>兩個希臘字：
　　　　　　　　　　　　　　　　　　　　　　　　　　　26

psyche 表示「靈魂」，而 logos 表示「…的研究」。這些字根最初結合於十六世
紀，<u>那時</u>人類的靈魂、精神，或心智被看做是與身
　　　27

體分開的東西。

　　　* psychology〔saɪ'kalədʒɪ〕*n.* 心理學
　　　　scientific〔ˌsaɪən'tɪfɪk〕*adj.* 科學的　　behavior〔bɪ'hevjə〕*n.* 行為
　　　　mind〔maɪnd〕*n.* 心；心智　　term〔tɝm〕*n.* 名詞用語
　　　　Greek〔grik〕*adj.* 希臘的　　psyche〔'saɪkɪ〕*n.* 靈魂；精神
　　　　soul〔sol〕*n.* 靈魂　　root〔rut〕*adj.* 根的
　　　　root word 字根　　combine〔kəm'baɪn〕*v.* 結合
　　　　be seen as 被視為　　distinct〔dɪ'stɪŋkt〕*adj.* 分開的 *<from>*

26. (**C**) 依句意，選 (C) *come from*「起源於」。而 (A) consist in「在於」，
(B) call for「需要」，(D) rely on「依賴」，均不合句意。

27. (**D**) 空格後為完整句，故應填關係副詞引導形容詞子句，表「時間」用
when，故選 (D)。而 (A) which 為「關代」，須加不完整句，做子句中
的主詞或受詞，在此不合。而 (B) unless「除非」，(C) until「直到」，
用法與句意皆不合。

　　許多人認為心理學家是那些提供意見、剖析人格、並幫助精神病患的人。
但心理學<u>不僅止於</u>個人問題的治療。心理學涵蓋的範圍很廣，可研究很多種類
　　　　　28
的現象。

* *think of* A *as* B　認為 A 是 B
psychologist〔saɪˈkɑlədʒɪst〕*n.* 心理學家
individual〔ˌɪndəˈvɪdʒʊəl〕*n.* 個人
dispense〔dɪˈspɛns〕*v.* 分發；分送　　advice〔ədˈvaɪs〕*n.* 意見；建議
analyze〔ˈænḷˌaɪz〕*v.* 分析　　personality〔ˌpɜsṇˈælətɪ〕*n.* 性格
treatment〔ˈtritmənt〕*n.* 治療　　personal〔ˈpɜsṇḷ〕*adj.* 個人的
scope〔skop〕*n.* 範圍　　investigate〔ɪnˈvɛstəˌget〕*v.* 調查；研究
enormous〔ɪˈnɔrməs〕*adj.* 巨大的　　range〔rendʒ〕*n.* 範圍；領域
phenomena〔fəˈnamənə〕*n. pl.* 現象【單數是 phenomenon】

28. (**C**) 依句意，選 (C) *more than*「不只是」。而 (A) in turn「依序地」，(B)
without doubt「無疑地」，(D) on average「平均而言」，則不合句意。

心理學家從多種互補的觀點來檢視各種現象。有些人對大腦做了詳細的生物學
研究；有些人探討我們如何處理訊息；有些人分析演化的角色；<u>還有一些人研</u>
　　　　　　　　　　　　　　　　　　　　　　　　　　　　　　29
究文化與社會的影響。他們的目的是要了解人性之謎。他們的研究發現可以幫
助人們了解自己、增進人際關係，並解決人們所面臨的問題。
　　　　　　　30

* examine〔ɪɡˈzæmɪn〕*v.* 檢視　　*a variety of* 各種的
complementary〔ˌkɑmpləˈmɛntərɪ〕*adj.* 互補的；補充的
perspective〔pəˈspɛktɪv〕*n.* 觀點（= *point of view*）
conduct〔kənˈdʌkt〕*v.* 進行；做　　detailed〔ˈditeld〕*adj.* 詳細的
study〔ˈstʌdɪ〕*n.* 研究　　biological〔ˌbaɪəˈlɑdʒɪkḷ〕*adj.* 生物學的

brain〔bren〕n. 大腦　　explore〔ɪk'splor〕v. 探討
process〔'prɑsɛs〕v. 處理分析　　evolution〔ˌɛvə'luʃən〕n. 進化；演化
influence〔'ɪnfluəns〕n. 影響　　mystery〔'mɪstərɪ〕n. 奧秘；謎
human nature 人性　　discovery〔dɪ'skʌvərɪ〕n. 發現
confront〔kən'frʌnt〕v. 使面對

29. (**A**) 表「有些…；有些…；還有一些…」的說法為 some…, others…,
still others…，故選 (A)。

30. (**D**) 依句意，跟別人的「關係」更好，故選 (D) ***relate***〔rɪ'let〕v. 使有關係
< *to* >。而 (A) detect〔dɪ'tɛkt〕v. 發現 < *in* >，(B) resist〔rɪ'zɪst〕v. 抵抗，
(C) accuse〔ə'kjuz〕v. 控告 < *of* >，用法及句意均不合。

三、文意選填：

第 31 至 40 題為題組

　　平底小船就是底部平坦的窄船，有點 ³¹(**E**) 像威尼斯的貢多拉船，但是沒有
曲線。平底小船通常可以 ³²(**B**) 承載多達四位成人，同時還有一個人會站在船後
方，用長長的篙來 ³³(**G**) 推動小船。

* punt〔pʌnt〕n. 平底小船　　flat-bottomed〔'flæt,bɑtəmd〕adj. 平底的
somewhat〔'sʌm,hwɑt〕adv. 有一點　　resemble〔rɪ'sɛmbl̩〕v. 像
Venetian〔və'niʃən〕adj. 威尼斯的
gondola〔'gɑndələ〕n. 貢多拉【威尼斯的平底遊覽船】
curve〔kɝv〕n. 彎曲；曲線　　remove〔rɪ'muv〕v. 除去
seat〔sit〕v. 可容納　　***up to*** 多達　　rear〔rɪr〕n. 後面
propel〔prə'pɛl〕v. 推動　　pole〔pol〕n. 長棍子　　v. 用篙撐船

　　這種設計是在中世紀時研發出來的，³⁴(**C**) 讓人們可以在淺水地區輕鬆地航
行。直到最近，平底小船才被那些在東英格蘭工作的商業化漁民拿來使用，但
現在平底小船幾乎 ³⁵(**D**) 僅供休閒娛樂。

* medieval〔ˌmidɪ'ivl̩〕adj. 中世紀的　　***allow for*** 考慮到；顧及
navigation〔ˌnævə'geʃən〕n. 航行　　shallow〔'ʃælo〕adj. 淺的
commercial〔kə'mɝʃəl〕adj. 商業的　　fen〔fɛn〕n. 沼澤地
East Anglia〔'ist'æŋglɪə〕東英格利亞【Anglia 為 England 的拉丁文名稱】
exclusively〔ɪk'sklusɪvlɪ〕adv. 專門地；僅
recreation〔ˌrɛkrɪ'eʃən〕n. 休閒；娛樂

　　沿著河流用篙撐船看起來既不費力又輕鬆，是一種輕鬆享受寧靜的夏日午後的一種方式。然而，表象卻可能 36 **(I) 騙**了你，駕馭一艘平底小船其實一點也不像看起來那麼的輕鬆又不費力。一來，撐船的篙可能會卡在河底的泥巴裡，還有，在小船後面駕駛船隻，37 **(F) 需要**技巧和靈敏度。

* effortless〔ˋɛfətlɪs〕*adj.* 不費力的
　relaxing〔rɪˋlæksɪŋ〕*adj.* 輕鬆愉快的　　look〔lʊk〕*n.* 外表
　deceiving〔dɪˋsivɪŋ〕*adj.* 騙人的　　steer〔stɪr〕*v.* 駕駛；掌舵
　neither…nor~ 既不…也不~　　***for one thing*** 一來；首先
　stuck〔stʌk〕*adj.* 卡住的；動彈不得的　　mud〔mʌd〕*n.* 泥巴
　take〔tek〕*v.* 需要；花費　　dexterity〔dɛksˋtɛrətɪ〕*n.* 靈巧；機靈

　　除非你的協調性非常地好，不然你嘗試直線地划小船的前幾次，將會帶給岸邊 38 **(J) 觀眾**一些娛樂。別擔心，你很快就可以抓到做這件事情的 39 **(A) 訣竅**，而且這真的很好玩！

* remarkably〔rɪˋmɑrkəblɪ〕*adv.* 非常地；格外地
　well-coordinated〔ˋwɛlkoˋɔrdn̩͵etɪd〕*adj.* 協調度很好的
　attempt〔əˋtɛmpt〕*n.* 企圖；嘗試　　direct〔dəˋrɛkt〕*v.* 指揮；操縱
　straight line 直線　　entertainment〔͵ɛntəˋtenmənt〕*n.* 娛樂
　onlooker〔ˋɑn͵lʊkə〕*n.* 觀眾　　bank〔bæŋk〕*n.* 河岸
　get the hang of N. 抓到~的訣竅　　***a great deal of*** 很多

　　遊歷劍橋的一項傳統樂趣，就是撐小船遊覽康河，而且每個人都至少要嘗試過一次才行！你可以在銀街橋、磨坊街、麥格達琳橋、基督學院花園、三一學院，或格蘭切斯特莊園 40 **(H) 雇用**平底小船。

* ***River Cam*** 康河【流經劍橋郡及劍橋大學的河流】
　traditional〔trəˋdɪʃən̩l〕*adj.* 傳統的　　delight〔dɪˋlaɪt〕*n.* 喜悅
　Cambridge〔ˋkembrɪdʒ〕*n.* 劍橋（郡、大學）　　***at least*** 至少
　hire〔haɪr〕*v.* 雇用　　***Silver Street Bridge*** 銀街橋【康河上的一座橋】
　mill〔mɪl〕*n.* 磨坊　　***Mill Lane*** 磨坊街【劍橋街道名】
　Magdalene Bridge 麥格達琳橋【康河上的一座橋，若在劍橋租平底船遊
　　康河，這裡就是遊河的終點】
　Jesus Green 基督學院花園【劍橋大學基督學院裡的大草坪】
　trinity〔ˋtrɪnətɪ〕*n.* 三位一體【基督教指神、聖靈、基督三者合一】
　Trinity College 三一學院【劍橋大學最有名，規模也最大的學院】
　Grantchester〔ˋgrænt`tʃɛstə〕*n.* 格蘭切斯特莊園【康河沿岸的村莊名】

四、閱讀測驗：

第 41 至 44 題為題組

　　如果你沒有 iPad，你應該讓 iPad 3 讓成為你的第一台 iPad 嗎？如果你已經有最初的 iPad 或 iPad 2，升級到新的 iPad 是值得的嗎？那如果你正在使用黑梅機，安卓平板電腦或是視窗小筆電，又該怎麼辦？要買、升級還是跳過等下一代（或是其他的選擇）是我們得考慮的底線。新的 iPad 只是個小小的升級還是必要的東西，以及需求的對象是誰？

　　* ***iPad*** iPad 平版電腦【一款蘋果公司於 2010 年 1 月 27 日發布的平板電腦】
　　original〔ə'rɪdʒənl〕*adj.* 最早的；最初的　　***be worth + V-ing*** 值得～
　　update〔ʌp'det〕*n. v.* 更新
　　BlackBerry 黑莓【加拿大的一家手提無線通信設備品牌，於 1999 年創立】
　　tablet〔'tæblɪt〕*n.* 平板　　***Android tablet*** 安卓平板電腦
　　Windows 視窗作業系統【由微軟所推出的一系列作業系統】
　　netbook〔'nɛt,bʊk〕*n.* 小筆電　　skip〔skɪp〕*v.* 跳過；忽略
　　bottom line 底線；（可接受的）最大限度
　　minor〔'maɪnɚ〕*adj.* 較小的；次要的　　***must have*** 必備品

　　這裡告訴你要考慮什麼。如果你在市場上尋找平板電腦，有更小、更便宜甚至還有在一至兩個特定的方面比 iPad 3 表現更好的選擇。然而，就一個完整的設備而言，沒有其他的平板電腦能集這麼多科技於一套裝軟體，容易上手，而賣如此的好價格。別想太美了。

　　* consider〔kən'sɪdɚ〕*v.* 考慮
　　in the market for 在市場上尋找～　　option〔'ɑpʃən〕*n.* 選擇
　　specific〔spɪ'sɪfɪk〕*adj.* 特定的　　device〔dɪ'vaɪs〕*n.* 裝置；發明
　　give away 贈送　　technology〔tɛk'nɑlədʒɪ〕*n.* 科技
　　easy-to-use *adj.* 方便使用的　　package〔'pækɪdʒ〕*n.* 套裝軟體
　　this〔ðɪs〕*adv.* 如此（= *so*）　　***not even close*** 差遠了

　　如果關注的是價格，考慮一下賣 $ 399 的 iPad 2，你會錯失一些酷炫的規格，但是它容易上手，而且它支援的作業系統僅次於 iPad 3。如果關注的是價格跟尺寸，考慮一下賣 $ 199 的黑莓平板電腦或是亞馬遜之火，你會錯過一些蘋果的 iOS 作業系統，但是你會覺得值回票價。

* issue〔ˋɪʃjʊ〕*n.*（值得關注的）問題　　***miss out on*** 錯失（機會）
 fantastic〔fænˋtæstɪk〕*adj.* 極棒的
 spec〔spɛk〕*n.* 規格（＝ *specification*）
 operating system 作業系統　　***be second to*** 次於
 BlackBerry PlayBook 黑莓平板電腦
 Amazon Kindle Fire 亞馬遜之火【2011 年 9 月 28 日亞馬遜公司推出的 7 英寸平板電腦】　　***iOS*** iOS 作業系統【由蘋果公司開發的作業系統】
 bang〔bæŋ〕*n.* 巨響　　buck〔bʌk〕*n.* 錢
 bang for one's ***buck*** 值回票價（＝ *value for one's money*）

　　如果你真的需要某個 iPad 缺乏的特色，像是有像桌上型電腦的介面，考慮安卓平板電腦，或是等待 Windows 8 平板電腦。較不易上手，硬碟較小，但是基本上比較有彈性且有配置性。但是認真來說，如果你在考慮你的第一台平板電腦，買新的 iPad 吧。

* feature〔ˋfitʃɚ〕*n.* 特色　　lack〔læk〕*v.* 缺乏
 desktop〔ˋdɛsk͵tɑp〕*n.* 桌上型電腦　　interface〔ˋɪntɚ͵fes〕*n.* 介面
 Windows 8 視窗 8【微軟預計 2012 年 9 月推出正式版的作業系統】
 slate〔slet〕*n.* 石板；寫字版（這裡是指「平板電腦」）
 hard drive 硬碟　　typically〔ˋtɪpɪk!ɪ〕*adv.* 典型地；大概；通常
 flexible〔ˋflɛksəb!〕*adj.* 有彈性的
 configurable〔kənˋfɪgjərəb!〕*adj.* 可配置的
 seriously〔ˋsɪrɪəslɪ〕*adv.* 正經地說

41.（**C**）本文最有可能取材自 _____。
　　(A) 新聞頭條　　　　　　　　　(B) 使用書
　　(C) 線上消費者報告　　　　　　(D) 科學及醫學期刊
　　* headline〔ˋhɛd͵laɪn〕*n.* 頭條　　manual〔ˋmænjʊəl〕*n.* 手冊
　　 journal〔ˋdʒɝn!〕*n.* 期刊　　medical〔ˋmɛdɪk!〕*adj.* 醫學的

42.（**A**）下列何者最能解釋第一段的 "**upgrading**" 這個字？
　　(A) 用新的版本替換某物。　　　(B) 重塑現有的結構。
　　(C) 讓某物更吸引人。　　　　　(D) 給消費者調查更高的分數。
　　* ***replace*** A ***with*** B 用 B 替代 A
　　 remodel〔riˋmɑd!〕*v.* 重塑；修改　　existing〔ɪgˋzɪstɪŋ〕*adj.* 現存的
　　 structure〔ˋstrʌktʃɚ〕*n.* 結構　　survey〔ˋsɝve〕*n.* 調查

43. (**D**) 新的 iPad 3 要多少錢？
    (A) 199 美元。　(B) 299 美元。　(C) 399 美元。　(D) 很難說。

44. (**B**) 作者給那些要買第一台平板電腦的人什麼建議？
    (A) 等待 iPad 4。　　　　　　　(B) 買 iPad 3。
    (C) 買 iPad 2。　　　　　　　　(D) 買黑莓平板電腦。

第 45 至 48 題為題組

　　非言語的溝通很重要。大多數的人會擔心他們說了什麼，然而言語的效果中，有百分之九十三和說話內容並無關聯。我們顯然需要留意非言語的溝通，因為它扮演的角色非常重要。

* nonverbal〔ˌnɑn'vɝbḷ〕*adj.* 不使用言語的；非言語的
  communication〔kə,mjunə'keʃən〕*n.* 溝通
  yet〔yɛt〕*conj.* 然而　　effectiveness〔ə'fɛktɪvnɪs〕*n.* 有效；效果
  related〔rɪ'letɪd〕*adj.* 有關的 < to >　　content〔'kɑntɛnt〕*n.* 內容
  pay attention to 住意　　tremendously〔trɪ'mɛndəslɪ〕*adv.* 非常

　　加州大學洛杉磯分校的一份研究調查顯示，我們說的話裡面，只有百分之七讓別人相信。研究也發現，我們說話的方式，佔他人相信要素的百分之三十八，而視覺訊息，則構成被相信成分的百分之五十五。當然，視覺訊息包括了別人所看見的東西。而這些就是和溝通效果有關的三個要素。

* **UCLA** 加州大學洛杉磯分校　　reveal〔rɪ'vil〕*v.* 顯示
  account for 佔…　　visual〔'vɪʒuəl〕*adj.* 視覺的
  message〔'mɛsɪdʒ〕*n.* 訊息　　major〔'medʒɚ〕*adj.* 主要的
  element〔'ɛləmənt〕*n.* 因素；成分
  involved〔ɪn'vɑlvd〕*adj.* 有關的 < in >

　　人們藉由他們的臉部表情和身體動作，所傳達出的情緒、慾望，與態度，會比他們用言語表達來得更為清楚——而且經常更加生動。查理・卓別林創造出一個令人難忘的角色，能不發一語，就傳達出各種情緒。

* express〔ɪk'sprɛs〕*v.* 表達　　emotion〔ɪ'moʃən〕*n.* 情緒
  desire〔dɪ'zaɪr〕*n.* 慾望　　attitude〔'ætə,tjud〕*n.* 態度；想法
  facial〔'feʃəl〕*adj.* 臉部的　　expression〔ɪk'sprɛʃən〕*n.* 表情
  movements〔'muvmənts〕*n. pl.* 動作；舉止

verbally〔'vɜblɪ〕*adv.* 言語上　　graphically〔'græfɪklɪ〕*adv.* 生動地
Charlie Chaplin〔'tʃɑrlɪ'tʃæplɪn〕*n.* 查理‧卓別林【1889-1977，英國
　喜劇與默劇演員】
unforgettable〔ˌʌnfɚ'gɛtəbl̩〕*adj.* 令人難忘的；使人印象深刻的
character〔'kærɪktɚ〕*n.* 角色　　convey〔kən'veˌ〕*v.* 傳達
single〔'sɪŋgl̩〕*adj.* 單一的

用熱忱傳達出的訊息，會比詞藻組織出色，但單調地用眼睛注視地板，且沒有
身體動作，所傳達出的訊息更有效。有些非言語動作具有普遍意義，像是表示
投降而將手舉過頭頂、敬禮、握手，和聳肩。

* deliver〔dɪ'lɪvɚ〕*v.* 傳達　　enthusiasm〔ɪn'θjuzɪˌæzəm〕*n.* 熱忱
effective〔ə'fɛktɪv〕*adj.* 有效的　　brilliantly〔'brɪljəntlɪ〕*adv.* 出色地
structured〔'strʌktʃəd〕*adj.* 有組織的　　monotone〔'mɑnəˌton〕*n.* 單調
focus on 聚焦；注視　　gesture〔'dʒɛstʃɚ〕*n.* 手勢；動作
universal〔ˌjunə'vɜsl̩〕*adj.* 普遍的　　raise〔rez〕*v.* 舉起
indicate〔'ɪndəˌket〕*v.* 表示　　surrender〔sə'rɛndɚ〕*n.* 投降
salute〔sə'lut〕*v.* 打招呼；敬禮　　*shake hands* 握手
shrug〔ʃrʌg〕*v.* 聳（肩）　　shoulder〔'ʃoldɚ〕*n.* 肩膀

雖然要如何精準地解讀身體姿勢與動作還有些爭論，但無疑的，非言語溝通在
任何面對面的交談中，是種非常有說服力的要素。

* debate〔dɪ'bet〕*n.* 爭論　　precisely〔prɪ'saɪslɪ〕*adv.* 準確地
interpret〔ɪn'tɜprɪt〕*v.* 解釋　　position〔pə'zɪʃən〕*n.* 姿勢
face-to-face〔'festə'fes〕*adj.* 面對面的
exchange〔ɪks'tʃendʒ〕*n.* 交換（意見等）
strong〔strɔŋ〕*adj.* 有說服力的

45.（**C**）本文沒有提到 ＿＿＿＿＿ 也是有效溝通的一部分。
　　(A) 說話的內容　　　　　　　(B) 說話的方式
　　(C) 說話的地點　　　　　　　(D) 對方看到什麼

46.（**D**）根據本文，視覺訊息佔被相信成分的百分之 ＿＿＿＿＿ 。
　　(A) 93　　　　　　　　　　　(B) 7
　　(C) 38　　　　　　　　　　　(D) 55

47.（**D**）"**monotone**" 這個字最適合用 ＿＿＿＿＿ 來取代。

    (A) 奇異的外表   (B) 滑稽的風格

    (C) 有趣的方式   (D) <u>單調的方式</u>

    * weird〔wɪrd〕*adj.* 奇異的   funny〔ˈfʌnɪ〕*adj.* 滑稽的

    fashion〔ˈfæʃən〕*n.* 樣式；方式   dull〔dʌl〕*adj.* 單調的

    manner〔ˈmænɚ〕*n.* 方式

48.（**A**）查理・卓別林 ＿＿＿＿＿ 來傳達自己的訊息。

    (A) <u>不必用言語</u>   (B) 用無窮盡的活力

    (C) 討論各種動作   (D) 用世界共通的語言

    * verbal〔ˈvɝbḷ〕*adj.* 言語表達的   restless〔ˈrɛstlɪs〕*adj.* 無休止的

    debate〔dɪˈbet〕*v.* 辯論

第 49 至 52 題爲題組

    把毛衣和長袖襯衫準備好——秋天在今晨八點四十四分正式到來。不過你可能暫時還不需要這些秋衣，本週的天氣狀況，會持續有夏天的感覺。

    * sweater〔ˈswɛtɚ〕*n.* 毛衣   long-sleeved〔ˈlɔŋˈslivd〕*adj.* 長袖的

    officially〔əˈfɪʃəlɪ〕*adv.* 正式地   *not…just yet* 暫時還不…

    condition〔kənˈdɪʃən〕*n.* 狀況

    根據國家氣象局今天的天氣預報說，高溫會到華氏 91 度，有晴朗的天氣，與逐漸往北移，風速爲時速八哩左右的西南西風。今晚的天氣會有點像秋天的感覺，氣溫下降到華氏 67 度，風速爲時速七哩，東風將轉爲西北西風。本週其他日子的天氣都差不多，高溫在華氏 90 度，而低溫則是華氏 6、70 度上下。

    * forecast〔ˈforˌkæst〕*n.* 天氣預報；預測   high〔haɪ〕*n.* 最高數字

    sunny〔ˈsʌnɪ〕*adj.* 晴朗的

    southwesterly〔ˌsauθˈwɛstɚlɪ〕*adj.* 來自西南的

    west-southwesterly〔ˈwɛstˌsauθˈwɛstɚlɪ〕*adj.* 西南西的

    mph 時速…哩（ = *miles per hour* ）

    northerly〔ˈnɔrðɚlɪ〕*adj.* 向北的   service〔ˈsɝvɪs〕*n.*（官署等）局

    National Weather Service 國家氣象局

    fall-like〔ˈfɔlˌlaɪk〕*adj.* 像秋天的   dip〔dɪp〕*v.* 下降

    degree〔dɪˈgri〕*n.* 度   easterly〔ˈistɚlɪ〕*adj.* 來自東方的

switch over 轉換；轉往

west-northwest (ˋwɛst͵nɔrθˋwɛst) *n.* 西北西

somewhat (ˋsʌm͵hwɑt) *adv.* 有點

similar (ˋsɪmələ) *adj.* 類似的　　　low (lo) *n.* 最低數字

　　今日預計高溫是 91 度，離今日的平均高溫 92 度只差一點點。記錄上的今日最高溫，是在 1949 年創下的 104 度。今晨的低溫是 72 度，而今日的平均低溫是 67 度，記錄上的今日最低溫是 1944 年出現的 51 度。

＊expected (ɪkˋspɛktɪd) *adj.* 預期的　　　shy (ʃaɪ) *adj.* 尚差…的 < *of* >

normal (ˋnɔrml) *adj.* 平均的；常態的

record (ˋrɛkəd) *adj.* 記錄的　　　set (sɛt) *v.* 創（紀錄）

　　秋分出現在今天早上八點四十四分，這時太陽會位在地球赤道的正上方。在秋分時，黑夜與白天的長度大約相等。過了這天以後，黑夜會漸漸變長，而白天會漸漸變短，一直到冬至為止，而今年的冬至，會在十二月二十一日出現。屆時白天又會漸漸變長。

＊autumnal (ɔˋtʌmnl) *adj.* 秋天的

equinox (ˋikwə͵nɑks) *n.* 秋分；春分

occur (əˋkɝ) *v.* 出現；發生　　　directly (dəˋrɛktlɪ) *adv.* 直接地

equator (ɪˋkwetə) *n.* 赤道　　　approximately (əˋprɑksəmɪtlɪ) *adv.* 大約

length (lɛŋθ) *n.* 長度　　　solstice (ˋsɑlstɪs) *n.* 至日【可指冬至或夏至】

gradually (ˋgrædʒʊəlɪ) *adv.* 逐漸地

49. (**C**) 本文主旨為何？

(A) 冬至又帶來奇怪的天氣。

(B) 氣象局第一次在網站上做氣象預告。

(C) <u>秋天到了，但氣溫還是像夏天。</u>

(D) 秋天的天氣可能就要來了。

＊***bring about*** 導致；造成　　　post (post) *v.* 公布；告示

website (ˋwɛb͵saɪt) *n.* 網站

summer-like (ˋsʌmə͵laɪk) *adj.* 像夏天的

remain (rɪˋmen) *v.* 繼續

be around the corner 就快到了

50.（**A**）本文的作者最有可能是個 _____ 。

　　(A) 氣象播報員　　　　　　　(B) 新聞主播
　　(C) 工程師　　　　　　　　　(D) 新聞特派員

　　* **be likely to** 可能　　weatherman〔'wɛðɚˌmæn〕*n.* 氣象播報員
　　anchorperson〔'æŋkɚˌpɝsn̩〕*n.* 新聞主播
　　engineer〔ˌɛndʒə'nɪr〕*n.* 工程師
　　correspondent〔ˌkɔrə'spɑndənt〕*n.* 特派員；通訊記者
　　news correspondent 新聞特派員

51.（**D**）根據本文，歷史記錄上今天的最高溫度是 _____ 度。

　　(A) 51　　　　(B) 72　　　　(C) 91　　　　(D) <u>104</u>

52.（**D**）秋分是 _____ 時發生。

　　(A) 當太陽往北移動　　　　　(B) 當太陽在最南端
　　(C) 當太陽離地球赤道最遠　　(D) <u>當太陽在赤道正上方</u>

　　* southernmost〔'sʌðɚnˌmost〕*adj.* 最南端的
　　directly〔də'rɛktlɪ〕*adv.* 正好

第 53 至 56 題為題組

　　根據最近一項研究，房間內有電視或電腦的中學生，在學年期間睡得比較少。他們會比沒有電視或電腦的同學，看更多電視、玩更多電腦遊戲，及更常上網。這項研究調查了四百四十四位，平均年齡十四歲的中學生，詢問他們的睡眠習慣、使用電腦和電視的情況，以及看電視或使用電腦時的飲食習慣。

　　* **middle school** 中學　　**school year** 學年
　　computer game 電玩遊戲　　surf〔sɝf〕*v.* 上（網）
　　Net〔nɛt〕*n.* 網際網路（ = *Internet* ）
　　surf the Net 上網搜尋；上網瀏覽（ = *surf the Internet* ）
　　peer〔pɪr〕*n.* 同儕　　examine〔ɪg'zæmɪn〕*v.* 調查；檢查
　　pupil〔'pjupl̩〕*n.* 學生　　average〔'ævərɪdʒ〕*adj.* 平均的

　　參與這項研究的人說，平均的就寢時間是晚上十一點零四分，而起床時間則是早上六點四十五分。週末時，平均就寢時間稍微晚一點——凌晨一點四十五分，然後起床更晚——早上十一點三十分。那些房間裡有電視或電腦的學童，平均會晚半個小時上床睡覺，但是會在同樣的時間起床。

* participant〔pɚˋtɪsəpənt〕*n.* 參與者　　report〔rɪˋport〕*v.* 報告
bedtime〔ˋbɛd͵taɪm〕*n.* 就寢時間　　*wake-up time* 起床時間
on average 平均而言

中學生平均一天看兩小時四十分的電視，並且用三小時四十五分的電腦。在週末，他們會比在一週內其餘的那幾天，多看半小時的電視，並且一天使用電腦四個小時。房間內有電視的兒童，比那些房內沒有電視的人，多看一小時的電視，而房內自己有電腦的，會比他們的同學多用一個小時的電腦。

* daily〔ˋdelɪ〕*adj.* 每日的　　*half an hour* 半小時

五分之一的學生說，他們經常會在電視機前面用餐，而百分之七十的學生說他們只有偶爾才會這樣做。而只有百分之十的學生回報說，從未在電視前面用餐。電腦被視為是一個較不吸引人的用餐地點，只有百分之十的學生會經常在電腦前用餐，百分之四十偶爾會，而半數從未在那裡用過餐。

* *a fifth of* 五分之一的　　*in front of* 在…前面　　*TV set* 電視機
regular〔ˋrɛgjəlɚ〕*adj.* 定期的　　basis〔ˋbesɪs〕*n.* 基礎
on a regular basis 定期地；經常地
occasionally〔əˋkeʒənlɪ〕*adv.* 偶爾
consider〔kənˋsɪdɚ〕*v.* 認為
attractive〔əˋtræktɪv〕*adj.* 吸引人的

根據這項研究，與媒體的接觸，和在電視或電腦前面用餐之間，有直接的關聯。愈常看電視或使用電腦的兒童，在螢光幕前用餐的機會就更多。

* connection〔kəˋnɛkʃən〕*n.* 關聯；關係
exposure〔ɪkˋspoʒɚ〕*n.* 接觸；暴露
media〔ˋmidɪə〕*n. pl.* 媒體　　screen〔skrin〕*n.* 螢光幕

53.(**B**) 根據本文，房間裡面有電視或是電腦的兒童 _____。
　(A) 想要的電動遊戲比較多　　(B) 睡得比較少
　(C) 上網比較在行　　(D) 吃得比較多
　* covet〔ˋkʌvɪt〕*v.* 垂涎；覬覦　　online〔ˋɑn͵laɪn〕*adj.* 線上的

54. (**C**) 本研究沒有問參與者 _____。
    (A) 他們吃飯的習慣　　　　　(B) 他們電腦及電視的使用情況
    (C) <u>他們的學校表現</u>　　　　　(D) 他們的睡眠習慣

    * performance〔pɚ'fɔrməns〕*n.* 表演；表現

55. (**D**) 本文的作者最有可能是一位 _____。
    (A) 人力資源部的經理　　　　(B) 熱心的環保運動者
    (C) 人權鬥士　　　　　　　　(D) <u>教育心理學者</u>

    * resource〔rɪ'sors〕*n.* 來源；資源
    human resources 人力資源
    devoted〔dɪ'votɪd〕*adj.* 熱心的
    environmentalist〔ɪnˌvaɪrən'mɛntḷɪst〕*n.* 環境保護論者
    human rights 人權　　activist〔'æktɪvɪst〕*n.* 行動者
    educational〔ˌɛdʒə'keʃənḷ〕*adj.* 教育性的
    psychologist〔saɪ'kɑlədʒɪst〕*n.* 心理學家

56. (**D**) 根據本文，下列何者爲非？
    (A) 受訪者一週平均每天使用電腦的時間爲三小時四十五分。
    (B) 受訪者說每天平均的上床時間是十一點零四分。
    (C) 房間裡有電視的受訪者說，週末平均起床時間是早上十一點半。
    (D) <u>房間裡有電腦的受訪者說，週六花四個小時在玩電腦。</u>

第貳部分：非選擇題

一、中譯英：

1. 河的兩岸有許多柳樹，長長的枝條在風中優雅地擺動著。

On $\begin{cases} \text{each side} \\ \text{either side} \\ \text{both sides} \end{cases}$ of the river are many willows, which have long branches

$\begin{cases} \text{that} \\ \text{which} \end{cases}$ wave / move / sway $\begin{cases} \text{gracefully} \\ \text{gently} \end{cases}$ in the wind.

2. 這項特色著實令人讚嘆，也使我的家鄉成為著名的觀光景點。

This feature is
$\begin{Bmatrix} \text{really} \\ \text{truly} \\ \text{definitely} \end{Bmatrix}$
$\begin{Bmatrix} \text{awesome} \\ \text{amazing} \\ \text{marvelous} \end{Bmatrix}$
and makes my hometown

a
$\begin{Bmatrix} \text{well-known} \\ \text{famous} \\ \text{renowned} \end{Bmatrix}$
$\begin{Bmatrix} \text{tourist attraction.} \\ \text{tourist spot.} \\ \text{sightseeing spot.} \end{Bmatrix}$

二、英文作文：

作文範例

To Whom It May Concern,　　　　　　　　　Jan. 28, 2013

　　My name is David Young and I am seeking a cashier's position at your downtown location. As a regular customer, I am very familiar with both McDonald's food quality and standards of service. You will find me to be an able, loyal and experienced employee. For the last three years, I have worked as a cashier for one of your competitors, Burger Clown. The position gave me valuable experience, which I am now ready to use at your establishment.

　　I am a responsible and outgoing individual. I love people and I genuinely enjoy serving others in any way possible. It is my dream to work for a professional organization such as McDonald's, where I will be given a chance for advancement, and maybe one day, become a manager. Of all my personal qualities, dependability is my most outstanding trait. I have never been late for work in over five years of employment.

　　I hope you give me this opportunity to prove my worth. Thank you for your time.

　　　　　　　　　　　　　　　　　　　　Sincerely,
　　　　　　　　　　　　　　　　　　　　David Young

To Whom It May Concern 敬啓者【用於推薦信或公開信】

cashier〔kæ'ʃɪr〕*n.* 櫃台收銀員

position〔pə'zɪʃən〕*n.* 工作；職位

location〔lo'keʃən〕*n.* 地點　　regular〔'rɛgjələ〕*adj.* 固定的

regular customer 老顧客；常客

loyal〔'lɔɪəl〕*adj.* 忠心的　　able〔'ebl̩〕*adj.* 能幹的

employee〔ˌɛmplɔɪ'i〕*n.* 員工

competitor〔kəm'pɛtətə〕*n.* 競爭者；對手

valuable〔'væljəbl̩〕*adj.* 重要的；寶貴的

establishment〔ə'stæblɪʃmənt〕*n.* 公司；企業

responsible〔rɪ'spɑnsəbl̩〕*adj.* 負責的

outgoing〔'aʊtˌgoɪŋ〕*adj.* 外向的

individual〔ˌɪndə'vɪdʒʊəl〕*n.* 個人

genuinely〔'dʒɛnjʊɪnlɪ〕*adv.* 眞誠地

professional〔prə'fɛʃənl̩〕*adj.* 專業的

organization〔ˌɔrgənə'zeʃən〕*n.* 組織；機構

advancement〔əd'vænsmənt〕*n.* 升遷

dependability〔dɪˌpɛndə'bɪlətɪ〕*n.* 可靠性

trait〔tret〕*n.* 特質　　worth〔wɜθ〕*n.* 價値

大學入學學科能力測驗英文模擬試題 ②

第壹部分：單選題 (佔72分)

一、詞彙 (佔15分)

說明：第 1 題至第 15 題，每題 4 個選項，其中只有一個是最適當的答案，畫記在答案卡之「選擇題答案區」。各題答對得 1 分；未作答、答錯、或畫記多於一個選項者，該題以零分計算。

1. Before you make a presentation, you must know your _____.
   Ask yourself what you really want to achieve.
   (A) authority　　(B) popularity　　(C) objective　　(D) security

2. Some people _____ most of their time on-line talking to friends
   from home on-line instead of making new friends in school.
   (A) acquaint　　(B) expend　　(C) fetch　　(D) quote

3. Rich as he is, he still lives in Spartan _____. He travels
   economy class and refuses to stay in five-star hotels.
   (A) simplicity　　(B) reluctance　　(C) permission　　(D) potential

4. Tom had a serious drinking problem. The doctor advised him to
   quit drinking completely or at least _____ his consumption.
   (A) defeat　　(B) emphasize　　(C) moderate　　(D) fasten

5. Though India is becoming wealthy, it still has 500 million people
   living on less than a dollar a day in complete _____.
   (A) awareness　　(B) circulation　　(C) charity　　(D) poverty

6. The roots of communication between parent and child begin to grow
   in early childhood. It is _____ for them to talk openly and
   honestly if they have no history of in-depth conversation.
   (A) shy　　(B) innocent　　(C) defensive　　(D) tough

7. The teen years can be tough for both parent and child. _____ are under stress to do well in school, get along with their family and make important life decisions.
   (A) Generations (B) Adolescents (C) Participants (D) Laymen

8. Young people's mental health problems can be real and painful, leading to school failure, loss of friends, or family _____.
   (A) conflict (B) familiarity (C) reputation (D) significance

9. In Taiwan, most children do not find themselves in life-threatening situations, but it is _____ for them to know about some safety issues before problems arise.
   (A) coherent (B) quarrelsome (C) considerable (D) crucial

10. The successful company is not the one with the most brains, but the one with the most brains acting in _____.
    (A) reference (B) intention (C) controversy (D) concert

11. For 20 years Dr. Johnson has suffered a serious mental problem but, _____, he is recognized as a proficient researcher able to help others with their medical problems.
    (A) originally (B) ironically (C) relatively (D) ideally

12. As the Internet makes people across the world feel closer, they slowly start _____ about the real world they live in.
    (A) concluding (B) retarding (C) forgetting (D) regretting

13. Every year, as the Chinese Moon Festival _____, Chinese people around the world buy mooncakes as gifts for family and friends.
    (A) approaches (B) segments (C) splashes (D) diminishes

14. Many people take listening for _____. They confuse hearing with listening. That is why they often misunderstand others.
    (A) threatened (B) granted (C) demonstrated (D) arrested

15. In a sluggish economy, many people are _____ from their employment, causing a large number of social and family problems.
   (A) laid off　　(B) called off　　(C) put off　　(D) taken off

二、綜合測驗（佔 15 分）

說明：第 16 題至第 30 題，每題一個空格，請依文意選出最適當的一個答案，畫記在答案卡之「選擇題答案區」。各題答對得 1 分；未作答、答錯、或畫記多於一個選項者，該題以零分計算。

第 16 至 20 題為題組

　　Walking is an endurance activity and you will need to replace energy when walking for two hours or more. Water is not enough on a long walk, but sports drinks can replenish you.

　　Sports drinks with sugar and salt better ___16___ both water and body salt when walking for more than an hour. They can prevent dehydration and hyponatremia. However, make sure to steer clear of those with fancy additives and herbs, ___17___ do you no good on a walk. Look for those with proper amounts of salt and carbohydrates. The popular high-caffeine energy drinks in small cans are not ___18___ for exercise hydration. They provide too much caffeine and not enough water. You can also make your own sports drinks at lower cost.

　　___19___, you should bring along fruit for the truly all-natural carbohydrate burst. Fruit snacks such as bananas are an excellent source of potassium. Apples, small oranges, and raisins are great packable snacks too, but be sure to ___20___ peels and cores appropriately. Toss them in the trash, not in the bushes or on the roadside.

16. (A) dominate　　(B) suppress　　(C) replace　　(D) represent
17. (A) what　　(B) which　　(C) that　　(D) and
18. (A) associated　　(B) innovated　　(C) recommended　　(D) accommodated
19. (A) If possible　　(B) If ever　　(C) If only　　(D) If not
20. (A) consist in　　(B) contribute to　　(C) reflect on　　(D) dispose of

第 21 至 25 題為題組

There was a time when the only interaction the general public had with space exploration was passive and through the media. ___21___, many people felt indifferent to space missions as they just did not connect with them on a personal level.

But that was before the twenty-first century, and today we ___22___ the opportunity to actively participate in the exploration of space by sending our names toward the stars. ___23___ the names of millions of individuals can sit on Mars or at least cling to a small celestial body revolving around the sun. The National Aeronautics and Space Administration (NASA) recently announced another opportunity to fly high. ___24___ can get their name aboard the Glory satellite, which is the first science mission dedicated to measuring the effects of particles in the atmosphere and ___25___ solar data for the purpose of creating a long-term climate record. Participants can get a printable certificate and have their names recorded on a microchip aboard the spacecraft.

21. (A) Nevertheless   (B) Consequently
    (C) Furthermore   (D) Afterwards
22. (A) have   (B) have been   (C) had   (D) had had
23. (A) When   (B) Because   (C) As   (D) Now
24. (A) Someone   (B) Nobody   (C) Anyone   (D) Those
25. (A) collecting   (B) collected   (C) collect   (D) to collect

第 26 至 30 題為題組

If you could be any animal on Earth, what would you be? A bird, because it can fly? Maybe that was a popular choice long ago, but now, birds are probably the most abused animals on the planet.

Unlike wild birds, birds sold in pet stores cannot fly because their wings are clipped. They are sold by the pet stores and frequently end up

___26___ or dead at an early age. Before being sold, they have to spend their lives in bird mills. Large parrots, ___27___, can live for over 70 years. Can you imagine spending 70 years trapped in a small cage? However, even if they are sold, they are not guaranteed a good life. Parrots are intelligent, social creatures that require exercise, companionship, a varied diet, and toys to be happy. But how many people buying birds on ___28___ are prepared to care for them adequately?

Besides, many pet stores breed birds for money, caring only about production and not about the well-being of the breeding animals and their offspring. They do not respect the natural breeding cycle and mate birds all year long. ___29___, there are many mutations.

While we hope that proper legislation will one day save the birds, in the meantime we can do nothing but love our birds and give them ___30___ they desperately need—proper care.

26. (A) abandoned　　　　　　　(B) abandoning
　　(C) coldheartedly　　　　　(D) sympathetically
27. (A) in contrast　　　　　　(B) in due time
　　(C) rather than　　　　　　(D) for example
28. (A) schedule　　(B) condition　　(C) impulse　　(D) occasion
29. (A) As a result　　　　　　(B) Despite this
　　(C) To begin with　　　　　(D) By no means
30. (A) if　　　　　　(B) what　　　　　(C) when　　　　　(D) which

三、文意選填（佔 10 分）

說明： 第 31 題至第 40 題，每題一個空格，請依文意在文章後所提供的 (A) 到 (J) 選項中分別選出最適當者，並將其英文字母代號畫記在答案卡之「選擇題答案區」。各題答對得 1 分；未作答、答錯、或畫記多於一個選項者，該題以零分計算。

第 31 至 40 題為題組

Americans tended to think that knowing English was sufficient for all their needs. That is why they cannot say ___31___ the most rudimentary phrase in any other language. However, many Americans now are belatedly realizing that the whole world does not ___32___ speak English, and that even many of those who have learned English as a second language prefer to converse in their ___33___ tongue.

A second language is now becoming a vital part of the basic preparation for an ___34___ number of careers. Even in those cases where the knowledge of a second language does not help graduates obtain a first job, many report that their foreign language skills do enhance their mobility and improve their chances for ___35___.

In addition to any technical skills that foreign language students choose to develop, they also have further ___36___ in the job market. Asked which of their college courses had been most valuable, people who were employed in the business world pointed not only to career-oriented courses ___37___ business management, but also to people-oriented subjects like psychology, and to classes that had helped them to develop communication skills.

And foreign language students, whose courses focus ___38___ on this aspect of learning, often possess better communication skills. They may have a language ability that enables them to achieve greater mental flexibility and command an awareness of a wider set of ___39___. Bilinguals can communicate more effectively with people of other countries and cultures, and they are more effective ___40___ too.

(A) options (B) necessarily (C) increasing (D) promotion
(E) even (F) such as (G) native
(H) problem-solver (I) advantages (J) heavily

四、閱讀測驗（佔 32 分）

說明： 第 41 題至第 56 題，每題 4 個選項，請分別根據各篇文章之文意選出最適當的一個答案，畫記在答案卡之「選擇題答案區」。各題答對得 2 分；未作答、答錯、或畫記多於一個選項者，該題以零分計算。

第 41 至 44 題為題組

Diwali, the festival of lights, celebrates the abundance of the autumn harvest. Dedicated to various gods and goddesses, the festival also marks an important date in the Indian calendar. This is the point from which the Hindus measure the "Vikram Samvat", the era established by King Vikram, who defeated the Huns and saved India from their potentially disastrous foreign rule.

Diwali also worships the gracious nature of the three goddesses, Lakshmi, Kali and Saraswati. The blessings of Lakshmi are essential in making lives prosperous and peaceful. They represent boundless wealth, health, friends and long life. Goddess Kali represents physical, mental and spiritual strength, which is necessary for an individual as well as a community to flourish. Goddess Saraswati stands for knowledge and wisdom, which is the ultimate in spirituality, for it leads to Enlightenment.

Over the years Diwali celebrations have changed in nature and character. Once only earthen lamps filled with oil and homemade wicks were used, while now candles and electric lamps are lit and sweets are made to welcome guests and gods. People buy gold and silver as a sign of good luck. Merchants and businessmen close their books and accounts, thanking the gods for a bountiful end of the year. Fireworks are lit in the evening and all the houses are wonderfully lit with lamps and lanterns. It is believed that lights can dispel darkness and evil spirits lingering in the neighborhood. Festival spirit is in full swing as sweets and sumptuous food are served at dinner. It seems all the heavens and humans rejoice as the new year begins and the eternal cycle of time is renewed.

41. Which of the following is NOT true of Diwali?
    (A) Diwali is the festival of lights and celebrates the autumn harvest.
    (B) Diwali marks the day when India was freed from a local tyrant.
    (C) Diwali is dedicated to a large number of gods and goddesses.
    (D) Diwali means all heavens and humans rejoice as the new year begins.

42. Diwali does NOT mainly worship _____.
    (A) Lakshmi　　(B) Saraswati　(C) Kali　　　(D) Lord Yama

43. Which of the following is NOT a common Diwali celebration activity now?
    (A) People use earthen lamps filled with homemade wicks.
    (B) People buy gold and silver as a sign of good luck.
    (C) Businessmen close their books and accounts.
    (D) Houses are lit with decorative lamps and lanterns.

44. According to the passage, people who want to use money to generate more money would worship _____.
    (A) Saraswati　　(B) Kali　　　(C) Lord Yama　(D) Lakshmi

第 45 至 48 題為題組

　　You walk up to your colleague to talk to him about an important issue at work. As soon as he starts talking, you have to turn your head away due to the stench coming from his mouth. Most men and women agree that bad breath is the biggest turnoff in a relationship. It can be quite damaging to self-esteem. A person can be made fun of at work, not just behind his back but also by a few casual remarks which can be quite hurtful.

　　Bad breath is also called halitosis and most people have suffered from it at some stage. It is particularly common after waking and eating some foods which can cause bad breath, such as garlic, onion, pastrami, and curry.

There are quite a few ways to determine if you have bad breath. Take a piece of clean cloth and rub it on your teeth. Wait for a few seconds and smell it. Or you can lick the back of your hand and smell it after it dries. If you do have a chronic breath problem, don't expect to get rid of it by popping some chewing gum or using a mouthwash, for these will only mask your bad breath and not treat it.

The first step in treating bad breath is to identify its cause. There may be a respiratory tract or sinus infections, or it may be associated with your lifestyle. For example, severe dieting causes a fruity odor. The most common cause tends to be poor oral hygiene, which allows bacteria to breed uninhibited and produces a foul smell by acting on organic substances in the mouth.

Most bad breath can be cured by proper dental hygiene measures. It is not a hard problem to take care of. In case of persistent bad breath due to no apparent reason, it is always best to consult your dentist.

45. What is the title of this passage?
   (A) The Prevention of Bad Breath
   (B) The Impact of Bad Breath
   (C) The Causes of Bad Breath
   (D) An Overview of Bad Breath

46. In which of the following magazines would you most likely find this passage?
   (A) *Stem Cells and Diseases*   (B) *Psychology Today*
   (C) *Skin Care for Children*   (D) *Natural Health*

47. Which of the following is NOT mentioned in this passage regarding bad breath?
   (A) The first step in treating bad breath is to identify the cause.
   (B) Bad breath is likely to be experienced by most people at least occasionally.
   (C) Avoid processed or spicy foods that contribute to bad breath.
   (D) There are some ways of checking if you have developed halitosis.

48. The author advised the readers to _____ if they do not
understand why they have continuing bad breath.
(A) consult a dentist   (B) eat a healthy diet
(C) maintain good oral hygiene   (D) quit severe dieting

第 49 至 52 題爲題組

Living things face a constant **barrage** of threats that challenge
their ability to survive and reproduce. They need to adapt to new
temperatures, climates, and atmospheric conditions, as well as
man-made threats. If a species is unable to cope with these threats
through adaptation, it may face extinction.

In recent evolutionary history, threats facing many organisms have
been driven primarily by the effects of a single species: humans. The
extent to which humans have altered this planet has initiated extinctions
on such a vast scale that many scientists believe we are now
experiencing a mass extinction.

Unlike other natural threats, man-made threats can be prevented by
changing our behavior. After examining how human activities have
adversely impacted life on earth, we can take steps to prevent future
damage. For example, the destruction of animal habitats for human use of
the land should be stopped. Activities such as the burning of fossil fuels
that alter the Earth's atmosphere and result in global climate changes
should be reduced. Pollutants like pesticides, herbicides, etc. should be
regulated. Besides, excessive fishing, hunting, poaching, and illegal
trade in endangered species should all be prohibited.

As humans, we have a unique ability to understand the consequences
of our actions. We are capable of learning about the effects our actions
have on the world around us and how changes in those actions could
help to alter future events. So let's do it here and now.

49. The purpose of this article is most likely to ＿＿＿＿＿＿＿.
　　(A) understand the exploitation of wild tribes
　　(B) emphasize the effect of endangered species on illegal markets
　　(C) examine natural threats and man-made threats to animals
　　(D) explore the pollutants and accidental deaths of wildlife

50. The author of this passage is most likely to be a ＿＿＿＿＿＿＿.
　　(A) human rights activist　　　　　(B) devoted environmentalist
　　(C) family physician　　　　　　　(D) news correspondent

51. Which of the following best explains the word "**barrage**" in the first
　　paragraph?
　　(A) A great waste of time.
　　(B) A quick burst of thunder.
　　(C) A type of machine that fires bullets.
　　(D) An overwhelming, concentrated attack.

52. The author advised the readers to ＿＿＿＿＿＿＿.
　　(A) destroy wildlife habitats
　　(B) prevent future damage to the earth
　　(C) burn fossil fuels to alter the Earth's atmosphere
　　(D) rationally trade endangered species

第 53 至 56 題為題組

　　On October 10, the Norwegian Nobel Committee awarded its 2008 Peace Prize to Martti Ahtisaari. The Committee said it honored the former Finnish president for his important efforts over more than three decades to resolve conflicts in Europe, Asia, Africa and the Middle East.

　　Ahtisaari worked as a primary school teacher before becoming a Finnish diplomat in 1956 and was a senior Finnish diplomat when, in 1977, he was named the U.N. envoy to Namibia, where guerrillas were battling South African apartheid rule. He later rose to undersecretary-general, and in 1988 was dispatched to Namibia to lead 8,000 U.N. peacekeepers during its transition to independence. He was chairman of the Bosnia-Herzegovina working group in the international peace conference on former Yugoslavia from 1992 to 1993, and was special adviser to the U.N. secretary-general on former Yugoslavia in 1993.

He had been mentioned as a possible Nobel Peace Prize winner since 2005. He was selected out of 197 nominees, including Chinese human rights lawyer Gao Zhisheng and AIDS and environmental activist Hu Jia, Russia's Lidia Yusupova, and Vietnam's Thich Quang Do. The honor went to former Vice President Al Gore and the U.N. Panel on Climate Change in 2007 and to anti-poverty activist and microcredit pioneer Muhammad Yunus in 2006.

As the Norwegian Nobel Committee said, "Throughout all his adult life, whether as a senior Finnish public servant and president or in an international capacity, often connected to the United Nations, Ahtisaari has worked for peace and reconciliation."

53. Who won the Nobel Peace Prize immediately before Ahtisaari?
    (A) Muhammad Yunus   (B) Wangari Maathai
    (C) Al Gore   (D) Mohamed ElBaradei

54. Who was NOT a 2008 Nobel Peace Prize candidate?
    (A) Thich Quang Do   (B) Gao Zhisheng
    (C) Lidia Yusupova   (D) Al Gore

55. Martti Ahtisaari did NOT resolve conflicts in _____.
    (A) Europe   (B) Africa
    (C) the Middle East   (D) South America

56. Martti Ahtisaari has NOT been _____.
    (A) chairman of the Bosnia-Herzegovina working group
    (B) a senior high school teacher
    (C) special adviser to the U.N. secretary-general
    (D) named the U.N. envoy to Namibia

第貳部分：非選擇題（佔 28 分）

一、中譯英（佔 8 分）

說明：1. 請將以下中文句子譯成正確、通順、達意的英文，並將答案寫在「答案卷」上。

2. 請依序作答，並標明題號。每題 4 分，共 8 分。

1. 身為在家裡負責煮飯的人，媽媽最怕的就是晚餐時間。

2. 她必須想盡辦法做出美味而健康的晚餐，同時要滿足家人不同的喜好。

二、英文作文（佔 20 分）

說明：1. 依提示在「答案卷」上寫一篇英文作文。

2. 文長約 100 至 120 個單詞（words）。

提示：你剛剛認識了一位住在美國的高中生筆友（英文名字必須假設為 Jerry 或 Cathy）。你（英文名字必須假設為 Fang 或 Liu），要寫一封信和他（她）敘述台灣高中生的生活，並請他（她）描述美國高中生的生活，彼此交換意見及想法。

請注意：必須使用上述的 Fang 或 Liu 在信末署名，**不得使用自己的真實中文或英文名字。**

大學入學學科能力測驗英文模擬試題 ② 詳解

第壹部分：單選題

一、詞彙：

1. (**C**) 在做簡報之前，你必須要先知道你的<u>目標</u>，問問自己真正想要達到的是什麼。

(A) authority〔ə'θɔrətɪ〕*n.* 權威　　authorities *n. pl.* 當局

(B) popularity〔͵pɑpjə'lærətɪ〕*n.* 名氣（= *fame*）；流行（= *vogue*）

(C) ***objective***〔əb'dʒɛktɪv〕*n.* 目標（= *goal*）

(D) security〔sɪ'kjʊrətɪ〕*n.* 安全

* presentation〔͵prɛznʹteʃən〕*n.* 報告

make a presentation 做簡報　　achieve〔ə'tʃiv〕*v.* 達到

2. (**B**) 有些人<u>花費</u>他們大部分時間，從家裡與朋友在線上交談，而不是在學校裡結交新朋友。

(A) acquaint〔ə'kwent〕*v.* 使熟悉 < *with* >

(B) ***expend***〔ɪk'spɛnd〕*v.* 花費（時間、金錢）（= *spend*）

(C) fetch〔fɛtʃ〕*v.*（去）拿來

(D) quote〔kwot〕*v.* 引用（= *cite*）

* on-line〔'ɑn͵laɪn〕*adv.* 在線上　　***instead of*** 而不是

make friends 交朋友

3. (**A**) 他雖然很富有，但仍然過著斯巴達式的<u>簡樸</u>生活。他搭乘經濟艙，而且拒絕入住五星級飯店。

(A) ***simplicity***〔sɪm'plɪsətɪ〕*n.* 簡樸　　***Spartan simplicity*** 簡樸生活

(B) reluctance〔rɪ'lʌktəns〕*n.* 不情願　　reluctant *adj.*

(C) permission〔pə'mɪʃən〕*n.* 許可（= *approval*）

(D) potential〔pə'tɛnʃəl〕*n.* 潛力　　*adj.* 潛在的；可能的

* Spartan〔'spɑrtn̩〕*adj.* 斯巴達式的

economy〔ɪ'kɑnəmɪ〕*adj.* 經濟的

economy class 經濟艙

five-star〔'faɪv'stɑr〕*adj.* 五星級的

4. (**C**) 湯姆有非常嚴重的酗酒問題，醫生勸他要徹底戒酒，或至少<u>節制</u>一下他的飲酒量。

(A) defeat〔dɪˈfit〕*v.* 打敗

(B) emphasize〔ˈɛmfəˌsaɪz〕*v.* 強調（ = *stress* ）

(C) *moderate*〔ˈmɑdəˌret〕*v.* 節制

(D) fasten〔ˈfæsn̩〕*v.* 繫上

* serious〔ˈsɪrɪəs〕*adj.* 嚴重的
drinking〔ˈdrɪŋkɪŋ〕*n.* 飲酒
advise〔ədˈvaɪz〕*v.* 勸告　　quit〔kwɪt〕*v.* 戒除
completely〔kəmˈplitlɪ〕*adv.* 完全地；徹底地
at least 至少　　consumption〔kənˈsʌmpʃən〕*n.* 吃；喝

5. (**D**) 雖然印度正走向富裕，但是仍有五億人口，每天花不到一美元在過活，非常<u>貧窮</u>。

(A) awareness〔əˈwɛrnɪs〕*n.* 察覺；意識

(B) circulation〔ˌsɝkjəˈleʃən〕*n.* 循環；（書報的）發行量

(C) charity〔ˈtʃærətɪ〕*n.* 慈善

(D) *poverty*〔ˈpɑvətɪ〕*n.* 貧窮

* India〔ˈɪndɪə〕*n.* 印度　　wealthy〔ˈwɛlθɪ〕*adj.* 富裕的
complete〔kəmˈplit〕*adj.* 完全的

6. (**D**) 親子之間的溝通基礎，是從童年初期就開始發展。如果彼此沒有深入對話的經歷，那對他們來說，率直且真誠地談話是很<u>困難的</u>。

(A) shy〔ʃaɪ〕*adj.* 害羞的；膽小的

(B) innocent〔ˈɪnəsn̩t〕*adj.* 天真的；清白的（ ↔ guilty ）

(C) defensive〔dɪˈfɛnsɪv〕*adj.* 防禦的（ ↔ aggressive *adj.* 攻擊的 ）

(D) *tough*〔tʌf〕*adj.* 困難的（ = *difficult* ）

* root〔rut〕*n.* 根源；基礎
communication〔kəˌmjunəˈkeʃən〕*n.* 溝通
childhood〔ˈtʃaɪldˌhʊd〕*n.* 童年時期
openly〔ˈopənlɪ〕*adv.* 率直地
honestly〔ˈɑnɪstlɪ〕*adv.* 真誠地
in-depth〔ˈɪnˈdɛpθ〕*adj.* 深入的

7. (**B**) 青少年時期，對父母和孩子來說，可能都不好應付。青少年的壓力很大，要在學校有好表現、要與家人和睦相處，以及要做出人生重要的決定。

　　(A) generation〔͵dʒɛnəˋreʃən〕 *n.* 世代

　　(B) ***adolescent***〔͵ædḷˋɛsn̩t〕 *n.* 青少年 (= *teenager*)　 *adj.* 青少年的

　　(C) participant〔pɚˋtɪsəpənt〕 *n.* 參與者

　　(D) layman〔ˋlemən〕 *n.* 門外漢 (= *outsider*)

　　* teen〔tin〕 *adj.* 十幾歲的　　 ***teen years*** 青少年時期
　　　 tough〔tʌf〕 *adj.* 困難的；難對付的
　　　 stress〔strɛs〕 *n.* 壓力
　　　 do well 表現好　　 ***under stress*** 承受壓力
　　　 get along with 與～相處　　 ***make a decision*** 做決定

8. (**A**) 年輕人的心理健康問題，有時是非同小可而且痛苦的，可能會導致學業上的失敗、失去朋友，或家庭衝突。

　　(A) ***conflict***〔ˋkɑnflɪkt〕 *n.* 衝突 (↔ *harmony* *n.* 和諧)

　　(B) familiarity〔fə͵mɪlɪˋærətɪ〕 *n.* 熟悉

　　(C) reputation〔͵rɛpjəˋteʃən〕 *n.* 名聲 (= *prestige*)

　　(D) significance〔sɪgˋnɪfəkəns〕 *n.* 意義；重要性

　　* mental〔ˋmɛntḷ〕 *adj.* 心理的　　 real〔ˋriəl〕 *adj.* 非同小可的
　　　 painful〔ˋpenfəl〕 *adj.* 痛苦的　　 ***lead to*** 導致
　　　 failure〔ˋfeljɚ〕 *n.* 失敗

9. (**D**) 在台灣，大部分的孩子並不覺得自己置身於生命受到威脅的狀況，但在問題發生之前，就讓他們了解一些關於安全的問題，是很重要的。

　　(A) coherent〔koˋhɪrənt〕 *adj.* 有條理的；前後連貫的 (= *consistent*)

　　(B) quarrelsome〔ˋkwɔrəlsəm〕 *adj.* 愛爭吵的

　　(C) considerable〔kənˋsɪdərəbḷ〕 *adj.* 相當大的

　　(D) ***crucial***〔ˋkruʃəl〕 *adj.* 非常重要的 (= *vital*)

　　* life-threatening〔ˋlaɪf͵θrɛtənɪŋ〕 *adj.* 威脅生命的
　　　 situation〔͵sɪtʃʊˋeʃən〕 *n.* 情況
　　　 issue〔ˋɪʃʊ〕 *n.* 問題　　 arise〔əˋraɪz〕 *v.* 發生

10. (**D**) 成功的公司，不是智囊團最多的那一個，而是有最多智囊團一起
齊力合作的那一個。

　　(A) reference〔ˈrɛfərəns〕 n. 參考

　　(B) intention〔ɪnˈtɛnʃən〕 n. 意圖；目的 (= *purpose*)

　　(C) controversy〔ˈkɑntrəˌvɝsɪ〕 n. 爭論 (= *dispute*)

　　(D) ***concert***〔ˈkɑnsɝt〕 n. 協力；演唱會

　　　　in concert 一起；合作

　　* brains〔brenz〕 n. pl. 智囊團　　act〔ækt〕 v. 行動表現

11. (**B**) 強森博士這二十年來一直有很嚴重的心理問題，但諷刺的是，他卻
被認為是專業的研究員，能幫助有醫學問題的人。

　　(A) originally〔əˈrɪdʒənlɪ〕 adv. 原本；最初 (= *at first* = *initially*)

　　(B) ***ironically***〔aɪˈrɑnɪklɪ〕 adv. 諷刺地　　irony n. 諷刺

　　(C) relatively〔ˈrɛlətɪvlɪ〕 adv. 相對地

　　(D) ideally〔aɪˈdiəlɪ〕 adv. 理想地

　　* suffer〔ˈsʌfɚ〕 v. 遭受　　mental〔ˈmɛntl̩〕 adj. 心理的
　　　recognize〔ˈrɛkəgˌnaɪz〕 v. 認為
　　　proficient〔prəˈfɪʃənt〕 adj. 精通的
　　　researcher〔rɪˈsɝtʃɚ〕 n. 研究員
　　　medical〔ˈmɛdɪkl̩〕 adj. 醫學的；醫療的

12. (**C**) 當網際網路讓全世界的人們感覺更接近的時候，他們也開始慢慢
遺忘了所生活的真實世界。

　　(A) conclude〔kənˈklud〕 v. 下結論　　conclusion n. 結論

　　(B) retard〔rɪˈtɑrd〕 v. 阻礙 (= *obstruct*)

　　(C) ***forget***〔fɚˈgɛt〕 v. 忘記

　　(D) regret〔rɪˈgrɛt〕 v. 後悔

　　* Internet〔ˈɪntɚˌnɛt〕 n. 網際網路

13. (**A**) 每年當中國中秋節接近的時候，世界各地的中國人都會購買月餅，當作禮物送給家人或朋友。

(A) ***approach*** 〔ə'protʃ〕 *v.* 接近 (= *come near*)

(B) segment 〔'sɛgmənt〕 *v.* 分割

(C) splash 〔splæʃ〕 *v.* (水) 濺起

(D) diminish 〔də'mɪnɪʃ〕 *v.* 減少 (= *reduce*)

* festival 〔'fɛstəvḷ〕 *n.* 節日　***Moon Festival*** 中秋節
mooncake 〔'mun,kek〕 *n.* 月餅

14. (**B**) 很多人都把聆聽當作是理所當然的，他們分不清楚聽見和聆聽，這就是他們時常誤解別人的原因。

(A) threatened 〔'θrɛtṇd〕 *adj.* 受到威脅的

(B) ***granted*** 〔'græntɪd〕 *adj.* 理所當然的
take sth. for granted 將某事視爲理所當然

(C) demonstrated 〔'dɛmən,stretɪd〕 *adj.* 被證明的

(D) arrested 〔ə'rɛstɪd〕 *adj.* 被逮捕的

* confuse 〔kən'fjuz〕 *v.* 混淆；分不清
misunderstand 〔,mɪsʌndə'stænd〕 *v.* 誤解

15. (**A**) 在經濟不景氣的時候，很多人被解雇，引起許多社會與家庭的問題。

(A) ***lay off*** (暫時) 解雇

(B) call off 取消 (= *cancel*)

(C) put off 拖延 (= *postpone*)

(D) take off 起飛

* sluggish 〔'slʌgɪʃ〕 *adj.* 不振的；不景氣的
employment 〔ɪm'plɔɪmənt〕 *n.* 職業；工作
a large number of 很多

二、綜合測驗：

第 16 至 20 題為題組

　　散步是一種耐力運動，如果散步超過兩個小時，你可能必須去補充點能量。就長程的步行來說，水是不夠的，要運動飲料才能夠替你補充精力。

　　散步超過一個小時的時候，含有糖和鹽的運動飲料，更適合<u>取代</u>水分和體內的鹽分。它們能夠預防脫水和低鈉血症。

16

* walking〔'wɔkɪŋ〕*n.* 散步　　endurance〔ɪn'djʊrəns〕*n.* 耐力

activity〔æk'tɪvətɪ〕*n.* 活動

replace〔rɪ'ples〕*v.* 取代；接替　　***sports drink*** 運動飲料

replenish〔rɪ'plɛnɪʃ〕*v.* 給～充注精力

16. (**C**)　(A) dominate〔'dɑmə‚net〕*v.* 支配；佔優勢

(B) suppress〔sə'prɛs〕*v.* 鎮壓

(C) ***replace***〔rɪ'ples〕*v.* 取代

(D) represent〔‚rɛprɪ'zɛnt〕*v.* 代表

　　不過，請一定要遠離<u>那些</u>對你在步行時沒有益處，又含有特別添加物或藥草的

17

飲品。去找那些<u>擁有</u>適量鹽分和碳水化合物的飲料。那些受到大眾喜愛，含有高咖啡因的小瓶罐裝飲料，並不<u>建議</u>用來補充運動流失的水分。它們提供過多

18

咖啡因，及不夠充足的水分。你也可以用低的成本製作你自己的運動飲料。

* prevent〔prɪ'vɛnt〕*v.* 預防

dehydration〔‚dihaɪ'dreʃən〕*n.* 脫水

hyponatremia〔‚haɪponə'trimɪə〕*n.* 低鈉血症

make sure to 確保　　steer〔stɪr〕*v.* 操控

steer clear of 避開　　fancy〔'fænsɪ〕*adj.* 特製的；花俏的

additive〔'ædətɪv〕*n.* 添加物

herb〔hɝb , ɝb〕*n.* 藥草；草本　　***do sb. good*** 對某人有益

look for 尋找　　proper〔'prɑpɚ〕*adj.* 適當的

carbohydrate〔‚kɑrbo'haɪdret〕*n.* 碳水化合物

17. (**B**) 空格應填關代，引導形容詞子句，又前有逗點，不可用 that，故選
(B) *which*。而 (A) what 爲複合關代，引導名詞子句，在此用法不合。

* caffeine（'kæfiɪn）*n.* 咖啡因　　*energy drink* 能量飲料
can（kæn）*n.* 罐子　　hydration（haɪ'dreʃən）*n.* 提供水分
provide（prə'vaɪd）*v.* 提供　　cost（kɔst）*n.* 成本

18. (**C**) (A) associate（ə'soʃɪ,et）*v.* 聯想
(B) innovate（'ɪnə,vet）*v.* 創新
(C) *recommend*（,rɛkə'mɛnd）*v.* 推薦
(D) accommodate（ə'kɑmə,det）*v.* 容納

　　<u>如果可能的話</u>，爲了瞬間補充眞正純天然的碳水化合物的瞬間供給，要
　　　　19
帶著水果。水果類點心，像是香蕉，就是很棒的鉀的來源。

* natural（'nætʃərəl）*adj.* 天然的
burst（bɝst）*n.* 突然爆發；瞬間供給
snack（snæk）*n.* 點心　　excellent（'ɛkslənt）*adj.* 極好的
source（sors）*n.* 來源　　potassium（pə'tæsɪəm）*n.* 鉀

19. (**A**) 依句意，「如果可能的話」，選 (A) *If possible*。而 (B) if ever「如果
曾經」，(C) if only「但願」，(D) if not「如果不是這樣的話」，均不
合句意。

蘋果、小柑橘和葡萄乾，也都是能打包好的好點心，但是，務必要適當<u>處理</u>
果皮和果核。把它們丟到垃圾堆裡，不要丟在樹叢或路邊。　　　　　20

* raisin（'rezn）*n.* 葡萄乾　　packable（'pækəbḷ）*adj.* 可打包的
be sure to V. 務必～　　peel（pil）*n.* 果皮
core（kor）*n.* 果核　　appropriately（ə'proprɪɪtlɪ）*adv.* 適當地
toss（tɔs）*v.* 扔；投擲　　trash（træʃ）*n.* 垃圾
bush（buʃ）*n.* 灌木叢　　roadside（'rod,saɪd）*n.* 路邊

20. (**D**) 依句意，選 (D) *dispose of*「處理」。而 (A) consist in「在於」，
(B) contribute to「促成；有助於」，(C) reflect on「仔細思考」，
則不合句意。

第 21 至 25 題為題組

　　很久之前，一般大眾與太空探險間唯一的互動是被動的，而且是要透過媒體的。<u>因此</u>，許多人對太空任務感到漠不關心，就像他們不會以個人的層級，
21
與太空任務產生連結。

* interaction〔͵ɪntə'ækʃən〕*n.* 互動
  the general public 一般大眾　　　　space〔spes〕*n.* 太空
  exploration〔͵ɛksplə'reʃən〕*n.* 探險　　　passive〔'pæsɪv〕*adj.* 被動的
  media〔'midɪə〕*n. pl.* 媒體【單數為 medium〔'midɪəm〕】
  indifferent〔ɪn'dɪfrənt〕*adj.* 漠不關心的　　　mission〔'mɪʃən〕*n.* 任務
  connect〔kə'nɛkt〕*v.* 連結　　　personal〔'pɜsn̩l̩〕*adj.* 個人的
  level〔'lɛvl̩〕*n.* 層面；地位

21. (**B**)　依句意，選 (B) ***Consequently***〔'kɑnsə͵kwɛntlɪ〕*adv.* 因此。而
　　(A) nevertheless〔͵nɛvəðə'lɛs〕*adv.* 然而，(C) furthermore〔'fɜðə͵mor〕
　　adv. 此外，(D) afterwards〔'æftəwədz〕*adv.* 後來，則不合句意。

　　但那是在二十一世紀以前的事了，現在我們可以藉著向星體發送自己的名字，而<u>得到</u>主動參與探索太空的機會。
22

* century〔'sɛntʃərɪ〕*n.* 世紀　　　opportunity〔͵ɑpə'tjunətɪ〕*n.* 機會
  actively〔'æktɪvlɪ〕*adv.* 主動地　　　participate〔pɑr'tɪsə͵pet〕*v.* 參與

22. (**A**)　現在我們「有」這樣的機會，用現在簡單式，選 (A) ***have***。

　　<u>現在</u>，可以把數百萬人的名字放在火星上，或至少能夠附著在一些繞著太陽公
23
轉的小天體之上。最近，美國航空暨太空總署宣布了另一個能夠高飛的機會。

* individual〔͵ɪndə'vɪdʒʊəl〕*n.* 個人　　　sit〔sɪt〕*v.* 坐落；放置
  Mars〔mɑrz〕*n.* 火星　　　cling〔klɪŋ〕*v.* 附著 < *to* >
  celestial〔sə'lɛstʃəl〕*adj.* 天體的　　　revolve〔rɪ'vɑlv〕*v.* 公轉
  aeronautics〔͵ɛrə'nɔtɪks〕*n.* 航空學
  administration〔əd͵mɪnə'streʃən〕*n.* 局；部門
  National Aeronautics and Space Administration 美國航空暨太空總署
  recently〔'risn̩tlɪ〕*adv.* 最近　　　announce〔ə'naʊns〕*v.* 宣布

23. (**D**) 空格後為完整句，故要選副詞，才不影響句子結構，故選 (D) *Now*
「現在」。而 (A) when，(B) because，和 (C) as「當～時候」，都是
連接詞，在此用法不合。

<u>任何人</u>都能夠把他的名字，放在葛洛莉號衛星上，這個衛星是第一個專門進
　　24

行測量大氣粒子以及<u>收集</u>太陽資料的科學任務，以建立長期的氣候紀錄。參
　　　　　　　　　　25

加者可以得到一張可印刷的證書，並讓自己的名字，紀錄在太空飛行器的微
晶片上。

* aboard〔ə'bord〕*adv.* 在（船、飛機、火車等）上
  satellite〔'sætḷˌaɪt〕*n.* 人造衛星
  be dedicated to + V-ing 致力於～
  measure〔'mɛʒɚ〕*v.* 測量　　effect〔ɪ'fɛkt〕*n.* 影響；效果
  particle〔'pɑrtɪkḷ〕*n.* 粒子　　atmosphere〔'ætməsˌfɪr〕*n.* 大氣（層）
  solar〔'solɚ〕*adj.* 太陽的　　data〔'detə〕*n. pl.* 資料
  for the purpose of 為了　　long-term〔'lɔŋˌtɝm〕*adj.* 長期的
  record〔*n.* 'rɛkɚd　*v.* rɪ'kɔrd〕*n. v.* 紀錄
  printable〔'prɪntəbḷ〕*adj.* 可印刷的
  certificate〔sɚ'tɪfəkɪt〕*n.* 證書
  microchip〔'maɪkroˌtʃɪp〕*n.* 微晶片
  spacecraft〔'spesˌkræft〕*n.* 太空船；太空飛行器

24. (**C**) 依句意，「任何人」都可以，選 (C) *Anyone*。而 (A) someone「某人」，
(B) nobody「沒有人」，(D) those「那些人」，均不合句意。

25. (**A**) and 為對等連接詞，須連接文法地位相同的單字、片語或子句，前面
是動名詞 measuring，故空格亦應填動名詞，選 (A) *collecting*。
collect〔kə'lɛkt〕*v.* 收集

第 26 至 30 題為題組

　　如果你能夠成為地球上任何一種動物，你想當什麼呢？想當隻小鳥，因為
牠會飛翔嗎？在很久以前，這或許是個很受歡迎的選擇，但是現在，鳥類可能
是在這星球上，受到最多虐待的動物了。

* ***on Earth*** 在地球上（ = *on the planet*）　　abuse〔ə'bjuz〕*v.* 虐待

　　跟野生鳥類不同，寵物店裡販售的鳥兒是不能飛的，因爲牠們的翅膀被剪過了。在寵物店裡被販售出的鳥，最後往往是<u>被拋棄</u>或夭折。而且在被賣出去之前，牠們得在鳥房裡度日。
26

> * wild〔waɪld〕*adj.* 野生的　　pet〔pɛt〕*n.* 寵物
>
> ***pet store*** 寵物店　　wing〔wɪŋ〕*n.* 翅膀
>
> clip〔klɪp〕*v.* 修剪　　frequently〔'frikwəntlɪ〕*adv.* 常常
>
> ***end up*** 最後　　mill〔mɪl〕*n.* 磨坊；工廠

26. (**A**) end up「最後…」，又 or 爲表選擇的對等連接詞，後面 dead 是形容詞，故空格亦應塡形容詞，選 (A) ***abandoned***〔ə'bændənd〕*adj.* 被拋棄的。而 (C) coldheartedly「冷淡地」，(D) sympathetically「同情地」，則用法不合。

<u>舉例來說</u>，大型的鸚鵡可以活七十年以上，你能想像被困在小小的鳥籠內度過
27
七十個年頭嗎？

> * parrot〔'pærət〕*n.* 鸚鵡　　imagine〔ɪ'mædʒɪn〕*v.* 想像
>
> trap〔træp〕*v.* 使困住　　cage〔kedʒ〕*n.* 鳥籠

27. (**D**) 依句意，選 (D) ***for example***「例如」。而 (A) in contrast「對比之下」，(B) in due time「在適當的時候」，(C) rather than「而不是…」，均不合句意。

然而，即使牠們被售出，也並不保證就會有好日子過。鸚鵡是聰明又愛社交的動物，牠們需要活動、友誼、各式各樣的食物和玩具，才會開心。但有多少人在一<u>衝動</u>之下買了鳥，就充分地準備好要照顧牠了？
28

> * ***even if*** 即使　　guarantee〔,gærən'ti〕*v.* 保證
>
> intelligent〔ɪn'tɛlədʒənt〕*adj.* 聰明的　　social〔'soʃəl〕*adj.* 社交的
>
> creature〔'kritʃɚ〕*n.* 動物；生物　　require〔rɪ'kwaɪr〕*v.* 需要
>
> companionship〔kəm'pænjənˌʃɪp〕*n.* 友誼
>
> varied〔'vɛrɪd〕*adj.* 各式各樣的　　diet〔'daɪət〕*n.* 飲食
>
> toy〔tɔɪ〕*n.* 玩具　　prepare〔prɪ'pɛr〕*v.* 準備
>
> adequately〔'ædəkwɪtlɪ〕*adv.* 適當地

28. (**C**) 依句意，選 (C) ***on impulse*** 「一衝動之下」。

impulse〔ˈɪmpʌls〕 *n.* 衝動
而 (A) on schedule「按照進度」，(B) on condition (that)「在…的條件下」，(D) on occasion(s)「有時候」，均不合句意。

　　此外，很多寵物店為了賺錢而繁殖鳥類，只在乎其產量，不在乎配種動物和牠們後代的健康。他們並不尊重自然界的繁殖循環週期，終年都讓鳥兒交配，<u>因而</u>出現很多突變。
29

　　* breed〔brid〕 *v.* 繁殖　　　production〔prəˈdʌkʃən〕 *n.* 產量
well-being〔ˈwɛlˈbiɪŋ〕 *n.* 健康　　offspring〔ˈɔf,sprɪŋ〕 *n.* 後代
respect〔rɪˈspɛkt〕 *v.* 尊重　　　cycle〔ˈsaɪkl〕 *n.* 循環
mate〔met〕 *v.* 使交配　　　mutation〔mjuˈteʃən〕 *n.* 【生物】突變

29. (**A**) 依句意，選 (A) ***As a result*** 「因此；結果」。而 (B) despite this「儘管如此」，(C) to begin with「首先；第一點」，(D) by no means「絕不」，均不合句意。

　　雖然我們希望有一天，有適當的立法能拯救這些鳥類，在這期間，我們所能做的，就是愛護我們的鳥，並給牠們最需要的<u>東西</u>——適當的照顧。
30

　　* proper〔ˈprɑpɚ〕 *adj.* 適當的　　legislation〔ˌlɛdʒɪsˈleʃən〕 *n.* 立法
one day （將來）有一天　　***in the meantime*** 在這期間
nothing but 僅僅　　desperately〔ˈdɛspərɪtlɪ〕 *adv.* 強烈地；拼命地
care〔kɛr〕 *n.* 照顧

30. (**B**) 空格應填複合關代，相當於先行詞加關係代名詞，引導名詞子句，故選 (B) ***what*** (= the thing that)。

三、文意選填：

第 31 至 40 題為題組

　　美國人大多覺得，懂英文就足以應付他們的需要。這就是為何他們 [31] **(E)** 甚至連其他語言中，最基本的片語都不會說的原因。但是，很多美國人終於恍然大悟，知道說並不是全世界都 [32] **(B)** 一定要說英語，就連許多學習英語當第二外語的人，也偏愛講自己 [33] **(G)** 本國的語言。

　* ***tend to*** 易於；傾向於　　sufficient〔sə'fɪʃənt〕*adj.* 足夠的
rudimentary〔,rudə'mɛntərɪ〕*adj.* 基本的
phrase〔frez〕*n.* 片語　　belatedly〔bɪ'letɪdlɪ〕*adv.* 爲時已晚地
realize〔'riə,laɪz〕*v.* 了解
necessarily〔'nɛsə,sɛrəlɪ〕*adv.* 必定；當然　　***prefer to*** 比較喜歡
converse〔kən'vɜs〕*v.* 交談　　native〔'netɪv〕*adj.* 本國的
tongue〔tʌŋ〕*n.* 舌頭；語言　　***native tongue*** 本國語言

　　第二外語現在已經在 [34](C) 越來越多職業的基本準備工作中，佔很重要的部分。即使是在某些例子中，有懂第二外語，並不會幫助畢業生找到第一份工作，很多人還是說他們的外語能力，確實能提高他們換工作的機動性，並增加他們 [35](D) 升遷 的機會。

　* vital〔'vaɪtḷ〕*adj.* 非常重要的　　preparation〔,prɛpə'reʃən〕*n.* 準備
increasing〔ɪn'krisɪŋ〕*adj.* 逐漸增加的　　career〔kə'rɪr〕*n.* 職業生涯
case〔kes〕*n.* 例子　　graduate〔'grædʒʊɪt〕*n.* 畢業生
obtain〔əb'ten〕*v.* 獲得　　report〔rɪ'port〕*v.* 報告
enhance〔ɪn'hæns〕*v.* 提高；增進　　mobility〔mo'bɪlətɪ〕*n.* 機動性
improve〔ɪm'pruv〕*v.* 改善　　promotion〔prə'moʃən〕*n.* 升遷

　　除了外文系學生選擇培養的任何技術性技能以外，他們在就業市場上還有更多的 [36](I) 優勢。當被問到哪一門大學課程最有價值時，任職於商業界的人指出，[37](F) 像是企管等以就業爲取向的課程，還有像是心理學等以人文爲導向的科目，還有幫助他們培養溝通技巧的課程。

　* ***in addition to*** 除了⋯之外（還有）　　technical〔'tɛknɪkḷ〕*adj.* 技術的
develope〔dɪ'vɛləp〕*v.* 培養　　advantage〔əd'væntɪdʒ〕*n.* 優點
job market 就業市場　　college〔'kalɪdʒ〕*n.* 大學
course〔kors〕*n.* 課程
employ〔ɪm'plɔɪ〕*v.* 雇用　　point〔pɔɪnt〕*v.* 指出
career-oriented〔kə'rɪr'orɪɛntɪd〕*adj.* 以就業爲導向的
such as 例如　　management〔'mænɪdʒmənt〕*n.* 管理
business management 企管
people-oriented〔'pipḷ'orɪɛntɪd〕*adj.* 以人文爲導向的
subject〔'sʌbdʒɪkt〕*n.* 科目　　psychology〔saɪ'kalədʒɪ〕*n.* 心理學
communication〔kə,mjunə'keʃən〕*n.* 溝通

　　而外文系學生的課程 [38] **(J)** 非常著重這方面的學習，他們通常有較好的溝通技巧。他們可能擁有語言能力，讓他們心理上有更多靈活度，而且讓他們知道有更多種 [39] **(A)** 選擇的組合。會說兩種語言的人，能跟其他國家、和文化的人，做更有效的溝通，而且也會是很有效率的 [40] **(H)** 問題解決者。

> * focus〔'fokəs〕 v. 集中　　heavily〔'hɛvɪlɪ〕 adv. 重重地；大大地
> aspect〔'æspɛkt〕 n. 方面　　possess〔pə'zɛs〕 v. 擁有
> achieve〔ə'tʃiv〕 v. 達到　　mental〔'mɛntl̩〕 adj. 心理的
> flexibility〔ˌflɛksə'bɪlətɪ〕 n. 彈性；適應性
> command〔kə'mænd〕 v. 擁有；掌握
> awareness〔ə'wɛrnɪs〕 n. 察覺；認識　　set〔sɛt〕 n. 一組；一套
> option〔'ɑpʃən〕 n. 選擇　　bilingual〔baɪ'lɪŋgwəl〕 n. 會說雙語的人
> effectively〔ə'fɛktɪvlɪ〕 adv. 有效率地
> problem-solver〔'prɑbləmˌsɑlvɚ〕 n. 問題解決者

四、閱讀測驗：

第 41 至 44 題為題組

　　排燈節是光的節慶，慶祝秋天的豐收。這個節日供奉各種神祇與女神，也是印度日曆上的一個相當重要的日子；因為它是印度人計算「印度曆」曆法的起點，印度曆是維克拉大帝所建立的，他擊敗匈奴，把印度人從可能具毀滅性的異族統治中，拯救出來。

> * Diwali〔dɪ'wɑli〕 n. 排燈節【又稱萬燈節、屠妖節，或是印度燈節，是印度教、錫克教與耆那教的共同節日，在這天人們點燈，要「以光明驅走黑暗，以善良戰勝邪惡」，在每年的 10 月或 11 月舉行】
> festival〔'fɛstəvl̩〕 n. 節慶　　celebrate〔'sɛləˌbret〕 v. 慶祝
> abundance〔ə'bʌndəns〕 n. 豐富；充裕　　autumn〔'ɔtəm〕 adj. 秋天的
> harvest〔'hɑrvɪst〕 n. 收穫　　dedicate〔'dɛdəˌket〕 v. 以～供奉 <to>
> various〔'vɛrɪəs〕 adj. 各式各樣的　　goddess〔'gɑdɪs〕 n. 女神
> mark〔mɑrk〕 v. 標明　　Indian〔'ɪndɪən〕 adj. 印度的
> calendar〔'kæləndɚ〕 n. 日曆　　Hindu〔'hɪndu〕 n. 印度人
> measure〔'mɛʒɚ〕 v. 測量；測定
> Vikram Samvat n. 印度教曆法【印度、孟加拉、尼泊爾所用的曆法，是由印度傳說中的偉大國王 Vikramaditya（維克拉姆帝亞）所創造的曆法】
> era〔'ɪrə〕 n. 時代；紀元　　establish〔ə'stæblɪʃ〕 v. 建立

King Vikram 維克拉國王【古印度王朝的國王維克拉瑪蒂亞】
defeat〔dɪ'fit〕v. 打敗　　　　Hun〔hʌn〕n. 匈奴人
India〔'ɪndɪə〕n. 印度　　　potentially〔pə'tɛnʃəlɪ〕adv. 可能地
disastrous〔dɪz'æstrəs〕adj. 災難的　　　rule〔rul〕v. 統治

　　排燈節也膜拜三位女神，拉克希米、迦利以及薩羅斯瓦蒂仁慈的本性。拉克希米的恩賜，對生命的豐饒與和平是不可或缺的，它們象徵無窮的財富、健康、朋友和長壽。迦利女神則代表對個人和團體的興盛都很重要的身、心、靈的力量。而薩羅斯瓦蒂女神則是象徵靈性極至的知識與智慧，因為其能引導啟蒙教化。

＊ worship〔'wɝʃɪp〕v. 信奉；膜拜　　gracious〔'greʃəs〕adj. 仁慈的
nature〔'netʃɚ〕n. 天性；本性
Lakshmi〔'lakʃmi〕n. 拉克希米【印度教中主管財富、光明、豐收、智慧、
　　命運、生育、豐饒跟勇氣的女神，又稱吉祥天女】
Kali〔'kalɪ〕n. 迦利【又稱時母，或迦梨，字面意思是「黑色」，是印度教中
　　與時間、永恆力量、死亡、新生有關的女神】
Saraswati〔'sʌrəs,wʌti〕n. 薩羅斯瓦蒂【印度教中的妙音佛母，主管音樂、
　　知識、藝術的女神，又稱辯才天女】
blessing〔'blɛsɪŋ〕n. 神恩；恩賜　　essential〔ə'sɛnʃəl〕adj. 必要的
prosperous〔'prɑspərəs〕adj. 繁榮的；順利的
peaceful〔'pisfəl〕adj. 寧靜的　　　represent〔,rɛprɪ'zɛnt〕v. 代表；象徵
boundless〔'baʊndlɪs〕adj. 無窮的　　wealth〔wɛlθ〕n. 財富
physical〔'fɪzɪkl̩〕adj. 身體的　　　mental〔'mɛntl̩〕adj. 心理的
spiritual〔'spɪrɪtʃʊəl〕adj. 精神的　　***as well as*** 以及
community〔kə'mjunətɪ〕n. 團體　　flourish〔'flɝɪʃ〕v. 興盛
stand for 代表　　wisdom〔'wɪzdəm〕n. 智慧
ultimate〔'ʌltəmɪt〕n. 終極的事物
spirituality〔,spɪrɪtʃʊ'ælətɪ〕n. 靈性
lead to 導致　　enlightenment〔ɪn'laɪtn̩mənt〕n. 啟蒙；教化

　　多年來，排燈節慶典在本質特色上已經改變了。曾經是只用充滿燈油的陶燈與家庭製的燈芯，現在則點亮了蠟燭和電燈，而且也製作甜食來迎接客人和神祇。人們購買金子和銀子作為好運的象徵。貿易商與生意人收起他們的帳簿和帳目，感謝神祇為一年帶來豐收的結果。在夜間，燃放起煙火，家家戶戶都因為點亮了燈和燈籠而變得很華麗。

* nature〔'netʃə〕n. 本質　　character〔'kærɪktə〕n. 特色
earthen〔'ɝθən〕adj. 陶製的　　lamp〔læmp〕n. 燈
be filled with 充滿了　　wick〔wɪk〕n. 燈芯
candle〔'kændḷ〕n. 蠟燭　　electric〔ɪ'lɛktrɪk〕adj. 電的
sweets〔swits〕n. pl. 甜食　　merchant〔'mɝtʃənt〕n. 商人
account〔ə'kaʊnt〕n. 帳目　　bountiful〔'baʊntəfəl〕adj. 豐富的
firework〔'faɪr,wɝk〕n. 煙火　　wonderfully〔'wʌndəfəlɪ〕adv. 富麗地
light〔laɪt〕v. 點燃【三態變化為：light-lighted-lit】
lantern〔'læntən〕n. 燈籠

一般相信，光能夠驅離黑暗，以及那些在附近地區流連的惡靈。節日氣氛在晚餐出現了甜品和豪華食物時，達到最高點。似乎所有的天神與人類，都隨著新年的開始和永續循環的時序的更新而感到欣喜。

* dispel〔dɪ'spɛl〕v. 驅離　　***evil spirit*** 惡靈
linger〔'lɪŋgə〕v. 徘徊　　neighborhood〔'nebə,hʊd〕n. 附近地區
in full swing 正全力進行中；正起勁
sumptuous〔'sʌmptʃʊəs〕adj. 豪華的　　heavens〔'hɛvən〕n. pl. 衆天神
rejoice〔rɪ'dʒɔɪs〕v. 高興；欣喜　　eternal〔ɪ'tɝnḷ〕adj. 永恆的
renew〔rɪ'nju〕v. 更新

41.（**B**）關於排燈節，下列何者為非？
　　(A) 排燈節是光明的節日，慶祝秋天的豐收。
　　(B) 排燈節那一天，是印度從印度暴君手中解放的日子。
　　(C) 排燈節會供奉很多神祇與女神。
　　(D) 排燈節代表所有天神與人類因新年的到來而歡欣。
　　* free〔fri〕v. 使自由　　tyrant〔'taɪrənt〕n. 暴君

42.（**D**）排燈節主要不是在讚頌 ＿＿＿＿＿＿＿。
　　　　(A) 拉克希米　　(B) 薩羅斯瓦蒂　　(C) 迦利　　　　(D) 雅馬國王

43.（**A**）下列何者不是現在普遍的排燈節慶祝活動？
　　　　(A) 人們使用裡面裝滿家庭製燈芯的陶燈。
　　　　(B) 人們購買金子跟銀子，作為好運的象徵。
　　　　(C) 商人會收起帳簿並停用戶頭。
　　　　(D) 家家戶戶都被裝飾性的燈泡還有燈籠點亮。

44. (**D**) 根據本文，希望能用錢滾錢的人們，會讚頌 ＿＿＿＿＿＿ 。
   (A) 薩羅斯瓦蒂
   (B) 迦利
   (C) 雅馬國王
   (D) <u>拉克希米</u>

   * generate〔ˋdʒɛnəˏret〕v. 產生

第 45 至 48 題爲題組

　　你走向你的同事，要跟他說一件重要的公事，但當他開口時，你就因爲從他口中跑出來的臭氣而把頭轉開。大部分的男女都同意，不好的氣味，是讓關係生厭的最大原因，自尊心也會受到相當的傷害。一個人在職場上，不僅可能是在背地裡，也可能在一些隨口說出的傷人言語中，淪爲笑柄。

   * colleague〔ˋkɑlig〕n. 同事　　　issue〔ˋɪʃʊ〕n. 問題；議題
   as soon as 一…就～　　***turn away*** 轉過身　　***due to*** 由於
   stench〔stɛntʃ〕n. 臭氣　　breath〔brɛθ〕n. 氣息
   turnoff〔ˋtɜnˏɔf〕n. 令人厭煩的事物
   relationship〔rɪˋleʃənˏʃɪp〕n. 關係
   damaging〔ˋdæmɪdʒɪŋ〕adj. 有害的
   self-esteem〔ˏsɛlfəˋstim〕n. 自尊心　　***make fun of*** 取笑
   at work 在職場上　　casual〔ˋkæʒʊəl〕adj. 隨便的
   remark〔rɪˋmɑrk〕n. 評論；話　　hurtful〔ˋhɜtfəl〕adj. 傷感情的

　　不好的氣味也叫作口臭，大部分人都曾經在一些時期經歷過。在起床後和吃下某些會引起口臭的食物後特別常見，像大蒜、洋蔥、五香燻牛肉和咖哩。

   * halitosis〔ˏhæləˋtosɪs〕n. 口臭　　***suffer from*** 遭受；罹患
   stage〔stedʒ〕n. 階段　　particularly〔pɚˋtɪkjələlɪ〕adv. 特別地
   common〔ˋkɑmən〕adj. 普遍的　　garlic〔ˋgɑrlɪk〕n. 大蒜
   onion〔ˋʌnjən〕n. 洋蔥　　pastrami〔pəˋstrɑmɪ〕n. 五香燻牛肉
   curry〔ˋkɜɪ〕n. 咖哩

　　有很多方法可判斷你是否有口臭。拿一小塊乾淨的布，摩擦你的牙齒。等待幾秒後去聞聞看它。或是你可以舔一下手背，等它乾掉後再去聞它。如果你真的有長期的口臭問題，別期待可以靠著嚼口香糖，或是用漱口水就可以擺脫它，因爲那都只能掩蓋口臭，而不是治療它。

* ***quite a few*** 很多的（＝ *many*）　　determine〔dɪˋtɝmɪn〕*v.* 判定
rub〔rʌb〕*v.* 摩擦　　lick〔lɪk〕*v.* 舔
dry〔draɪ〕*v.* 變乾　　chronic〔ˋkrɑnɪk〕*adj.* 慢性的；長期的
expect〔ɪkˋspɛkt〕*v.* 期待　　***get rid of*** 擺脫
pop〔pɑp〕*v.* 把東西突然放入
chewing gum 口香糖　　mouthwash〔ˋmaʊθ͵wɑʃ〕*n.* 漱口水
mask〔mæsk〕*v.* 掩飾　　treat〔trit〕*v.* 治療

　　治療口臭的第一步，就是要知道它的原因。可能是呼吸道或鼻竇感染，也可能和你的生活方式有關，舉例來說，激烈節食會引起如水果般的臭味。最常見的原因，或許是口腔不衛生，讓細菌無受限地繁殖，然後在口腔中與有機物質起作用，而產生一股腐敗的氣味。

* identify〔aɪˋdɛntə͵faɪ〕*v.* 確認　　cause〔kɔz〕*n.* 原因
respiratory〔rɪˋspaɪrə͵torɪ〕*adj.* 呼吸的
tract〔trækt〕*n.* 管；道　　sinus〔ˋsaɪnəs〕*n.* 鼻竇
infection〔ɪnˋfɛkʃən〕*n.* 感染
be associated with 與～有關　　severe〔səˋvɪr〕*adj.* 劇烈的
fruity〔ˋfrutɪ〕*adj.* 水果味的　　odor〔ˋodɚ〕*n.* 氣味；臭氣
oral〔ˋorəl〕*adj.* 口部的　　hygiene〔ˋhaɪdʒin〕*n.* 衛生
bacteria〔bækˋtɪrɪə〕*n. pl.* 細菌　　breed〔brid〕*v.* 產生
uninhibited〔͵ʌnɪnˋhɪbɪtɪd〕*adj.* 無拘束的
foul〔faʊl〕*adj.* 腐敗的　　***act on*** 對～起作用
organic〔ɔrˋgænɪk〕*adj.* 有機的　　substance〔ˋsʌbstəns〕*n.* 物質

　　大部分的口臭，可以用適當的牙齒清潔方法來治療。這並不是難以應付的問題。如果是持續性的、沒有明顯原因的口臭，那最好一定要去看牙醫。

* cure〔kjʊr〕*v.* 治療　　dental〔ˋdɛnt!〕*adj.* 牙齒的
measure〔ˋmɛʒɚ〕*n.* 措施；方法　　***take care of*** 處理
in case of 如果　　persistent〔pɚˋzɪstənt〕*adj.* 持續的
apparent〔əˋpærənt〕*adj.* 明顯的
consult〔kənˋsʌlt〕*v.* 請教；找…看病
dentist〔ˋdɛntɪst〕*n.* 牙醫

45.（ **D** ） 本文的標題為何？

　　 (A) 預防口臭　　　　　　　　 (B) 口臭的影響

　　 (C) 口臭的原因　　　　　　　 (D) 口臭概述

　　 * prevention〔prɪˋvɛnʃən〕 *n.* 預防　　impact〔ˋɪmpækt〕 *n.* 影響

　　　introduction〔͵ɪntrəˋdʌkʃən〕 *n.* 介紹　　overview〔ˋovɚ͵vju〕 *n.* 概述

46.（ **D** ） 你最有可能在哪本雜誌裡面看到這篇文章？

　　 (A) 幹細胞與疾病　　　　　　 (B) 今日心理學

　　 (C) 照顧兒童肌膚　　　　　　 (D) 自然健康

　　 * stem〔stɛm〕 *n.* 莖；主幹　　cell〔sɛl〕 *n.* 細胞

　　　 stem cell 幹細胞　　psychology〔saɪˋkɑlədʒɪ〕 *n.* 心理學

47.（ **C** ） 關於口臭，本文中沒有提到下列哪一點？

　　 (A) 治療口臭的第一步，就是確認口臭的原因。

　　 (B) 很多人可能至少偶爾都會有口臭。

　　 (C) 不要吃可能會引起口臭的加工食品，或辛辣的食物。

　　 (D) 有一些方法可以確認是否罹患口臭。

　　 * *be likely to* + *V.* 可能～

　　　experience〔ɪkˋspɪrɪəns〕 *v.* 經歷；罹患

　　　 at least 至少　　occasionally〔əˋkeʒənḷɪ〕 *adv.* 偶爾

　　　regarding〔rɪˋgɑrdɪŋ〕 *prep.* 關於

　　　 processed food 加工食品　　spicy〔ˋspaɪsɪ〕 *adj.* 辛辣的

　　　 contribute to 導致　　check〔tʃɛk〕 *v.* 檢查；確認

　　　develop〔dɪˋvɛləp〕 *v.* 罹患（疾病）

48.（ **A** ） 作者勸讀者，如果他們不知道為何口臭的症狀持續，要 ＿＿＿＿＿＿ 。

　　 (A) 去看牙醫　　　　　　　　 (B) 吃健康的飲食

　　 (C) 維持良好的口腔衛生　　　 (D) 停止激烈節食

第 49 至 52 題為題組

　　生物面臨到持續如密集炮火般，不間斷的威脅，挑戰著牠們生存與繁殖的能力。牠們必須適應新的溫度、氣候和大氣狀況，以及人類造成的威脅。如果某個物種無法藉由適應來應付這些威脅，那牠就可能會面臨滅絕。

＊ ***living things*** 生物　　constant〔'kɑnstənt〕*adj.* 持續不斷的
barrage〔bə'rɑʒ〕*n.* 密集的炮火　　threat〔θrɛt〕*n.* 威脅
challenge〔'tʃælɪndʒ〕*v.* 挑戰　　ability〔ə'bɪlətɪ〕*n.* 能力
survive〔sə'vaɪv〕*v.* 存活　　reproduce〔‚riprə'djus〕*v.* 繁殖
adpat to 適應　　atmospheric〔‚ætməs'fɛrɪk〕*adj.* 大氣的
condition〔kən'dɪʃən〕*n.* 情況　　***as well as*** 以及
man-made〔'mæn‚med〕*adj.* 人造的
species〔'spiʃɪz〕*n.* 物種【單複數同形】　　***cope with*** 應付；處理
adaptation〔‚ædəp'teʃən〕*n.* 適應　　extinction〔ɪk'stɪŋkʃən〕*n.* 絕種

　　在最近的演化史中，很多生物面臨的威脅，主要都是由單一的物種，也就是人類，所造成的影響。人們改變這個星球的程度，引發的滅絕規模如此巨大，使讓許多科學家都深信，我們正經歷一場大量的滅絕。

＊ recent〔'risn̩t〕*adj.* 最近的　　evolutionary〔‚ɛvə'luʃən‚ɛrɪ〕*adj.* 演化的
organism〔'ɔrgən‚ɪzəm〕*n.* 生物　　drive〔draɪv〕*v.* 驅使；驅動
primarily〔'praɪ‚mɛrəlɪ〕*adv.* 主要地　　effect〔ɪ'fɛkt〕*n.* 影響
single〔'sɪŋgl̩〕*adj.* 單一的　　extent〔ɪk'stɛnt〕*n.* 程度
alter〔'ɔltɚ〕*v.* 改變　　initiate〔ɪ'nɪʃɪ‚et〕*v.* 開始
vast〔væst〕*adj.* 巨大的　　scale〔skel〕*n.* 規模
experience〔ɪk'spɪrɪəns〕*v.* 經歷　　mass〔mæs〕*adj.* 大量的；大規模的

　　不像其他自然威脅，人類所造成的威脅，是可以透過改變我們的行為而避免的。在檢視人類的活動，是如何不利地衝擊地球上的生物後，我們可以著手預防未來的傷害。例如，人類使用土地，而對動物棲息地造成的破壞，應該要被阻止。像是燃燒石化燃料等的活動，會改變地球的大氣，並造成全球氣候改變，也應該要減少。諸如殺蟲劑、除草劑等污染物，應該受到管制。此外，過度的捕魚、狩獵、盜獵和非法買賣瀕臨絕種的動物，都應該要被禁止。

＊ prevent〔prɪ'vɛnt〕*v.* 預防；避免　　behavior〔bɪ'hevjɚ〕*n.* 行為
examine〔ɪg'zæmɪn〕*v.* 檢查　　adversely〔æd'vɝslɪ〕*adv.* 不利地
impact〔ɪm'pækt〕*v.* 衝擊　　***take steps*** 採取措施
damage〔'dæmɪdʒ〕*n.* 傷害　　***for example*** 例如
destruction〔dɪ'strʌkʃən〕*n.* 破壞　　habitat〔'hæbə‚tæt〕*n.* 棲息地
fossil〔'fɑsl̩〕*adj.* 化石的　　fuel〔'fjuəl〕*n.* 燃料
fossil fuel 石化燃料　　alter〔'ɔltɚ〕*v.* 改變

atmosphere〔'ætməsˌfɪr〕*n.* 大氣（層）　　*result in* 導致
global〔'globḷ〕*adj.* 全球的　　reduce〔rɪ'djus〕*v.* 降低
pollutant〔pə'lutn̩t〕*n.* 污染物　　pesticide〔'pɛstɪˌsaɪd〕*n.* 殺蟲劑
herbicide〔'hɝbəˌsaɪd〕*n.* 除草劑　　*etc.* 等等（= *et cetera*〔ɛt'sɛtərə〕）
regulate〔'rɛgjəˌlet〕*v.* 管制　　excessive〔ɪk'sɛsɪv〕*adj.* 過度的
poaching〔'potʃɪŋ〕*n.* 盜獵　　trade〔tred〕*v.* 貿易；交易
endangered〔ɪn'dendʒəd〕*adj.* 瀕臨絕種的
endangered species 瀕臨絕種的動物　　prohibit〔pro'hɪbɪt〕*v.* 禁止

　　身為人類，我們擁有能夠明白行為會導致何種後果的獨特能力。我們能夠得知我們的行為，對週遭的世界會有什麼影響，以及行為的轉變，能對改變未來的事件有什麼幫助。所以，讓我們現在就立刻著手吧。

* unique〔ju'nik〕*adj.* 獨特的　　consequence〔'kɑnsəˌkwɛns〕*n.* 後果
be capable of + *V-ing* 能夠~　　*learn about* 得知
effect〔ɪ'fɛkt〕*n.* 影響　　event〔ɪ'vɛnt〕*n.* 事件
here and now 在此時此地；立刻；馬上

49. (**C**) 本文的目的最有可能是要 ＿＿＿＿＿＿ 。
　　(A) 了解對蠻荒部落的開發
　　(B) 強調瀕臨絕種動物對非法市場的影響
　　(C) 檢視自然以及人類對動物所造成的威脅
　　(D) 探索污染物，以及野生動物的意外死亡

* *be likely to V.* 有可能~
　exploitation〔ˌɛksplɔɪ'teʃən〕*n.* 開發；剝削
　emphasize〔'ɛmfəˌsaɪz〕*v.* 強調　　*accidental death* 意外死亡
　wildlife〔'waɪldˌlaɪf〕*n.* 野生動物

50. (**B**) 本文的作者最有可能是一位 ＿＿＿＿＿＿ 。
　　(A) 人權鬥士　　　　　　　　(B) 全心投入的環保人士
　　(C) 家庭醫師　　　　　　　　(D) 新聞特派員

* *human rights* 人權　　activist〔'æktɪvɪst〕*n.* 行動者
　devoted〔dɪ'votɪd〕*adj.* 專心致力的
　environmentalist〔ɪnˌvaɪrən'mɛntḷɪst〕*n.* 環保人士
　physician〔fə'zɪʃən〕*n.*（內科）醫師
　correspondent〔ˌkɔrə'spɑndənt〕*n.* 通訊記者；特派員

51. (**D**) 下列何者最能夠解釋第一段的 "**barrage**" 這個字？
　　(A) 很浪費時間。　　　　　　　(B) 突如其來的打雷。
　　(C) 一種發射子彈的機器。　　　(D) <u>壓倒性的、集中的攻擊。</u>

　　* burst〔bɝst〕*n.* 突然爆發　　　thunder〔ˈθʌndɚ〕*n.* 雷；雷鳴
　　fire〔faɪr〕*v.* 發射　　bullet〔ˈbʊlɪt〕*n.* 子彈
　　overwhelming〔ˌovɚˈhwɛlmɪŋ〕*adj.* 壓倒性的
　　concentrated〔ˈkɑnsṇˌtretɪd〕*adj.* 集中的　　attack〔əˈtæk〕*n.* 攻擊

52. (**B**) 作者建議讀者要 ＿＿＿＿＿＿＿。
　　(A) 破壞野生動物棲息地
　　(B) <u>預防往後對地球的傷害</u>
　　(C) 燃燒石化燃料以改變地球的大氣
　　(D) 在合理範圍內買賣瀕臨絕種的動物

　　* advise〔ədˈvaɪz〕*v.* 勸告；建議　　　destroy〔dɪˈstrɔɪ〕*v.* 破壞
　　rationally〔ˈræʃənḷɪ〕*adv.* 理性地；合理地

第 53 至 56 題爲題組

　　十月十日，挪威諾貝爾委員會，將其 2008 年度的諾貝爾和平獎，頒發給馬爾蒂‧阿赫蒂薩里。委員會表示，他們給予芬蘭前總統這份榮譽，是由於他三十年來，對於解決在歐、亞、非和中東的衝突，做了很大的貢獻。

　　* Norwegian〔nɔrˈwidʒən〕*adj.* 挪威的　　committee〔kəˈmɪtɪ〕*n.* 委員會
　　Norwegian Nobel Committee 諾貝爾委員會【諾貝爾和平獎的評定機構】
　　award〔əˈwɔrd〕*v.* 頒發　　***peace prize*** 和平獎
　　Martti Ahtisaari〔ˈmɑrtɪˈɑhtɪsɑrɪ〕*n.* 馬爾蒂‧阿赫蒂薩里【1937-，曾任
　　　芬蘭總統以及聯合國副秘書長，是 2008 年諾貝爾和平獎得主】
　　honor〔ˈɑnɚ〕*v.* 授與榮譽　　former〔ˈfɔrmɚ〕*adj.* 前任的
　　Finnish〔ˈfɪnɪʃ〕*adj.* 芬蘭的　　decade〔ˈdɛked〕*n.* 十年
　　resolve〔rɪˈzɑlv〕*v.* 解決　　conflict〔ˈkɑnflɪkt〕*n.* 衝突
　　Middle East〔ˈmɪdḷˈist〕中東【指利比亞、巴基斯坦、土耳其、阿拉伯
　　　半島之間的地區】

　　在 1956 年成爲芬蘭外交官之前，阿赫蒂薩里是個小學老師。1977 年，他被指派爲聯合國駐那米比亞大使時，他已經是位資深的外交官了，在那米比亞，游擊隊正爲了南非種族隔離制度而戰。

＊ ***work as*** 擔任　　***primary school*** 小學

diplomat〔'dɪplə‚mæt〕 *n.* 外交官　　senior〔'sinjɚ〕 *adj.* 資深的

name〔nem〕 *v.* 任命；指名　　***U.N.*** 聯合國（＝ *United Nations*）

envoy〔'ɛnvɔɪ〕 *n.* 使節　　Namibia〔nə'mɪbɪə〕 *n.* 那米比亞【南非國家】

guerrilla〔gə'rɪlə〕 *n.* 游擊隊　　battle〔'bætl〕 *v.* 戰鬥

South African 南非的　　apartheid〔ə'pɑrthet〕 *n.* 種族隔離制度

rule〔rul〕 *n.* 規定

隨後，他升任副秘書長，1988 年，在那米比亞要獨立時，他被派到那裡，領導八千名聯合國維持和平部隊。1992 到 1993 年，他是波士尼亞－赫塞哥維納聯邦共合國，代表出席前南斯拉夫國際和平會議的工聯團體主席，並在 1993 年，擔任聯合國秘書長關於前南斯拉夫問題的特別顧問。

＊ rise〔raɪz〕 *v.* 晉升　　undersecretary〔‚ʌndɚ'sɛkrə‚tɛrɪ〕 *n.* 次長

undersecretary-general 副秘書長　　dispatch〔dɪ'spætʃ〕 *v.* 派遣

U.N. peacekeepers 聯合國維持和平部隊

transition〔træn'zɪʃən〕 *n.* 過渡時期

independence〔‚ɪndɪ'pɛndəns〕 *n.* 獨立　　chairman〔'tʃɛrmən〕 *n.* 主席

Bosnia-Herzegovina〔‚bɑznɪə‚hɝtsə'govɪnə〕 *n.* 波士尼亞－赫塞哥維納
　　聯邦共合國【簡稱波赫，前南斯拉夫共和國的會員之一，90年代南斯拉夫
　　內戰時獨立】

working group 工聯團體

international〔‚ɪntɚ'næʃənḷ〕 *adj.* 國際（間）的

conference〔'kɑnfərəns〕 *n.* 會議

Yugoslavia〔‚jugo'slɑvɪə〕 *n.* 南斯拉夫【南歐國家，首都貝爾格勒】

adviser〔əd'vaɪzɚ〕 *n.* 顧問

secretary-general〔'sɛkrə‚tɛrɪ'dʒɛnərəl〕 *n.* 秘書長

從 2005 年起，他就開始被提到是可能的諾貝爾和平獎的得主。他從 197 位被提名人中雀屏中選，那些人包括中國人權律師高智晟，和愛滋及環保鬥士胡佳、俄羅斯的尤瑟波娃，還有越南的釋廣度。這份榮耀於 2007 年時，給了前美國副總統艾爾·高爾，和聯合國氣候變遷研究小組。而於 2006 年時，則是給了對抗貧窮，提出微型貸款的先驅穆罕默德·尤納斯。

＊ mention〔'mɛnʃən〕 *v.* 提到　　select〔sə'lɛkt〕 *v.* 選擇

nominee〔‚nɑmə'ni〕 *n.* 被提名人　　lawyer〔'lɔjɚ〕 *n.* 律師

Gao Zhisheng　*n.* 高智晟【1966-，中國人權律師】

AIDS〔edz〕*n.* 愛滋病（＝*acquired immunodeficiency syndrome*）

environmental〔ɪn,vaɪrən'mɛntḷ〕*adj.* 環境的

activist〔'æktɪvɪst〕*n.* 行動家

Hu Jia　*n.* 胡佳（胡嘉）【1973-，中國的環保及愛滋病行動者】

Russia〔'rʌʃə〕*n.* 俄羅斯

Lidia Yusupova　*n.* 莉蒂亞・尤瑟波娃【俄羅斯車臣的人權律師】

Vietnam〔,viɛt'nɑm〕*n.* 越南

Thich Quang Do　*n.* 釋廣度【釋廣度為法號，他是促進民主發展的主要推手】

vice〔vaɪs〕*adj.* 副的　　***vice president***　副總統

Al Gore　*n.* 艾爾・高爾【1948-，全名 Albert Arnold Gore，美國第四十五任
　　副總統，與聯合國氣候委員會共同獲得諾貝爾和平獎】

panel〔'pænḷ〕*n.* 研究小組　　anti-〔'æntɪ〕【字首】表示「反對；對抗」。

poverty〔'pɑvətɪ〕*n.* 貧窮　　microcredit〔,maɪkro'krɛdɪt〕*n.* 微型貸款

pioneer〔,paɪə'nɪr〕*n.* 先驅

Muhammad Yunus　*n.* 穆罕默德・尤納斯【發明「微型貸款」，提供服務給
　　無法得到貸款的貧窮創業者，與孟加拉鄉村銀行共同獲得諾貝爾和平獎】

　　就像挪威諾貝爾委員會所說的：「在他的成年生活期間，無論是擔任資深的
芬蘭公職人員、總統，還是一個常常與聯合國接觸的國際要角，阿赫蒂薩里一
直都在為和平與和諧而努力。」

　* throughout〔θru'aʊt〕*prep.* 遍及；在整個…期間

　　adult〔ə'dʌlt〕*adj.* 成年的　　***public servant***　司儀；公職人員

　　capacity〔kə'pæsətɪ〕*n.* 身分　　connect〔kə'nɛkt〕*v.* 連接

　　reconciliation〔,rɛkən,sɪlɪ'eʃən〕*n.* 調停；和諧

53. (**C**) 誰就在阿赫蒂薩里之前拿到諾貝爾和平獎？

　　(A) 穆罕默德・尤納斯　　　　　(B) 旺加里・馬塔伊

　　(C) 艾爾・高爾　　　　　　　　(D) 穆罕默德・埃爾巴拉迪

　* immediately〔ɪ'midɪɪtlɪ〕*adv.* 立刻；就在…（之前或之後）

　　Wangari Maathai　*n.* 旺加里・馬塔伊【1940-，肯亞的社會運動者，
　　　東、西非洲的第一位女博士，發起綠帶運動與非洲減債運動】

　　Mohamed ElBaradei　*n.* 穆罕默德・埃爾巴拉迪【1942-，國際原子能
　　　委員會總幹事，致力於反對核子武器運動，2005 年獲得諾貝爾和平獎】

54. (**D**) 誰不是 2008 年諾貝爾和平獎的候選人？

　　(A) 釋廣度　　　　　　　　　(B) 高智晟

　　(C) 莉蒂亞‧尤瑟波娃　　　　(D) <u>艾爾‧高爾</u>

　　* candidate〔ˈkændə,det〕*n.* 候選人

55. (**D**) 馬爾蒂‧阿赫蒂薩里沒有解決在 ＿＿＿＿＿＿ 的衝突。

　　(A) 歐洲　　　(B) 非洲　　　(C) 中東　　　(D) <u>南美洲</u>

56. (**B**) 馬爾蒂‧阿赫蒂薩里沒有當過 ＿＿＿＿＿＿。

　　(A) 波士尼亞‧赫塞哥維納工聯團體的主席

　　(B) <u>高中老師</u>

　　(C) 聯合國秘書長的特別顧問

　　(D) 被提名的聯合國駐那米比亞使節

第貳部分：非選擇題

一、中譯英：

1. 身爲在家裡負責煮飯的人，媽媽最怕的就是晚餐時間。

As the person $\left\{ \begin{array}{l} \text{in charge of} \\ \text{responsible for} \end{array} \right\}$ cooking in my family, Mother

$\left\{ \begin{array}{l} \text{is most anxious about dinner time.} \\ \left. \begin{array}{l} \text{dreads} \\ \text{fears} \\ \text{worries about} \end{array} \right\} \text{dinnertime (the) most.} \end{array} \right.$

2. 她必須想盡辦法做出美味而健康的晚餐，同時要滿足家人不同的喜好。

She has to $\left\{ \begin{array}{l} \text{focus her attention} \\ \text{put her mind to it} \end{array} \right\}$ to $\left\{ \begin{array}{l} \text{prepare} \\ \text{make} \end{array} \right\}$ a $\left\{ \begin{array}{l} \text{tasty} \\ \text{delicious} \\ \text{tasteful} \end{array} \right\}$

and healthy dinner while $\left\{ \begin{array}{l} \text{satisfying} \\ \text{gratifying} \end{array} \right\}$ the different $\left\{ \begin{array}{l} \text{favorites} \\ \text{inclinations} \\ \text{preferences} \end{array} \right\}$

of my family.

二、英文作文：

作文範例

Dear Jerry,   Jan. 28, 2013

    I am so excited! You are my first American pen pal. I have
so many questions for you. First, what is life like in the U.S.? Do
American high school students have the same schedule and amount
of homework we have in Taiwan? I hope not! Ha ha. You see,
here in Taiwan we spend most of our time either in school or
studying. We don't have a lot of free time to ourselves. I would
imagine that American kids have more time to themselves.

    Please describe your life when you write me back. As for me,
I don't have a lot to talk about right now. Everything revolves
around school. My parents are very strict and push me hard to
achieve high marks. That might sound boring to you, but my
parents say it's in my best interest. When I graduate, I can go to
a good college and follow my dream career.

    I'm looking forward to your letter.

                                                    Best wishes,
                                                    Fang

pen pal 筆友   schedule〔'skɛdʒʊl〕*n.* 課程表；時程表
free time 自由時間；休閒時間（= *leisure time*）
as for 至於   ***revolve around*** 以…為中心
strict〔strɪkt〕*adj.* 嚴格的   ***put sb. hard*** （把某人）逼得很緊
achieve〔ə'tʃiv〕*v.* 達到   mark〔mɑrk〕*n.* 分數
in one's (best) interest 為了某人好；對某人有利
career〔kə'rɪr〕*n.* 工作；事業   ***look forward to + N/V-ing*** 期待

大學入學學科能力測驗英文模擬試題 ③

第壹部分：單選題（佔72分）

一、詞彙（佔15分）

說明：第1題至第15題，每題4個選項，其中只有一個是最適當的答案，畫記在答案卡之「選擇題答案區」。各題答對得1分；未作答、答錯、或畫記多於一個選項者，該題以零分計算。

1. As the mountain biking fashion spreads, several countries have started to hold national mountain-bike _____.
   (A) documents　　(B) formations　　(C) championships (D) constructions

2. Parkinson's disease is a nervous disorder that affects muscle control and is _____ by trembling of the arms and legs, muscular rigidity, and poor balance.
   (A) retreated　　　(B) marked　　　(C) removed　　　(D) stretched

3. About one-third of drowning victims are experienced swimmers who become overconfident and swim too far from _____.
   (A) shore　　　(B) guidance　　(C) measure　　(D) division

4. All children have the right to life. Governments should _____ that children survive and develop healthily.
   (A) acquaint　　(B) enquire　　(C) ensure　　(D) assure

5. Prompted by water _____, the government issued water-use restrictions, which included bans on watering lawns and filling swimming pools.
   (A) mechanics　　(B) permits　　(C) certificates　　(D) shortages

6. Once used, tissue paper products are not _____ or recyclable. They are not a type of waste with the potential to be recycled.
   (A) terrific　　(B) common　　(C) favorable　　(D) recoverable

7. New York City used to be a leading center of global finance, but the recent severe economic and financial _____ has ended its leadership.

(A) fatigue   (B) crisis   (C) opposition   (D) circulation

8. When you are afraid, keep your mind on what you have to do. And if you are _____ prepared, you will not be afraid.

(A) thoroughly   (B) ideally   (C) relatively   (D) sincerely

9. Many teachers discuss the material in different words, perhaps adding illustrations to _____ the material.

(A) adjust   (B) simplify   (C) defeat   (D) upload

10. It is very _____ to go on a date alone with a person you know only from a chat room on the Internet. You'd better not do it!

(A) inquisitive   (B) essential   (C) influential   (D) dangerous

11. Giving a presentation without knowing your audience has little _____ of success. Consider your audience carefully.

(A) fortune   (B) chance   (C) companion   (D) request

12. In shallow shore areas with low waves and weak currents, sea grasses flourish and provide protected habitats where many species of animals _____ their eggs.

(A) expose   (B) move   (C) lay   (D) afford

13. Traditionally, ships were distinguished from boats by size, but common usage has _____ the distinction between boats and ships.

(A) blurred   (B) threatened   (C) demonstrated   (D) arrested

14. Taking lecture notes in class _____ listening skills, helping the reader to recognize main ideas and to understand the organization of the material.

(A) compensates   (B) develops   (C) negotiates   (D) substitutes

15. The lack of rainfall has _____ the worst forest fire conditions
    ever recorded in America's history. More than one million acres
    have been burned.
    (A) contributed to   (B) resulted from
    (C) took to   (D) dealt with

二、綜合測驗（佔 15 分）

說明： 第 16 題至第 30 題，每題一個空格，請依文意選出最適當的一個答案，
         畫記在答案卡之「選擇題答案區」。各題答對得 1 分；未作答、答錯、
         或畫記多於一個選項者，該題以零分計算。

第 16 至 20 題為題組

    Modern people often feel pressure to meet our society's preferences
in looks. It can become hard for one to achieve success in life and love
___16___ he or she fits a certain image. In the last few decades, the
desired look has been extremely thin. It is important, therefore, to be aware
that habits you develop in order to achieve or maintain a low weight can
become excessive and make you ___17___ potentially serious illnesses,
one of which is an eating disorder.

    The difference between trying to lose weight and having an eating
disorder is not easy to detect. Serious eating problems may ___18___ as
a simple wish, such as the desire to fit into a favorite swimsuit, but
eventually become a preoccupation in the person's life. When a
person's diet and fitness routine becomes extremely strict and inflexible
and interferes with his or her ability to enjoy life and stay in good
health, ___19___ his or her self worth is determined by his or her size,
that is a sign of an eating disorder.

    If you have an eating disorder, don't ___20___. Talk to someone
you trust, and ask for support. Usually the best way of dealing with an
eating disorder is just a change of attitude and behavior.

16. (A) while   (B) despite   (C) unless   (D) as
17. (A) familiar with (B) vulnerable to (C) similar to (D) popular with
18. (A) end up   (B) drop in   (C) start out   (D) stand by
19. (A) so   (B) but   (C) or   (D) for
20. (A) show it off   (B) speed it up
  (C) give it a try   (D) keep it a secret

第 21 至 25 題為題組

 Feng Shui is the Chinese practice of positioning objects, especially graves, buildings, and furniture, based on a belief in patterns of yin and yang and the flow of chi that have positive and negative effects. It teaches that we are in a constant energy exchange with everything around us. ___21___, it is very important to create a Feng Shui home that has a happy and healthy energy.

 The best way to have a Feng Shui harmonized house is by ___22___ it in mind from the moment of buying it. If it contains many sharp edges or triangular shapes inside or outside the house, it is said to have poisoned arrows, which are very bad for the inhabitants of a building and hurt them in many areas of their lives. If there is a road ending in front of your house, you should ___23___ the house from your list of choices.

 Your house should also ___24___ its environment and with other buildings surrounding it. A house that contains any menacing shapes towards a neighboring house would bring you problems with your neighbors. Besides, you should avoid houses ___25___ trees right in front of the entrance.

21. (A) However   (B) Thus   (C) Instead   (D) Later
22. (A) taking   (B) having   (C) doing   (D) making
23. (A) design   (B) seize   (C) observe   (D) remove
24. (A) be in favor of   (B) be in charge of
  (C) be in harmony with   (D) be in conflict with
25. (A) with   (B) in   (C) for   (D) at

第 26 至 30 題為題組

　　Rising sea levels due to global warming are reportedly threatening the existence of many Indian Ocean islands. A group of scientists who met in Arusha for the launch of the International Year of Planet Earth for Africa said that the islands of Mafia and Zanzibar in Tanzania are most ___26___ to disappear under seawaters due to global warming. They predicted that all the islands off Tanzania's mainland coast could be under water by 2100 following a disastrous ___27___ in sea levels caused by the melting of polar ice. According to the scientists, this scenario is "___28___" unless something is done soon.

　　Islands that are known to have been submerged in the past ___29___ Maziwi, near Pangani in the Tanga Region , and Fungu la Nyani, on the Rufiji River estuary. At present, other islands, such as Ras Nungwi, located off the northern coast of Zanzibar Island, which has already lost 100 meters of its beach to the sea, and the Mbudya and Bongoyo islands, are threatened by global warming.

　　It seems ___30___ measures should be taken to save these beautiful islands, which are among the leading tourist destinations of the world.

26. (A) regular　　　(B) superficial　　(C) likely　　　(D) accurate
27. (A) arise　　　　(B) raise　　　　(C) arouse　　　(D) rise
28. (A) very possible　　　　　　(B) very dogmatic
　　(C) too improbable　　　　　(D) too dangerous
29. (A) include　　　(B) including　　(C) that include　(D) to include
30. (A) drowsy　　　(B) drastic　　　(C) dreadful　　(D) dreary

三、文意選填（佔 10 分）

說明：　第 31 題至第 40 題，每題一個空格，請依文意在文章後所提供的 (A) 到 (J) 選項中分別選出最適當者，並將其英文字母代號畫記在答案卡之「選擇題答案區」。各題答對得 1 分；未作答、答錯、或畫記多於一個選項者，該題以零分計算。

第 31 至 40 題為題組

Many people think that cats are afraid of water. They're not.
Occasionally, one can see a cat ___31___ spontaneously into the water.
Nature documentary fans can ___32___ to the fact that many of the cats'
larger ___33___, such as tigers and jaguars, love to swim.

So why isn't your cat likely to stick a ___34___ into the pool? For
the same reasons it always drives you ___35___: it has a cleanliness
fetish, and it's ___36___. Your cat refuses to have a good time. It won't
get wet because it figures it isn't ___37___ the effort needed to dry and
clean itself with its tongue to enjoy something as ___38___ as marine
frolic. Unless you ___39___ it and stock your pool with fish, your cat is
likely to remain ___40___.

(A) starve　　　(B) attest　　　(C) paw　　　(D) nuts
(E) leap　　　(F) worth　　　(G) relatives　　　(H) landlocked
(I) lazy　　　(J) superficial

四、閱讀測驗（佔 32 分）

說明：　第 41 題至第 56 題，每題 4 個選項，請分別根據各篇文章之文意選出最
　　　　適當的一個答案，畫記在答案卡之「選擇題答案區」。各題答對得 2 分；
　　　　未作答、答錯、或畫記多於一個選項者，該題以零分計算。

第 41 至 44 題為題組

Is your heart strong? By some calculations, a healthy heart can
produce enough energy in an hour to lift a one-ton car off the ground.
That is pretty strong, but what happens if your heart is not healthy?
A damaged heart does not work very well, perhaps leaving your body
starved for oxygen. Even worse, if your arteries are damaged and your
heart does not get enough blood, you may have trouble lifting your own
body out of a hospital bed, much less lifting a car off the ground.

You do have some control over how healthy your heart is. What you do, what you eat and how you live can actually change how your heart works. You actually have the power to make your heart stronger with just a few changes in your lifestyle. If you have ever worked out, you have certainly felt the immediate effects of exercise. Your heart speeds up as your body demands more oxygen, your breathing rate increases and you start to sweat to cool your body. In the long-term, not only does regular exercise increase good cholesterol, but it also decreases bad cholesterol. It means there may be less plaque built up in the arteries. Less plaque means blood can flow freely to and from the heart. It is amazing that something as simple as moving your body can have such dramatic benefits!

41. The title of this article is most likely to be _____.
    (A) Focus on Your Heart
    (B) Exercise for a Strong, Healthy Heart
    (C) How to Reduce Coronary Artery Disease
    (D) High Blood Pressure and High Cholesterol

42. Which of the following is NOT mentioned in the passage as something that affects the way our hearts work?
    (A) What we do.　　　　(B) How we live our lives.
    (C) What we eat.　　　　(D) Where we live.

43. What is NOT an immediate effect of exercise?
    (A) Good cholesterol is increased.
    (B) The heartbeat speeds up.
    (C) Sweating to cool off the body.
    (D) Breathing rate increases.

44. The author mainly advised the readers to _____.
    (A) eat less cholesterol　　　　(B) protect their health
    (C) clear out the plaque　　　　(D) get regular exercise

In this tight economy, where gas prices are high and funds are low, many families are opting for purchase-less mall excursions. There they can get out of the house and take in some sights, expending little more than the fuel it takes to get there. Savvy marketers are taking this opportunity to **tantalize** bored Americans with free gifts and maintain their brand images through tough economic times.

For example, Coca-Cola promoted its sponsorship of the 2008 Beijing Olympics and offered thousands of free, commemorative Coke bottles specially designed by Chinese artists to visitors at Simon Malls. The free gifts came with cards prompting those who received them to visit Coke's website and download free music associated with each bottle. The promotion was part of a teen-focused event featuring giveaways in the shopping malls. Other companies such as Sprint and ABC Family gave away network programming-based T-shirts that visitors could customize on-site.

As consumers come to malls expecting entertainment, even if hosting a mall event requires extra staffing, advertising, and purchasing security, this type of promotion is still highly recommended. After all, handing out freebies and samples can keep brands in consumers' minds, even when their wallets are closed.

45. In which of the following magazines would you most likely find this passage?
   (A) *World Entertainment*   (B) *Technology Update*
   (C) *Business Management*   (D) *Tourist Guidebook*

46. Which of the following best explains the word "**tantalize**" in the first paragraph?
   (A) to examine   (B) to distract
   (C) to urge   (D) to tempt

47. According to the passage, hosting a mall event does NOT require

_____.

(A) extra staffing 　　　　(B) putting out advertisements
(C) purchasing security 　　(D) charging admission

48. Which of the following is NOT mentioned in this passage?
(A) It usually takes several months to plan the promotional activities.
(B) Sprint and ABC Family gave away customized T-shirts for promotion.
(C) Corporations are trying to maintain their brand images through tough economic times.
(D) Coca-Cola promoted the 2008 Beijing Olympics by offering free, specially designed Coke bottles.

第 49 至 52 題為題組

　Infectious diseases are no laughing matter. If you are coughing and blowing your nose all over the place but still feel tempted to go to work, try to resist and get some rest. Not all diseases are contagious, but it is better to be safe than sorry. Avoid sharing drinks or personal items with people. Remember, prevention is the best cure.

　There are four main kinds of germs that cause infectious diseases. Bacteria are single-cell germs that have the ability to multiply rapidly and release chemicals that will make you sick. Examples of bacterial, transmittable diseases are cholera, diphtheria, scarlet fever and tuberculosis. Viruses are capsules containing genetic information and they use your own cells to multiply. Contagious viral diseases include AIDS, smallpox, pneumonia and SARS. Fungi are vegetable-like mushrooms or mildew that will make you ill, and protozoa are single-cell predators that are looking for a host where they can eat and live, like malaria.

When dealing with an infectious disease, the first step is to identify the infection. The infection becomes a disease when cells in your body become damaged and the symptoms of illness appear. White blood cells and antibodies will attempt to protect your body from the infection, which results in fevers, coughing, sneezing or other ailments. Once the disease takes hold, medication will be needed.

49. The author of this passage is most likely to be a(n) _____.
    (A) high-ranking engineer   (B) human resources manager
    (C) family physician   (D) educational psychologist

50. The four main kinds of germs that cause infectious diseases do NOT include _____.
    (A) antibiotics   (B) fungi   (C) bacteria   (D) viruses

51. According to the passage, SARS is a contagious disease caused by a _____.
    (A) predator   (B) fungus   (C) bacteria   (D) virus

52. Which of the following is NOT mentioned in this passage?
    (A) When the symptoms of illness appear, don't force yourself to work.
    (B) Medications that treat one person are ineffective against treating another.
    (C) Not all diseases are infectious or dangerous.
    (D) Antibodies protect our bodies from the infection, which results in ailments.

第 53 至 56 題為題組

A large number of websites allow university students to buy ready-made term papers. Some even lure elementary students by doing their homework for them. That flood of paperwork makes it virtually impossible to ferret out **plagiarism**. But recent research reveals that writing has its own "fingerprint" that can tell teachers who the writer is.

In February 1996, a novel titled "Primary Colors" was published by an anonymous author in the United States. The protagonist, a governor in the southern U.S. who has an affair with a librarian during the campaign, closely resembled Bill Clinton, and the novel was full of information that only a close acquaintance of Clinton could have. The first suspect was Joe Klein, then a columnist for *Newsweek*. He first denied the accusations, but subsequently admitted it. Prof. Donald Foster, a forensic linguist and text analyst for the FBI, showed that the novel was written in a similar style as Klein's columns by statistical analysis of the sentences.

Statistical text analysis done to track down an author can have a success rate of up to 90 percent, but it varies from language to language. Even so, a database can always be expanded by analyzing more texts, and this method can soon be used at a practical level to detect plagiarism in students' work.

53. What is the main idea of this passage?
    (A) The scientific application of statistical modeling and classification is ineffective.
    (B) Linguistic analysis offers clues to authorship.
    (C) Text analysis is a method for retrieving relevant stories from a collection of stories.
    (D) The application of text analysis is important in politics.

54. Who is the author of the novel titled "Primary Colors"?
    (A) Bill Clinton.   (B) Donald Foster.
    (C) Joe Klein.   (D) An unknown author.

55. Which of the following best explains the word "**plagiarism**" in the first paragraph?
    (A) Taking part in a game.   (B) Suffering from a disease.
    (C) Joining a gang.   (D) Copying another's work.

56. According to the passage, which of the following is NOT true?
    (A) A large number of ready-made term papers are available online.
    (B) The text analysis method can soon be applied in the academic fields.
    (C) The FBI text analyst identified the author by analyzing the sentences statistically.
    (D) Statistical text analysis is always successful in tracking down an author.

第貳部分：非選擇題（佔 28 分）

一、中譯英（佔 8 分）

說明： 1. 請將以下中文句子譯成正確、通順、達意的英文，並將答案寫在「答案卷」上。

2. 請依序作答，並標明題號。每題 4 分，共 8 分。

1. 聽說湯姆在上個禮拜的期中考作弊被抓到了，他懊悔不已。

2. 不管他有多難過，他現在唯一能做的事就是勇敢面對現實。

二、英文作文（20 ％）

說明： 1. 依提示在「答案卷」上寫一篇英文作文。

2. 文長約 100 至 120 個單詞（words）。

提示：你去一家餐廳吃飯，受到差勁的服務。你（英文名字必須假設為 Marie Stokes 或 Tom Cruise），要寫一封投訴信，跟經理講述你不好的用餐經驗。

請注意：必須使用上述的 Marie Stokes 或 Tom Cruise 在信末署名，**不得使用自己的真實中文或英文名字**。

大學入學學科能力測驗英文模擬試題 ③ 詳解

第壹部分：單選題

一、詞彙：

1. (**C**) 由於騎越野自行車的流行普及，有幾個國家已經開始舉辦全國性的越野自行車錦標賽。

    (A) document〔'dɑkjəmənt〕*n.* 文件　　documentary *n.* 紀錄片

    (B) formation〔fɔr'meʃən〕*n.* 形成

    (C) *championship*〔'tʃæmpiən‚ʃip〕*n.* 錦標賽；冠軍（資格）

        champion *n.* 冠軍

    (D) construction〔kən'strʌkʃən〕*n.* 建造　　constructive *adj.*

    * *mountain biking* 騎越野自行車　　fashion〔'fæʃən〕*n.* 流行

      spread〔sprɛd〕*v.* 普及；流傳　　hold〔hold〕*v.* 舉辦

2. (**B**) 帕金森氏症是一種會影響肌肉控制的神經系統疾病，<u>以手腳顫抖、肌肉僵硬，和平衡不佳為特徵</u>。

    (A) retreat〔rɪ'trit〕*v.* 撤退　*n.* 避難處；撤退

    (B) *mark*〔mɑrk〕*v.* 以…為特徵；做記號　*n.* 記號；分數

    (C) remove〔rɪ'muv〕*v.* 除去（ = *take away* ）；遷移

    (D) stretch〔strɛtʃ〕*v.* 伸展

    * *Parkinson's disease* 帕金森氏症　　nervous〔'nɜvəs〕*adj.* 神經的

      disorder〔dɪs'ɔrdə〕*n.* 失調；疾病　　muscle〔'mʌsl̩〕*n.* 肌肉

      trembling〔'trɛmblɪŋ〕*n.* 顫抖　　muscular〔'mʌskjələ〕*adj.* 肌肉的

      rigidity〔rɪ'dʒɪdətɪ〕*n.* 僵硬　　balance〔'bæləns〕*n.* 平衡

3. (**A**) 大約三分之一的溺水受害者都有豐富的游泳經驗，他們因為過於自信，而游離岸邊太遠。

    (A) *shore*〔ʃor〕*n.* （湖、海）岸　　on shore 在岸上

    (B) guidance〔'gaɪdn̩s〕*n.* 指導　　guide *v.* 引導（ = *lead* ）

    (C) measure〔'mɛʒə〕*v.* 測量　*n.* 措施

    (D) division〔də'vɪʒən〕*n.* 分割；不一致（ = *disagreement* ）

    * drown〔draʊn〕*v.* 溺水；淹死　　victim〔'vɪktɪm〕*n.* 受害者

      experienced〔ɪk'spɪrɪənst〕*adj.* 經驗豐富的

      overconfident〔'ovə'kɑnfədənt〕*adj.* 過於自信的

4. (**C**) 所有兒童都有生存的權利。政府應該<u>確保</u>兒童得以生存，並健康地發育。

    (A) acquaint〔ə'kwɛnt〕*v.* 使熟悉   acquaintance *n.* 認識的人

    (B) enquire〔ɪn'kwaɪr〕*v.* 詢問（= *inquire*）   enquire into 調查

    (C) ***ensure***〔ɪn'ʃur〕*v.* 保證；確保

    (D) assure〔ə'ʃur〕*v.* 向～保證

    * right〔raɪt〕*n.* 權利   survive〔sə'vaɪv〕*v.* 存活

    develop〔dɪ'vɛləp〕*v.* 發育

5. (**D**) 水源<u>短缺</u>促使政府發佈用水管制，其中包括禁止在草坪上灑水以及泳池蓄水。

    (A) mechanic〔mə'kænɪk〕*n.* 機械工人；技工   mechanical *adj.*

    (B) permit〔'pɝmɪt〕*n.* 許可證 〔pə'mɪt〕*v.* 允許

    (C) certificate〔sə'tɪfəkɪt〕*n.* 證書   certify *v.* 證明

    (D) ***shortage***〔'ʃɔrtɪdʒ〕*n.* 短缺

    * prompt〔prɑmpt〕*v.* 驅使；促使   issue〔'ɪʃu〕*v.* 發佈

    restriction〔rɪ'strɪkʃən〕*n.* 限制   ban〔bæn〕*n.* 禁止 < *on* >

    water〔'wɔtə〕*v.* 在…上灑水   lawn〔lɔn〕*n.* 草坪

6. (**D**) 面紙類的產品，一旦經過使用，就<u>不能回收</u>或再利用。它們是一種不可能回收的廢棄物。

    (A) terrific〔tə'rɪfɪk〕*adj.* 極好的

    (B) common〔'kɑmən〕*adj.* 常見的；普通的

    (C) favorable〔'fevərəbl̩〕*adj.* 有利的（= *advantageous*）

    (D) ***recoverable***〔rɪ'kʌvərəbl̩〕*adj.* 可收回的；可恢復的

        recover *v.* 恢復

  * ***tissue paper*** 面紙

    recyclable〔rɪ'saɪkləbl̩〕*adj.* 可回收再利用的

    type〔taɪp〕*n.* 類型   waste〔west〕*n.* 廢棄物

    potential〔pə'tɛnʃəl〕*n.* 可能性；潛力

    recycle〔ri'saɪkl̩〕*v.* 回收；再利用

7. (**B**) 紐約市以前是全球金融的領導中心，但最近嚴重的經濟與金融危機，結束了它的領導地位。

    (A) fatigue〔fəˋtig〕*n.* 疲勞（= *tiredness*）

    (B) ***crisis***〔ˋkraɪsɪs〕*n.* 危機　　crises *n. pl.*

    (C) opposition〔ˏɑpəˋzɪʃən〕*n.* 抵抗；反對 < *to* >　　oppose *v.*

    (D) circulation〔ˏsɝkjəˋleʃən〕*n.* 循環；發行（量）

        circulate *v.*

    * ***used to V.*** 以前～　　leading〔ˋlidɪŋ〕*adj.* 領導的

      finance〔ˋfaɪnæns〕*n.* 金融　　severe〔səˋvɪr〕*adj.* 嚴重的

      economic〔ˏikəˋnɑmɪk〕*adj.* 經濟的

      financial〔fəˋnænʃəl〕*adj.* 金融的

      leadership〔ˋlidɚˏʃɪp〕*n.* 領導地位

8. (**A**) 當你害怕時，就專注在你必須要做的事上面。而如果你完全準備好，你就不會害怕。

    (A) ***thoroughly***〔ˋθɝolɪ〕*adv.* 完全地（= *completely* = *totally*）

    (B) ideally〔aɪˋdiəlɪ〕*adv.* 理想上；完美地（= *perfectly*）

    (C) relatively〔ˋrɛlətɪvlɪ〕*adv.* 相對地；比較上　　relative *adj.*

    (D) sincerely〔sɪnˋsɪrlɪ〕*adv.* 由衷地

    * ***keep*** *one's* ***mind on*** 專注於

      prepared〔prɪˋpɛrd〕*adj.* 準備好的

9. (**B**) 許多教師用不同的方法討論這份教材，也許是加上圖解說明，以使教材變簡單。

    (A) adjust〔əˋdʒʌst〕*v.* 調整；使適應（= *accustom*）

    (B) ***simplify***〔ˋsɪmpləˏfaɪ〕*v.* 簡化　　simplicity *n.*

    (C) defeat〔dɪˋfit〕*v.* 打敗（= *beat*）

    (D) upload〔ʌpˋlod〕*v.* 上傳（↔ download *v.* 下載）

    * material〔məˋtɪrɪəl〕*n.* 資料；材料

      in different words 以不同的話來詮釋；用不同方法解釋

      add〔æd〕*v.* 增加；補充

      illustration〔ˏɪləsˋtreʃən〕*n.* 插圖；圖解

10. (**D**) 跟一個從網路聊天室上認識的人單獨約會，是非常<u>危險的</u>事，
你最好別這樣做！

(A) inquisitive〔ɪn'kwɪzətɪv〕*adj.* 好問的；好打聽的（= *curious*）
(B) essential〔ə'sɛnʃəl〕*adj.* 必要的　　essence *n.* 本質
(C) influential〔ˌɪnflʊ'ɛnʃəl〕*adj.* 有影響力的　　influence *n. v.* 影響
(D) ***dangerous***〔'dendʒərəs〕*adj.* 危險的

* ***go on a date*** 去約會　　alone〔ə'lon〕*adv.* 單獨地
chat room 聊天室　　Internet〔'ɪntəˌnɛt〕*n.* 網際網路
had better + V. 最好～

11. (**B**) 不了解你的觀衆就發表演說，成功的<u>機會</u>很小。你應該仔細考慮到你
的觀衆。

(A) fortune〔'fɔrtʃən〕*n.* 運氣（= *luck*）；財富（= *wealth*）
(B) ***chance***〔tʃæns〕*n.* 機會（= *opportunity*）
(C) companion〔kəm'pænjən〕*n.* 同伴
(D) request〔rɪ'kwɛst〕*n. v.* 請求；要求（= *demand*）

* presentation〔ˌprɛzn̩'teʃən〕*n.* 演說；演出
give a presentation 發表演說；上台報告
audience〔'ɔdɪəns〕*n.* 觀衆；聽衆
consider〔kən'sɪdə〕*v.* 考慮

12. (**C**) 海草在波浪小且洋流弱的淺灘區長得很茂密，提供受保護的棲息
地，讓很多種動物在那邊<u>產卵</u>。

(A) expose〔ɪk'spoz〕*v.* 暴露；使接觸
(B) move〔muv〕*v.* 移動；使感動
(C) ***lay***〔le〕*v.* 產卵；放置【三態變化：lay-laid-laid】
(D) afford〔ə'fɔrd〕*v.* 負擔得起　　affordable *adj.* 可負擔得起的

* shallow〔'ʃælo〕*adj.* 淺的　　wave〔wev〕*n.* 波浪
current〔'kɜənt〕*n.* 洋流　　***sea grass*** 海草
flourish〔'flɝɪʃ〕*v.* 茂盛　　protected〔prə'tɛktɪd〕*adj.* 受保護的
habitat〔'hæbəˌtæt〕*n.* 棲息地
species〔'spiʃɪz〕*n.* 物種【單複數同形】

13. (**A**) 傳統上，船艦和小船是以大小來區別的，但一般語法已經<u>模糊</u>了小船
與船艦之間的差別。

(A) ***blur*** ﹝ blɜ ﹞ *v.* 使模糊　　*n.* 模糊物；朦朧的狀況

(B) threaten ﹝ˈθrɛtṇ﹞ *v.* 威脅　　threatening *adj.* 威脅的

(C) demonstrate ﹝ˈdɛmən͵stret﹞ *v.* 示威；示範

　　demonstration *n.* 示威遊行

(D) arrest ﹝əˈrɛst﹞ *v.* 逮捕

* traditionally ﹝ trəˈdɪʃənl̩ɪ ﹞ *adv.* 傳統上　　ship ﹝ ʃɪp ﹞ *n.* 船；艦

distinguish ﹝ dɪˈstɪŋgwɪʃ ﹞ *v.* 區別 < *from* >

boat ﹝ bot ﹞ *n.* (小) 船　　usage ﹝ˈjusɪdʒ﹞ *n.* 用法；語法

distinction ﹝ dɪˈstɪŋkʃən ﹞ *n.* 區別；差別

14. (**B**) 在課堂上聽課做筆記所<u>培養</u>出的聽力技巧，能幫助讀者認清主要的
概念，並了解教材的架構。

(A) compensate ﹝ˈkɑmpən͵set﹞ *v.* 補償　　compensation *n.*

(B) ***develop*** ﹝ dɪˈvɛləp ﹞ *v.* 培養　　development *n.*

(C) negotiate ﹝ nɪˈgoʃɪ͵et ﹞ *v.* 談判；交涉　　negotiable *adj.*

　　negotiation *n.*

(D) substitute ﹝ˈsʌbstə͵tjut﹞ *v.* 用～代替　　*n.* 替代品

* ***take notes*** 做筆記　　lecture ﹝ˈlɛktʃɚ﹞ *n.* 講課；演講

skill ﹝ skɪl ﹞ *n.* 技巧；技能　　recognize ﹝ˈrɛkəg͵naɪz﹞ *v.* 認出

organization ﹝͵ɔrgənəˈzeʃən﹞ *n.* 組織；架構

15. (**A**) 缺乏降雨<u>導致</u>美國有史以來，情況最嚴重的一場森林大火。有超過
一百萬英畝的森林燒毀。

(A) ***contribute to*** 導致；造成

(B) result from 起因於；由…引起

(C) take to 喜歡　　　　　(D) deal with 處理

* lack ﹝ læk ﹞ *n.* 缺乏　　rainfall ﹝ˈren͵fɔl﹞ *n.* 降雨 (量)

condition ﹝ kənˈdɪʃən ﹞ *n.* 情況　　record ﹝ rɪˈkɔrd ﹞ *v.* 紀錄

ever recorded in history 有歷史紀錄以來

acre ﹝ˈekɚ﹞ *n.* 英畝

二、綜合測驗：

第 16 至 20 題為題組

現代人為了要符合社會所偏好的外表，經常會覺得有壓力。除非符合某種
　　　　　　　　　　　　　　　　　　　　　　　　　　　　　　　　16
形象，否則一個人要在生活或愛情裡取得成功，有可能會很困難。在最近幾十
年中，大家所在意的是極度苗條的外表。因此，有一件重要的事必須要知道，
那就是你為了達到、或維持低體重所培養的習慣，可能會變得太過度，並讓你
容易得到潛在的嚴重疾病，而其中一種就是飲食失調。
17

> * modern〔ˈmɑdən〕adj. 現代的　　pressure〔ˈprɛʃə〕n. 壓力
> meet〔mit〕v. 符合　　preference〔ˈprɛfərəns〕n. 偏愛
> looks〔lʊks〕n. pl. 外表　　achieve〔əˈtʃiv〕v. 達到；獲得
> fit〔fɪt〕v. 符合（= match）　　certain〔ˈsɝtn̩〕adj. 某種的
> image〔ˈɪmɪdʒ〕n. 形象　　decade〔ˈdɛked〕n. 十年
> desired〔dɪˈzaɪrd〕adj. 所期望的；所想要的
> extremely〔ɪkˈstrimlɪ〕adv. 極度地
> thin〔θɪn〕adj. 瘦的；苗條的　　aware〔əˈwɛr〕adj. 知道的；感覺到的
> develop〔dɪˈvɛləp〕v. 培養　　***in order to*** 為了
> maintain〔menˈten〕v. 維持　　excessive〔ɪkˈsɛsɪv〕adj. 過度的
> potentially〔pəˈtɛnʃəlɪ〕adv. 潛在地　　illness〔ˈɪlnɪs〕n. 疾病
> disorder〔dɪsˈɔrdə〕n. 失調　　***eating disorder*** 飲食失調

16. (**C**) 依句意，選 (C) ***unless*** 「除非」。而 (A) while 「當…時候」，(B) despite
「儘管」，(D) as 「因為」，均不合句意。

17. (**B**) 依句意，選 (B) ***vulnerable to*** 「易受…傷害的；易受…影響的」。
vulnerable〔ˈvʌlnərəbl̩〕adj. 易受傷害的
而 (A) be familiar with 「對…熟悉」，(C) be similar to 「和…相似」，
(D) be popular with 「受…歡迎」，則不合句意。

　　想要減重和患有飲食失調之間的差別，是不容易發現的。嚴重的飲食問
題，可能一開始是一個簡單的願望，像是想穿進一件最喜愛泳裝的願望，但
　　　　　　18
是到最後卻變成了生活中很在意的事。

* ***lose weight*** 減重　　detect〔dɪˈtɛkt〕v. 發現
　fit into 被容納　　swimsuit〔ˈswɪm,sut〕n. 泳裝
　eventually〔ɪˈvɛntʃʊəlɪ〕adv. 最後
　preoccupation〔pri,ɑkjəˈpeʃən〕n. 耿耿於懷的事；全神貫注之事

18. (**C**) 依句意，選 (C) ***start out as***「一開始是…」。而 (A) end up「最後…」，
　　　(B) drop in「順道拜訪」, (D) stand by「站在一旁；袖手旁觀；待命」，
　　　則不合句意。

當一個人的飲食控制與健身規劃變得過於嚴格死板，並妨礙到了享受人生與維
持健康的能力時，<u>或者是</u>個人的自我價值是由身材來決定時，就是飲食失調的
徵兆。
19

* diet〔ˈdaɪət〕n. 飲食控制　　fitness〔ˈfɪtnɪs〕n. 健康
　routine〔ruˈtin〕n. 例行公事；常規　　***fitness routine*** 健身規劃
　strict〔strɪkt〕adj. 嚴格的
　inflexible〔ɪnˈflɛksəbl̩〕adj. 不能變通的
　interfere〔,ɪntɚˈfɪr〕v. 妨礙 < *with* >
　stay〔ste〕v. 保持　　***self worth*** 自我價值
　determine〔dɪˈtɝmɪn〕v. 決定 (= *decide*)
　size〔saɪz〕n. 身材；大小　　sign〔saɪn〕n. 徵兆

19. (**C**) 依句意，選 (C) ***or***「或者」。而 (A) so「所以」, (B) but「但是」,
　　　(D) for「因為」，均不合句意。

如果你飲食失調，不要<u>隱瞞這件事</u>。告訴你信任的人並請求幫助。通常處
20
理飲食失調的最佳辦法，就只是改變態度和行為而已。

* ***ask for*** 請求　　support〔səˈport〕n. 支持；援助
　deal with 應付；處理　　attitude〔ˈætə,tjud〕n. 態度
　behavior〔bɪˈhevjɚ〕n. 行為

20. (**D**) 依句意，選 (D) ***keep it a secret***「保密；隱瞞」。而 (A) show off「炫
　　　耀」, (B) speed up「加速」, (C) give it a try「試試看」，則不合句意。

第 21 至 25 題爲題組

　　風水是中國擺設物體的習俗，尤其是墳墓、建築物，和家具，都是以相信陰陽的模式，以及氣的流動，會產生正面和負面的影響爲根據。風水教導我們，我們不斷的和周圍的事物交換能量。<u>因此</u>，創造一個有快樂與健康能量的風水住宅，是一件非常重要的事。
21

> * **Feng Shui** 風水　　　practice〔ˈpræktɪs〕n. 作法；習俗（= custom）
> position〔pəˈzɪʃən〕v. 擺設位置　　object〔ˈɑbdʒɪkt〕n. 物體
> grave〔grev〕n. 墳墓　　building〔ˈbɪldɪŋ〕n. 建築物
> furniture〔ˈfɜnɪtʃɚ〕n. 家具　　***based on*** 根據
> belief〔bəˈlif〕n. 相信；信仰 < in >　　pattern〔ˈpætən〕n. 模式
> flow〔flo〕n. 流動　　positive〔ˈpɑzətɪv〕adj. 正面的
> negative〔ˈnɛgətɪv〕adj. 負面的　　effect〔ɪˈfɛkt〕n. 影響
> constant〔ˈkɑnstənt〕adj. 不斷的　　energy〔ˈɛnədʒɪ〕n. 能量
> exchange〔ɪksˈtʃendʒ〕n. 交換

21.（**B**）依句意，選 (B) ***Thus***〔ðʌs〕adv. 因此。而 (A) however「然而」，
　　　 (C) instead「作爲代替；相反地」，(D) later「後來」，均不合句意。

　　想擁有風水調和的住宅的最佳方法，就是從買房子的那一刻起，就在心中<u>記著</u>這件事。如果房子內外有許多銳利的邊緣，或是三角的形狀，據說會有毒
22
箭，對建築物內居民極爲不利，會傷害到他們生活中的許多方面。如果有一條路的終點就在你的房子前面，你應該將它從你的購屋選擇中<u>移除</u>。
23

> * harmonized〔ˈhɑrmə.naɪzd〕adj. 調和的；和諧的
> contain〔kənˈten〕v. 包含　　sharp〔ʃɑrp〕adj. 銳利的
> edge〔ɛdʒ〕n. 邊緣　　triangular〔traɪˈæŋgjələ〕adj. 三角形的
> shape〔ʃep〕n. 形狀　　***it is said to*** 據說
> poisoning〔ˈpɔɪzn〕n. 毒　　arrow〔ˈæro〕n. 箭
> inhabitant〔ɪnˈhæbətənt〕n. 居民　　area〔ˈɛrɪə〕n. 領域
> list〔lɪst〕n. 表；目錄　　choice〔tʃɔɪs〕n. 選擇

22.（**B**）***have sth. in mind*** 將某事牢記在心

23.（**D**）依句意，選 (D) ***remove***〔rɪˈmuv〕v. 移除。而 (A) design〔dɪˈzaɪn〕v.
　　　 設計，(B) seize〔siz〕v. 抓住，(C) observe〔əbˈzɜv〕v. 觀察；遵守，
　　　 均不合句意。

你的房子也應該要和環境，以及周圍的其他建築物<u>很協調</u>。一棟對於鄰近
　　　　　　　　　　　　　　　　　　　　　　　24　　　　　　　　　　24
住宅而言，一棟有任何脅迫外形的房屋，會為你帶來與鄰居之間的問題。此外，
你應該避免大門正前方<u>有</u>樹的房子。
　　　　　　　　　25

* surround〔 sə'raʊnd 〕v. 圍繞　　menacing〔'mɛnɪsɪŋ 〕adj. 險惡的
  neighboring〔'nebərɪŋ 〕adj. 鄰近的　　avoid〔 ə'vɔɪd 〕v. 避免
  entrance〔'ɛntrəns 〕n. 入口；大門

24. (**C**) 依句意，選 (C) *be in harmony with*「與⋯調和」。
    harmony〔'hɑrmənɪ 〕n. 和諧；調和
    而 (A) be in favor of「贊成」，(B) be in charge of「負責」，
    (D) be in conflict with「與⋯衝突」，均不合句意。

25. (**A**) 依句意，正前方「有」樹，選 (A) *with*。

第 26 至 30 題為題組

　　由於全球暖化而上升的海平面，據報導會威脅到許多印度洋島嶼的存亡。
一群科學家為非洲而發起國際地球年活動，齊聚在阿魯沙市，他們說坦尚尼亞
的馬非亞島與占吉巴島，最有<u>可能</u>因為全球暖化，而消失於海水中。
　　　　　　　　　　　　　　　　　　　　26

* rising〔'raɪzɪŋ 〕adj. 上升的　　*sea level* 海平面　　*due to* 由於
  global warming 全球暖化　　reportedly〔 rɪ'portɪdlɪ 〕adv. 據報導
  threaten〔'θrɛtn̩ 〕v. 威脅　　existence〔 ɪg'zɪstəns 〕n. 存在
  Indian Ocean 印度洋　　launch〔 lɔntʃ 〕n. 發起
  international〔ˌɪntɚ'næʃənl̩ 〕adj. 國際的
  planet〔'plænɪt 〕n. 行星【常指「地球」】
  the International Year of Planet Earth 國際地球年【聯合國大會宣布
  　　2008 年為國際地球年，目標是加強人們對地球科學的認識，並將這個領域
  　　的知識，用於改善全球環境上】
  seawater〔'siˌwɔtɚ 〕n. 海水

26. (**C**) 依句意，選 (C) *be likely to* + *V.*「可能～」。而 (A) regular〔'rɛgjələ 〕
    adj. 規律的，(B) superficial〔ˌsupɚ'fɪʃəl 〕*adj.* 表面的；膚淺的
    (D) accurate〔'ækjərɪt 〕*adj.* 準確的，均不合句意。

他們預測，在極地融冰造成的嚴重海平面<u>上升</u>後，坦尙尼亞大陸沿海的島嶼，
27

到西元 2100 年時，可能都會位在水面下。根據科學家的說法，除非馬上採取行動，否則這種局面<u>非常有可能</u>出現。
28

> * predict〔prɪ′dɪkt〕v. 預測　　off〔ɔf〕prep. 在…的外海
> mainland〔′menˌlænd〕adj. 大陸的；本土的　　coast〔kost〕n. 海岸
> following〔′faləwɪŋ〕prep. 在…之後
> disastrous〔dɪz′æstrəs〕adj. 引起災害的；(災害) 嚴重的
> melt〔mɛlt〕v. 融化　　polar〔′polɚ〕adj. 極地的
> scenario〔sɪ′nɛrɪˏo〕n. 局面；情況　　unless〔ən′lɛs〕conj. 除非

27.(**D**)　(A) arise〔ə′raɪz〕v. 發生　　　　(B) raise〔rez〕v. 提高
　　　　　　 (C) arouse〔ə′rauz〕v. 喚起　　　　(D) *rise*〔raɪz〕n. 上升

28.(**A**)　依上下句意，選 (A) *very possible*「很有可能的」。而 (B) dogmatic
　　　　　　〔dɔg′mætɪk〕adj. 武斷的，(C) improbable〔ɪm′prabəbļ〕adj. 未必發生
　　　　　　的，(D) dangerous「危險的」，均不合句意。

過去已知的下沈島嶼，<u>包括</u>在坦加地區靠近潘加尼區的馬士威島，以及位
29

在魯非吉河河口的 Fungu la Nyani 島。目前其他的島嶼，像是位於占吉巴島北
海岸的 Ras Nungwi 島，海灘已經被海淹沒掉一百公尺，而 Mbudya 島與
Bongoyo 島也受到了全球暖化的威脅。

> * submerge〔səb′mɝdʒ〕v. 淹沒　　*in the past* 在過去
> *Maziwi* 馬士威島【已消失的島嶼名】
> *Pangani* 潘加尼區【坦加地區內的一區】
> *Tanga Region* 坦加地區　　estuary〔′ɛstʃʊˏɛrɪ〕n. 河口
> *at present* 目前　　locate〔′loket , lo′ket〕v. 使位於

29.(**A**)　空格應填動詞，故選 (A) *include*〔ɪn′klud〕v. 包括。

似乎應該要採取<u>強烈的</u>措施，以拯救這些美麗的島嶼，它們都是全世界主
30

要的觀光地區。

* measure〔'mɛʒɚ〕 *n.* 措施　　***take measures*** 採取措施
leading〔'lidɪŋ〕 *adj.* 一流的；主要的　　tourist〔'tʊrɪst〕 *adj.* 觀光的
destination〔ˌdɛstə'neʃən〕 *n.* 目的地

30. (**B**) (A) drowsy〔'draʊzɪ〕 *adj.* 睏的；想睡的
(B) ***drastic***〔'dræstɪk〕 *adj.* 激烈的
(C) dreadful〔'drɛdfəl〕 *adj.* 可怕的
(D) dreary〔'drɪrɪ〕 *adj.* 荒涼的

三、文意選填：

第 31 至 40 題為題組

　　很多人認為貓會怕水。牠們其實不怕。有時候我們會看到貓自動地
³¹ (**E**) 跳進水中。自然紀錄片的愛好者可以 ³² (**B**) 證實這件事，就是許多較大的
貓科 ³³ (**G**) 動物，例如老虎還有美洲豹，都很喜歡游泳。

* ***be afraid of*** 害怕　　occasionally〔ə'keʒənlɪ〕 *adv.* 偶爾
leap〔lip〕 *v.* 跳；跳躍
spontaneously〔spɑn'tenɪəslɪ〕 *adv.* 自動自發地
documentary〔ˌdɑkjə'mɛntərɪ〕 *n.* 紀錄片
natural documentary 自然紀錄片　　fan〔fæn〕 *n.* 迷；愛好者
attest〔ə'tɛst〕 *v.* 證實　　relative〔'rɛlətɪv〕 *n.* 近親；親緣動物
such as 例如　　jaguar〔'dʒægwɑr〕 *n.* 美洲豹

　　那為什麼你的貓不會把 ³⁴ (**C**) 爪子伸進池子裡呢？同樣的原因可能會讓你
³⁵ (**D**) 抓狂：因為貓有潔癖，而且貓很 ³⁶ (**I**) 懶惰。

* ***be likely to*** + ***V.*** 可能～　　stick〔stɪk〕 *v.* 伸出　　paw〔pɔ〕 *n.* 腳掌
drive〔draɪv〕 *v.* 驅使　　nut〔nʌt〕 *n.* 堅果；瘋子
drive *sb.* ***nuts*** 使某人抓狂　　cleanliness〔'klɛnlɪnɪs〕 *n.* 愛乾淨
fetish〔'fitɪʃ〕 *n.* 盲目愛好　　***cleanliness fetish*** 潔癖

你的貓不想好好玩一下。牠不想弄濕，因為牠發現，去享受像在水中嬉鬧這種
³⁸ (**J**) 膚淺的遊戲而弄濕後，用舌頭他自己弄乾並且弄乾淨，所需要的功夫不太
³⁷ (**F**) 值得。除非你讓牠 ³⁹ (**A**) 餓肚子，然後在池子裡放魚，不然你的貓還是會
保持 ⁴⁰ (**H**) 離水遠遠的。

* refuse〔rɪˋfjuz〕v. 拒絕　　***have a good time*** 玩得愉快
figure〔ˋfɪgjə〕v. 料想　　***be worth*** + ***N.*** 值得～
dry〔draɪ〕v. 使變乾　　tongue〔tʌŋ〕n. 舌頭
superficial〔͵supəˋfɪʃəl〕adj. 表面的；膚淺的
marine〔məˋrin〕adj. 海洋的；水的　　frolic〔ˋfrɑlɪk〕n. 玩耍；嬉戲
starve〔stɑrv〕v. 使挨餓
stock〔stɑk〕v. 存放；在（河裡）放著（魚）< ***with*** >
landlocked〔ˋlænd͵lɑkt〕adj. 與（海）水隔絕的；內陸的

四、閱讀測驗：

第 41 至 44 題為題組

　　你的心臟強壯嗎？經過某些計算，一顆健康的心臟在一個小時中，可以產生足夠的能量，將一噸重的汽車抬離地面。這相當強壯，但是如果你的心臟不健康會怎麼樣呢？一顆受損的心臟不會運作得很好，也許會讓你的身體極度缺乏氧氣。更糟的是，如果你的動脈受損，而心臟得不到足夠的血液，你可能很難讓自己的身體離開醫院的病床，更不用說要把車子抬離地面了。

* calculation〔͵kælkjəˋleʃən〕n. 計算　　produce〔prəˋdjus〕v. 產生
lift〔lɪft〕v. 舉起；抬高　　ton〔tʌn〕n. 噸
work〔wɝk〕v. 運作　　leave〔liv〕v. 使處於（某種狀態）
damaged〔ˋdæmɪdʒd〕adj. 受損害的　　starve〔stɑrv〕v. 飢餓；極缺乏
oxygen〔ˋɑksədʒən〕n. 氧氣　　***even worse*** 更糟的是
artery〔ˋɑrtərɪ〕n. 動脈（↔ vein n. 靜脈）
have trouble (***in***) + ***V-ing*** 做…有困難　　***much less*** 更不用說

　　你對心臟的健康狀況的確有一些控制權。你所做的事、所吃的東西，以及所過的生活，真的能改變你心臟的運作情狀。只要在你的生活方式上做一些改變，你其實有能力使自己的心臟更強壯。

* actually〔ˋæktʃʊəlɪ〕adv. 實際上　　lifestyle〔ˋlaɪf͵staɪl〕n. 生活方式

　　如果你曾經運動過，你一定有感受過運動的立即效果。由於你的身體需要更多的氧，所以心臟就會加速跳動，你的呼吸速率會增加，然後你就會開始流汗，來讓身體冷卻。

* ***work out*** 運動　　certainly〔ˋsɝtṇlɪ〕adv. 一定

immediate〔ɪ'midɪɪt〕*adj.* 立即的　　effect〔ɪ'fɛkt〕*n.* 效果；影響
speed up 加速　　demand〔dɪ'mænd〕*v.* 需要
breathing〔'briðɪŋ〕*n.* 呼吸　　rate〔ret〕*n.* 速率
sweat〔swɛt〕*v.* 流汗　　cool〔kul〕*v.* 使冷卻

長期來看，規律的運動不但會增加好的膽固醇，還會減少壞的膽固醇。這表示
累積在動脈裡的阻塞物可能會比較少。阻塞物較少代表血液可以自由地從心臟
流出跟流入。令人驚訝的是，像動動身體這樣簡單的事，會有如此大的好處！

　　* long-term〔'lɔŋ,tɝm〕*n.* 長期　　regular〔'rɛgjələ〕*adj.* 規律的
　　cholesterol〔kə'lɛstə,rol〕*n.* 膽固醇
　　plaque〔plæk〕*n.* (血液中硬化的) 阻塞物
　　build up 累積；增加　　flow〔flo〕*v.* 流動
　　to and from 往返於　　amazing〔ə'mezɪŋ〕*adj.* 令人驚訝的
　　dramatic〔drə'mætɪk〕*adj.* 戲劇性的；(程度) 大的
　　benefit〔'bɛnəfɪt〕*n.* 好處

41. (**B**) 本文的標題最有可能是 ＿＿＿＿＿＿＿。
　　(A) 注意你的心臟　　　　　　　(B) 為了有強壯、健康的心臟而運動
　　(C) 如何減少冠狀動脈疾病　　　(D) 高血壓以及高膽固醇
　　* coronary〔'kɔrə,nɛrɪ〕*adj.* 冠狀的　　***high blood pressure*** 高血壓

42. (**D**) 本文沒有提到下列何者會影響我們心臟的運作？
　　(A) 我們所做的事。　　　　　　(B) 我們如何過生活。
　　(C) 我們所吃的東西。　　　　　(D) 我們住在哪裡。
　　* work〔wɝk〕*v.* 運作

43. (**A**) 下列何者不是運動會有的立即效果？
　　(A) 增加好的膽固醇。　　　　　(B) 心跳加速。
　　(C) 流汗以使身體冷卻。　　　　(D) 呼吸速率增加。
　　* heartbeat〔'hɑrt,bit〕*n.* 心跳　　***cool off*** 使冷卻

44. (**D**) 作者主要是建議讀者要 ＿＿＿＿＿＿＿。
　　(A) 少吃膽固醇　　　　　　　　(B) 保護自己的健康
　　(C) 清除硬化阻塞物　　　　　　(D) 定期運動
　　* ***clear out*** 清除

第 45 至 48 題為題組

　　在油價高而財源少的這種經濟困難的情況下，許多家庭選擇少買一點的購物中心之旅。在那裡，人們可以離開住所，看一些風景，所花的錢與到達那邊的油錢幾乎差不多。精明的市場人員正抓住這個機會，以免費禮物來吸引無聊的美國人，並在這段經濟艱困的時期裡，維持住自家品牌的形象。

* tight〔taɪt〕*adj.* 緊的　　economy〔ɪˈkɑnəmɪ〕*n.* 經濟
tight economy 經濟艱難　　gas〔gæs〕*n.* 汽油
funds〔fʌndz〕*n. pl.* 資金；現款　　low〔lo〕*adj.*（錢）不夠的；缺乏的
opt〔ɑpt〕*v.* 選擇 *< for >*　　purchase〔ˈpɝtʃəs〕*v. n.* 購買
excursion〔ɪkˈskɝʒən〕*n.* 短程旅行　　***take in*** 參觀；遊覽
sight〔saɪt〕*n.* 風景名勝；景點　　expend〔ɪkˈspɛnd〕*v.* 花費（= *spend*）
little more than 與…幾乎一樣；與…差不多的　　fuel〔ˈfjuəl〕*n.* 燃料
savvy〔ˈsævɪ〕*adj.* 精通的　　marketer〔ˈmɑrkɪtɚ〕*n.* 市場行銷人員
opportunity〔ˌɑpɚˈtjunətɪ〕*n.* 機會
tantalize〔ˈtæntḷˌaɪz〕*v.* 逗弄；吊胃口　　brand〔brænd〕*n.* 品牌
image〔ˈɪmɪdʒ〕*n.* 形象　　tough〔tʌf〕*adj.* 艱難的
tough economic times 經濟困難時期

　　舉例來說，可口可樂推廣它對二〇〇八年北京奧運的贊助，並提供給西門購物中心的遊客，好幾千個由中國藝術家特別設計的免費可樂紀念瓶。免費禮物上附著卡片，鼓勵那些收到它們的人，參觀可口可樂的網站，並下載和每個瓶子有關的免費音樂。

* promote〔prəˈmot〕*v.* 推廣　　sponsorship〔ˈspɑnsɚˌʃɪp〕*n.* 贊助
Olympics〔oˈlɪmpɪks〕*n.* 奧運會　　offer〔ˈɔfɚ〕*v.* 提供
thousands of 數以千計的
commemorative〔kəˈmɛməˌretɪv〕*adj.* 紀念的
specially〔ˈspɛʃəlɪ〕*adv.* 特別地　　design〔dɪˈzaɪn〕*v.* 設計
visitor〔ˈvɪzɪtɚ〕*n.* 訪客　　***come with*** 和…一起
prompt〔prɑmpt〕*v.* 促使；鼓勵　　website〔ˈwɛbˌsaɪt〕*n.* 網站
download〔ˈdaʊnˌlod〕*v.* 下載　　***be associated with*** 和…有關

這項促銷方法是有點針對青少年的活動，以購物中心的贈品為其特色。其他像 Sprint 以及 ABC Family 公司，則贈送參訪者由網路程式設計，而且可以在網站上訂做的 T 恤。

* promotion〔prə'moʃən〕n. 促銷；推廣
teen-focused〔'tin'fokəst〕adj. 以青少年為主的
event〔ɪ'vɛnt〕n. 事件；大型活動　　feature〔'fitʃɚ〕v. 以…為特色
giveaway〔'gɪvə,we〕n. 贈品　　*shopping mall* 購物中心
give away 贈送　　network〔'nɛt,wɝk〕n. 網路
programming〔'progræmɪŋ〕n.（電腦）程式設計
programming-based adj. 用程式製作的
customize〔'kʌstəm,aɪz〕v. 訂做　　on-site〔'ɑn,saɪt〕adv. 在網站上

　　由於消費者到購物中心都很期待有樂趣，所以即使主辦一場商場大型活動需要額外的人力、廣告，以及購物的安全措施，這種促銷活動仍然受到高度的推薦。畢竟分發免費贈品與試用品，就算消費者的皮夾是緊閉的，卻可以讓品牌留在他們的心中。

* consumer〔kən'sumɚ〕n. 消費者　　expect〔ɪk'spɛkt〕v. 期待
entertainment〔,ɛntɚ'tenmənt〕n. 娛樂；樂趣
even if 即使　　host〔host〕v. 主辦　　require〔rɪ'kwaɪr〕v. 需要
extra〔'ɛkstrə〕adj. 額外的　　staffing〔'stæfɪŋ〕n. 人力配備
advertising〔'ædvɚ,taɪzɪŋ〕n. 廣告　　purchase〔'pɝtʃəs〕v. 購買
security〔sɪ'kjurəti〕n. 安全措施　　highly〔'haɪli〕adv. 高度地
recommend〔,rɛkə'mɛnd〕v. 推薦　　*after all* 畢竟　　*hand out* 分發
freebie〔'fribi〕n. 免費贈品　　sample〔'sæmpl〕n. 試用品
wallet〔'wɑlɪt〕n. 皮夾

45.（**C**）你最有可能在哪一本雜誌中看到這篇文章？
　　(A) 世界娛樂　　　　　　　　(B) 科技最新資訊
　　(C) 商業管理　　　　　　　　(D) 旅遊指南
　　* technology〔tɛk'nɑlədʒɪ〕n. 科技　　update〔'ʌp,det〕n. 最新資訊
　　　management〔'mænɪdʒmənt〕n. 管理
　　　tourist〔'turɪst〕adj. 旅遊的；觀光的　　guidebook〔'gaɪd,buk〕n. 指南

46.（**D**）下列何者最能解釋第一段的 "**tantalize**" 這個字？
　　(A) 檢查　　(B) 使分心　　(C) 催促　　(D) 誘惑
　　* examine〔ɪg'zæmɪn〕v. 檢查　　distract〔dɪ'strækt〕v. 使分心
　　　urge〔ɝdʒ〕v. 催促　　tempt〔tɛmpt〕v. 誘惑

47. (**D**) 根據本文，舉辦大型商場活動不需要 ＿＿＿＿＿＿。
    (A) 額外的人力配置　　　　　　(B) 刊登廣告
    (C) 購物安全措施　　　　　　　(D) 收取入場費

    * *put out* 發表；發佈　　charge〔tʃɑrdʒ〕v. 收（費）
    admission〔əd'mɪʃən〕n. 入場費

48. (**A**) 本文中沒有提到下列何者？
    (A) 通常要花好幾個月來計畫促銷活動。
    (B) Sprint 還有 ABC Family 贈送定做的 T 恤來促銷。
    (C) 許多公司都想要在經濟困難時期，維持品牌形象。
    (D) 可口可樂公司藉由提供免費、特別設計的可樂瓶，推廣 2008 年
        北京奧運。

    * corporation〔ˌkɔrpə'reʃən〕n. 公司　　maintain〔men'ten〕v. 維持

第 49 至 52 題為題組

　　傳染病可不是開玩笑的事。如果你正在咳嗽並到處擤鼻涕，卻還是很想去
上班的話，試著忍住別去並且休息。不是所有疾病都會傳染，但安全總比遺憾
來得好。避免與人一起共用飲料或私人物品。要記得，預防是最好的治療。

    * infectious〔ɪn'fɛkʃəs〕adj. 有傳染性的　　laughing〔'læfɪŋ〕adj. 可笑的
    matter〔'mætɚ〕n. 事情　　cough〔kɔf〕v. 咳嗽
    blow〔blo〕v. 擤（鼻涕）　　*blow one's nose* 擤鼻涕
    all over the place 到處　　tempt〔tɛmpt〕v. 誘惑
    feel tempted to V. 很想～　　resist〔rɪ'zɪst〕v. 抵抗；忍耐
    rest〔rɛst〕n. 休息　　contagious〔kən'tedʒəs〕adj. 會傳染的
    it's better to be safe than sorry 安全總比後悔好
    share〔ʃɛr〕v. 分享；共用　　personal〔'pɝsn̩l〕adj. 私人的
    item〔'aɪtəm〕n. 物品　　prevention〔prɪ'vɛnʃən〕n. 預防
    cure〔kjur〕n. 治療

　　有四種主要的病菌會引起傳染病。細菌是單細胞的病菌，它們有快速繁殖
的能力，還會釋放能讓你生病的化學物質。細菌性傳染病的例子有霍亂、白喉、
猩紅熱，與肺結核。

    * germ〔dʒɝm〕n. 病菌　　bacteria〔bæk'tɪrɪə〕n. pl. 細菌

cell〔sɛl〕*n.* 細胞　　single-cell〔'sɪŋl̩'sɛl〕*adj.* 單細胞的

multiply〔'mʌltə,plaɪ〕*v.* 繁殖　　rapidly〔'ræpɪdlɪ〕*adv.* 快速地

release〔rɪ'lis〕*v.* 釋放　　chemical〔'kɛmɪkl̩〕*n.* 化學物質

bacterial〔bæk'tɪrɪəl〕*adj.* 細菌的

transmittable〔træns'mɪtəbl̩〕*adj.* 會傳染的

cholera〔'kɑlərə〕*n.* 霍亂　　diphtheria〔dɪf'θɪrɪə〕*n.* 白喉

scarlet fever〔'skɑrlɪt'fivɚ〕*n.* 猩紅熱【scarlet *adj.* 深紅色的】

tuberculosis〔tju,bɝkjə'losɪs〕*n.* 肺結核

病毒是包含基因訊息的囊苞，它們會利用人本身的細胞來繁殖。病毒傳染性疾病包括愛滋病、天花、肺炎，以及非典型肺炎。黴菌是會讓你生病，狀似蔬菜的蕈或黴，而原蟲是單細胞的掠食者，會尋找可讓它們吞噬與寄宿的宿主，像瘧疾。

* virus〔'vaɪrəs〕*n.* 病毒　　capsule〔'kæpsl̩〕*n.* 膠囊囊苞

contain〔kən'ten〕*v.* 包含；帶有　　genetic〔dʒə'nɛtɪk〕*adj.* 基因的

viral〔'vaɪrəl〕*adj.* 病毒的

AIDS 愛滋病；後天免疫缺乏症候群（= *Acquired Immune Deficiency Syndrome*）　　smallpox〔'smɔl,pɑks〕*n.* 天花

pneumonia〔nju'monjə〕*n.* 肺炎

SARS 急性呼吸道綜合症；非典型肺炎（= *Severe Acute Respiratory Syndrome*）　　fungi〔'fʌndʒaɪ〕*n. pl.* 黴菌；菌類【單數為 fungus】

mushroom〔'mʌʃrum〕*n.* 蕈；蘑菇　　mildew〔'mɪl,dju〕*n.* 黴

protozoa〔,protə'zoə〕*n.* 原生動物；原蟲【由單細胞組成，一般透過顯微鏡才看得到】　　predator〔'prɛdətɚ〕*n.* 掠食者；補食者

look for 尋找　　host〔host〕*n.*（寄生動植物的）宿主

malaria〔mə'lɛrɪə〕*n.* 瘧疾

　　處理傳染性的疾病時，第一步就是要辨識出感染。當你身體裡的細胞受到損害，而有疾病症狀出現時，感染就變成是一種疾病了。白血球和抗體會試圖保護你的身體免於感染，而感染會導致發燒、咳嗽、打噴嚏，或其他疾病。一旦確定感染疾病，就需要藥物治療了。

* *deal with* 應付；處理　　identify〔aɪ'dɛntə,faɪ〕*v.* 確認

infection〔ɪn'fɛkʃən〕*n.* 感染　　microbe〔'maɪkrob〕*n.* 微生物

damaged〔'dæmɪdʒd〕*adj.* 受損的　　symptom〔'sɪmptəm〕*n.* 症狀

illness〔'ɪlnɪs〕*n.* 疾病　　*white blood cell* 白血球

antibody〔'æntɪˌbadɪ〕n. 抗體　　attempt〔ə'tɛmpt〕v. 試圖
protect…from~ 保護…免受~　　***result in*** 導致；造成
fever〔'fivɚ〕n. 發燒　　sneeze〔sniz〕v. 打噴嚏
ailment〔'elmənt〕n. 疾病　　***take hold*** 生根；固定下來；確立
medication〔ˌmɛdɪ'keʃən〕n. 藥物治療；藥物

49.（**C**）本文的作者最有可能是一位 _____。
　　(A) 高階的工程師　　　　　　(B) 人力資源經理
　　(C) 家庭醫師　　　　　　　　(D) 教育心理學家
　　* high-ranking〔'haɪ'ræŋkɪŋ〕adj. 高位階的
　　　engineer〔ˌɛndʒə'nɪr〕n. 工程師　　***human resources*** 人力資源
　　　physician〔fə'zɪʃən〕n.（內科）醫師
　　　psychologist〔saɪ'kɑlədʒɪst〕n. 心理學家

50.（**A**）會引起傳染性疾病的四種主要病菌不包括 _____。
　　(A) 抗生素　　(B) 黴菌　　(C) 細菌　　(D) 病毒
　　* antibiotics〔ˌæntɪbaɪ'ɑtɪks〕n. 抗生素

51.（**D**）根據本文，非典型肺炎是一種由 _____ 所引起的傳染性疾病。
　　(A) 掠食者　　(B) 黴菌　　(C) 細菌　　(D) 病毒

52.（**B**）本文沒有提到下列何者？
　　(A) 當疾病的症狀出現時，不要強迫自己去工作。
　　(B) 治療某一個人的藥物，會對治療其他人無效。
　　(C) 不是所有疾病都會傳染或很危險。
　　(D) 抗體會保護我們的身體不受感染，而感染會引發疾病。
　　* treat〔trit〕v. 治療　　ineffective〔ˌɪnə'fɛktɪv〕adj. 無效的

第 53 至 56 題為題組

　　有很多網站可以讓大學生買到現成的學期報告。有些網站甚至以幫小學生做功課來吸引他們。這種書面作業氾濫的情形，使得要找出抄襲行為幾乎是不可能的。但最近有研究顯示，作品有自己的「指紋」，可以告訴老師作者是誰。

　　* ***a large number of*** 很多的　　website〔'wɛbˌsaɪt〕n. 網站
　　ready-made〔'rɛdɪ'med〕adj. 現成的　　term〔tɝm〕n. 學期
　　term paper 學期報告　　lure〔lʊr〕v. 引誘（= tempt = attract）

elementary〔͵ɛləˈmɛntərɪ〕*adj.* 初等的；小學的
flood〔flʌd〕*n.* 氾濫的情形
paperwork〔ˈpepɚ͵wɝk〕*n.* 文書工作：（學生的）書面作業
virtually〔ˈvɝtʃʊəlɪ〕*adv.* 幾乎（= *nearly*）
ferret〔ˈfɛrɪt〕*v.* 搜出；找出 < *out* >（= *find out*）
plagiarism〔ˈpledʒə͵rɪzəm〕*n.* 抄襲；剽竊　reveal〔rɪˈvil〕*v.* 顯示
fingerprint〔ˈfɪŋgɚ͵prɪnt〕*n.* 指紋　writer〔ˈraɪtɚ〕*n.* 作者

一九九六年二月，有一本書名叫作《原色》的小說，由一位匿名作家在美國出版。書中的主角是美國南部的一位州長，他在競選期間和一位圖書館員有曖昧關係，和比爾‧柯林頓非常相似，而且書中充滿了只有與柯林頓親近認識的人，才會有的資訊。

* title〔ˈtaɪtl̩〕*v.* 以⋯爲標題　primary〔ˈpraɪ͵mɛrɪ〕*adj.* 主要的
primary colors 原色（指紅、黃、藍等）
anonymous〔əˈnɑnəməs〕*adj.* 匿名的　author〔ˈɔθɚ〕*n.* 作家
protagonist〔proˈtægənɪst〕*n.* 主角　governor〔ˈgʌvənɚ〕*n.* 州長
affair〔əˈfɛr〕*n.* 曖昧關係；外遇　***have an affair*** 有外遇
librarian〔laɪˈbrɛrɪən〕*n.* 圖書館員　campaign〔kæmˈpen〕*n.* 競選活動
closely〔ˈkloslɪ〕*adv.* 接近地　resemble〔rɪˈzɛmbl̩〕*v.* 相似
Bill Clinton 比爾‧柯林頓【美國第四十二任總統】
acquaintance〔əˈkwentəns〕*n.* 認識的人

頭號嫌疑犯是喬‧克萊恩，他那時是新聞週刊的專欄作家。他一開始否認這些指控，但隨後又承認了。唐納德‧福斯特教授是一位鑑識語言學家，也是美國聯邦調查局的文學作品分析師，他指出將句子做統計分析之後，這本小說的寫作風格，與克萊恩的專欄很相似。

* suspect〔ˈsʌspɛkt〕*n.* 嫌疑犯　columnist〔ˈkɑləmnɪst〕*n.* 專欄作家
Newsweek 新聞週刊【一本在紐約出版的新聞類週刊】
deny〔dɪˈnaɪ〕*v.* 否認　accusation〔͵ækjəˈzeʃən〕*n.* 指控
subsequently〔ˈsʌbsɪk͵wɛntlɪ〕*adv.* 隨後（= *afterward*）
admit〔ədˈmɪt〕*v.* 承認　***Prof.*** 教授（= *professor*）
forensic〔fəˈrɛnsɪk〕*adj.* 鑑識的　linguist〔ˈlɪŋgwɪst〕*n.* 語言學家
forensic linguist 鑑識語言學家【屬於應用語言學的領域，牽涉到有關語言、法律、犯罪這三者間的關係】

text〔tɛkst〕*n.* 內文；本文　　analyst〔'ænḷɪst〕*n.* 分析師

text analyst 文本分析師；作品分析師

the FBI 美國聯邦調查局（= *the Federal Bureau of Investigation*）

column〔'kɑləm〕*n.* 特約專欄　　statistical〔stə'tɪstɪkḷ〕*adj.* 統計的

analysis〔ə'næləsɪs〕*n.* 分析

　　用來查出作者身份的統計作品分析，可以有高達百分之九十的成功率，但是這項分析的成功率因語言而異。即使如此，永遠可以藉由分析更多作品，將資料庫一直擴充下去，而這個方法很快就能被用在實務層面上，以查出學生的作品是否有抄襲。

　　* track〔træk〕*v.* 追蹤　　***track down*** 查出　　***up to*** 高達

vary〔'vɛrɪ〕*v.* 不同

vary from language to language 每個語言都不同

even so 即使如此　　database〔'detəˌbes〕*n.* 資料庫

expand〔ɪk'spænd〕*v.* 擴充　　analyze〔'ænḷˌaɪz〕*v.* 分析

method〔'mɛθəd〕*n.* 方法　　practical〔'præktɪkḷ〕*adj.* 實際的；實用的

level〔'lɛvḷ〕*n.* 角度；層面　　detect〔dɪ'tɛkt〕*v.* 查出

53.（**B**）本文的主旨為何？

　　(A) 統計模式與分類的科學應用是無效的。

　　(B) 語言分析提供作者身份的線索。

　　(C) 作品分析是一種在一系列故事中，追查出相關故事的方法。

　　(D) 作品分析法的應用對政治學來說很重要。

　　* application〔ˌæplə'keʃən〕*n.* 應用　　modeling〔'mɑdḷɪŋ〕*n.* 模型製作

classification〔ˌklæsəfə'keʃən〕*n.* 分類

ineffective〔ˌɪnə'fɛktɪv〕*adj.* 無效的

linguistic〔lɪŋ'gwɪstɪk〕*adj.* 語言的　　clue〔klu〕*n.* 線索

authorship〔'ɔθɚˌʃɪp〕*n.* 作者身份；出處

retrieve〔rɪ'triv〕*v.* 尋回　　relevant〔'rɛləvənt〕*adj.* 相關的

collection〔kə'lɛkʃən〕*n.* 蒐集（品）

politics〔'pɑləˌtɪks〕*n.* 政治學

54.（**C**）誰是《原色》這本小說的作者？

　　(A) 比爾·柯林頓。　　　　　　(B) 唐納德·福斯特。

　　(C) 喬·克萊恩。　　　　　　　(D) 不知名的作者。

55. (**D**) 下列何者最能解釋第一段的 "**plagiarism**" 這個字？

  (A) 參加一項遊戲。   (B) 罹患一種疾病。

  (C) 加入幫派。   (D) 抄襲別人的作品。

  * *take part in* 參加 *suffer from* 罹患（疾病）

  gang〔gæŋ〕*n.* 幫派 copy〔ˋkɑpɪ〕*v.* 抄寫；模仿

  work〔wɝk〕*n.* 作品

56. (**D**) 根據本文，下列何者為非？

  (A) 很多現成的學期報告，在網路上都找得到。

  (B) 作品分析法很快就可以被應用在學術領域。

  (C) 美國聯邦調查局的作品分析師，利用統計來分析句子以辨識作者。

  (D) 在查出作者這方面，統計的作品分析法總是很成功。

  * available〔əˋveləbḷ〕*adj.* 可獲得的

  online〔ˏɑnˋlaɪn〕*adv.* 在網路上

  statistically〔stəˋtɪstɪklɪ〕*adv.* 統計上

第貳部分：非選擇題

一、中譯英：

1. 聽說湯姆在上個禮拜的期中考作弊被抓到了，他現在懊悔不已。

 It is said that Tom was caught cheating in the mid-term exam

 last week, and now he
$$\begin{cases} \text{is quite remorseful.} \\ \text{regrets it very much.} \\ \text{feels a lot of regret} \end{cases}$$

2. 不管他有多難過，他現在唯一能做的事就是勇敢面對現實。

 No matter how
$$\begin{cases} \text{upset} \\ \text{troubled} \\ \text{distressed} \end{cases}$$
he feels,
$$\begin{cases} \text{all (that)} \\ \text{the only thing (that)} \\ \text{what} \end{cases}$$

 he can do now is (to)
$$\begin{cases} \text{face the music.} \\ \text{face the consequences.} \end{cases}$$

二、英文作文：

作文範例

Dear Sir,   Feb. 28, 2013

    Two nights ago, I was at your restaurant and I received very poor service. It seemed like the workers did not care about their jobs or their customers. The waitress was very cold. Even though we tried to cheer her up with our jokes, she never smiled. Then the food came and it wasn't what we ordered, so we sent it back to the kitchen. This seemed to make both the waitress and the assistant manager very unhappy. No one came to the table to apologize and it was another 20 minutes before the food came. I called the waitress several times but she ignored me. Some of my friends were so mad they were ready to walk out!

    Finally, when it came time to pay the bill, the waitress had disappeared. I finally approached the cashier and asked to pay with my credit card, when I was told it was "cash only." My friends had left and I didn't have enough cash on me, so I had to call my father to bring money from home. To say the least, I was very embarrassed and disappointed. Is this the kind of business you want to run?

                                           Sincerely,
                                           Marie Stokes

describe〔dɪ'skraɪb〕v. 描述   **it seems like** 似乎～
customer〔'kʌstəmə〕n. 顧客   waitress〔'wetrɪs〕n. 女服務生
cold〔kold〕adj. 冷淡的   **cheer sb. up** 使～振作；使～興奮
assisant〔ə'sɪstənt〕adj. 副的；助理的   **assistant manager** 副理
apologize〔ə'polə,dʒaɪz〕v. 道歉   ignore〔ɪg'nor〕v. 忽視
mark〔mork〕n. 分數   **pay the bill** 付帳
approach〔ə'protʃ〕v. 靠近；走近
cashier〔kæ'ʃɪr〕n. 收銀員   **cash only** 只收現金
to say the least 至少可以這麼說   run〔rʌn〕v. 經營

大學入學學科能力測驗英文模擬試題 ④

第壹部分：單選題（佔72分）

一、詞彙（佔15分）

說明： 第1題至第15題，每題4個選項，其中只有一個是最適當的答案，畫記在答案卡之「選擇題答案區」。各題答對得1分；未作答、答錯、或畫記多於一個選項者，該題以零分計算。

1. Without a doubt Santa Catalina is the _____ of Panama's beaches, enjoying some of the best waves of Central and South America.
   (A) result　　　　(B) progress　　　(C) jewel　　　　(D) guidance

2. Millions of people suffer the memory loss of dementia, yet this _____ ailment still remains shrouded in fear and mystery.
   (A) overtaking　(B) devastating　(C) finishing　　(D) representing

3. If you loathe cold weather, you can _____ going in and out, starting your exercise inside with a nice warm up, then head out, and come back until you are warm again.
   (A) alternate　　(B) apply　　　　(C) involve　　　(D) withhold

4. After the heavy rains, floodwaters have covered more than 20 villages, and at least three thousand people have been _____ to safer areas.
   (A) evicted　　　(B) evolved　　　(C) evacuated　　(D) evoked

5. The luxury shopping mall is believed by many social scientists to represent India's _____ towards a brand-new identity.
   (A) response　　(B) resemblance　(C) impression　(D) aspiration

6. Global surveys show that India has the fastest _____ number of billionaires and millionaires in the world.
   (A) stirring　　　(B) reinforcing　(C) spreading　　(D) growing

7. If your teacher speaks too fast, leave large empty _____ in your notes for filling in information you missed. Use symbols that will help you remember what is missing.
   (A) tendency   (B) spaces   (C) documents   (D) ancestors

8. Human beings are born with an ability to use their arms and legs to stay _____ on the surface of water, but the instinct disappears shortly after birth.
   (A) afloat   (B) awake   (C) alleviative   (D) adequate

9. When the theme park was _____ opened to the public on Saturday, an all-day celebration took place.
   (A) submissively   (B) officially   (C) exclusively   (D) narrowly

10. New York City's concert houses, museums, galleries, and theaters _____ an ensemble of cultural richness rivaled by few cities.
    (A) conduct   (B) reduce   (C) inspect   (D) constitute

11. Today aspirin is listed as a principal ingredient in more than 50 over-the-counter drugs and, in the United States alone, over 80 billion tablets are _____ annually.
    (A) publicized   (B) consumed   (C) conned   (D) conspired

12. The crocodile is a large reptile commonly regarded as a vicious killer, and its smile and tears have become bywords for _____.
    (A) definition   (B) deterioration   (C) deception   (D) description

13. Passengers were left _____ when the buses carrying them got stuck on the highway.
    (A) stranded   (B) outwitted   (C) overlapped   (D) conformed

14. Mountain biking is a recreational sport that is enjoying _____ popularity. More and more people are using mountain bikes for touring and for daily travel.
    (A) irritating   (B) increasing   (C) campaigning   (D) entitling

15. All the information we have collected in relation to that case
    _____ very little.
    (A) adds up to   (B) makes up for
    (C) comes up with   (D) puts up with

二、綜合測驗（佔 15 分）

說明： 第 16 題至第 30 題，每題一個空格，請依文意選出最適當的一個答案，
      畫記在答案卡之「選擇題答案區」。各題答對得 1 分；未作答、答錯、
      或畫記多於一個選項者，該題以零分計算。

第 16 至 20 題為題組

In a world increasingly plagued by droughts and water shortages,
conserving water has become not only a virtue but the standard. In
Taiwan, if you want people to use ___16___ water, you need to make it
more expensive, especially for those who use the most. It means the
more water you use, the more you will have to pay.

But the tricky part is how much to ___17___ the price and for whom.
Government officials have spent six months considering various pricing
possibilities and now they are making the citizens more "watertight" and
economical with water. ___18___ expected, those who use relatively
little water will see their bills increase only about 25 NT dollars per
month, while citizens with above average water use will see their bills
increase ___19___ as much as 110 NT dollars.

However, water officials do not want too drastic a reduction ___20___
that would also mean a drastic reduction in their revenue. In addition to
encouraging conservation, the rate increases also are expected to result in
a revenue increase for the nation.

16. (A) more   (B) much   (C) less   (D) fewer
17. (A) rise   (B) raise   (C) arise   (D) arouse
18. (A) What   (B) It   (C) As   (D) That
19. (A) by   (B) in   (C) at   (D) with
20. (A) so   (B) such   (C) despite   (D) because

第 21 至 25 題為題組

As the news of toxic Chinese milk spreads, soymilk is getting progressively popular. In fact, soymilk has long been a popular alternative for people who are unable to drink cow's milk. And now more and more people are ___21___ choosing soy milk because of the added health benefits.

The benefits of soy are still being disputed, ___22___ it is generally accepted that soymilk contains a high number of very healthy compounds and ___23___ it is high in protein. Because it is made from beans, soymilk also contains considerably more fiber than cow's milk. In addition, many soymilk manufacturers are adding calcium to their products.

___24___ the extra protein and fiber, the biggest benefit of soymilk is the isoflavones, which are actually chemicals very similar to the hormone estrogen. Isoflavones are connected with a whole host of health issues, ___25___ the most prevalent being the prevention of many cancers, heart disease, osteoporosis and more.

So you might seriously consider adding soymilk to, or substitute it for, your coffee or tea.

21. (A) tentatively   (B) deliberately   (C) reluctantly   (D) consecutively
22. (A) even   (B) but   (C) lest   (D) if
23. (A) if   (B) as   (C) when   (D) that
24. (A) Because   (B) Despite   (C) Besides   (D) Unless
25. (A) with   (B) for   (C) as   (D) and

第 26 至 30 題為題組

Anxiety is a basic human emotion consisting of fear and uncertainty that appears when an individual encounters some difficulties. In some instances, such as avoiding dangerous situations, anxiety can be helpful.

___26___, when taken to extremes, it may produce unfavorable results.

One of the most threatening events that cause anxiety in students today is testing. When students develop an extreme fear of performing poorly on an examination, they experience test anxiety. It ___27___ a variety of negative factors including psychological distress, academic failure, and insecurity. Many students have the ability to do well on exams but may not do so ___28___ high levels of test anxiety. The overemphasis of our society on testing has already limited their educational and vocational opportunities.

Students are encouraged to develop good, ___29___ sleep habits, especially during the week of the test, and maintain a healthy diet and exercise regularly. They should also ___30___ cramming and develop good study habits and good test taking skills. They should wear comfortable clothes during the exam and keep a comfortable and relaxed body posture during the test.

26. (A) Therefore　　(B) Moreover　　(C) However　　(D) Instead
27. (A) results from　(B) stands up for　(C) reacts to　　(D) calls for
28. (A) apart from　　(B) except for　　(C) because of　　(D) regardless of
29. (A) consistent　　(B) infatuated　　(C) approximate　(D) unknowing
30. (A) forge　　　　(B) avoid　　　　(C) confiscate　　(D) wave

三、文意選填（佔 10 分）

說明：第 31 題至第 40 題，每題一個空格，請依文意在文章後所提供的 (A) 到 (J) 選項中分別選出最適當者，並將其英文字母代號畫記在答案卡之「選擇題答案區」。各題答對得 1 分；未作答、答錯、或畫記多於一個選項者，該題以零分計算。

第 31 至 40 題為題組

Contact with electrical current is potentially fatal. The ___31___ of electric shock on the body depends not only on the strength of the current, but also on such factors as wetness of the skin, area of contact, duration of contact, constitution of the victim, and ___32___ the victim is well-grounded. The signs and symptoms of electric shock include a mild tingling, spasm of the muscles, headache, irregular breathing or lack of breathing, loss of consciousness, and ___33___ death. Electricity ___34___ through the body can cause injury to the skin and internal organs. If electricity passes through the heart, the heart muscle may be damaged and the heart's rhythm ___35___, leading to cardiac arrest.

The person ___36___ first-aid to a victim of electric shock should not touch the individual's body until the ___37___ of the shock is turned off. Because of the potential for internal injuries, victims of electrical injury should not be moved unless they are in ___38___ danger. The first-aid provider should monitor the victim for symptoms of shock. If the victim has stopped breathing and has no pulse, CPR should be performed after the airway, breathing, and circulation have been ___39___. When the victim's vital signs are stable, the ___40___ of the burn should be treated using the same methods used for other burns.

(A) checked   (B) whether or not   (C) passing   (D) interrupted
(E) effect   (F) source   (G) sometimes   (H) site
(I) providing   (J) immediate

四、閱讀測驗（佔 32 分）

說明： 第 41 題至第 56 題，每題 4 個選項，請分別根據各篇文章之文意選出最適當的一個答案，畫記在答案卡之「選擇題答案區」。各題答對得 2 分；未作答、答錯、或畫記多於一個選項者，該題以零分計算。

第 41 至 44 題為題組

As an integral part of almost all water-based activities, swimming involves movement through the water by using one's arms, legs, and body in motions called strokes. The most common strokes are the crawl, backstroke, breaststroke, butterfly, and sidestroke. Some people learn to swim by imitating others while others take lessons at swim clubs, community centers, schools, or recreational facilities. Beginners first put their heads in the water and blow bubbles by exhaling. Gradually, they progress to floating, treading water, and ultimately learning the techniques of the major strokes.

Students can use various pieces of equipment during the lessons. Water wings are inflatables worn around the upper arms to keep the students floating. Kickboards are buoyant boards that students can rest their arms on; this keeps their upper bodies afloat and allows them to concentrate on kicking correctly. Pull-buoys are foam floats that swimmers hold between their thighs to keep the lower body high and flat on the surface of the water. By using them, students can learn the arm and upper body movements of various strokes. Another one is paddles, which are small, firm boards fitted over the hands to force students to pull their arms through the water correctly. Fins worn on the feet also allow swimmers to go faster and to develop proper body position and power.

As swimming builds endurance, muscle strength and cardiovascular fitness, if you want to work out and stay cool at the same time, swimming is where it is at.

41. What is the best title for this article?
   (A) The Great Popularity of Swimming
   (B) Learning to Swim
   (C) The True Origin of Swimming
   (D) The Great Versatility of Swimming

42. According to the passage, beginners start learning how to swim by _____.
   (A) floating and treading water   (B) watching the major strokes
   (C) taking lessons at swim clubs
   (D) putting their heads in the water and blowing bubbles

43. Which of the following equipment is NOT mentioned in this passage?
   (A) Swimming goggles.　　　　(B) Water wings.
   (C) Kickboards.　　　　　　　(D) Pull-buoys.

44. Which of the following equipment helps learners better learn the arm and upper body movements?
   (A) Swimming goggles.　　　　(B) Water wings.
   (C) Kickboards.　　　　　　　(D) Pull-buoys.

第 45 至 48 題爲題組

　　As one of seven designated state sponsors of terrorism, North Korea has long been knowingly selling weapons to separatist groups, along with counterfeiting, providing sanctuary for five hijackers of a Japanese airliner, and other criminal activities like the midair bombing of Korean Airlines Flight 858 in 1987. That attack is thought to have been a tactic to scare tourists away from the 1988 Summer Olympics in Seoul. Besides, North Korea was also behind the 1996 assassination of a South Korean diplomat in Vladivostok, Russia.

　　But recently, North Korea was removed from the terrorism blacklist after it agreed to comply with full inspections of its nuclear facilities. The U.S. State Department said the inspection agreement and the decision to take North Korea off the list of countries sponsoring terrorism were in the interests of national security and consistent with the "action-for-action" principle of the negotiations. North Korea allowed atomic experts to conduct forensic tests at all of its nuclear facilities. It also permitted experts to verify whether it had told the truth about transfers of nuclear technology and an alleged uranium enrichment program.

　　North Korea's removal from the list followed days of intense internal debate in Washington and consultations with U.S. negotiating partners China, South Korea, Russia and Japan.

Even so, verifying North Korea's nuclear proliferation is a serious challenge, because it is one of the most secret and opaque regimes, if not the most, in the entire world. This is going to be a bumpy road ahead.

45. What is the main idea of this article?
   (A) North Korea blocked access to its undeclared sites of nuclear weapons.
   (B) North Korea agreed to resume disabling its main plutonium facility.
   (C) North Korea was removed from the terrorism blacklist.
   (D) The world heightened tensions with North Korea.

46. What is the author's attitude towards verifying North Korea's nuclear proliferation?
   (A) optimistic   (B) indifferent
   (C) enthusiastic   (D) skeptical

47. North Korea's criminal activities do NOT include _____.
   (A) counterfeiting and providing sanctuary for hijackers
   (B) bombing Korean Airlines Flight 858
   (C) selling weapons to separatist groups
   (D) assassinating a Russian diplomat

48. According to the passage, which of the following is NOT true?
   (A) North Korea used to be one of five designated state sponsors of terrorism.
   (B) Only recently was North Korea removed from the terrorism blacklist.
   (C) North Korea finally allowed atomic experts to conduct forensic tests at its nuclear facilities.
   (D) The decision to remove North Korea from the watch list was made after international negotiations.

<u>第 49 至 52 題為題組</u>

Computer technology is now altering the traditional ways people handle stress. Online support groups can range from serving as one therapeutic component of a comprehensive mental health treatment plan to serving as the sole support system. They attract a broad variety of members who may previously have avoided peers and their traditional support system. Satisfied members report feeling validation and support while dissatisfied members, though small in number, express frustration caused by technological problems and by the absence of visual, auditory and interpersonal cues.

Online support groups can be accessed through use of a computer and modem in conjunction with an Internet service provider (ISP). Once connected through an ISP, users can reach online support groups through Internet portals or through specialized websites.

Online support groups provide an alternative vehicle of support for people in distress by linking people with similar issues. They have the potential to improve the access and delivery of support to a wide range of people, including some who would not seek face-to-face support at all. Finally, they reduce the sense of isolation caused by geographic or physical/medical constraints and increase feelings of validation. However, they are not appropriate for everyone.

49. The title of this article is most likely to be _____.
   (A) The Limitations of Online Support Groups
   (B) Different Online Support Groups for Caregivers
   (C) The Strengths of Online Support Groups
   (D) How to Find Online Support Groups

50. From this passage, we may infer that the author ＿＿＿＿＿＿＿.
    (A) is an instinctively sharp customer
    (B) has a positive opinion of online support groups
    (C) is a professional aroma therapist
    (D) is an unsophisticated computer programmer

51. According to the passage, which of the following strengths is NOT mentioned in this passage regarding online support groups?
    (A) Increased access to support.
    (B) Improved feelings of self-worth.
    (C) Effectiveness.   (D) Limited language skills.

52. For whom would an online support group be most appropriate?
    (A) Someone who needs traditional counseling sessions.
    (B) Someone who is isolated in a remote location.
    (C) Someone who participates in too many after-school programs.
    (D) Someone who likes to communicate honestly and openly.

第 53 至 56 題爲題組

　　Animals such as snakes, dogs, cats, small rodents like squirrels, certain insects, and spiders may bite humans with dangerous consequences. Bites inflicted by **venomous** snakes, for example, require immediate first-aid measures. The victim should be taken as soon as possible to the nearest emergency medical facility. In the interim, the first-aid provider should not cut the area around the bite, attempt to suck out the venom, or apply ice to the wound. The focus of first aid should be to prevent the venom from spreading rapidly through the individual's bloodstream. The victim should be kept quiet to avoid stimulating circulation of the venom. In addition, the bite area should be kept at a lower level than the rest of the body. The wound should be washed thoroughly with soap and water, blotted dry, and loosely covered with a sterile dressing.

Biting insects include fleas, mosquitoes, bedbugs, lice, chiggers, and gnats. Bites from these insects should be washed to prevent infection, and cold compresses or topical medications applied to alleviate itching and pain.

Bites from other animals should be thoroughly washed, treated with an antibiotic ointment, and bandaged. The victim should seek medical attention if the bite is severe. Bites from other humans are particularly prone to serious bacterial infection and should be treated by a medical professional. Bites from most spiders can be treated like those of other biting insects. But bites from black widow spiders require medical help and should be treated similarly to poisonous snakebites.

53. Before the victim of the snakebite is taken to the nearest emergency medical facility, the first-aid provider should _____.
   (A) apply ice to the wound
   (B) keep the bite at a lower level than the rest of the body
   (C) attempt to suck out the blood
   (D) cut the area around the bite

54. Which of the following is NOT mentioned regarding biting insects?
   (A) chiggers   (B) bedbugs   (C) dragonflies   (D) mosquitoes

55. According to the passage, bites from _____ are most vulnerable to serious bacterial infection.
   (A) spiders   (B) snakes   (C) dogs   (D) humans

56. Which of the following best explains the word "**venomous**" in the first paragraph?
   (A) ill-mannered   (B) mischievous
   (C) wandering   (D) poisonous

第貳部分：非選擇題（佔 28 分）

一、中譯英（佔 8 分）

說明： 1. 請將以下中文句子譯成正確、通順、達意的英文，並將答案寫在「答案卷」上。

2. 請依序作答，並標明題號。每題 4 分，共 8 分。

1. 青少年看漫畫來消磨時間或紓解壓力。

2. 有的漫畫很幽默、很有創意，以致很多青少年沉溺其中。

二、英文作文（佔 20 分）

說明： 1. 依提示在「答案卷」上寫一篇英文作文。

2. 文長約 100 至 120 個單詞（words）。

提示：你在坐捷運時弄丟了皮包，有位好心人撿到你的皮包並歸還給你。你（英文名字必須假設為 Frank Dodd 或 Aretha Franklin），要寫一封投給撿到你皮包的人（英文名字必須假設為 Mr. Thomas），說明你為何弄丟皮包，並表達感謝之意。

請注意：必須使用上述的 Frank Dodd 或 Aretha Franklin 在信末署名，**不得使用自己的真實中文或英文名字。**

大學入學學科能力測驗英文模擬試題 ④ 詳解

第壹部分：單選題

一、詞彙：

1. (**C**) 無庸置疑地，聖卡塔利娜島是巴拿馬海灘上的一顆<u>寶石</u>，有中南美洲一些最棒的浪潮。

    (A) result〔rɪˋzʌlt〕 *n.* 結果（ = *consequence* ）

    (B) progress〔ˋprɑgrɛs〕 *n.* 進步（ ↔ regress ）

    (C) ***jewel***〔ˋdʒuəl〕 寶石【可數】   jewelry *n.* 珠寶類【不可數】

    (D) guidance〔ˋgaɪdn̩s〕 *n.* 引導；指示   parental guidance 輔導級

    * ***without a doubt*** 無庸置疑地（ = *undoubtedly* ）

    Panama〔ˋpænə͵mɑ〕 *n.* 巴拿馬【位於中美洲與南美洲相接地帶的一個國家】

    wave〔wev〕 *n.* 波浪   ***Central and South America*** 中南美洲

2. (**B**) 數百萬計的人們蒙受著癡呆的失憶之苦，然而這種<u>毀滅性的</u>疾病，迄今仍籠罩在恐懼與謎霧之中。

    (A) overtaking〔͵ovəˋtekɪŋ〕 *adj.* 突然侵襲的

    (B) ***devastating***〔ˋdɛvəs͵tetɪŋ〕 *adj.* 毀滅性的

    (C) finishing〔ˋfɪnɪʃɪŋ〕 *adj.* 最後修飾的

    (D) representing〔͵rɛprɪˋzɛntɪŋ〕 *adj.* 象徵的；代表的

    * suffer〔ˋsʌfɚ〕 *v.* 遭受（苦難）   ***memory loss*** 失憶

    dementia〔dɪˋmɛnʃɪə〕 *n.* 痴呆   yet〔jɛt〕 *adv.* 迄今仍（未）

    ailment〔ˋelmənt〕 *n.* 疾病   remain〔rɪˋmen〕 *v.* 依然（是）

    shroud〔ʃraʊd〕 *v.* 遮蔽；覆蓋   fear〔fɪr〕 *n.* 恐懼

    mystery〔ˋmɪstrɪ〕 *n.* 神秘；謎

3. (**A**) 如果你很厭惡寒冷的天氣，你可以<u>交替</u>進出。先在室內好好地做暖身運動，然後再出去，直到你又暖和了再回來。

    (A) ***alternate***〔ˋɔltɚ͵net〕 *v.* 交替；輪流

    (B) apply〔əˋplaɪ〕 *v.* 將～運用在 < *to* >；申請 < *to* / *for* >；

        把～塗在 < *to* / *on* >

    (C) involve〔ɪnˋvɑlv〕 *v.* 牽涉；包含（ = *contain* = *include* ）

    (D) withhold〔wɪθˋhold〕 *v.* 保留（ = *retain* ）；不給予

　　* loathe〔loð〕*v.* 極厭惡　　***in and out*** 進進出出地
　　inside〔'ɪn'saɪd〕*adv.* 在屋內　　***warm up*** 暖身

4. (**C**) 大雨過後，有超過二十座村莊遭受洪水覆蓋，至少三千位居民被<u>撤離</u>到較安全的區域。

　　(A) evict〔ɪ'vɪkt〕*v.* 逐出；趕走
　　(B) evolve〔ɪ'vɑlv〕*v.* 演化　　evolution *n.* 演化；進化
　　(C) ***evacuate***〔ɪ'vækju,et〕*v.* 撤離；疏散　　evacuation *n.* 撤離
　　(D) evoke〔ɪ'vok〕*v.* 喚起【e = ex (= *out*) + voke (= *call*)】
　　* floodwater〔'flʌd,wɔtə〕*n.* 洪水　　cover〔'kʌvə〕*v.* 覆蓋
　　at least 至少　　area〔'ɛrɪə〕*n.* 地區

5. (**D**) 許多社會科學家相信，高檔的購物中心，代表著印度追求全新自我的<u>渴望</u>。

　　(A) response〔rɪ'spɑns〕*n.* 反應；回答 (= *reply*)　　respond *v.*
　　(B) resemblance〔rɪ'zɛmbləns〕*n.* 類似　　resemble *v.* 相像
　　(C) impression〔ɪm'prɛʃən〕*n.* 印象　　impress *v.* 給予 (人) 印象
　　(D) ***aspiration***〔,æspə'reʃən〕*n.* 渴望　　aspire *v.* 渴望
　　* luxury〔'lʌkʃərɪ〕*adj.* 奢華的；高級的 (= *high-class*)
　　represent〔,rɛprɪ'zɛnt〕*v.* 代表；象徵　　India〔'ɪndɪə〕*n.* 印度
　　brand-new〔'brænd'nju〕*adj.* 全新的
　　identity〔aɪ'dɛntətɪ〕*n.* 認同

6. (**D**) 全球性的調查顯示出，印度億萬富翁及百萬富翁的<u>成長</u>數量，是世界最快的。

　　(A) stir〔stɝ〕*v.* 攪拌；煽動 (= *excite*)
　　(B) reinforce〔,riɪn'fors〕*v.* 加強 (= *strengthen*)
　　(C) spread〔sprɛd〕*v.* 宣傳；散播 (= *scatter* = *disperse*)
　　(D) ***grow***〔gro〕*v.* 成長【恆用主動】　　growing *adj.* 成長中的
　　* survey〔sə'νe〕*n.* 調查　　billionaire〔,bɪljən'ɛr〕*n.* 億萬富翁
　　millionaire〔,mɪljən'ɛr〕*n.* 百萬富翁

7. (**B**) 如果你的老師說話太快，在你的筆記上留下大片空<u>白</u>，來填入遺漏的資訊。可使用符號來幫助你想起遺漏的東西。

    (A) tendency〔'tɛndənsɪ〕*n.* 傾向；趨勢（= *trend*）

    (B) ***space***〔spes〕*n.* 空間；空白；間格

    (C) document〔'dɑkjəmənt〕*n.* 文件（= *file*）

    (D) ancestor〔'ænsɛstɚ〕*n.* 祖先（= *forefather*）（↔ descendant）

    * empty〔'ɛmptɪ〕*adj.* 空的   note〔not〕*n.* 筆記   ***fill in*** 填入

    information〔ˌɪnfɚ'meʃən〕*n.* 訊息   symbol〔'sɪmbl̩〕*n.* 符號

8. (**A**) 人們與生俱有利用手腳<u>漂浮</u>在水面上的能力，但這項本能在出生不久後就消失了。

    (A) ***afloat***〔ə'flot〕*adj.*（在水面、空氣中）漂浮的

    (B) awake〔ə'wek〕*adj.* 醒著的（↔ asleep）   *v.* 喚醒（= *wake*）

    (C) alleviative〔ə'livɪˌetɪv〕*adj.* 減輕的

    (D) adequate〔'ædəkwɪt〕*adj.* 充足的（= *sufficient*）

    * ***human beings*** 人類   ***be born with*** 與生俱來

    ability〔ə'bɪlətɪ〕*n.* 能力   surface〔'sɝfɪs〕*n.* 表面；水面

    instinct〔'ɪnstɪŋkt〕*n.* 本能   disappear〔ˌdɪsə'pɪr〕*v.* 消失

9. (**B**) 這個主題樂園在星期六<u>正式</u>對外開幕時，舉行了一整天的慶祝活動。

    (A) submissively〔səb'mɪsɪvlɪ〕*adv.* 順從地

    (B) ***officially***〔ə'fɪʃəlɪ〕*adv.* 正式地；官方地

    (C) exclusively〔ɪk'sklusɪvlɪ〕*adv.* 專門地；僅

    (D) narrowly〔'nærolɪ〕*adv.* 狹窄地；勉強地

    * theme〔θim〕*n.* 主題   ***theme park*** 主題樂園   ***the public*** 大眾

    celebration〔ˌsɛlə'breʃən〕*n.* 慶祝活動   ***take place*** 舉行；發生

10. (**D**) 紐約市的音樂廳、博物館、畫廊和劇院，<u>構成</u>了僅有幾個城市能與其匹敵的整體富饒文化。

    (A) conduct〔kən'dʌkt〕*v.* 指揮（= *direct*）；管理（= *manage*）

    (B) reduce〔rɪ'djus〕*v.* 減少（= *diminish*）

    (C) inspect〔ɪn'spɛkt〕*v.* 檢查（= *examine*）

    (D) ***constitute***〔'kɑnstəˌtjut〕*v.* 構成（= *compose* = *make up*）

　　* concert〔'kɑnsɝt〕*n.* 音樂會　　***concert house*** 音樂廳
　　　museum〔mju'ziəm〕*n.* 博物館
　　　gallery〔'gælərɪ〕*n.* 畫廊　　　theater〔'θiətə〕*n.* 劇院
　　　ensemble〔ɑn'sɑmbḷ〕*n.* 整體；總效果
　　　cultural〔'kʌltʃərəl〕*adj.* 文化的
　　　richness〔'rɪtʃnɪs〕*n.* 富足；豐富
　　　rival〔'raɪvḷ〕*v.* 競爭

11.（**B**）現在，阿斯匹靈在五十種以上的非處方用藥中，被列為主要成分，
　　　　　光是在美國，每年就<u>吃掉</u>超過八百億顆藥錠。

　　　(A) publicize〔'pʌblɪ,saɪz〕*v.* 宣傳（= *advertise*）
　　　(B) ***consume***〔kən'sum〕*v.* 吃；喝；消耗　　consumption *n.*
　　　(C) con〔kɑn〕*v.* 欺騙（= *cheat*）
　　　(D) conspire〔kən'spaɪr〕*v.* 密謀策劃　　conspiracy *n.*

　　　* aspirin〔'æspərɪn〕*n.* 阿斯匹靈
　　　　principal〔'prɪnsəpḷ〕*adj.* 主要的
　　　　ingredient〔ɪn'gridɪənt〕*n.* 成分　　counter〔'kaʊntə〕*n.* 櫃檯
　　　　over-the-counter〔'ovəðə'kaʊntə〕*adj.* 不需要醫生處方籤的；成藥的
　　　　billion〔'bɪljən〕*n.* 十億　　tablet〔'tæblɪt〕*n.* 藥片；錠
　　　　annually〔'ænjʊəlɪ〕*adv.* 每年

12.（**C**）鱷魚被公認為一種兇殘的殺手級大型爬蟲類，牠的微笑和眼淚，成為
　　　　　<u>欺騙</u>的代名詞。

　　　(A) definition〔,dɛfə'nɪʃən〕*n.* 定義；清晰度　　define *v.*
　　　(B) deterioration〔dɪ,tɪrɪə'reʃən〕*n.* 惡化　　deteriorate *v.*
　　　(C) ***deception***〔dɪ'sɛpʃən〕*n.* 欺騙　　deceive *v.*
　　　(D) description〔dɪ'skrɪpʃən〕*n.* 描述　　describe *v.*

　　　* crocodile〔'krɑkə,daɪl〕*n.* 鱷魚　　reptile〔'rɛptḷ〕*n.* 爬蟲類動物
　　　　commonly〔'kɑmənlɪ〕*adv.* 通常地　　***be regarded as*** 被視為
　　　　vicious〔'vɪʃəs〕*adj.* 惡毒的（= *wicked*）
　　　　killer〔'kɪlə〕*n.* 殺手　　tear〔tɪr〕*n.* 眼淚
　　　　byword〔'baɪ,wɝd〕*n.* 代名詞；綽號

13. (**A**) 載著他們的巴士，在公路上塞住動彈不得時，乘客們陷入<u>進退兩難</u>的窘境。

    (A) ***strand*** 〔 strænd 〕 *v.* 使～進退兩難

         be stranded 處於困境；陷入兩難 (*= be in a dilemma*)

    (B) outwit 〔 aʊt'wɪt 〕 *v.* 智勝 (*= outmaneuver*)

    (C) overlap 〔͵ovɚ'læp 〕 *v.* (時間、空間) 重疊

    (D) conform 〔 kən'fɔrm 〕 *v.* 遵守 < *to* > (*= abide by = comply with*)

    * passenger 〔'pæsn̩dʒɚ 〕 *n.* 乘客   carry 〔'kærɪ 〕 *v.* 運載

        stuck 〔 stʌk 〕 *adj.* 困住的   highway 〔'haɪ͵we 〕 *n.* 公路

14. (**B**) 騎越野單車是一種<u>越來越</u>受歡迎的休閒運動，越來越多人騎越野單車旅行，或用在日常通勤。

    (A) irritating 〔'ɪrə͵tetɪŋ 〕 *adj.* 令人生氣的 (↔ pleasant)

    (B) ***increasing*** 〔 ɪn'krisɪŋ 〕 *adj.* 逐漸增加的 (↔ decreasing)

    (C) campaign 〔 kæm'pen 〕 *v.* 發起 (宣傳、競選等) 運動

    (D) entitle 〔 ɪn'taɪtl̩ 〕 *v.* 授權 (*= authorize*)；命名 (*= name*)

    * ***mountain biking*** 騎越野單車

       recreational 〔͵rɛkrɪ'eʃənl̩ 〕 *adj.* 休閒的

       popularity 〔͵pɑpjə'lærətɪ 〕 *n.* 歡迎

       daily 〔'delɪ 〕 *adj.* 每天的   travel 〔'trævl̩ 〕 *n.* 移動；來回

15. (**A**) 關於這個案例，我們所能收集到的資料，<u>結果是</u>十分有限的。

    (A) ***add up to*** 結果是 (*= turn out to be*)；加起來總和

         (*= amount to*)

    (B) make up for 補償 (*= compensate for*)

    (C) come up with 想到；追上 (*= catch up with*)

    (D) put up with 忍受 (*= tolerate = endure = bear*)

    * information 〔͵ɪnfɚ'meʃən 〕 *n.* 資料

       collect 〔 kə'lɛkt 〕 *v.* 收集   ***in relation to*** 有關

       case 〔 kes 〕 *n.* 案例；問題

二、綜合測驗：

第 16 至 20 題為題組

　　在越來越受到乾旱和缺水困擾的世界裡，節約用水不僅是一種美德，更成為一個規範。在台灣，如果你希望大家能<u>少</u>用點水，那你就必須要讓水價更貴一點，尤其是對那些用量最大的人。也就是說，你用越多水，就要付越多錢。

* increasingly〔ɪnˈkrisɪŋlɪ〕*adv.* 越來越多地
  plague〔pleg〕*v.* 煩擾　　drought〔draʊt〕*n.* 乾旱
  shortage〔ˈʃɔrtɪdʒ〕*n.* 短缺　　conserve〔kənˈsɝv〕*v.* 節約
  virtue〔ˈvɝtʃʊ〕*n.* 美德　　standard〔ˈstændəd〕*n.* 規範

16.(**C**) 依句意，要用「更少的」水，選 (C) *less*。而 (D) fewer「較少的」，
　　　　 修飾可數名詞，在此用法不合。

　　但棘手的部分是，價格該<u>提高</u>多少，還有，該對誰漲價呢。政府官員們花了六個月去思考不同的定價的可能性，現在，他們要讓百姓們更「滴水不漏」，而且更節約用水。

* tricky〔ˈtrɪkɪ〕*adj.* 棘手的　　official〔əˈfɪʃəl〕*n.* 官員
  consider〔kənˈsɪdə〕*v.* 考慮　　various〔ˈvɛrɪəs〕*adj.* 各式各樣的
  price〔praɪs〕*v.* 定價格　　possibility〔ˌpɑsəˈbɪlətɪ〕*n.* 可能性
  citizen〔ˈsɪtəzn̩〕*n.* 老百姓；公民
  watertight〔ˈwɔtəˈtaɪt〕*adj.* 防水的 (= *waterproof*)【這裡一語雙關；tight
  　有「吝嗇的」意思，這裡指的是「對水很吝嗇」，就是少用水。】
  economical〔ˌikəˈnɑmɪkl̩〕*adj.* 節儉的 (= *saving*)

17.(**B**) (A) rise〔raɪz〕*v.* 上升　　　　　(B) *raise*〔rez〕*v.* 提高
　　　　 (C) arise〔əˈraɪz〕*v.* 發生　　　　 (D) arouse〔əˈraʊz〕*v.* 喚起

<u>一如預期的</u>，那些用水相對較少的人，會發現他們的帳單，每個月才增加了台幣二十五元左右，而那些用水高於平均值的市民，則會發現帳單增加<u>幅度</u>高達一百一十元。

* expect〔ɪkˈspɛkt〕*v.* 預期　　relatively〔ˈrɛlətɪvlɪ〕*adv.* 相對地
  bill〔bɪl〕*n.* 帳單　　average〔ˈævərɪdʒ〕*n.* 平均值

18. (**C**)　依句意，「正如」預期，選 (C) *As*。

19. (**A**)　表「差距」，介系詞用 *by*，選 (A)。

　　然而，自來水官員們並不希望用水量有很劇烈的削減，<u>因爲這也表示收益</u>
　　　　　　　　　　　　　　　　　　　　　　　　　　　　　20
有大幅的減少。除了鼓勵節約外，水費增加，也預期將爲國家帶來更多的收益。

　　* drastic（'dræstɪk）*adj.* 劇烈的　　revenue（'rɛvə,nju）*n.* 收益；營業額
　　 in addition to 除了～之外（還有）　　encourage（ɪn'kɝɪdʒ）*v.* 鼓勵
　　 conservation（,kɑnsə'veʃən）*n.* 節約　　rate（ret）*n.* 費用
　　 increase（'ɪnkris）*n.* 增加　　 ***result in*** 導致

20. (**D**)　依句意，選 (D) *because*「因爲」。而 (A) so「所以」，(B) such「如此
　　　　　的」，(C) despite「儘管」，均不合句意。

第 21 至 25 題爲題組

　　隨著中國毒奶的新聞散佈開來，豆漿越來越受到歡迎了。事實上，對於不
能喝牛奶的人來說，豆漿一直以來都是受歡迎的替代品。而且因爲它附加健康
上的好處，現在越來越多人<u>刻意</u>選擇豆漿了。
　　　　　　　　　　　　21

　　* toxic（'tɑksɪk）*adj.* 有毒的　　soymilk（'sɔɪ,mɪlk）*n.* 豆漿
　　 progressively（prə'grɛsɪvlɪ）*adv.* 逐漸地
　　 in fact 事實上　　alternative（ɔl'tɝnətɪv）*n.* 選擇；替換物
　　 unable（ʌn'ebḷ）*adj.* 不能～的（= *incapable*）　　 ***because of*** 因爲
　　 added（'ædɪd）*adj.* 附加的　　benefit（'bɛnəfɪt）*n.* 好處

21. (**B**)　(A) tentatively（'tɛntətɪvlɪ）*adv.* 暫時地；試驗性地
　　　　　(B) ***deliberately***（dɪ'lɪbərɪtlɪ）*adv.* 故意地
　　　　　(C) reluctantly（rɪ'lʌktəntlɪ）*adv.* 不情願地
　　　　　(D) consecutively（kən'sɛkjətɪvlɪ）*adv.* 連續地

　　大豆的益處仍受爭議，<u>但是普遍都接受豆漿含有多種非常健康的化合物</u>，
　　　　　　　　　　　　22
而且它蛋白質含量很高。因爲豆漿是由大豆製的，所以<u>豆漿</u>也比牛奶含有更多
　　　　　　　　　　　　　　　　　　　　　　　　23
纖維。另外，很多豆漿的製造業者會在他們的產品中添加鈣質。

* soy〔sɔɪ〕*n.* 大豆；黃豆　　dispute〔dɪ'spjut〕*v.* 爭論；討論
generally〔'dʒɛnərəlɪ〕*adv.* 普遍地　　accept〔ək'sɛpt〕*v.* 接受
contain〔kən'ten〕*v.* 包含　　compound〔'kɑmpaʊnd〕*n.* 化合物
protein〔'protiɪn〕*n.* 蛋白質
considerably〔kən'sɪdərəblɪ〕*adv.* 可觀地　　fiber〔'faɪbɚ〕*n.* 纖維
in addition 另外　　manufacturer〔͵mænjə'fæktʃərɚ〕*n.* 製造業者
calcium〔'kælsɪəm〕*n.* 鈣　　product〔'prɑdəkt〕*n.* 產品

22.(**B**) 依句意，選 (B) *but*「但是」。而 (A) even「甚至」, (C) lest「以免」,
(D) if「如果」，均不合句意。

23.(**D**) and 為對等連接詞，連接兩個由 that 引導的名詞子句，故選 (D)。

除了多的纖維和蛋白質，豆漿最大的好處，是大豆異黃酮，它其實是一種
　　24
和雌激素很類似的化學物質。

* extra〔'ɛkstrə〕*adj.* 額外的　　isoflavone〔͵aɪso'flevon〕*n.* 大豆異黃酮
actually〔'æktʃʊəlɪ〕*adv.* 事實上　　chemical〔'kɛmɪkl̩〕*n.* 化學製品
similar to 類似…的　　hormone〔'hɔrmon〕*n.* 賀爾蒙
estrogen〔'ɛstrədʒɛn〕*n.* 雌激素

24.(**C**) 依句意，選 (C) *Besides*「除了…之外（還有）」。而 (A) because「因
為」, (B) despite「儘管」, (D) unless「除非」，則不合句意。

大豆異黃酮與很多健康的議題有關，最盛行的，有預防多種癌症、心臟疾病，
還有骨質疏鬆症等。　　25

* *be connected with* 和～有關　　*a whole host of* 很多的
issue〔'ɪʃʊ〕*n.* 議題　　prevalent〔'prɛvələnt〕*adj.* 普遍的；流行的
prevention〔prɪ'vɛnʃən〕*n.* 預防
cancer〔'kænsɚ〕*n.* 癌症　　*heart disease* 心臟疾病
osteoporosis〔͵ɑstɪopə'rosɪs〕*n.* 骨質疏鬆症

25.(**A**) 空格後面沒有主要動詞，故選介系詞，此處須用表「附帶狀態」的
介系詞 *with*，選 (A)。

所以，你可以認眞考慮把豆漿加入，或是用豆漿來取代你的咖啡或茶了。

* seriously ('sɪrɪəslɪ) adv. 認眞地

substitute ('sʌbstə,tjut) v. 用～取代　　*substitute* A *for* B 用 A 取代 B

第 26 至 30 題爲題組

焦慮，是一種由恐懼跟不安所組成的人類基本情緒，當個體遇到一些困難時就會出現。在某些例子當中，像是避開危險的情況時，焦慮是很有幫助的。然而，若太過焦慮，可能會產生不利的後果。
26

* anxiety (æŋ'zaɪətɪ) n. 焦慮　　basic ('besɪk) adj. 基本的

emotion (ɪ'moʃən) n. 情緒　　*consist of* 由…組成

uncertainty (ʌn'sɝtntɪ) n. 不安　　appear (ə'pɪr) v. 出現

individual (,ɪndə'vɪdʒuəl) n. 個體　　encounter (ɪn'kauntɚ) v. 遭遇

instance ('ɪnstəns) n. 例子　　avoid (ə'vɔɪd) v. 避開

situation (,sɪtʃu'eʃən) n. 境遇　　extreme (ɪk'strim) n. 極端

take sth. to extremes 把…帶到極端

produce (prə'djus) v. 生產　　unfavorable (ʌn'fevərəbl̩) adj. 不利的

26. (**C**) 依句意，選 (C) *However*「然而」。而 (A) therefore「因此」，(B) moreover「此外」，(D) instead「作爲代替；相反地」，均不合句意。

現在，造成學生焦慮的事情中，最具威脅的就是考試。當學生對於考試表現不佳而顯露出極度恐懼的症狀時，他們正感受到考試焦慮。它起因於很多種負面因素，包括心理的痛苦、學業失敗，與不安。
27

* threatening ('θrɛtn̩ɪŋ) adj. 有威脅的　　event (ɪ'vɛnt) n. 事件

develop (dɪ'vɛləp) v. (症狀) 顯露

perform (pɚ'fɔrm) v. 表現　　poorly ('purlɪ) adv. 差勁地

a variety of 各種不同的　　negative ('nɛgətɪv) adj. 負面的

psychological (,saɪkə'lɑdʒɪkl̩) adj. 心理的

distress (dɪ'strɛs) n. 痛苦

academic (,ækə'dɛmɪk) adj. 學術的

failure ('feljɚ) n. 失敗　　insecurity (,ɪnsɪ'kjurətɪ) n. 不安

27. (**A**) 依句意，選 (A) *result from*「起因於；由於」。而 (B) stand up for「支持；為⋯辯護」，(C) react to「對⋯起反應」，(D) call for「需要」，均不合句意。

　　很多學生都擁有把考試考好的能力，但卻<u>因為</u>高度的考試焦慮而考差了。我們
28
的社會過度強調考試，這已經侷限了他們在教育和職業上的機會。

* overemphasis〔͵ovɚˈɛmfəsɪs〕*n.* 過度強調　　limit〔ˈlɪmɪt〕*v.* 限制
vocational〔voˈkeʃənḷ〕*adj.* 職業的

28. (**C**) 依句意，選 (C) *because of*「因為；由於」。而 (A) apart from「除了⋯之外」，(B) except for「除了⋯之外」，(D) regardless of「不管；不論」，均不合句意。

　　學生們被鼓勵要培養良好的、<u>一致的</u>睡眠習慣，尤其是在考試週這期間，
29
還要維持健康的飲食和規律的運動。他們還應該<u>避免</u>用死背的，要培養出好的
30
讀書習慣和考試技巧。他們考試時，應該要穿著舒適的衣服，並在考試中，保持舒適且放鬆的姿勢。

* habit〔ˈhæbɪt〕*n.* 習慣　　maintain〔menˈten〕*v.* 維持
regularly〔ˈrɛgjələ⋅lɪ〕*adv.* 規律地　　cram〔kræm〕*v.* 強記；填鴨式教學
skill〔skɪl〕*n.* 技巧　　comfortable〔ˈkʌmfɚtəbḷ〕*adj.* 舒適的（= *cozy*）
relaxed〔rɪˈlækst〕*adj.* 放鬆的
posture〔ˈpastʃɚ〕*n.* 姿勢（= *pose*）

29. (**A**)　(A) *consistent*〔kənˈsɪstənt〕*adj.* 一致的
　　　　　(B) infatuated〔ɪnˈfætʃuͺetɪd〕*adj.* 入迷的；熱中的
　　　　　(C) approximate〔əˈprɑksəmɪt〕*adj.* 大概的
　　　　　(D) unknowing〔ʌnˈnoɪŋ〕*adj.* 未察覺的

30. (**B**)　(A) forge〔fɔrdʒ〕*v.* 仿冒
　　　　　(B) *avoid*〔əˈvɔɪd〕*v.* 避免
　　　　　(C) confiscate〔ˈkɑnfɪsͺket〕*v.* 沒收
　　　　　(D) wave〔wev〕*v.* 揮動

三、文意選填：

第 31 至 40 題為題組

　　跟電流接觸可能會致命。電擊對身體的 [31](E) 影響不只要看電流的強度，還要看某些因素而定，例如皮膚的溼度、接觸的位置、接觸的時間長短、受害者的體質，還有受害者 [32](B) 是否有受過良好的訓練。

* contact（ˊkɑntækt）n. v. 接觸　　electrical（ɪˊlɛktrɪkḷ）adj. 使用電氣的
　current（ˊkɜənt）n. (電)流　　potentially（pəˊtɛnʃəlɪ）adv. 可能地
　fatal（ˊfetḷ）adj. 致命的　　effect（ɪˊfɛkt）n. 效果；影響
　electric（ɪˊlɛktrɪk）adj. 帶電的；電擊的　　shock（ʃɑk）n. 衝擊
　depend on 依賴　　*not only…but also~* 不但…而且~
　strength（strɛŋθ）n. 力量　　factor（ˊfæktɚ）n. 因素
　wetness（ˊwɛtnɪs）n. 潮濕　　duration（djuˊreʃən）n. 持續期間
　constitution（ˌkɑnstəˊtjuʃən）n. 結構；體質
　victim（ˊvɪktɪm）n. 受害者　　*whether or not* 是否
　well-grounded（ˊwɛlˊgraʊndɪd）adj. 有充分根據的；受過基本訓練的

　　電擊的徵兆跟症狀包括輕微的刺痛、肌肉痙攣、頭痛、呼吸不穩或無法呼吸、失去意識，[33](G) 有時還會死亡。[34](C) 流經身體的電力，會對皮膚還有內臟造成傷害。如果電力流經心臟，心臟肌肉可能會受傷，而且心跳的節奏會 [35](D) 中斷，導致心跳停止。

* sign（saɪn）n. 徵兆　　symptom（ˊsɪmptəm）n. 症狀；前兆
　mild（maɪld）adj. 溫和的　　tingle（ˊtɪŋgḷ）v. 刺痛
　spasm（ˊspæzəm）n. 痙攣　　muscle（ˊmʌsḷ）n. 肌肉
　irregular（ɪˊrɛgjələ）adj. 不規則的　　breathing（ˊbriðɪŋ）n. 呼吸
　consciousness（ˊkɑnʃəsnɪs）n. 意識　　*loss of consciousness* 失去意識
　electricity（ɪˌlɛkˊtrɪsətɪ）n. 電流　　*pass through* 通過
　cause（kɔz）v. 引起　　injury（ˊɪndʒərɪ）n. 傷害
　internal（ɪnˊtɜnḷ）adj. 內部的　　organ（ˊɔrgən）n. 器官
　internal organs 內臟　　damage（ˊdæmɪdʒ）v. 傷害
　rhythm（ˊrɪðəm）n. 節律；節奏　　interrupt（ˌɪntəˊrʌpt）v. 中斷
　lead to 導致　　cardiac（ˊkɑrdɪˌæk）adj. 心臟的
　arrest（əˊrɛst）n. 逮捕；停止　　*cardiac arrest* 心跳停止

若有受害者遭受電擊，^{36}**(I)** 提供急救的人，在電擊的 ^{37}**(F)** 來源被關掉之前，都不應該觸碰受害者。因為身體內部有可能受傷，除非受害者有 ^{38}**(J)** 立即的危險，否則不能移動受到電擊的傷者。

* provide〔prə'vaɪd〕v. 提供　　first-aid〔'fɝst'ed〕n. 急救
　touch〔tʌtʃ〕v. 觸碰　　individual〔͵ɪndə'vɪdʒʊəl〕n. 個人
　source〔sors〕n. 來源　　***turn off*** 關掉
　because of 因為；由於　　potential〔pə'tɛnʃəl〕n. 可能性
　immediate〔ɪ'midɪɪt〕adj. 立即的

提供急救的人應該要觀察受害者遭受電擊後的症狀。如果受害者已經沒有呼吸跟脈搏，^{39}**(A)** 確認過呼吸道、呼吸、血液循環後，應該要執行心肺復甦術。當受害者的生命跡象很穩定時，治療遭受電擊燒傷 ^{40}**(H)** 處的方法，就跟治療其他燒傷所使用的方法一樣。

* provider〔prə'vaɪdɚ〕n. 提供者　　monitor〔'manətɚ〕v. 監控；觀察
　breathe〔brið〕v. 呼吸　　pulse〔pʌls〕n. 脈搏
　CPR 心肺復甦術（= ___cardiopulmonary___〔͵kardɪo'pʌlmənɛrɪ〕adj. 心肺的
　　+ ___resuscitation___〔rɪ͵sʌsə'teʃən〕n. 復甦）
　perform〔pɚ'fɔrm〕v. 執行　　airway〔'ɛr͵we〕n. 呼吸道
　circulation〔͵sɝkjə'leʃən〕n.（血液）循環　　check〔tʃɛk〕v. 檢查
　vital signs 生命跡象　　stable〔'stebḷ〕adj. 穩定的
　site〔saɪt〕n.（事件發生的）地點
　burn〔bɝn〕n.（電擊、火等）燒傷
　treat〔trit〕v. 治療　　method〔'mɛθəd〕n. 方法

四、閱讀測驗：

<u>第 41 至 44 題為題組</u>

作為幾乎每一種水上活動不可或缺的一部分，游泳需要透過一個人的手臂、腿和身體在水中一起動，這被稱為游法。最普遍的游法有自由式、仰式、蛙式、蝶式和側泳。

* integral〔'ɪntəgrəl〕adj.（構成整體）不可或缺的
　water-based〔'wɔtɚ͵best〕adj. 以水為主的；水上的
　activity〔æk'tɪvətɪ〕n. 活動　　involve〔ɪn'vɑlv〕v. 包含；需要

movement〔'muvmənt〕 *n.* 動作　　motion〔'moʃən〕 *n.* 運動；移動
in motion 在動作中　　stroke〔strok〕 *n.* 游法；划
common〔'kɑmən〕 *adj.* 普遍的　　crawl〔krɔl〕 *n.* 自由式
backstroke〔'bæk,strok〕 *n.* 仰式　　breaststroke〔'brɛst,strok〕 *n.* 蛙式
butterfly〔'bʌtə,flaɪ〕 *n.* 蝶式　　sidestroke〔'saɪd,strok〕 *n.* 側泳

有些人是在其他人在游泳社團、社區中心、學校或是娛樂設施中上課時，模仿
他人而學會游泳。初學者首先將他們的頭部放進水裡，藉著吐氣吹出泡泡。漸
漸地進步到漂浮、踩水，最後才學習主要游法的技巧。

　＊imitate〔'ɪmə,tet〕 *v.* 模仿　　***take lessons*** 上課
club〔klʌb〕 *n.* 俱樂部；社團　　community〔kə'mjunətɪ〕 *n.* 社區
recreational〔,rɛkrɪ'eʃənļ〕 *adj.* 娛樂的　　facility〔fə'sɪlətɪ〕 *n.* 設施
beginner〔bɪ'gɪnə〕 *n.* 初學者　　blow〔blo〕 *v.* 吹
bubble〔'bʌbļ〕 *n.* 氣泡　　exhale〔ɛks'hel〕 *v.* 吐出
gradually〔'grædʒʊəlɪ〕 *adv.* 漸漸地　　progress〔prə'grɛs〕 *v.* 進展
float〔flot〕 *v.* 漂浮　 *n.* 漂浮物　　tread〔trɛd〕 *v.* 行走；踩
ultimately〔'ʌltəmɪtlɪ〕 *adv.* 最終地　　technique〔tɛk'nik〕 *n.* 技巧
major〔'medʒə〕 *adj.* 主要的

　　在課程中，學生可以使用各式各樣的裝備。浮袋是套在上手臂，讓學生保
持漂浮的一種充氣物。浮板是可以讓學生把手臂擱在上面，有浮力的板子，這
可以使他們的上半身保持漂浮，讓他們能夠專注在正確地踢水上。浮力筒是一
種海綿材質漂浮物，讓學生夾在大腿間，讓下半身平穩浮出水面上。藉著使用
它們，學生可以學習使用各種游法的手臂及上半身的動作。另外一個是人工蹼，
它是一種裝在手上，小且堅硬的板子，讓學生在水中正確地用他們的手臂划行。
穿在腳上的蛙鞋，也讓泳者更快速移動，並養成正確的身體姿勢和力量。

　＊equipment〔ɪ'kwɪpmənt〕 *n.* 裝備　　***water wings*** 浮袋
inflatable〔ɪn'fletəbļ〕 *n.* 充氣物　　upper〔'ʌpə〕 *adj.* 上部的
upper arm 上臂　　kickboard〔'kɪk,bord〕 *n.* 浮板
buoyant〔'bɔɪənt〕 *adj.* 有浮力的　　board〔bord〕 *n.* 板子
rest〔rɛst〕 *v.* 擱置　　***upper body*** 上半身
afloat〔ə'flot〕 *adj.* 漂浮的　　allow〔ə'laʊ〕 *v.* 讓；使能夠
concentrate〔'kɑnsņ,tret〕 *v.* 專注　　kick〔kɪk〕 *v.* 踢

correctly〔kəˋrɛktlɪ〕*adv.* 正確地　　pull〔pʊl〕*v.* 划；拉
buoy〔bɔɪ〕*n.* 浮筒；救生衣　　pull-buoy *n.* 浮力筒
foam〔fom〕*n.* 泡沫材料　　thigh〔θaɪ〕*n.* 大腿
lower body 下半身　　surface〔ˋsɝfɪs〕*n.* 表面
paddle〔ˋpædḷ〕*n.* 槳；蹼　　firm〔fɝm〕*adj.* 堅固的
fit over 固定在…之上　　force〔fors〕*v.* 強迫
fin〔fɪn〕*n.* 魚鰭；蛙鞋　　proper〔ˋprɑpɚ〕*adj.* 正確的
position〔pəˋzɪʃən〕*n.* 位置

　由於游泳能夠培養耐力、肌力和心血管的健康，如果你想要運動，而且同時想保持涼爽，游泳就是你很好的選擇。

　＊ endurance〔ɪnˋdjʊrəns〕*n.* 耐力　　strength〔strɛŋθ〕*n.* 力量
　　cardiovascular〔ˌkɑrdɪoˋvæskjulɚ〕*adj.* 心血管的
　　fitness〔ˋfɪtnɪs〕*n.* 健康；良好　　***work out*** 運動
　　sth. ***be where*** *sth.* ***be at*** （某事）是很好的

41.（ **B** ）本文最佳標題為何？
　　(A) 游泳廣受歡迎　　　　　(B) 學習游泳
　　(C) 游泳的真正起源　　　　(D) 游泳的許多用途
　　＊ popularity〔ˌpɑpjəˋlærətɪ〕*n.* 流行；通俗
　　　origin〔ˋɔrədʒɪn〕*n.* 起源
　　　versatility〔ˌvɝsəˋtɪlətɪ〕*n.* 多用途

42.（ **D** ）根據本文，初學者藉著 ＿＿＿＿＿＿ 開始學習游泳。
　　(A) 漂浮與踩水　　　　　　(B) 觀看主要的游法
　　(C) 在游泳俱樂部上課
　　(D) 把頭放到水中然後吐氣吹泡泡

43.（ **A** ）文中沒有提到下列哪一項設備？
　　(A) 蛙鏡。　　(B) 浮袋。　　(C) 浮板。　　(D) 浮力筒。
　　＊ goggles〔ˋgɑgḷz〕*n. pl.* 蛙鏡

44.（ **D** ）下列哪個設備較能幫助學習者學會手臂還有上半身的動作？
　　(A) 蛙鏡。　　(B) 浮袋。　　(C) 浮板。　　(D) 浮力筒。

第 45 至 48 題為題組

北韓被指為七個資助恐怖主義的國家之一，長久以來都存心販售武器給分離派團體，連同從事偽造活動、提供庇護給五名劫持日籍班機的劫機犯，以及其他的犯罪行動，譬如在 1987 年，大韓航空 858 次班機的空中爆炸事件，而此次的攻擊，被視為是要嚇跑 1988 年首爾夏季奧運的旅客的策略。除此之外，北韓還幕後主使了 1996 年，南韓外交官在俄國海參威的遇刺事件。

      * designate〔ˈdɛzɪɡ͵net〕*v.* 指出；任命　　state〔stet〕*n.* 國家
sponsor〔ˈspɑnsɚ〕*n.* 資助者　　terrorism〔ˈtɛrə͵rɪzəm〕*n.* 恐怖主義
North Korea 北韓　　knowingly〔ˈnoɪŋlɪ〕*adv.* 存心地
weapon〔ˈwɛpən〕*n.* 武器　　separatist〔ˈsɛpə͵retɪst〕*n.* 分離派的人
along with 一起；連同　　counterfeit〔ˈkaʊntɚfɪt〕*v.* 從事偽造活動
sanctuary〔ˈsæŋktʃʊ͵ɛrɪ〕*n.* 庇護；庇護所（ = *refuge* ）
hijacker〔ˈhaɪ͵dʒækɚ〕*n.* 劫機犯　　airliner〔ˈɛr͵laɪnɚ〕*n.* 大型客機
criminal〔ˈkrɪmənḷ〕*adj.* 犯罪的　　activity〔ækˈtɪvətɪ〕*n.* 活動
midair〔mɪdˈɛr〕*adj.* 空中的　　bomb〔bɑm〕*v.* 炸毀
Korean Airlines 大韓航空　　flight〔flaɪt〕*n.* (飛機的) 班次
attack〔əˈtæk〕*n.* 攻擊　　tactic〔ˈtæktɪk〕*n.* 戰術；策略
scare〔skɛr〕*v.* 嚇走 < *away* >　　tourist〔ˈtʊrɪst〕*n.* 觀光客
Olympics〔oˈlɪmpɪks〕*n.* 奧運
Summer Olympics 夏季奧運【即一般奧運會】
Seoul〔sol〕*n.* 首爾【南韓首都】
assassination〔ə͵sæsn̩ˈeʃən〕*n.* 暗殺　　***South Korean*** 南韓的
diplomat〔ˈdɪplə͵mæt〕*n.* 外交官
Vladivostok〔͵vlædɪˈvɑstɑk〕*n.* 海參威【俄國與中國、北韓接壤的重要港口】
Russia〔ˈrʌʃə〕*n.* 俄羅斯

但最近，北韓同意遵守對自己的核能設備作全面監控後，就被從恐怖主義黑名單中除名了。美國國務院表示，監控協議，以及將北韓從資助恐怖主義的國家名單除名的決定，是為了國家安全的利益，以及為了讓協議中「你一步，我一步」的原則不互相矛盾。北韓同意讓原子專家，對其所有的核能設備，做鑑定測試，並讓專家證實，其對核能技術轉移，與謠傳有鈾富集計畫這件事，是否說了實話。

* remove〔rɪˈmuv〕v. 除去　　blacklist〔ˈblækˌlɪst〕n. 黑名單
agree〔əˈgri〕v. 同意　　comply〔kəmˈplaɪ〕v. 服從 < *with* >
inspection〔ɪnˈspɛkʃən〕n. 檢查　　nuclear〔ˈnjuklɪɚ〕adj. 核子的
facility〔fəˈsɪlətɪ〕n. 設備　　*The U.S. State Department* 美國國務院
agreement〔əˈgrimənt〕n. 協議　　*take off* 除去
interest〔ˈɪntərɪst〕n. 利益　　*in the interest(s) of* 爲了…的利益
security〔sɪˈkjurətɪ〕n. 安全　　*national security* 國家安全
consistent〔kənˈsɪstənt〕adj. 一致的；不矛盾的
action-for-action 你一步，我一步　　principle〔ˈprɪnsəpḷ〕n. 原則
negotiation〔nɪˌgoʃɪˈeʃən〕n. 協商　　atomic〔əˈtɑmɪk〕adj. 原子的
expert〔ˈɛkspɝt〕n. 專家　　conduct〔kənˈdʌkt〕v. 執行；做
forensic〔fəˈrɛnsɪk〕adj. 鑑識的　　test〔tɛst〕n. 測試
permit〔pɚˈmɪt〕v. 允許　　verify〔ˈvɛrəˌfaɪ〕v. 證實
transfer〔ˈtrænsfɝ〕n. 轉移　　technology〔tɛkˈnɑlədʒɪ〕n. 科技
alleged〔əˈlɛdʒd〕adj. 謠傳的　　uranium〔juˈrenɪəm〕n. 鈾
enrichment〔ɪnˈrɪtʃmənt〕n. 富集　　program〔ˈprogræm〕n. 計畫

　　將北韓從名單中撤除，在美國總府華盛頓，以及美國與協商夥伴，中國、
南韓、俄國和日本的磋商會議中，引發好幾天激烈的內部討論。

* removal〔rɪˈmuvḷ〕n. 撤除　　intense〔ɪnˈtɛns〕adj. 激烈的
internal〔ɪnˈtɝnḷ〕adj. 內部的　　debate〔dɪˈbet〕n. 辯論；討論
Washington〔ˈwɑʃɪŋtən〕n. 華盛頓【美國首府，爲了和西北端的華盛頓州
　有所區別，常稱 Washington, D.C.】
consultation〔ˌkɑnsḷˈteʃən〕n. 諮商
negotiate〔nɪˈgoʃɪˌet〕v. 協商　　partner〔ˈpɑrtnɚ〕n. 夥伴

　　即使如此，要證實北韓的核能擴散，仍是一項嚴峻的挑戰，因爲即使不是
位居世界第一，它也是世界上最神秘且不透明化的政體之一。眼前會是一條顛
簸之路。

* *even so* 即使如此　　proliferation〔proˌlɪfəˈreʃən〕n. 擴散
serious〔ˈsɪrɪəs〕adj. 嚴峻的　　challenge〔ˈtʃælɪndʒ〕n. 挑戰
secret〔ˈsikrɪt〕adj. 神秘的　　opaque〔oˈpek〕adj. 不透明的
regime〔rɪˈʒim〕n. 政體　　entire〔ɪnˈtaɪr〕adj. 整個的
bumpy〔ˈbʌmpɪ〕adj. 顛簸的　　ahead〔əˈhɛd〕adv. 在前方

45.(**C**) 本文的主旨為何?

　　(A) 北韓不讓他人接近未公開的核子武器基地。

　　(B) 北韓答應再次停用主要的鈽元素裝置。

　　(C) <u>北韓被從恐怖主義黑名單中移除。</u>

　　(D) 世界對北韓的緊張情勢升高。

　　* block〔blɑk〕v. 阻礙　　　access〔'æksɛs〕n. 管道
　　　undeclared〔͵ʌndɪ'klɛrd〕adj. 未申報的　　　site〔saɪt〕n. 地點
　　　resume〔rɪ'zum〕v. 恢復　　disable〔dɪs'ebḷ〕v. 使無能力
　　　plutonium〔plu'tonɪəm〕n. 鈽【放射元素】
　　　heighten〔'haɪtn̩〕v. 升高　　tension〔'tɛnʃən〕n. 緊張（的情勢）

46.(**D**) 作者對於證實北韓核能擴散的態度為何?

　　(A) 樂觀的　　　　　　　　　　(B) 冷淡的

　　(C) 狂熱的　　　　　　　　　　(D) <u>懷疑的</u>

　　* optimistic〔͵ɑptə'mɪstɪk〕adj. 樂觀的
　　　indifferent〔ɪn'dɪfrənt〕adj. 冷淡的；漠不關心的
　　　enthusiastic〔ɪn͵θjuzɪ'æstɪk〕adj. 狂熱的
　　　skeptical〔'skɛptɪkḷ〕n. 懷疑的

47.(**D**) 北韓的犯罪行為「不」包含 ＿＿＿＿＿＿ 。

　　(A) 從事偽造活動並提供劫機犯庇護所

　　(B) 炸掉大韓航空的 858 班機

　　(C) 販售武器給離間份子

　　(D) <u>暗殺俄國的外交官</u>

48.(**A**) 根據本文,下列何者為非?

　　(A) <u>北韓曾經被指為是五個資助恐怖主義的國家之一。</u>

　　(B) 直到最近,北韓才被從恐怖主義的黑名單中移除。

　　(C) 北韓終於准許原子能專家,對它的核子設備,做鑑定測試。

　　(D) 把北韓從觀察名單中移除,是經由國際協商後才做出的決定。

第 49 至 52 題為題組

　　電腦科技現在正在改變人們傳統處理壓力的方式。網路上的支持團體範圍，從作為全面性心理健康醫療計畫中治療的一個部分，到單獨的支持系統。它們吸引各式各樣的成員，這些人之前可能曾經拒絕過同伴和傳統支持系統。滿意的成員回報，感覺到認同和支持，而不滿意的成員，雖然是少數，但他們表示挫折是由科技問題，和缺乏視覺、聽覺上的人際線索所引起的。

* technology〔tɛk'nɑlədʒɪ〕 *n.* 科技　　alter〔'ɔltɚ〕 *v.* 改變
traditional〔trə'dɪʃənḷ〕 *adj.* 傳統的　　handle〔'hændḷ〕 *v.* 處理
stress〔strɛs〕 *n.* 壓力　　online〔ˌɑn'laɪn〕 *adj.* 線上的
support group 支持團體　　***range from*** A ***to*** B（範圍）從 A 到 B 都有
therapeutic〔ˌθɛrə'pjutɪk〕 *adj.* 治療上的
component〔kəm'ponənt〕 *n.* 成分
comprehensive〔ˌkɑmprɪ'hɛnsɪv〕 *adj.* 全面的
mental〔'mɛntḷ〕 *adj.* 心理的　　treatment〔'tritmənt〕 *n.* 治療
serve as 作為　　sole〔sol〕 *adj.* 單一的　　attract〔ə'trækt〕 *v.* 吸引
a variety of 各式各樣的　　broad〔brɔd〕 *adj.* 廣大的
member〔'mɛmbɚ〕 *n.* 成員　　previously〔'privɪəslɪ〕 *adv.* 以前；事先
peer〔pɪr〕 *n.* 同儕　　satisfied〔'sætɪsˌfaɪd〕 *adj.* 滿意的
validation〔ˌvælə'deʃən〕 *n.* 認同；確認
dissatisfied〔dɪs'sætɪsˌfaɪd〕 *adj.* 不滿意的
express〔ɪk'sprɛs〕 *v.* 表達　　frustration〔frʌs'treʃən〕 *n.* 挫折
technological〔ˌtɛknə'lɑdʒɪkḷ〕 *adj.* 科技的　　absence〔'æbsns〕 *n.* 缺乏
visual〔'vɪʒuəl〕 *adj.* 視覺的　　auditory〔'ɔdəˌtorɪ〕 *adj.* 聽覺的
interpersonal〔ˌɪntɚ'pɝsnḷ〕 *adj.* 人與人之間的　　cue〔kju〕 *n.* 線索

　　線上的支持團體可以透過電腦和數據機，連上網路服務供應商而取得。一旦連結到網際網路服務，使用者就可以透過入口網站，或透過專門的網頁找到線上支持團體。

* access〔'æksɛs〕 *v.* 接近；取得　　modem〔'modɛm〕 *n.* 數據機
conjunction〔kən'dʒʌŋkʃən〕 *n.* 結合；連結
in conjunction with 連同　　provider〔prə'vaɪdɚ〕 *n.* 提供者
ISP 網際網路服務供應商　　connect〔kə'nɛkt〕 *v.* 連結
portal〔'portḷ〕 *n.* 開端；大門　　specialized〔'spɛʃəlˌaɪzd〕 *adj.* 專門的
website〔'wɛbˌsaɪt〕 *n.* 網站

　　線上支持團體藉著連結有類似問題的人，提供痛苦的人一種可選擇的支持媒介。它們可能可以改善取得支持的管道，並將支持送達廣泛的人群，包括某些一點都不想尋求面對面支持的人。最後，它們減少了由於地理遙遠，或身體／醫療限制所帶來的孤獨感，並增加認同感，不過，它們並非適合每一個人。

* **alternative** (ɔ'tɜnətɪv) *adj.* 可選擇的　　**vehicle** ('viɪkḷ) *n.* 媒介物
　distress (dɪ'strɛs) *n.* 苦惱　　**link** (lɪŋk) *v.* 連接
　issue ('ɪʃu) *n.* 議題；問題　　**potential** (pə'tɛnʃəl) *n.* 可能性；潛力
　improve (ɪm'pruv) *v.* 改善　　**delivery** (dɪ'lɪvərɪ) *n.* 傳送
　not…at all 一點也不…　　**seek** (sik) *v.* 尋求
　face-to-face ('festə'fes) *adj.* 面對面的　　**reduce** (rɪ'djus) *v.* 減少
　sense (sɛns) *n.* 感覺　　**isolation** (,aɪsḷ'eʃən) *n.* 孤獨
　geographic (,dʒiə'græfɪk) *adj.* 地理的　　**physical** ('fɪzɪkḷ) *adj.* 身體的
　medical ('mɛdɪkḷ) *adj.* 醫學的　　**constraint** (kən'strent) *n.* 限制；約束
　appropriate (ə'proprɪɪt) *adj.* 適合的

49. (**C**) 本文的標題最有可能是 ＿＿＿＿＿＿＿。
　　(A) 網路支持團體的限制
　　(B) 給看護者不同的網路支持團體
　　(C) <u>網路支持團體的優點</u>　　(D) 如何找到網路支持團體
　　* **limitation** (,lɪmə'teʃən) *n.* 限制；極限
　　　caregiver ('kɛr,gɪvɚ) *n.* 照料者；看護者

50. (**B**) 根據本文，我們可以推論作者 ＿＿＿＿＿＿＿。
　　(A) 是個直覺很敏銳的顧客
　　(B) <u>對網路支持團體有很正面的觀感</u>
　　(C) 是專業的芳香治療師　　(D) 是個天真的電腦程式設計師
　　* **infer** (ɪn'fɝ) *v.* 推論
　　　instinctively (ɪn'stɪŋktɪvlɪ) *adv.* 本能地；直覺地
　　　sharp (ʃɑrp) *adj.* 敏銳的　　**positive** ('pɑzətɪv) *adj.* 正面的；積極的
　　　opinion (ə'pɪnjən) *n.* 意見　　**professional** (prə'fɛʃənḷ) *adj.* 專業的
　　　aroma (ə'romə) *n.* 香味　　**therapist** ('θɛrəpɪst) *n.* 治療家
　　　unsophisticated (,ʌnsə'fɪstɪ,ketɪd) *adj.* 不諳世故的；天真的
　　　programmer ('progræmɚ) *n.* 程式設計者；節目編排者

51.(**D**) 根據本文，哪項關於網路支持團體的優點沒有提到？
　　(A) 較多管道可以得到支持。　　(B) 對自我價值有所提升。
　　(C) 有效性。　　(D) 有語言能力的限制。

　　* regarding〔rɪˋgɑrdɪŋ〕prep. 關於　　increased〔ɪnˋkrist〕adj. 較多的
　　improved〔ɪmˋpruvd〕adj. 改善的
　　self-worth〔ˋsɛlfˋwɝθ〕n. 自我價值

52.(**B**) 網路支持團體最適合哪一種人？
　　(A) 需要傳統諮詢講習的人。　　(B) 獨自住在偏遠地區的人。
　　(C) 參加太多課後活動的人。　　(D) 喜歡真誠又直率地講話的人。

　　* counseling〔ˋkaʊnslɪŋ〕n. 指導　　session〔ˋsɛʃən〕n. 講習會
　　isolate〔ˋaɪsḷˏet〕v. 使孤立　　remote〔rɪˋmot〕adj. 遙遠的
　　location〔loˋkeʃən〕n. 地方　　participate〔pɑrˋtɪsəˏpet〕v. 參加
　　after-school〔ˋæftɚ skul〕adj. 課後的
　　communicate〔kəˋmjunəˏket〕v. 溝通
　　honestly〔ˋɑnɪstlɪ〕adv. 真誠地　　openly〔ˋopənlɪ〕adv. 率直地

第 53 至 56 題為題組

　　像是蛇、狗、貓、小型齧齒動物，譬如松鼠、某些昆蟲和蜘蛛，這些動物，咬了人後，可能會有危險的後果。舉例來說，被毒蛇咬到後，需要立即的急救措施。

　　* rodent〔ˋrodṇt〕n. 齧齒動物　　squirrel〔ˋskwɝəl〕n. 松鼠
　　certain〔ˋsɝtṇ〕adj. 若干的　　insect〔ˋɪnsɛkt〕n. 昆蟲
　　spider〔ˋspaɪdɚ〕n. 蜘蛛　　bite〔baɪt〕v. 咬　　n. 咬傷（的傷口）
　　consequence〔ˋkɑnsəˏkwɛns〕n. 後果　　inflict〔ɪnˋflɪkt〕v. 施加（傷害）
　　venomous〔ˋvɛnəməs〕adj. 有毒的　　immediate〔ɪˋmidɪɪt〕adj. 立刻的
　　first-aid〔ˋfɝstˋed〕n. adj. 急救（的）　　measure〔ˋmɛʒɚ〕n. 措施

　　必須盡快將傷者送到最近的緊急醫療設施。同時，施予急救者不該把被咬傷的附近切除、不該試著把毒液吸出來，或把冰塊敷在傷口上。急救的要點，應該是阻止毒液在人體的血流中迅速擴散。傷者必須保持冷靜，避免刺激毒液的循環。此外，咬傷的區域應該要保持在比身體其他部分還低的地方。傷口必須用肥皂和水徹底地清洗、用毛巾吸乾，再用消毒過的包紮用品寬鬆地覆蓋在上面。

* victim〔'vɪktɪm〕*n.* 受害者　　emergency〔ɪ'mɜdʒənsɪ〕*adj.* 緊急的
medical〔'mɛdɪkl̩〕*adj.* 醫療的　　facility〔fə'sɪlətɪ〕*n.* 設施
interim〔'ɪntərɪm〕*n.* 中間時間　***in the interim*** 在那時候
attempt〔ə'tɛmpt〕*v.* 嘗試；企圖　　suck〔sʌk〕*v.* 吸
venom〔'vɛnəm〕*n.* 毒；毒液　　***apply*** A ***to*** B　將 A 塗於 B 上
wound〔wund〕*n.* 傷口　　focus〔'fokəs〕*n.* 焦點
first aid 急救　　***prevent*** sth. ***from*** V-ing　使某物不受～
rapidly〔'ræpɪdlɪ〕*adv.* 迅速地　　individual〔ˌɪndə'vɪdʒʊəl〕*n.* 個人
bloodstream〔'blʌd,strim〕*n.* 血流　　stimulate〔'stɪmjə,let〕*v.* 刺激
circulation〔ˌsɜkjə'leʃən〕*n.* 循環　　***in addition*** 除此之外
level〔'lɛvl̩〕*n.* 水平；高度　　rest〔rɛst〕*n.* 剩餘部分
thoroughly〔'θɜolɪ〕*adv.* 徹底地　　blot〔blɑt〕*v.* 吸乾
loosely〔'luslɪ〕*adv.* 鬆地　　cover〔'kʌvɚ〕*v.* 蓋；遮蔽
sterile〔'stɛrəl〕*adj.* 殺菌過的　　dressing〔'drɛsɪŋ〕*n.* 繃帶；包紮用品

　　會咬人的昆蟲，包括跳蚤、蚊子、臭蟲、蝨子、沙蚤和蚋。被這些昆蟲咬到的傷口，應該清洗乾淨以防感染，可以施予冰敷或是局部的藥物，以減輕搔癢和痛苦。

* flea〔fli〕*n.* 跳蚤　　mosquito〔mə'skito〕*n.* 蚊子
bedbug〔'bɛd,bʌg〕*n.* 臭蟲　　louse〔laus〕*n.* 蝨子【複數為 lice】
chigger〔'tʃɪgɚ〕*n.* 沙蚤　　gnat〔næt〕*n.* 蚋
infection〔ɪn'fɛkʃən〕*n.* 感染　　compress〔'kɑmprɛs〕*n.* 繃帶；壓布
cold compress 冷敷　　topical〔'tɑpɪkl̩〕*adj.* 局部的
medication〔ˌmɛdɪ'keʃən〕*n.* 藥物　　alleviate〔ə'livɪ,et〕*v.* 減輕
itching〔'ɪtʃɪŋ〕*n.* 癢

　　來自其他動物的咬傷，應該要徹底地清潔，用有抗生素的軟膏治療並包紮。如果是嚴重的咬傷，患者應該要尋求醫療照顧。被其他人咬傷，特別容易有嚴重的細菌感染，必須要由醫學專業人士來治療。被大部分的蜘蛛咬傷，要像被其他昆蟲咬到一樣來治療。但是被黑寡婦蜘蛛咬傷，所需要的醫療幫助，要像是被毒蛇咬傷一樣。

* treat〔trit〕*v.* 治療　　antibiotic〔ˌæntɪbaɪ'ɑtɪk〕*adj.* 抗生的
ointment〔'ɔɪntmənt〕*n.* 軟膏　　bandage〔'bændɪdʒ〕*v.* 用繃帶包紮
attention〔ə'tɛnʃən〕*n.* 照顧　　***medical attention*** 醫療照顧
severe〔sə'vɪr〕*adj.* 嚴重的　　particularly〔pə'tɪkjələ·lɪ〕*adv.* 尤其地

be prone to 容易~ bacterial〔bæk'tɪrɪəl〕*adj.* 細菌的
professional〔prə'fɛʃənḷ〕*n.* 專業人士 widow〔'wɪdo〕*n.* 寡婦
black widow spider 黑寡婦蜘蛛 similarly〔'sɪmələlɪ〕*adv.* 相似地
poisonous〔'pɔɪznəs〕*adj.* 有毒的 snakebite〔'snek,baɪt〕*n.* 蛇咬傷

53.（**B**）在被咬傷的人被送到最近的緊急醫療設施之前，急救的施行者應該

　　　　　　　　　。
(A) 把冰塊敷在傷口上 (B) 讓傷口保持在身體較低的位置
(C) 試著吸出血液 (D) 把咬傷的附近區域切除

54.（**C**）關於會咬人的昆蟲，文章中沒有提到哪一個？
(A) 沙蚤 (B) 臭蟲 (C) 蜻蜓 (D) 蚊子
* dragonfly〔'drægən,flaɪ〕*n.* 蜻蜓

55.（**D**）根據本文，被 　　　　　　 咬傷最容易受到細菌感染。
(A) 蜘蛛 (B) 蛇 (C) 狗 (D) 人
* vulnerable〔'vʌlnərəbḷ〕*adj.* 脆弱的
be vulnerable to 易受…影響的

56.（**D**）下列哪個字最能解釋第一段的 "**venomous**" 這個字？
(A) 沒有禮貌的 (B) 頑皮的 (C) 流浪的 (D) 有毒的
* ill-mannered〔'ɪl'mænəd〕*adj.* 沒禮貌的
mischievous〔'mɪstʃɪvəs〕*adj.* 頑皮的
wandering〔'wɑndərɪŋ〕*adj.* 流浪的；蜿蜒的

第貳部分：非選擇題
一、中譯英：

1. 青少年看漫畫來消磨時間或紓解壓力。

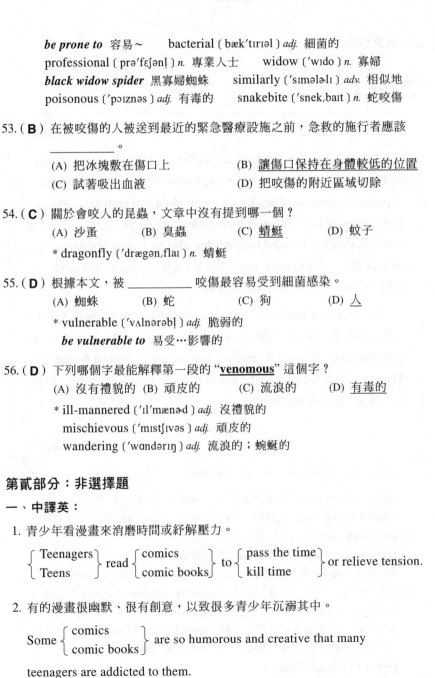

2. 有的漫畫很幽默、很有創意，以致很多青少年沉溺其中。

Some $\left\{ \begin{array}{l} \text{comics} \\ \text{comic books} \end{array} \right\}$ are so humorous and creative that many

teenagers are addicted to them.

二、英文作文：

作文範例

Dear Mr. Thomas,   Jan. 28, 2013

I'm still surprised to have my wallet back—with all the money and credit cards intact. Believe me, I never in my wildest dreams expected to have someone knock on my door and return the property I so carelessly lost. What an incredible thing for you to do! And I'm not only shocked by your honesty, but also by your willingness to deliver the wallet to my home. The average person would have called to arrange for me to pick it up.

In the past, when I lost something precious, like my wallet or my cell phone, my first reaction was to kiss it goodbye. I certainly never expected to get it back. Therefore, you are a very special person, Mr. Thomas. If all the kids in the world had you for a role model, there would be no need for prisons.

Sincerely,
Frank Dodd

surprised〔sə'praɪzd〕*adj.* 驚訝的　　wallet〔'walɪt〕*n.* 皮夾
intact〔ɪn'tækt〕*adj.* 完好的　　property〔'prɑpɚtɪ〕*n.* 財產；所有物
carelessly〔'kɛrlɪslɪ〕*adv.* 不小心地
incredible〔ɪn'krɛdəbḷ〕*adj.* 令人難以置信的
shocked〔ʃɑkt〕*adj.* 震驚的　　willingness〔'wɪlɪŋnɪs〕*n.* 願意
deliver〔dɪ'lɪvɚ〕*v.* 遞送；交付　***average person*** 一般人；平常人
arrange〔ə'rendʒ〕*v.* 安排；準備　　precious〔'prɛʃəs〕*adj.* 珍貴的
reaction〔rɪ'ækʃən〕*n.* 反應　***kiss goodbye*** 吻別；被迫放棄
model〔'mɑdḷ〕*n.* 榜樣；典範　***role model*** 模範
prison〔'prɪzn̩〕*n.* 監獄

大學入學學科能力測驗英文模擬試題 ⑤

第壹部分：單選題（佔 72 分）

一、詞彙（佔 15 分）

說明： 第 1 題至第 15 題，每題 4 個選項，其中只有一個是最適當的答案，畫記在答案卡之「選擇題答案區」。各題答對得 1 分；未作答、答錯、或畫記多於一個選項者，該題以零分計算。

1. Jack studies Latin because he wants to read Latin poetry in its _____ form.
   (A) major   (B) minor   (C) original   (D) central

2. Mother Teresa is _____ for her devotion to helping the sick and the poor in India.
   (A) discouraged (B) committed   (C) wondered   (D) admired

3. The young man was not able to control his bodily _____ after a motorbike accident.
   (A) functions   (B) situations   (C) connections   (D) limitations

4. Many people held a _____ outside the building, accusing the banks of giving them the wrong information about investment products.
   (A) protect   (B) protest   (C) cure   (D) defect

5. Though Ms. Su Li-wen did not win a medal, she is viewed as the most _____ of Taiwanese athletes in the Beijing Olympics.
   (A) extracurricular   (B) sarcastic
   (C) intentional   (D) outstanding

6. The government should take _____ action on the weakening economy; more and more people are losing their jobs.
   (A) serene   (B) inactive   (C) immediate   (D) negative

7. You can write my number down for future _____; you might need it some day.
   (A) reference   (B) schedule   (C) relation   (D) regard

8. Jack is very _____ in his job and that's why he was promoted so fast.
   (A) careless   (B) competent   (C) inaccurate   (D) flexible

9. A nearly pollution-free motorcycle was introduced recently to provide a(n) _____ to the problem of pollution on Taiwan's streets.
   (A) division   (B) solution   (C) production   (D) addition

10. Mountain climbers should always _____ themselves with the best, just in case an accident happens.
    (A) equip   (B) embrace   (C) celebrate   (D) acquire

11. Too much sun exposure might cause skin cancer, but many youths seem unaware of this danger in the _____ of a bronzed body.
    (A) pursue   (B) chase   (C) glance   (D) pursuit

12. Be sure to stir the soup _____, so it won't get burned on the bottom.
    (A) constantly   (B) recklessly   (C) reluctantly   (D) eventually

13. Mrs. Chen is always _____ about how rich her husband is and how many expensive things he buys her.
    (A) boasting   (B) bearing   (C) imposing   (D) calculating

14. It is _____ that Kim would speak ill of you; she is such a nice girl.
    (A) generous   (B) unforgiving   (C) critical   (D) unlikely

15. If you can't _____ the information you require from this book, you'll have to go to the library.
    (A) retain   (B) maintain   (C) obtain   (D) regain

二、綜合測驗（佔 15 分）

說明：　第 16 題至第 30 題，每題一個空格，請依文意選出最適當的一個答案，
　　　　畫記在答案卡之「選擇題答案區」。各題答對得 1 分；未作答、答錯、
　　　　或畫記多於一個選項者，該題以零分計算。

第 16 至 20 題為題組

　　We all forget things once in a while. Maybe we've forgotten to
send a card for someone's birthday or to return a(n) ___16___ library
book. Forgetting stuff is a part of life and it often becomes more
common ___17___ people age. But Alzheimer's disease, which ___18___
some older people, is different from everyday forgetting. It is a
condition that permanently influences the brain, and over time, makes it
harder to remember even basic stuff, like how to tie a shoe. ___19___,
the person may have trouble remembering the names of family members,
or even who he or she is. This can be very sad for the person and his or her
family. Researchers have found medicines that seem to ___20___ the
disease ___20___. And there's hope that someday there will be a cure.

16. (A) best-selling　(B) overdue　　(C) lately　　(D) outdated
17. (A) as　　　　　(B) despite　　(C) with　　　(D) though
18. (A) effects　　　(B) infects　　(C) affects　　(D) benefits
19. (A) Contrarily　　(B) Delightedly　(C) At first　　(D) Eventually
20. (A) turn ; up　　(B) rid ; of　　(C) put ; up　　(D) slow ; down

第 21 至 25 題為題組

　　For thousands of years, black cats have been seen as mysterious
animals with supernatural powers. They have been associated ___21___
witches and even death. It was believed that witches could change into
cats and ___22___ that change nine times. Some believe this to be the
origin of the belief ___23___ cats have nine lives.

　　There are many superstitions related to cats, partly because the cat
has lived with humans for such a long time. Superstitions ___24___ on

the black cat are some of the most well-known today. Do you worry
when a black cat crosses your path? It may depend on where you live in
the world. In Britain and Japan, when a black cat crosses your path, it is
considered good luck; ___25___, if you live in the USA or some European
countries, it is bad luck to have a black cat cross in front of you.

21. (A) with   (B) to   (C) for   (D) by
22. (A) do   (B) make   (C) have   (D) take
23. (A) when   (B) which   (C) why   (D) that
24. (A) centered   (B) center   (C) to center   (D) being centered
25. (A) for example   (B) that is to say   (C) however   (D) as a result

第 26 至 30 題爲題組

One of the things that makes Punahou very special is its location.
___26___ in Hawaii, the campus is covered with large, open-air playing
fields and lush trees, making it a year-round green beauty. ___27___
nearly 30 academic buildings, the school has a quarter-mile outdoor
track, eight tennis courts, and an ___28___ swimming pool. Every year
the junior class organizes the Punahou Carnival, a two-day whirlwind
event which generates money for the class's senior year. Every
February the front fields are transformed into a full-fledged carnival,
complete ___29___ games, food, and all sorts of amusement park rides.
The carnival is a favorite island ___30___ and is so popular that it
manages to bring in over a million dollars over the course of two days.

26. (A) To situate   (B) Situating
    (C) Situated   (D) Having situated
27. (A) On account of   (B) In addition to
    (C) As a result   (D) Despite
28. (A) Olympic-sized   (B) Olympic-in-size
    (C) Olympic-sizing   (D) Olympic-large
29. (A) by   (B) for   (C) in   (D) with
30. (A) situation   (B) play   (C) contest   (D) event

三、文意選填（佔 10 分）

說明：第 31 題至第 40 題，每題一個空格，請依文意在文章後所提供的 (A) 到 (J) 選項中分別選出最適當者，並將其英文字母代號畫記在答案卡之「選擇題答案區」。各題答對得 1 分；未作答、答錯、或畫記多於一個選項者，該題以零分計算。

第 31 至 40 題為題組

　　In 1974, a little girl was born without arms and abandoned in a marketplace. She was brought to the Liukuei Christian Orphanage, ___31___ in the mountainous region of Kaohsiung County. Believing that the baby was "sent by the Lord," Father Yang, the orphanage's founder, named the infant Yang En-dian, ___32___ "grace and benevolence from God."

　　Little ___33___ Father Yang know that the child would grow up and develop a legendary friendship with then-President Chiang Ching-kuo. Out of ___34___, President Chiang developed a special attachment ___35___ the child and arranged for her to receive ___36___ in Taipei to help straighten her spine and allow her to stand unaided. He even arranged for her to learn Chinese brush painting and calligraphy. The child became famous ___37___ a picture of her and President Chiang was made into a postage stamp.

　　Yang did not let the president ___38___. She learned to paint with her feet and earned her own ___39___ by selling her art works. She said that the light colors used in her paintings signified her smile and happiness. Whatever the type of painting, ___40___ is certain is that behind each painting rest years of her efforts to achieve the standard she has set. It is certain that Yang will continue using her feet to create miracles for people who appreciate her paintings.

(A) what　　(B) after　　(C) located　　(D) did　　(E) down

(F) to　　(G) surgery　　(H) pity　　(I) which means　(J) living

四、閱讀測驗（佔 32 分）

說明：第 41 題至第 56 題，每題 4 個選項，請分別根據各篇文章之文意選出最適當的一個答案，畫記在答案卡之「選擇題答案區」。各題答對得 2 分；未作答、答錯、或畫記多於一個選項者，該題以零分計算。

第 41 至 44 題為題組

People have seen the birth of a new language, one invented by deaf children. A recent study shows that a sign language that emerged over two decades ago now counts as a true language. It began in a school for the deaf in Managua, Nicaragua, which was founded in 1977. With instruction only in lip-reading and speaking Spanish, neither very successful, and no exposure to adult signing, the children were left to their own devices.

Their first **pantomime-like gestures** evolved into a grammar of increasing complexity as new children learned the signs and elaborated. Now it has a formal name: Nicaraguan Sign Language, (NSL), and is so distinct that it would not be understood by American and British signers.

NSL, now with 800 signers worldwide, aged from 4 to 45, counts as a language, according to a recently published study. "We're seeing evolution in action, but what's evolving here isn't an organism. It's a language system," Dr Ann Senghas, of Barnard College of Columbia University, said. The new language bears remarkable similarities to other languages, supporting the theory that children are born with an innate understanding of language.

41. What is the main idea of the passage?
    (A) NSL is rejected because not many people understand it.
    (B) Deaf children need to have a new language for their communication.
    (C) A new sign language system has been developed to help the deaf.
    (D) Children can learn a language without being taught formally.

42. Where might this passage appear?
    (A) A fashion magazine.　　　(B) A science journal.
    (C) A travel brochure.　　　(D) A dictionary.

43. What does "**pantomime-like gestures**" refer to?
　　(A) Using many bodily movements.
　　(B) Being difficult for children to understand.
　　(C) Easy to pick up.
　　(D) Similar to animal gestures.

44. Which of the following statements is TRUE?
　　(A) NSL was first invented by schoolteachers in Nicaragua.
　　(B) Theoretically speaking, NSL and other languages have nothing in common.
　　(C) When NSL was first invented, it was widely accepted by deaf children.
　　(D) Signers in other countries might have difficulty understanding NSL.

第 45 至 48 題爲題組

　　Have you ever heard of Frank Towers? He is the questionable figure who supposedly survived three doomed ships in the 1900s. Some considered him one of the luckiest men alive. He was **said** to be a middle-aged fireman in the engine room. Some considered him an ordinary, hardworking person, but he had the ability to avoid dying in some of the most horrible ocean liner accidents ever recorded.

　　He was said to have been a crew member on the Titanic at the time that the ship hit the iceberg. Two years later, he was working on the *Empress of Ireland* when she collided with the *Storstad*. Over one thousand people died in that disaster. He was then employed on the *Lusitania*. In May of 1915, it was hit by a U-20 torpedo. He apparently lived through that without a scratch as well. If you are beginning to doubt this man's existence, you are probably not too far from the truth. No records have ever been found listing a man by the name of Frank Towers working on any of the three ships.

　　The legend of Frank Towers seems to be another case of an urban folk tale and humanity's desire to see man triumph over a tragic situation. Fact or fiction, Frank Towers is one of the multiple characters that help color the history books.

45. What does "**said**" mean in the passage?
    (A) Reported.   (B) Promoted.   (C) Set-up.   (D) Sighted.

46. What might be the best title for the passage?
    (A) "Frank Towers, a Man of Mystery"
    (B) "Saving the Impossible"
    (C) "The Legend of Frank Towers Debunked"
    (D) "How to Survive a Sinking Ship"

47. Which of the following best describes the purpose of the passage?
    (A) A stitch in time saves nine.
    (B) Don't believe everything you read.
    (C) Seeing is believing.
    (D) There are many layers of an onion.

48. According to the passage, what is an urban folk tale?
    (A) An interesting news story.   (B) An unproven story.
    (C) A mystery story.   (D) A triumph over tragedy.

第 49 至 52 題為題組

　　One of the most dangerous drugs for pregnant women to consume is alcohol. Because alcohol is delivered quickly into the blood and passes quickly into the tissues and membranes, the human fetus is particularly vulnerable to its effects. In fact, the negative effects on a fetus are so obvious that babies born after exposure to alcohol are said to be suffering from fetal alcohol syndrome.

　　As a pregnant woman drinks alcohol, the alcohol is passed into her bloodstream almost simultaneously. Moreover, because the bloodstream of the fetus is tied to that of the mother, the alcohol passes directly into the bloodstream of the fetus as well. Furthermore, the concentration of alcohol in the fetus is exactly the same as in the mother. For the mother, this concentration is not a problem because her liver can remove one ounce of alcohol from her system per hour. However, the fetus's liver is not completely developed. The rate at which it is able to take the alcohol from the blood of the fetus is much slower. Eventually, the alcohol will be returned to the mother's system by passing across the placenta, but this process is slow. By the time this takes place, major neurological damage may have already occurred. Research has shown that as little as one drink of alcohol can produce significant, irreversible damage to the fetus. Babies born after exposure to alcohol generally exhibit facial distortion, inability to concentrate, and difficulty in remembering. Simply speaking, it is a must that pregnant women avoid alcohol.

49. What is the passage mainly about?
   (A) Women and drugs.
   (B) The dangers of pregnancy.
   (C) The dangers of drinking while pregnant.
   (D) Drinking and the human body.

50. How much time does it take alcohol to enter a woman's bloodstream after she takes a drink?
   (A) About one hour.　　　(B) A few seconds.
   (C) Several minutes.　　　(D) At least 24 hours.

51. What can be inferred from the passage?
   (A) Drugs have a greater effect on a fetus than they do on its mother.
   (B) It takes only one alcoholic drink to kill a fetus.
   (C) Large fetuses are not adversely affected by alcohol.
   (D) Fathers should also avoid alcohol when expecting a child.

52. According to the passage, how is alcohol finally returned to the mother's system?
   (A) It is carried through the bloodstream.
   (B) It is transferred across the placenta.
   (C) It is expelled by the fetus's liver.
   (D) It is not completely returned.

第 53 至 56 題爲題組

   Now an accepted practice, education of the blind was not always commonplace. In ancient civilizations, the blind were not generally considered members of normal society, and they survived primarily by begging. And although many civilizations provided the blind with places to live, it was not until the early 19th century that a significant advance in their education was made, when Louis Braille devised a method of reading for the blind, based on the sense of touch. Braille's idea for his system was derived from a similar system invented by Charles Barbier to provide the possibility for communication on battlefields during the night. Braille modified the system somewhat, basing his on six possible positions, arranged in two vertical rows of three positions each. The absence or presence of raised dots in each position determines the letter, number, or punctuation sign. Since this invention, the education of the blind has improved immensely.

With the Braille system, schools for blind children were soon established; almost 40 existed by the turn of the century. An even greater advance was made when the blind began to be incorporated into normal classes. Today, most blind children are educated in normal classes, and **many** continue with their educations to the college and graduate school levels.

53. The passage is mainly concerned with ＿＿＿＿＿＿.
    (A) the Barbier system   (B) mistreatment of the blind
    (C) education of the blind   (D) systems of reading

54. The word "**many**" in the last sentence of the last paragraph refers to ＿＿＿＿＿＿.
    (A) blind children   (B) normal classes
    (C) teenagers   (D) high school students

55. Which of the following does the author NOT mention as an advancement in the education of the blind?
    (A) the development of a reading system
    (B) the establishment of graduate schools for the blind
    (C) the integration of the blind into normal classes
    (D) the establishment of schools for blind children

56. It can be inferred from the passage that Charles Barbier's system of communication _____.
   (A) was based on the sense of touch
   (B) was used earlier so that the blind could read
   (C) had two rows of three positions
   (D) did not have only six possible positions

第貳部分：非選擇題（佔 28 分）

一、中譯英（佔 8 分）

說明： 1. 請將以下中文句子譯成正確、通順、達意的英文，並將答案寫在「答案卷」上。

2. 請依序作答，並標明題號。每題 4 分，共 8 分。

1. 肢體語言能抵過千言萬語；小小的動作或手勢就能傳達很多意思。

2. 注意自己的肢體語言，能幫助你給別人正面的印象。

二、英文作文（佔 20 分）

說明： 1. 依提示在「答案卷」上寫一篇英文作文。

2. 文長約 100 至 120 個單詞（words）。

提示：你和朋友有晚餐的約定，但是你失約。你（英文名字必須假設為 Robin 或 Lisa），要寫一封道歉信給你的朋友（英文名字必須假設為 John 或 Mindy），說明你為何失約，並如何補償此次的約定。

請注意：必須使用上述的 Robin 或 Lisa 在信末署名，**不得使用自己的真實中文或英文名字**。

大學入學學科能力測驗英文模擬試題 ⑤ 詳解

第壹部分：單選題

一、詞彙：

1. (**C**) 傑克學拉丁文是因爲他想用<u>原文</u>來閱讀拉丁詩集。
    (A) major〔'medʒɚ〕 *adj.* 較大的；主要的 (= *principal* = *chief*)
    (B) minor〔'maɪnɚ〕 *adj.* 較小的；次要的 (= *secondary* = *subordinate*)
    (C) ***original***〔ə'rɪdʒən!〕 *adj.* 原本的
    (D) central〔'sɛntrəl〕 *adj.* 中心的
    * poetry〔'po‧ɪtrɪ〕 *n.* 詩　　form〔fɔrm〕 *n.* 形式；語形

2. (**D**) 泰瑞莎修女由於致力於幫助印度的病人和窮人而受到<u>景仰</u>。
    (A) discourage〔dɪs'kɝɪdʒ〕 *v.* 使氣餒 (↔ encourage)
    (B) commit〔kə'mɪt〕 *v.* 委託；犯 (罪)　　commit suicide 自殺
    (C) wonder〔'wʌndɚ〕 *v.* 好奇；驚訝
    (D) ***admire***〔əd'maɪr〕 *v.* 欽佩 (= *adore*)
    * Mother〔'mʌðɚ〕 *n.* 修女　　devotion〔dɪ'voʃən〕 *n.* 奉獻
    the sick 病人　　***the poor*** 窮人　　India〔'ɪndɪə〕 *n.* 印度

3. (**A**) 這位年輕人在一場摩托車意外事故後，失去控制身體<u>機能</u>的能力。
    (A) ***function***〔'fʌŋkʃən〕 *n.* 機能；功能
    (B) situation〔͵sɪtʃu'eʃən〕 *n.* 情況
    (C) connection〔kə'nɛkʃən〕 *n.* 關聯　　in connection with 關於
    (D) limitation〔͵lɪmə'teʃən〕 *n.* 限制　　limit *v.*
    * bodily〔'badɪlɪ〕 *adj.* 身體的　　motorbike〔'motɚ͵baɪk〕 *n.* 摩托車

4. (**B**) 許多人在這棟建築外舉行<u>抗議</u>，控訴銀行給他們不正確的投資產品訊息。
    (A) protect〔prə'tɛkt〕 *v.* 保護　　protection *n.*
    (B) ***protest***〔'protɛst〕 *n.* 抗議　　〔prə'tɛst〕 *v.* 抗議
    (C) cure〔kjur〕 *n.* 治療法 (= *remedy*)
    (D) defect〔dɪ'fɛkt〕 *n.* 缺陷；缺點 (= *shortcoming*)
    * hold〔hold〕 *v.* 舉行　　accuse〔ə'kjuz〕 *v.* 指控
    investment〔ɪn'vɛstmənt〕 *n.* 投資　　product〔'pradəkt〕 *n.* 產品

5. (**D**) 雖然蘇麗文小姐並沒有奪得獎牌，但她卻被視爲在北京奧運中最<u>傑出</u>的台灣運動員。

　　(A) extracurricular〔͵ɛkstrəkə'rɪkjələ〕*adj.* 課外的

　　(B) sarcastic〔sɑr'kæstɪk〕*adj.* 諷刺的

　　(C) intentional〔ɪn'tɛnʃənḷ〕*adj.* 有意的；故意的　　intention *n.*

　　(D) ***outstanding***〔'aʊt'stændɪŋ〕*adj.* 傑出的（ = *prominent* ）

　　* medal〔'mɛdḷ〕*n.* 獎牌　　***be viewed as*** 被視爲

　　　Beijing〔'beˈdʒɪŋ〕*n.* 北京　　Olympics〔o'lɪmpɪks〕*n.* 奧運會

　　　the Olympics 奧運會（ = *the Olympic games* ）

6. (**C**) 政府應該對日漸疲軟的經濟採取<u>立即</u>行動；失業人口越來越多了。

　　(A) serene〔sə'rin〕*adj.* 平靜的（ = *calm* ）

　　(B) inactive〔ɪn'æktɪv〕*adj.* 不活潑的；無活動力的

　　(C) ***immediate***〔ɪ'midɪɪt〕*adj.* 立即的　　immediately *adv.*

　　(D) negative〔'nɛgətɪv〕*adj.* 否定的；負面的（ ↔ positive ）

　　* ***take action*** 採取行動　　weaken〔'wikən〕*v.* 衰弱

　　　economy〔ɪ'kɑnəmɪ〕*n.* 經濟　　***lose one's job*** 失業

7. (**A**) 你可以寫下我的電話號碼以供將來<u>參考</u>，有天你可能會需要它。

　　(A) ***reference***〔'rɛfərəns〕*n.* 參考　　for reference only 僅供參考

　　(B) schedule〔'skɛdʒul〕*n.* 預定表　　*v.* 安排時間

　　　on schedule 按照進度　　behind schedule 進度落後

　　(C) relation〔rɪ'leʃən〕*n.* 關聯　　in / with relation to 有關

　　(D) regard〔rɪ'gɑrd〕*n.* 關於；尊敬　　regarding *prep.* 關於

　　* ***write down*** 寫下；記下

8. (**B**) 傑克工作<u>能力</u>很強，這就是他能迅速升遷的原因。

　　(A) careless〔'kɛrlɪs〕*adj.* 粗心的（ ↔ careful ）

　　(B) ***competent***〔'kɑmpətənt〕*adj.* 能勝任的；能幹的

　　(C) inaccurate〔ɪn'ækjərɪt〕*adj.* 不正確的（ = *inexact* ）

　　(D) flexible〔'flɛksəbḷ〕*adj.* 有彈性的（ ↔ inflexible ）

　　* promote〔prə'mot〕*v.* 升職

9. (**B**) 最近有種幾乎無污染的摩托車問世，提供台灣街道污染問題一個<u>解決之道</u>。

　　(A) division〔dəˋvɪʒən〕n. 分割；部門 (= department)

　　(B) **solution**〔səˋluʃən〕n. 解決之道 < to >

　　(C) production〔prəˋdʌkʃən〕n. 製造；生產

　　　　in production 生產中

　　(D) addition〔əˋdɪʃən〕n. 附加；加法

　　　　in addition 此外　　in addition to 除了～之外 (還有)

　　* nearly〔ˋnɪrlɪ〕adv. 幾乎　　pollution〔pəˋluʃən〕n. 污染

　　　pollution-free〔pəˋluʃənˋfri〕adj. 無污染的

　　　introduce〔ˌɪntrəˋdjus〕v. 使 (商品) 問世

　　　provide〔prəˋvaɪd〕v. 提供

10. (**A**) 登山者永遠都必須<u>配置</u>最好的裝備，以防萬一意外發生。

　　(A) **equip**〔ɪˋkwɪp〕v. 使配備 (用具) < with >　　equipment n.

　　(B) embrace〔ɪmˋbres〕v. 擁抱 (= hug)；包含 (= contain)

　　(C) celebrate〔ˋsɛləˌbret〕v. 慶祝

　　(D) acquire〔əˋkwaɪr〕v. 獲得 (= obtain)

　　* climber〔ˋklaɪmɚ〕n. 登山者　　**in case** 以防萬一

　　　accident〔ˋæksədənt〕n. 意外

11. (**D**) 過量的陽光曝曬會引發皮膚癌，但很多年輕人在<u>追求</u>身體曬成古銅色的時候，似乎沒察覺到這樣的危險。

　　(A) pursue〔pɚˋsu〕v. 追趕；追求

　　(B) chase〔tʃes〕v. 追趕 (獵物等)

　　(C) glance〔glæns〕n. 一瞥　　at a glance 一看就⋯

　　(D) **pursuit**〔pɚˋsut〕n. 追求　　in the pursuit of sth. 追求某事物

　　* exposure〔ɪkˋspoʒɚ〕n. 暴露

　　　cause〔kɔz〕v. 引起　　cancer〔ˋkænsɚ〕n. 癌症

　　　unaware〔ˌʌnəˋwɛr〕adj. 未察覺的

　　　bronzed〔brɑnzd〕adj. (皮膚曬得) 古銅色的

12. (**A**) 煮湯一定要<u>經常</u>攪拌，這樣底部才不會燒焦。

　　(A) ***constantly*** 〔'kɑnstəntlɪ〕*adv.* 經常地　　constancy *n.* 不變

　　(B) recklessly 〔'rɛklɪslɪ〕*adv.* 魯莽地 (↔ cautiously)

　　(C) reluctantly 〔rɪ'lʌktəntlɪ〕*adv.* 不情願地 (↔ willingly)

　　(D) eventually 〔ɪ'vɛntʃʊəlɪ〕*adv.* 最後 (= *ultimately*)

　　* ***be sure to*** 一定要　　stir 〔stɜ〕*v.* 攪拌

　　　burn 〔bɜn〕*v.* 燒焦　　bottom 〔'bɑtəm〕*n.* 底部

13. (**A**) 陳太太總愛<u>吹噓</u>說她的丈夫多有錢，又買了多少昂貴的東西給她。

　　(A) ***boast*** 〔bost〕*v.* 吹噓；(物、地方) 以擁有…而自豪

　　(B) bear 〔bɛr〕*v.* 有；忍受 (= *endure* = *tolerate* = *stand*)

　　(C) impose 〔ɪm'poz〕*v.* 強加

　　(D) calculate 〔'kælkjə,let〕*v.* 計算 (= *count*)

14. (**D**) <u>金</u>不太可能會說你的壞話，她是個好女孩。

　　(A) generous 〔'dʒɛnərəs〕*adj.* 慷慨的 (↔ stingy)

　　(B) unforgiving 〔,ʌnfə'gɪvɪŋ〕*adj.* 不寬恕的

　　(C) critical 〔'krɪtɪkl〕*adj.* 批評的　　criticize *v.* 批評

　　(D) ***unlikely*** 〔ʌn'laɪklɪ〕*adj.* 不可能的 (↔ likely)

　　* ***speak ill of*** *sb.* 說某人的壞話

15. (**C**) 如果無法在這本書中<u>獲得</u>你需要的資訊，那就必須去圖書館找。

　　(A) retain 〔rɪ'ten〕*v.* 保留 (= *withhold*)

　　(B) maintain 〔men'ten〕*v.* 維持

　　(C) ***obtain*** 〔əb'ten〕*v.* 獲得　　obtainable *adj.* 可獲得的

　　(D) regain 〔rɪ'gen〕*v.* 復得 (= *recover*)

　　* require 〔rɪ'kwaɪr〕*v.* 需要

二、綜合測驗：

<u>第 16 至 20 題為題組</u>

　　我們偶爾都會忘記事情，可能是忘記寄生日卡給某人，或是忘記去還圖書館<u>過期的</u>書。

16

　　* ***once in a while*** 有時　　return 〔rɪ'tɜn〕*v.* 歸還

16. (**B**) (A) best-selling〔'bɛst'sɛlɪŋ〕 *adj.* 暢銷的
　　　　　(B) ***overdue***〔'ovɚ'dju〕 *adj.* 過期的
　　　　　(C) lately〔'letlɪ〕 *adv.* 最近
　　　　　(D) outdated〔,aut'detɪd〕 *adj.* 過時的；落伍的

忘記事物是生活的一部分，而且它通常會隨著人年齡的增長而更為常見。但是
　　　　　　　　　　　　　　　　　　17
某些老人罹患的阿茲海默症，和每天忘東忘西的情況是不一樣的。
　　　　　18

　　　* stuff〔stʌf〕 *n.* 事物　　　age〔edʒ〕 *v.* 變老
　　　　Alzheimer's disease〔'alts,haɪmɚz , dɪziz〕 *n.* 阿茲海默症【又稱老年癡呆
　　　　　症，是一種持續性神經功能障礙。阿茲海默症的成因未明，目前仍無治療方法。
　　　　　它侵襲人的腦部，患者會漸漸喪失記憶並且出現語言和情緒障礙。當病情漸
　　　　　趨嚴重時，病患在生活各方面都需要他人的協助，像是洗澡、吃東西、上廁
　　　　　所等，因此病患親友的生活往往也跟著受到很大的影響】

17. (**A**) 依句意，選 (A) *as*「當…時候；隨著」。而 (B) despite「儘管」，
　　　　　(C) with「隨著」，均為介系詞，後面不可接句子，在此不合；
　　　　　(D) though「雖然」，則不合句意。

18. (**C**) (A) effect〔ɪ'fɛkt〕 *n.* 影響
　　　　　(B) infect〔ɪn'fɛkt〕 *v.* 感染
　　　　　(C) ***affect***〔ə'fɛkt〕 *v.* (疾病等) 侵襲；影響
　　　　　(D) benefit〔'bɛnəfɪt〕 *v.* 對～有益

阿茲海默症會對腦部產生永久的影響，隨著時間過去，記憶一些基本的事物，
像是如何把鞋帶綁好之類的事情會有困難。最後，會忘記家人的姓名，甚至連
　　　　　　　　　　　　　　　　　　　　　　19
自己是誰都不一定知道。

　　　* condition〔kən'dɪʃən〕 *n.* 情況
　　　　permanently〔'pɝmənəntlɪ〕 *adv.* 永久地　　influence〔'ɪnfluəns〕 *v.* 影響
　　　　have trouble (in) V-ing 做～有困難　　　***family member*** 家庭成員

19. (**D**) (A) contrarily〔'kɑntrɛrəlɪ〕 *adv.* 相反地
　　　　　(B) delightedly〔dɪ'laɪtɪdlɪ〕 *adv.* 高興地
　　　　　(C) at first 起初
　　　　　(D) ***eventually***〔ɪ'vɛntʃuəlɪ〕 *adv.* 最後

這對罹患這種疾病的病人，以及他的家人來說，都是一件很難過的事。研究人員已經找到可能可以<u>減緩</u>這種疾病的藥物。希望未來有一天解藥可以問世。
20

* researcher〔rɪˋsɝtʃɚ〕*n.* 研究員　　medicine〔ˋmɛdəsṇ〕*n.* 藥物
cure〔kjʊr〕*n.* 治療法

20.(**D**) 依句意，選 (D) *slow down*「減緩」。而 (A) turn up「把（音量）開大」，(B) rid…of～「除去…中的～」，(C) put up「張貼」，均不合句意。

<u>第 21 至 25 題為題組</u>

幾千年來，黑貓被視爲一種擁有超自然力量的神秘動物。牠們一直被<u>和女巫、甚至是死亡聯想在一起</u>。
21

* mysterious〔mɪsˋtɪrɪəs〕*adj.* 神秘的
supernatural〔͵supɚˋnætʃrəl〕*adj.* 超自然的
associate〔əˋsoʃɪ͵et〕*v.* 將…聯想在一起　　witch〔wɪtʃ〕*n.* 女巫

21.(**A**) *be associated with* 和…聯想在一起；和…有關

據信女巫可以變成貓，而且還可以<u>變</u>九次。有些人認爲，<u>這</u>就是相信貓有九條命的由來。
22　　　　　23

* time〔taɪm〕*n.* 次數　　origin〔ˋɔrədʒɪn〕*n.* 由來；起源

22.(**B**) *make a change* 做改變

23.(**D**) that 引導名詞子句，做 belief 的同位語。

有許多與貓有關的迷信，一部分是因爲貓和人類一起生活了很久。以黑貓<u>爲主題</u>的迷信，有些是現在最著名的。
24

* superstition〔͵supɚˋstɪʃən〕*n.* 迷信　　*related to* 關於
partly〔ˋpɑrtlɪ〕*adv.* 部分地

24.(**A**) 空格應塡 which are centered，又關代與 be 動詞可同時省略，故選
(A) *centered*。　　*be centered on* 以…爲中心；以…爲主題

黑貓橫跨你前方道路的時候，你會擔心嗎？這要看你住在地球上的哪個地方。在英國和日本，黑貓越過你前方的路被視爲好運；<u>然而</u>，若你住在美國或是某些歐洲國家，那就變成是惡運嘍。
25

* cross〔krɔs〕*v.* 越過　　　path〔pæθ〕*n.* 道路
  depend on 視～而定　　consider〔kən'sɪdə〕*v.* 認爲
  be considered (to be) 被視爲　　***good luck*** 好運

25. (**C**) 依句意，選 (C) ***however*** 「然而」。而 (A) for example 「例如」，(B) that is to say 「也就是說」，(D) as a result 「因此；結果」，均不合句意。

第 26 至 30 題爲題組

　　普納荷大學之所以特別的原因之一，就是它的位置。它<u>位於</u>夏威夷，校園
26
被遼闊的露天操場和茂盛的樹木所覆蓋，一年四季都青翠美麗。

* ***Punahou*** 普納荷大學【位於夏威夷的私立名校，包含 1 到 12 年級基礎教育，美國現任總統歐巴馬，跟國父孫中山先生都畢業於此】
  location〔lo'keʃən〕*n.* 位置
  Hawaii〔hə'waɪ‧i〕*n.* 夏威夷【美國唯一在海外的一州】
  campus〔'kæmpəs〕*n.* 校園　　cover〔'kʌvə〕*v.* 覆蓋
  open-air〔'opən'ɛr〕*adj.* 露天的　　field〔fild〕*n.* 場地
  playing field 遊戲場；操場　　lush〔lʌʃ〕*adj.* 青翠的
  year-round〔'jɪr,raʊnd〕*adj.* 整年的

26. (**C**) 原句爲：***Because the campus is situated*** in Hawaii, ... 可改成分詞構句，去掉連接詞及相同主詞，is 改成 being，又 being 可省略，故選 (C) ***Situated***。　　***be situated in*** 位於

<u>除了</u>近三十棟學院大樓<u>外</u>，這間學校還擁有四分之一哩的戶外跑道，八座網球
27　　　　　　27
場，和一個<u>奧運</u>規格的游泳池。每年低年級的班級，爲了往後升上高年級，都
28
會籌辦爲期兩天，招募資金的短期「普納荷嘉年華會」。

　* academic〔͵ækəˋdɛmɪk〕adj. 學院的　　quarter〔ˋkwɔrtɚ〕n. 四分之一
　　outdoor〔ˋaʊt͵dor〕adj. 戶外的　　track〔træk〕n. 跑道
　　court〔kort〕n. 球場　　***tennis court*** 網球場
　　junior〔ˋdʒunjɚ〕adj. 低年級的　　organize〔ˋɔrgən͵aɪz〕v. 組織；籌畫
　　carnival〔ˋkɑrnəvl̩〕n. 嘉年華會
　　whirlwind〔ˋhwɝl͵wɪnd〕adj. 旋風式的
　　generate〔ˋdʒɛnə͵ret〕v. 產生　　senior〔ˋsinjɚ〕adj. 高年級的

27. (**B**) 依句意，選 (B) ***In addition to***「除了…之外（還有）」。而 (A) on
　　account of「由於」，(C) as a result「因此；結果」，(D) despite「儘
　　管」，均不合句意。

28. (**A**) 複合形容詞可由形容詞、副詞或名詞在前，加上現在分詞、過去分
　　詞，或名詞-ed，而「形容詞＋名詞-ed」表「具有某種特徵的」，
　　故選 (A) ***Olympic-sized***「奧運規格的」。
　　Olympic〔oˋlɪmpɪk〕adj. 奧運的

每年二月，前院都會被改造成<u>有齊全設施的</u>嘉年華會會場，遊戲、食物以及各
　　　　　　　　　　　　　29
種遊樂設施一應俱全。這個嘉年華會是島上人民最愛的<u>大事</u>，由於受到廣大的
　　　　　　　　　　　　　　　　　　　　　　30
歡迎，它可以在為期兩天的活動過程中，獲得超過一百萬美金的收益。

　* transform〔trænsˋfɔrm〕v. 使變成　　***be transformed into*** 被改變成
　　full-fledged〔ˋfʊlˋflɛdʒd〕adj. 發育齊全的；完善的；成熟的
　　complete〔kəmˋplit〕v. 使完備　　sort〔sort〕n. 種類
　　amusement〔əˋmjuzmənt〕n. 樂趣　　***amusement park*** 遊樂園
　　ride〔raɪd〕n. 遊樂設施　　***manage to*** 設法完成
　　bring in 產生（利潤、收入）　　course〔kors〕n. 過程
　　over the course of 在…的期間

29. (**D**) 表「有～」介系詞用 ***with***，選 (D)。

30. (**D**) (A) situation〔͵sɪtʃʊˋeʃən〕n. 情況　　(B) play〔ple〕n. 戲劇
　　(C) contest〔ˋkɑntɛst〕n. 比賽
　　(D) ***event***〔ɪˋvɛnt〕n. 事件；大型活動

三、文意選填：

第 31 至 40 題為題組

　　1974 年，一個生來就沒有雙臂的小女孩，被遺棄在市場裡。她被帶到
³¹**(C)** 位於高雄縣山區的六龜基督教育幼院。育幼院的創辦人楊神父深信這個嬰
孩是「上帝所派來的」，替她取名為「楊恩典」，³²**(I)** 意思是「來自上帝的恩寵與仁
慈」。

　　　* abandon〔ə'bændən〕v. 遺棄　　marketplace〔'mɑrkɪt,ples〕n. 市場
　　　Christian〔'krɪstʃən〕adj. 基督教的　　orphanage〔'ɔrfənɪdʒ〕n. 孤兒院
　　　locate〔'loket , lo'ket〕v. 座落　　mountainous〔'mauntṇəs〕adj. 多山的
　　　region〔'ridʒən〕n. 地區　　county〔'kauntɪ〕n. 縣　　***the Lord*** 上帝
　　　Father〔'fɑðə〕n.（大寫）神父　　founder〔'faundə〕n. 創辦人
　　　infant〔'ɪnfənt〕n. 嬰兒　　grace〔gres〕n. 恩寵
　　　benevolence〔bə'nɛvələns〕n. 慈愛

　　楊神父 ³³**(D)** 完全不知道這個孩子能夠長大，並和當時的總統蔣經國先生，
發展出一段傳奇性的友誼。出於 ³⁴**(H)** 同情，蔣總統 ³⁵**(F)** 和這個孩子產生特別
的情感連結，並幫她安排到台北接受 ³⁶**(G)** 手術，來幫助她矯正脊椎，使她能獨
自站立，他甚至還安排她去學習中國的水墨畫和書法。自從她與蔣總統的合照
被做成郵票 ³⁷**(B)** 後，這個孩子就開始成名了。

　　　* develop〔dɪ'vɛləp〕v. 發展　　legendary〔'lɛdʒənd,ɛrɪ〕adj. 傳奇的
　　　friendship〔'frɛnd,ʃɪp〕n. 友誼　　then〔ðɛn〕adv. 當時
　　　president〔'prɛzədənt〕n. 總統　　pity〔'pɪtɪ〕n. 同情
　　　out of pity 出於同情　　attachment〔ə'tætʃmənt〕n. 感情
　　　arrange〔ə'rendʒ〕v. 安排　　receive〔rɪ'siv〕v. 接收
　　　surgery〔'sɝdʒərɪ〕n. 手術　　straighten〔'stretṇ〕v. 使～變直
　　　spine〔spaɪn〕n. 脊椎　　allow〔ə'lau〕v. 讓；允許
　　　unaided〔ʌn'edɪd〕adj. 未受幫助的；獨立的　　brush〔brʌʃ〕n. 刷子
　　　Chinese brush painting 中國水墨畫　　calligraphy〔kə'lɪgrəfɪ〕n. 書法
　　　postage〔'postɪdʒ〕n. 郵資　　stamp〔stæmp〕n. 郵票

　　楊恩典並沒有讓總統 ³⁸**(E)** 失望，她用雙腳學習畫畫，並靠著出售自己的藝
術作品養 ³⁹**(J)** 活自己。她說她在繪畫中所使用的明亮色彩，代表她的微笑與快
樂。

* ***let** sb. **down*** 使失望　　***earn** one's **living*** 賺取生活費；養活自己
  art works 藝術作品　　light〔laɪt〕*adj.* 明亮的
  signify〔'sɪgnə,faɪ〕*v.* 意味著；表示

不論繪畫的種類爲何，可以肯定的 [40](A) 是，每幅畫背後，都有著她爲了要達到這個程度的標準，所付出的多年努力。無疑的是，楊恩典會繼續用她的雙腳，爲欣賞她的作品的人，創造更多奇蹟。

* rest〔rɛst〕*v.* 落在　　achieve〔ə'tʃiv〕*v.* 達到
  standard〔'stændəd〕*n.* 水平；標準　　continue〔kən'tɪnju〕*v.* 繼續
  create〔krɪ'et〕*v.* 創造　　miracle〔'mɪrəkl〕*n.* 奇蹟
  appreciate〔ə'priʃɪ,et〕*v.* 欣賞

四、閱讀測驗：

第 41 至 44 題爲題組

　　人們見證了由耳朵聽不見的孩子們所發明的新語言的誕生。最近的一項研究顯示，有種在二十多年前出現的手語，現在已經被視爲是眞正的語言。1977年，它首度出現於尼加拉瓜首都馬拿瓜的聾人學校。只用唇讀法和西班牙語教導孩子都不怎麼成功，孩子們也沒有接觸過成人手語，讓孩子們只能用自己發明的方法。

* invent〔ɪn'vɛnt〕*v.* 發明　　deaf〔dɛf〕*adj.* 聾的
  recent〔'risn̩t〕*adj.* 最近的　　***sign language*** 手語
  emerge〔ɪ'mɝdʒ〕*v.* 出現　　decade〔'dɛked〕*n.* 十年
  count〔kaʊnt〕*v.* 算入；包含
  Managua〔mə'nɑgwə〕*n.* 馬拿瓜【尼加拉瓜首都】
  Nicaragua〔,nɪkə'rɑgwə〕*n.* 尼加拉瓜【中美洲國家】
  found〔faʊnd〕*v.* 創立　　instruction〔ɪn'strʌkʃən〕*n.* 教導
  lip〔lɪp〕*n.* 唇　　lip-read〔'lɪp,rid〕*v.* 唇讀
  Spanish〔'spænɪʃ〕*n.* 西班牙語　　exposure〔ɪk'spoʒɚ〕*n.* 接觸
  adult〔ə'dʌlt〕*adj.* 成人的　　device〔dɪ'vaɪs〕*n.* 方法；發明

　　孩子們最初類似比手畫腳的手勢，因爲新進小孩的學習與揣摩，演變爲越來越複雜的語法。現在它有個正式的名稱：「尼加拉瓜手語」。因爲它很不一樣，所以連英美的手語人士都無法了解。

* pantomime〔'pæntə,maɪm〕*n.* 比手畫腳　　gesture〔'dʒɛstʃɚ〕*n.* 手勢
evolve〔ɪ'valv〕*v.* 演進　　grammar〔'græmɚ〕*n.* 文法
increasing〔ɪn'krisɪŋ〕*adj.* 越來越多的；逐漸的
complexity〔kəm'plɛksətɪ〕*n.* 複雜　　elaborate〔ɪ'læbə,ret〕*v.* 琢磨
formal〔'fɔrml̩〕*adj.* 正式的　　distinct〔dɪ'stɪŋkt〕*adj.* 不同的
signer〔'saɪnɚ〕*n.* 打手語者

　　根據一項最新出版的研究，尼加拉瓜手語被視爲一種語言，全球有八百多位手語人士使用，年齡從四歲到四十五歲都有。哥倫比亞大學巴納德學院的安‧珊荷絲博士說：「我們看見正在進行中的演變，但進化的不是一種生物，而是一個語言系統。」令人訝異的是，這個新的語言與其他語言有相當類似的地方，這更加可以說明孩子對語言有與生俱來的理解力。

* worldwide〔'wɝld'waɪd〕*adj.* 遍及全球的
publish〔'pʌblɪʃ〕*v.* 發表；出版
evolution〔,ɛvə'luʃən〕*n.* 演化；進化
in action 在活動中的　　organism〔'ɔrgən,ɪzəm〕*n.* 生物
bear〔bɛr〕*v.* 具有　　remarkable〔rɪ'markəbl̩〕*adj.* 令人驚訝的
similarity〔,sɪmə'lærətɪ〕*n.* 類似　　support〔sə'port〕*v.* 支持
theory〔'θiərɪ〕*n.* 理論　　innate〔ɪ'net〕*adj.* 天生的；與生俱來的
understanding〔,ʌndɚ'stændɪŋ〕*n.* 了解

41.(**D**) 這篇文章的主旨爲何？
　　(A) 尼加拉瓜手語被棄置不用，因爲沒有很多人了解它。
　　(B) 失聰的孩子需要一種新語言作爲溝通方法。
　　(C) 一種新的手語系統被發展出來，以幫助聾人。
　　(D) <u>不須經由正式地教導，孩子就能學會語言。</u>
　　* reject〔rɪ'dʒɛkt〕*v.* 丟棄　　formally〔'fɔrmlɪ〕*adv.* 正式地

42.(**B**) 這篇文章可能會出現在哪裡？
　　(A) 時尙雜誌。　　　　　　　(B) <u>科學期刊。</u>
　　(C) 旅遊手冊。　　　　　　　(D) 字典。
　　* appear〔ə'pɪr〕*v.* 出現　　journal〔'dʒɝnl̩〕*n.* 期刊
　　brochure〔bro'ʃur〕*n.* 小册子

43. (**A**) "**pantomime-like gestures**" 指的是什麼？

(A) 運用很多身體的動作。　　　(B) 孩子們很難了解。

(C) 很容易學會。　　　　　　　(D) 類似於動物的手勢。

* bodily 〔ˈbɑdɪlɪ〕 *adj.* 身體的　　movement 〔ˈmuvmənt〕 *n.* 動作

　pick up　（無形中）學會　　*similar to* 類似

44. (**D**) 下列敘述何者正確？

(A) 尼加拉瓜手語，最早是由尼加拉瓜的學校老師所發明。

(B) 理論上來說，尼加拉瓜手語和其他的語言完全沒有共同之處。

(C) 當尼加拉瓜手語一開始被發明時，它廣泛地被失聰的孩子接受。

(D) 其他國家的手語人士要了解尼加拉瓜手語可能會有困難。

* theoretically 〔ˌθiəˈrɛtɪkḷɪ〕 *adv.* 理論上

　in common 共同的　　widely 〔ˈwaɪdlɪ〕 *adv.* 廣泛地

第 45 至 48 題為題組

　　你曾經聽過法蘭克・塔爾斯這個人嗎？他是一位可疑的人物。據說他在 1900 年代，從三次不可能存活的船難中生還。有些人認為他是世上最幸運的人。據說他是一位任職於船艦引擎室裡的中年消防員。有些人認為他只是個平凡、努力工作的人，不過卻擁有在幾個歷史紀錄上最可怕的遠洋客輪意外中，死裡逃生的能力。

* questionable 〔ˈkwɛstʃənəbḷ〕 *adj.* 可疑的　　figure 〔ˈfɪgjɚ〕 *n.* 人物

　supposedly 〔səˈpozɪdlɪ〕 *adv.* 據說　　survive 〔sɚˈvaɪv〕 *v.* 生還

　doomed 〔dumd〕 *adj.* 天命已盡的　　alive 〔əˈlaɪv〕 *adj.* 活著的

　middle-aged 〔ˈmɪdḷˈedʒd〕 *adj.* 中年的　　fireman 〔ˈfaɪrmən〕 *n.* 消防員

　engine 〔ˈɛndʒən〕 *n.* 引擎　　ordinary 〔ˈordṇˌɛrɪ〕 *adj.* 普通的

　ability 〔əˈbɪlətɪ〕 *n.* 能力　　liner 〔ˈlaɪnɚ〕 *n.* 客輪

　ocean liner 遠洋客輪

　　據說他在鐵達尼號撞上冰山的時候，在船上服役當船員。兩年後，愛爾蘭皇后號撞上挪威貨船時，他也正好在愛爾蘭皇后號上工作，而超過一千人死於那場船難。然後他受雇於露西塔尼亞號，1915 年 5 月，船隻被 U-20 魚雷擊沉。顯然，他也毫髮無傷地活了下來。如果你開始懷疑這個人是否真實存在，那你的方向就對了。沒有任何紀錄顯示，有位叫做法蘭克・塔爾斯的人曾經在這三艘船的任何一艘中工作過。

* **be said to** 據說　　**crew member** 機務（或船務）人員
  at the time that 在～的時候　　hit〔hɪt〕v. 撞上
  iceberg〔'aɪs͵bɝg〕n. 冰山　　empress〔'ɛmprɪs〕n. 皇后；女皇
  Ireland〔'aɪrlənd〕n. 愛爾蘭　　collide〔kə'laɪd〕v. 相撞
  disaster〔dɪz'æstə〕n. 災害　　employ〔ɪm'plɔɪ〕v. 雇用
  torpedo〔tɔr'pido〕n. 魚雷　　apparently〔ə'pærəntlɪ〕adv. 明顯地
  scratch〔skrætʃ〕n. 刮痕　　**without a scratch** 毫髮無傷
  as well 也　　doubt〔daʊt〕v. 懷疑
  existence〔ɪg'zɪstəns〕n. 存在　　probably〔'prɑbəblɪ〕adv. 可能
  record〔'rɛkəd〕n. 紀錄　　list〔lɪst〕v. 列出清單

　　法蘭克‧塔爾斯的傳奇似乎是另一種都市民間故事，以及人類對於戰勝悲劇的渴望。眞實或杜撰的都好，法蘭克‧塔爾斯只是眾多之中一位替史書增添色彩的角色罷了。

* legend〔'lɛdʒənd〕n. 傳奇　　case〔kes〕n. 例子；案例
  urban〔'ɝbən〕adj. 都市的　　folk〔fok〕adj. 民俗的；民間的
  tale〔tel〕n. 故事　　**urban folk tale** 都市傳說
  humanity〔hju'mænətɪ〕n.（集合名詞）人類　　desire〔dɪ'zaɪr〕n. 渴望
  triumph〔'traɪəmf〕n. 勝利　　tragic〔'trædʒɪk〕adj. 悲劇的
  fiction〔'fɪkʃən〕n. 杜撰的故事　　multiple〔'mʌltəpl̩〕adj. 多數的
  character〔'kærɪktə〕n. 角色　　color〔'kʌlə〕v. 著色
  history book 史書

45.（**A**）在本文中，"**said**" 指的是什麼？
　　(A) 被報導。　　(B) 被拔擢。　　(C) 被設置。　　(D) 被看見。
　　* promote〔prə'mot〕v. 促銷；拔擢　　sight〔saɪt〕v. 發現；看出

46.（**C**）何者會是本文的最佳標題？
　　(A)「法蘭克‧塔爾斯，謎樣的男人」
　　(B)「拯救不可能的事情」　　(C)「揭開法蘭克‧塔爾斯的傳奇」
　　(D)「如何在沉沒的船隻中生還」
　　* mystery〔'mɪstrɪ〕n. 神秘；謎　　**the impossible** 不可能之事
　　　debunk〔dɪ'bʌŋk〕v. 揭穿　　sinking〔'sɪŋkɪŋ〕adj. 下沉的；沉沒的

47. (**B**) 下列何者最能解釋本文的目的？
    (A) 及時縫一針，可省掉九針；及時行事，事半功倍。
    (B) <u>別相信你讀的每一件事。</u>
    (C) 眼見為憑。
    (D) 洋蔥有很多層（指真相被隱匿，需要層層發掘）。
    * describe〔dɪˈskraɪb〕v. 描述　　purpose〔ˈpɝpəs〕n. 目的
     stitch〔stɪtʃ〕n. 一針；一縫　　layer〔ˈleɚ〕n. 層
     onion〔ˈʌnjən〕n. 洋蔥

48. (**B**) 根據這篇文章，什麼是都市傳說？
    (A) 有趣的新聞故事。　　　　　(B) <u>未經證實的故事。</u>
    (C) 神秘的故事。　　　　　　　(D) 戰勝悲劇。
    * unproven〔ʌnˈpruvən〕adj. 未經證實的
     tragedy〔ˈtrædʒədɪ〕n. 悲劇

第 49 至 52 題為題組

　　對孕婦來說，吃下去最危險的其中一種藥物，就是酒精，因為酒精會迅速輸送到血液裡，並很快地通過組織和細胞膜。人類的胎兒特別容易受到這種傷害的影響。事實上，這種對胎兒的負面影響非常明顯，接觸過酒精的寶寶出生後，據說會罹患胎兒酒精症候群。

    * pregnant〔ˈprɛgnənt〕adj. 懷孕的　　consume〔kənˈsum〕v. 吃；喝
     alcohol〔ˈælkəˌhɔl〕n. 酒精　　deliver〔dɪˈlɪvɚ〕v. 傳送
     tissue〔ˈtɪʃu〕n. 組織　　　　membrane〔ˈmɛmbren〕n. 膜
     fetus〔ˈfitəs〕n. 胎兒　　particularly〔pɚˈtɪkjələˌlɪ〕adv. 特別地
     vulnerable〔ˈvʌlnərəbl̩〕adj. 易受傷害的　　　effect〔ɪˈfɛkt〕n. 影響
     obvious〔ˈɑbvɪəs〕adj. 明顯的　　exposure〔ɪkˈspoʒɚ〕n. 接觸
     suffer from 罹患（疾病）　　fetal〔ˈfitl̩〕adj. 胎兒的
     syndrome〔ˈsɪnˌdrom〕n. 症候群
     fetal alcohol syndrome 胎兒酒精症候群【簡稱 FAS，懷孕期間喝酒的
       婦女可能會產下罹患 FAS 的嬰兒，酒精可能會使胎兒生長遲緩、腦部跟神
       經系統受損，這些都是永久的傷害，醫生建議懷孕期間最好完全不碰酒精】

　　當孕婦飲酒時，酒精幾乎會同時通過她的血液。而且，由於胎兒的血液與母親相連，酒精也會立刻通過胎兒的血液。再者，在胎兒體內的酒精濃度，和母親是完全相同的。對母親來說，這種濃度不會造成問題，因為母親的肝臟每小時可以從身體裡面分解掉一盎司的酒精。

> ＊ bloodstream〔'blʌd,strim〕n. (體內的) 血流
> simultaneously〔,saɪml'tenɪəslɪ〕adv. 同時地
> *be tied to* 和～連結　directly〔də'rɛktlɪ〕adv. 立即地
> *as well* 也　concentration〔,kansn'treʃən〕n. 濃度
> exactly〔ɪg'zæktlɪ〕adv. 正好；恰好
> liver〔'lɪvɚ〕n. 肝臟　remove〔rɪ'muv〕v. 移除
> ounce〔auns〕n. 盎司【重量單位，簡寫作 oz.】　per〔pɚ〕prep. 每～

　　然而，胎兒的肝臟還沒發育完全，胎兒的肝臟能從血液中分解酒精的速率也緩慢得多。最後，酒精會穿過胎盤回到母親的循環系統，但這個過程很慢。等到這個過程發生的時候，主要神經可能已經受損了。

> ＊ completely〔kəm'plitlɪ〕adv. 完整地　rate〔ret〕n. 速率
> return〔rɪ'tɝn〕v. 返回　placenta〔plə'sɛntə〕n. 胎盤
> process〔'prasɛs〕n. 過程　*take place* 發生
> neurological〔,njurə'ladʒɪkəl〕adj. 神經的　occur〔ə'kɝ〕v. 發生

　　研究顯示，只要喝一點點酒，就會對胎兒造成顯著、無法復原的傷害。接觸過酒精出生的寶寶，通常會出現臉部扭曲、注意力無法集中，和記憶困難的症狀。簡單來說，孕婦絕對不可飲酒。

> ＊ research〔'risɝtʃ〕n. 研究　produce〔prə'djus〕v. 產生
> significant〔sɪg'nɪfəkənt〕adj. 顯著的
> irreversible〔,ɪrɪ'vɝsəbl̩〕adj. 不可逆轉的
> exhibit〔ɪg'zɪbɪt〕v. 顯示　facial〔'feʃəl〕adj. 面部的
> distortion〔dɪs'tɔrʃən〕n. 變形　inability〔,ɪnə'bɪlətɪ〕n. 無能力
> concentrate〔'kansn̩,tret〕v. 專心　must〔mʌst〕n. 必要的事

49.(**C**) 本篇文章主要關於？
　　(A) 女人和藥物。　　　　　　(B) 懷孕的危險。
　　(C) 懷孕時飲酒的危險。　　　(D) 飲酒和人體。

50.(**B**) 女人喝酒後，酒精要花多久的時間進入她的血液中？
  (A) 大約一小時。   (B) <u>幾秒鐘。</u>
  (C) 幾分鐘。   (D) 至少二十四小時。

51.(**A**) 文中暗指什麼？
  (A) <u>比起對母親，藥物對胎兒有更大的影響。</u>
  (B) 只要一杯酒精性飲料就能使胎兒致死。
  (C) 大的胎兒不會受到酒精的不良影響。
  (D) 懷孕期間，父親也應該拒酒。

  * infer (ɪn'fɝ) v. 推論 alcoholic (ˌælkə'hɔlɪk) adj. 含酒精的
  adversely (æd'vɝslɪ) adv. 不利地 expect (ɪk'spɛkt) v. 懷孕

52.(**B**) 根據這篇文章，酒精最後是如何回到媽媽的系統？
  (A) 透過血液運送。   (B) <u>透過胎盤轉移。</u>
  (C) 由胎兒的肝臟排出。   (D) 它不會完全返回。

  * carry ('kærɪ) v. 運送 transfer (træns'fɝ) v. 轉移
  expel (ɪk'spɛl) v. 排出

第 53 至 56 題為題組

  現在盲人接受的訓練和教育是經過認可的，但以前並不是這樣。在古文明時期，盲人通常不被視為是正常社會的一份子，而且主要靠乞討維生。雖然許多文明提供盲人生活的處所，但直到十九世紀初，路易士‧布萊爾設計出以觸摸的方式來幫助盲人閱讀的方法之後，盲人的教育才有顯著的進步。

  * accepted (ək'sɛptɪd) adj. 公認的
  practice ('præktɪs) n. 練習；慣例
  blind (blaɪnd) adj. 看不見的 ***the blind*** 盲人
  commonplace ('kɑmən,ples) adj. 普遍的
  ancient ('enʃənt) adj. 古代的
  civilization (ˌsɪvlə'zeʃən) n. 文明 survive (sə'vaɪv) v. 生存
  primarily ('praɪ,mɛrəlɪ) adv. 主要地 beg (bɛg) v. 乞討
  century ('sɛntʃərɪ) n. 世紀 advance (əd'væns) n. 進步
  devise (dɪ'vaɪz) v. 設計；想出 method ('mɛθəd) n. 方法
  base (bes) v. 使（以…）為根據 sense (sɛns) n. 感覺

布萊爾這套系統的構想，源自於由查爾斯‧巴比爾，他為了提供戰地夜間通訊的而發明類似的系統。布萊爾小幅修正巴比爾的系統，根據他自己的六點可能相關位置，將六個點排列在兩直排，每排各有三個位置上。每個位置上有或沒有凸起的點，決定了字母、數字或標點符號。自從有了這個發明之後，大大改善了盲人教育。

* derive〔dəˈraɪv〕v. 源自＜from＞
  communication〔kə,mjunəˈkeʃən〕n. 通訊
  battlefield〔ˈbætl̦,fild〕n. 戰場　　modify〔ˈmɑdə,faɪ〕v. 修正
  arrange〔əˈrendʒ〕v. 排列　　vertical〔ˈvɜtɪkl̦〕adj. 垂直的
  row〔ro〕n. 行；排　　absence〔ˈæbsn̦s〕n. 缺乏
  raised〔rezd〕adj. 凸起的　　dot〔dɑt〕n. 點
  determine〔dɪˈtɜmɪn〕v. 決定
  punctuation〔,pʌŋktʃuˈeʃən〕n. 標點　　***punctuation sign*** 標點
  invention〔ɪnˈvɛnʃən〕n. 發明　　improve〔ɪmˈpruv〕v. 改善
  immensely〔ɪˈmɛnslɪ〕adv. 廣大地

　　有了布萊爾系統後，給盲童就讀的學校很快就設立了，要進入下一個世紀的時候，已經設立了將近四十所學校。更大的進步在於盲人開始併入正規班級讀書。而今，大多數的盲童在正規班級接受教育，並有許多人進入大學和研究所階段繼續學業。

* establish〔əˈstæblɪʃ〕v. 建立　　exist〔ɪgˈzɪst〕v. 存在
  turn〔tɜn〕n. 轉捩點　　incorporate〔ɪnˈkɔrpə,ret〕v. 併入
  college〔ˈkɑlɪdʒ〕n. 大學　　***graduate school*** 研究所
  level〔ˈlɛvl̦〕n. 程度；階段

53.(**C**) 本文主要是關於 ＿＿＿＿＿＿。
  (A) 巴比爾系統　　　　　　(B) 虐待盲人
  (C) 盲人的教育　　　　　　(D) 閱讀系統
  * ***be concerned with*** 和…有關
    mistreatment〔mɪsˈtritmənt〕n. 虐待

54.(**A**) 在本文最後一段，最後一句話中的 "**many**" 指的是 ＿＿＿＿＿＿。
  (A) 盲童　　(B) 正規班級　　(C) 青少年　　(D) 高中生

55. (**B**) 下列何者不是作者提到的，有關盲人教育的進步？
　　　(A) 閱讀系統的發展。　　　　(B) 盲人研究所的設立。
　　　(C) 盲人與正規班級的整合。　(D) 盲童學校的設立。
　　　* mention〔'mɛnʃən〕v. 提到　　integration〔ˌɪntə'greʃən〕n. 整合

56. (**A**) 可以從本文中推論出，查爾斯・巴比爾的溝通系統 ＿＿＿＿＿＿。
　　　(A) 以觸感為基礎
　　　(B) 為了讓盲人能閱讀，在更早之前就被使用了
　　　(C) 有兩排各三個位置
　　　(D) 不只有六個可能位置
　　　* **be based on** 以～為基礎　　**so that** 以便於

第貳部分：非選擇題

一、中譯英：

1. 肢體語言能抵過千言萬語；小小的動作或手勢就能傳達很多意思。

Body language $\begin{Bmatrix} \text{merits / is equal to} \\ \text{is worth / is worthy of} \end{Bmatrix}$ a thousand words;

little movements can $\begin{Bmatrix} \text{communicate / tell / transmit} \\ \text{express / project / suggest} \\ \text{convey / express} \end{Bmatrix}$ much meaning.

2. 注意自己的肢體語言，能幫助你給別人正面的印象。

$\begin{Bmatrix} \text{Keeping an eye on / Watching} \\ \text{Paying heed to / Heeding} \\ \text{Paying attention to / Monitoring} \end{Bmatrix}$ your body language can help you

$\begin{Bmatrix} \text{give a positive impression.} \\ \text{present a positive image.} \\ \text{make} \begin{Bmatrix} \text{a positive impression.} \\ \text{a good impression.} \end{Bmatrix} \end{Bmatrix}$

二、英文作文：

作文範例

Dear Mindy,   Jan. 28, 2013

　　Please forgive me for missing our dinner date last evening. No doubt, you are very angry with me. Please accept my apology. I'd like to make it up to you. Would you please allow me to treat you to dinner at the same restaurant next week?

　　I didn't have a chance to give you the details on the phone, but I really had a bad day. First, I forgot about my math homework, which was due today. Then my mother gave me extra chores since my brother is sick. I kept thinking I could get everything finished, but that didn't happen. If you agree to meet me next week, I promise that I'll show up this time. Forgiven?

Sincerely,

Robin

no doubt 無疑地　　*be angry with* 對…生氣
apology〔əˋpɑlədʒɪ〕*n.* 道歉　　*make it up to* 對…做補償
treat〔trit〕*v.* 款待；請客
detail〔ˋditel〕*n.* 細節　　*have a bad day* 過得不順
due〔dju〕*adj.* 到期的　　chore〔tʃor〕*n.* 雜務
show up 出現　　promise〔ˋprɑmɪs〕*v.* 保證

大學入學學科能力測驗英文模擬試題 ⑥

第壹部分：單選題（佔 72 分）

一、詞彙（佔 15 分）

說明： 第 1 題至第 15 題，每題 4 個選項，其中只有一個是最適當的答案，畫記在答案卡之「選擇題答案區」。各題答對得 1 分；未作答、答錯、或畫記多於一個選項者，該題以零分計算。

1. After heavy _____ over the last 24 hours, flash flooding has turned the village into a virtual island, making movement difficult.
   (A) warrant　　(B) amendment　　(C) rainfall　　(D) security

2. The grand building _____ comfortably in the heart of New Delhi is India's brand-new luxury shopping mall, and it is proving to be a big draw for India's newly wealthy.
   (A) flocking　　(B) nestling　　(C) clustering　　(D) populating

3. Emotional blocks that might _____ with academic success include boredom, daydreaming, stress, anger and frustration. They all reduce concentration in the classroom.
   (A) interfere　　(B) accelerate　　(C) deprive　　(D) dissatisfy

4. Stress can lead to sickness that will blow your schedule apart, and exercise is the best known way of _____ anxiety-producing stress.
   (A) conveying　　(B) defying　　(C) reducing　　(D) devising

5. Paper towels and napkins are wasteful of forest resources. Better _____ to cleaning up messes are cloth napkins at meals, and rags, sponges, or towels.
   (A) processions　　(B) memorials　　(C) registration　　(D) alternatives

6. Traditionally, children have been considered the property of their parents and have _____ had few entitlements in their own right.
   (A) consecutively
   (B) intensively
   (C) respectfully
   (D) consequently

7. Parents should accept their responsibilities and not expect the school and teachers to take over their _____ as parents.
   (A) assets   (B) obligations   (C) appliances   (D) deficits

8. To lose weight, you must stay _____, because thirst sometimes presents itself as hunger pains.
   (A) hydrated   (B) paralyzed   (C) deceived   (D) testified

9. In China, according to brokers, the number of people buying homes has decreased _____. And in some neighborhoods, especially in southeast China, prices have even dropped by 40 percent.
   (A) economically
   (B) dramatically
   (C) objectively
   (D) dogmatically

10. Taking lecture notes in class keeps the student's attention focused on the lecture, thereby increasing _____, retention and understanding.
    (A) delegation
    (B) access
    (C) restriction
    (D) concentration

11. Do you put off important tasks? That is called _____.
    (A) admission
    (B) procrastination
    (C) circulation
    (D) extension

12. Due to heavy rains, many people were _____ on the bridge. The villagers went to their rescue, but the tractor could not reach there because of the flowing water.
    (A) acquainted   (B) acquired   (C) stranded   (D) smothered

13. Jumping on the trendy mooncake bandwagon, ice cream giant
　　Häagen Dazs has created a line of _____, ice cream-filled
　　mooncakes for those who can afford costly mooncakes.
　　(A) high-end　　　(B) low-cal　　　(C) upside-down　(D) out-of-date

14. By taking lecture notes in class, not only does the student record
　　_____ facts, but the teacher's points and perspectives are
　　recorded as well.
　　(A) inherent　　　(B) significant　　(C) various　　　(D) lengthy

15. Social media is now _____ mass market. It is hard to find a
　　trade publication that does not talk about it.
　　(A) definitively　(B) scarcely　　　(C) consciously　(D) ideally

二、綜合測驗（佔 15 分）

說明： 第 16 題至第 30 題，每題一個空格，請依文意選出最適當的一個答案，
　　　畫記在答案卡之「選擇題答案區」。各題答對得 1 分；未作答、答錯、
　　　或畫記多於一個選項者，該題以零分計算。

第 16 至 20 題為題組

　　　16　for national parks were first heard in the 19th century in
Africa, as industrial towns grew ever bigger and suburbs swelled. Even
so, Africa's wildlife was still hunted heavily from the 19th century well
into the 20th century. By 1920, big-game hunters had almost depleted
several wildlife populations and settlers had deforested large tracts of
land. The once vast　17　of elephants that had roamed Eastern
Cape, a province in southeast South Africa, was reduced to just 11
animals, and the zebra also faced extinction.

　　As a result, South Africa took the first steps to reverse these trends
　18　parks and preserves. Addo Elephant National Park, established
in 1931, now has more than 200 elephants within its borders.

The park, ___19___ 241 sq km, is also home to Cape buffalo, black rhinoceros, and 180 species of birds. Mountain Zebra National Park, established in 1937, protects more than 200 mountain zebra, several antelope species, and 200 bird species. Within the 62 sq km park ___20___ mountains, steep ravines, several aloe species, and numerous varieties of flowering shrubs.

16. (A) Rehearsals   (B) Proposals
     (C) Dispersals   (D) Disposals

17. (A) school   (B) herd   (C) swarm   (D) pack

18. (A) by creating   (B) to create
     (C) that create   (D) of creating

19. (A) encompass   (B) encompassing
     (C) surpassed   (D) surpassing

20. (A) are   (B) is   (C) have   (D) has

第 21 至 25 題為題組

Cancer is an abnormal growth of cells. They rapidly reproduce ___21___ restriction of space, having to share nutrients with other cells, or signals sent from the body to stop reproduction. They are shaped differently from healthy cells and may unexpectedly spread to many areas of the body.

As the number of cells in each body tissue is tightly controlled, the number of new cells made ___22___ the number needed to replace dying cells plus the number needed for growth and development. ___23___ normal cells, however, tumors are clusters of cells capable of growing and dividing uncontrollably. Their growth is not regulated.

Tumors can be benign or malignant. Benign tumors tend to grow slowly and do not spread, ___24___ malignant tumors grow rapidly, can invade and destroy nearby normal tissues, and can spread throughout the body. The term "cancer" is used when a tumor is malignant.

Cancer can also be "locally invasive" and "metastatic." When it is locally invasive, the tumor invades the tissues surrounding it by sending out cancerous cells into the normal tissue. When it is __25__, the tumor sends cells into other tissues distant from it. In fact, cancer is not just one disease but rather a group of diseases.

21. (A) with   (B) for   (C) despite   (D) on
22. (A) equal   (B) equaling   (C) to equal   (D) equals
23. (A) Within   (B) Above   (C) Unlike   (D) Beneath
24. (A) whereas   (B) since   (C) unless   (D) lest
25. (A) immune   (B) metastatic (C) hysterical   (D) eligible

第 26 至 30 題為題組

Victor saw a sign in the window of a restaurant that __26__ "Unusual Breakfast." Always an adventurous eater, Victor went in and sat down. The waitress brought him his pot of tea and asked him what he wanted to eat.

"What does your unusual breakfast include?" he asked politely.

"Baked tongue of chicken!" she replied with a __27__.

"Baked tongue of chicken? Baked tongue of chicken! Do you have any idea __28__ disgusting that is? I would never even __29__ eating anything that came out of a chicken's mouth!" Victor snapped.

__30__, the waitress asked, "What would you like then?"

"Oh, just bring me some scrambled eggs," Victor replied.

26. (A) spoke   (B) read   (C) uttered   (D) told
27. (A) grain   (B) grin   (C) grief   (D) groan
28. (A) what   (B) how   (C) such   (D) so
29. (A) regard   (B) consider   (C) reflect   (D) ponder
30. (A) Undaunted   (B) Unequaled (C) Undesired   (D) Unexpired

三、文意選填（佔 10 分）

說明： 第 31 題至第 40 題，每題一個空格，請依文意在文章後所提供的 (A) 到 (J) 選項中分別選出最適當者，並將其英文字母代號畫記在答案卡之「選擇題答案區」。各題答對得 1 分；未作答、答錯、或畫記多於一個選項者，該題以零分計算。

第 31 至 40 題為題組

Chronic fatigue syndrome (CFS) is a condition that causes extreme tiredness. It is a disease that was first named in the 1980s. Even now, as ___31___ numbers of people are being diagnosed with CFS, many people inside and outside the health ___32___ still doubt its existence or maintain that it is a psychological ailment. People previously healthy and ___33___ energy may experience a variety of symptoms, including extreme fatigue, weakness, sore throat, headaches and difficulty ___34___. People with CFS have fatigue that lasts for six months or longer. CFS does not have a known cause, but appears to result from a ___35___ of factors.

Non-specific symptoms of fatigue, tiredness, exhaustion, and aches make CFS difficult to ___36___ and similar to other conditions ___37___ lupus, multiple sclerosis, fibromyalgia and Lyme disease. People with CFS are often unable to perform normally at work and home ___38___ their long-term fatigue and problems with short-term memory. The hallmark symptoms of CFS are overwhelming fatigue and weakness that make it extremely difficult to perform ___39___ and daily tasks, like getting out of bed, dressing, and eating. The illness can severely ___40___ school, work, and leisure activities, and cause physical and emotional symptoms that can last for months or even years.

(A) routine   (B) professions   (C) concentrating   (D) combination

(E) increasing   (F) such as   (G) full of   (H) affect

(I) diagnose   (J) because of

四、閱讀測驗（佔 32 分）

說明： 第 41 題至第 56 題，每題 4 個選項，請分別根據各篇文章之文意選出最適當的一個答案，畫記在答案卡之「選擇題答案區」。各題答對得 2 分；未作答、答錯、或畫記多於一個選項者，該題以零分計算。

第 41 至 44 題為題組

Walk into any Internet cafe in China, and you will see a lot of people with an IM window open chatting with friends, perhaps while playing online games or conducting a search. In the office, the breeze of chat flows through the open IM window as people work their Excel spreadsheets. They may keep windows open for QQ and MSN to share information widely. Both are popular instant-messaging services in China.

The Chinese IM market is dominated by Tencent Holdings Inc., of Shenzhen, with its QQ platform. QQ's active accounts have reached 315 million, a figure that is boosted by people opening multiple accounts. QQ is China's No. 1 IM service, with a 79.6% market share. The closest rival, Microsoft Corp.'s Microsoft Messenger (MSN), which mainly targets business users, had about 16.5 million active accounts by the first quarter of 2008.

In China, hundreds of millions of people subscribe to QQ, and many of them have more than 100 QQ friends in their contacts list. They tend to keep several premium QQ numbers, each of which costs 10 yuan ($1.43) a month. In addition to messaging, they read the news on QQ.com and participate in discussions in QQ chat groups. They log in after connecting to the Internet, in the office and at home, most of them spending over 10 hours on it every day, while spending only 10 minutes chatting with real friends.

As many young Chinese grew up with the product, they generally do not ask one another for email addresses, but ask for QQ numbers.

They have also developed a QQ lifestyle and even a new online language, "Language from Mars," mainly used in QQ chatting and in Qzone, a multimedia blog service. For example, 3Q means "thank you."

41. The author of this passage is most likely to be a(n) ＿＿＿＿＿＿.
    (A) devoted environmentalist　(B) news correspondent
    (C) educational psychologist　(D) high-ranking engineer

42. According to the passage, which company owns China's most popular instant-messaging service?
    (A) Microsoft Corp.　(B) Google Inc.
    (C) Yahoo Inc.　(D) Tencent Holding Inc.

43. According to the passage, which of the following is NOT true?
    (A) QQ is China's most popular IM service, for it has a 79.6% market share.
    (B) Each of the premium QQ numbers costs $1.43 a month.
    (C) "Language from Mars" is widely used in QQ chatting and in Qzone.
    (D) Chinese people use IM services to play online games.

44. What is the author's attitude toward the popularity of China's IM service?
    (A) interested　(B) indifferent
    (C) pessimistic　(D) furious

第 45 至 48 題為題組

　　Forensics, or medical jurisprudence, is the application of science to law. It uses highly developed technologies to uncover scientific evidence in a variety of fields. Modern forensic science has a broad range of applications. However, it is most commonly used to investigate criminal cases involving a victim, such as assault, robbery, kidnapping, rape, or murder.

The central figure in the forensic investigation of crimes is the medical examiner, whose responsibility is to visit the crime scene, conduct an autopsy (an examination of the body), examine the medical evidence and laboratory reports, study the victim's medical history, and put all this information together in a report to the district attorney. The medical examiner's ability to properly collect and process forensic samples can affect the ability of the prosecution to prove the crime during a trial.

Medical examiners are usually physicians specializing in forensic pathology, which is the study of structural and functional changes in the body as a result of injury. Their training and qualifications most often include a medical degree and an apprenticeship in a medical examiner's office. Depending on the requirements of the particular state, city, or county, the medical examiner may also be required to be certified as a forensic pathologist by the American Board of Pathology. At present, the United States has no national system of medical examiners and has no federal law requiring that coroners be licensed physicians.

45. The title of this article is most likely to be _____.
    (A) Investigation of the Crime Scene
    (B) The American Board of Criminalistics
    (C) Forensics and the Medical Examiner
    (D) The Medical Evidence and Laboratory Reports

46. According to the passage, who plays the most important role in the forensic investigation of crimes?
    (A) physician   (B) judge
    (C) district attorney   (D) coroner

47. The medical examiner's responsibility does NOT include
    _____.
    (A) conducting an autopsy   (B) studying the laboratory reports
    (C) visiting the crime scene
    (D) making an oral report to the district attorney

48. According to the passage, which of the following is NOT true?
    (A) The U.S. government issues certificates to licensed medical examiners.
    (B) Forensic science applies science and medicine to criminal and civil law.
    (C) Medical examiners can provide physical evidence to prove a crime.
    (D) Medical examiners generally specialize in forensic pathology.

第 49 至 52 題為題組

　　Knowing how to give a good massage is like having a talent. Being able to massage yourself is beneficial, especially if you are prone to body aches and pains. There is more than one kind of massage therapy technique that is practiced. Baby massage, for example, is a massage therapy technique that does not require a lot of training. Many parenting classes offer information on this type of gentle and soothing technique to help calm babies down and help their circulation.

　　Some other massage therapy methods require more formal training. Swedish massage therapy is one that helps people to relax and takes away the pain of sore muscles and joints. It involves stroking, deep prodding, gentle shaking and tapping motions to loosen up the tired muscles. The sports massage therapy technique is designed to help athletes warm up their bodies prior to competing and to help them recover after a race or competition. Sports medicine uses massage both as a preventive and a curative treatment.

　　Massage therapy can be very effective in helping reduce stress and rejuvenate you when your muscles are tired or sore. It is becoming more recognized and has finally come to the point where many medical plans allow massage as part of routine medical care, having seen the benefits of massage in reducing pain and alleviating stress and fatigue. Some massage therapy techniques are used to relax people while other methods treat specific areas for aches and pains.

49. In which of the following magazines would you most likely find this passage?
    (A) *Psychology Today*
    (B) *Stem Cells and Diseases*
    (C) *World Entertainment*
    (D) *Natural Health*

50. How many massage therapies are mentioned in this passage?
    (A) 2
    (B) 3
    (C) 4
    (D) 5

51. According to the passage, which of the following is NOT true?
    (A) Massages help parents calm down a baby and help its circulation.
    (B) Baby massage requires intensive training.
    (C) Massages may now be considered as part of routine medical care to alleviate fatigue.
    (D) Sports medicine uses massages not only for prevention but for treatment as well.

52. What is this passage about?
    (A) The benefits of massage therapy methods.
    (B) The impact of massage therapy methods.
    (C) The great popularity of massage therapy methods.
    (D) The wide variety of massage therapy methods.

第 53 至 56 題為題組

　　Diego Chiapello, legally blind since birth, isn't one of Italy's famous "**mama's boys**" who live with their parents into adulthood. The 27-year-old lives alone in Milan, works as a network administrator, loves diving and dreams of sailing across the Atlantic with a sight-impaired crew.

　　Obviously, he's not your average disabled person—but especially so in Italy. The country has more barriers to integration than almost anywhere else on the Continent: among European countries, Italy ranks third from the bottom in accessibility for the disabled, ahead of only

Greece and Portugal. People who use wheelchairs, especially, find it difficult to navigate the country's cobblestone streets, ride buses or visit restaurants, shops and museums. Less than a quarter of Italy's disabled hold jobs, compared with 47 percent for Europe.

But the biggest obstacle for the country's physically challenged may, in fact, be the fabled Italian family. Because of the social stigma that still attaches to disabilities, "they tend to keep disabled people at home" and out of public view, explains Giovanni Marri, head of an employment training center in Milan that caters to the handicapped. Thus while 15 percent of the country's families include a disabled person, according to surveys, only 2 percent of Italians report going to school with a disabled person and only 4 percent work with one.

Italians are beginning to recognize the problem. Over the past decade, the government has passed laws targeting everything from workplace discrimination to accessibility requirements. A recent study by the European Union found that 85 percent of Italians admit that public transportation and infrastructure are inadequate for the handicapped, and 97 percent say action is needed. But the biggest barrier is psychological. "Italian companies are afraid of hiring disabled people," says Chiapello. The only way to alter that, he says, is for Italy's disabled to do what he did—get out of the house and demand change.

53. Which of the following words best describes "**mama's boys**"?
　　(A) Adorable　　(B) Optimistic　(C) Dependent　　(D) Desirable

54. In this passage, Chiapello is cited as an example of ＿＿＿＿＿＿＿＿.
　　(A) unusual disabled Italians
　　(B) courageous blind sailors
　　(C) typical handicapped people
　　(D) vulnerable disabled Europeans

55. Italy's general public will most probably agree that _____.

(A) physical inadequacies are the biggest obstacle for the disabled

(B) things should be done to remove the barriers against the disabled

(C) workplace prejudices toward the disabled are hardly recognizable

(D) disabled people should reduce their needs to go to public places

56. What is the passage mainly about?

(A) Italy does not do enough to aid the disabled.

(B) Italy's disabled people should get out of their houses.

(C) Italian people have been blind to troubles of the disabled.

(D) Italian ways of aiding the disabled should be encouraged.

第貳部分：非選擇題（佔 28 分）

一、中譯英（佔 8 分）

說明：1. 請將以下中文句子譯成正確、通順、達意的英文，並將答案寫在「答案卷」上。

2. 請依序作答，並標明題號。每題 4 分，共 8 分。

1. 全球暖化是有史以來最嚴重的問題之一，我們都應該關注這個議題。

2. 騎腳踏車已經成為一股潮流，不僅可以節省能源，也是很好的一種運動方式。

二、英文作文（佔 20 分）

說明：1. 依提示在「答案卷」上寫一篇英文作文。

2. 文長約 100 至 120 個單詞（words）。

提示：你的朋友剛剛和他（她）的男（女）朋友分手。你（英文名字必須假設為 Stanley 或 Alice），要寫一封信給你的朋友（英文名字必須假設為 Paul 或 Tracy），安慰他（她），並設想一個讓他（她）忘記情傷的方法。

請注意：必須使用上述的 Stanley 或 Alice 在信末署名，**不得使用自己的真實中文或英文名字**。

大學入學學科能力測驗英文模擬試題 ⑥ 詳解

第壹部分：單選題

一、詞彙：

1. (**C**) 下了二十四小時的大雨後，瞬間氾濫讓村莊著實成為一座小島，使行動變得困難。

    (A) warrant (ˈwɔrənt) *n.* 授權書；正當權利

    (B) amendment (əˈmɛndmənt) *n.* 修正案

    (C) ***rainfall*** (ˈrenˌfɔl) *n.* 降雨（量）

    (D) security (sɪˈkjurətɪ) *n.* 安全；防護   secure *adj.* 安全的

    * flash (flæʃ) *adj.* 瞬間的   flooding (ˈflʌdɪŋ) *n.* 氾濫

    turn A ***into*** B 將 A 變成 B   virtual (ˈvɝtʃuəl) *adj.* 實際上的

    movement (ˈmuvmənt) *n.* 移動；遷徙

2. (**B**) 穩穩地座落在新德里中心的雄偉建築，是印度的全新高級購物中心，也確實吸引了印度新富人士。

    (A) flock (flɑk) *v.* 聚集 *n.*（鳥、羊）群；（人）群

    (B) ***nestle*** (ˈnɛsḷ) *v.* 座落 (= *sit* = *stand* = *lie*)

    (C) cluster (ˈklʌstɚ) *v.* 群聚 (= *gather* = *assemble*)；叢生

    (D) populate (ˈpɑpjəˌlet) *v.* 居住於

    * grand (grænd) *adj.* 雄偉的

    New Delhi (njuˈdɛlɪ) *n.* 新德里【印度首都】

    India (ˈɪndɪə) *n.* 印度   brand-new (ˈbrændˈnju) *adj.* 嶄新的

    luxury (ˈlʌkʃərɪ) *adj.* 高級的   prove (pruv) *v.* 證明是

    draw (drɔ) *n.* 吸引人的事物   ***the newly wealthy*** 新富人士

3. (**A**) 情緒障礙包含厭煩、做白日夢、壓力、生氣和挫折，可能會妨礙學業成就。它們都會降低在課堂上的專注。

    (A) ***interfere*** (ˌɪntɚˈfɪr) *v.* 妨礙 < *with* >；干涉 < *in* >

    (B) accelerate (ækˈsɛləˌret) *v.* 加速 (= *hasten* = *quicken*)

    (C) deprive (dɪˈpraɪv) *v.* 剝奪   deprived *adj.* 貧窮的

    (D) dissatisfy (dɪsˈsætɪsˌfaɪ) *v.* 使不滿

* emotional〔ɪˈmoʃənḷ〕*adj.* 情緒的　　block〔blɑk〕*n.* 阻礙
academic〔͵ækəˈdɛmɪk〕*adj.* 學術的　　boredom〔ˈbordəm〕*n.* 厭煩
daydream〔ˈde͵drim〕*v.* 做白日夢　　stress〔strɛs〕*n.* 壓力
frustration〔frʌsˈtreʃən〕*n.* 挫折
concentration〔͵kɑnsṇˈtreʃən〕*n.* 專注

4. (**C**) 壓力會導致足以打消你計畫的疾病，而運動是已知的最佳方法，可以<u>降低</u>因焦慮產生的壓力。

(A) convey〔kənˈve〕*v.* 傳送 (= *transport*)；表達 (= *communicate*)
(B) defy〔dɪˈfaɪ〕*v.* 違抗 (= *disobey*)
(C) ***reduce***〔rɪˈdjus〕*v.* 降低 (= *lessen* = *diminish*)
(D) devise〔dɪˈvaɪz〕*v.* 想出 (= *conceive*)；發明 (= *invent*)

* ***blow apart*** 破壞　　***lead to*** 導致　　schedule〔ˈskɛdʒul〕*n.* 計畫
anxiety〔æŋˈzaɪətɪ〕*n.* 焦慮　　produce〔prəˈdjus〕*v.* 產生

5. (**D**) 紙巾和餐巾紙都很浪費森林資源。用餐時，清理雜亂更好的<u>替代品</u>有餐巾布、舊布、海綿或毛巾。

(A) procession〔prəˈsɛʃən〕*n.* 行列 (= *parade* = *file*)
(B) memorial〔məˈmorɪəl〕*n.* 紀念碑（館、物）
(C) registration〔͵rɛdʒɪˈstreʃən〕*n.* 掛號；註冊　　register *v.*
(D) ***alternative***〔ɔlˈtɝnətɪv〕*n.* 替代品；可供選擇之物
　　(= *choice* = *option*)　　*adj.* 替代的

* ***paper towel*** 紙巾　　napkin〔ˈnæpkɪn〕*n.* 餐巾
wasteful〔ˈwestfəl〕*adj.* 浪費的　　***be wasteful of*** 浪費
resource〔rɪˈsors〕*n.* 資源　　***clean up*** 清理　　mess〔mɛs〕*n.* 雜亂
rag〔ræg〕*n.* 破布；舊布　　sponge〔spʌndʒ〕*n.* 海綿

6. (**D**) 傳統上，孩子被視為是父母的財產，<u>因此</u>他們自己本身沒有什麼權力。

(A) consecutively〔kənˈsɛkjətɪvlɪ〕*adv.* 連續地；接連地
(B) intensively〔ɪnˈtɛnsɪvlɪ〕*adv.* 強烈地；密集地　　intensity *n.*
(C) respectfully〔rɪˈspɛktfəlɪ〕*adv.* 恭敬地
(D) ***consequently***〔ˈkɑnsə͵kwɛntlɪ〕*adv.* 因此
　　consequence *n.* 結果　　consequent *adj.* 隨之發生的

* traditionally〔trəˈdɪʃənḷɪ〕*adv.* 傳統地

property〔'prɑpətɪ〕n. 財產
entitlement〔ɪn'taɪtl̩mənt〕n. 應得的權力
in one's own right 憑本身的條件

7.（**B**）父母應該要承擔他們的責任，而不是去期待校方和老師，去接手他們身為父母親該有的<u>義務</u>。

   (A) asset〔'æsɛt〕n. 資產【常用複數】；有價值的特質或技能

   (B) *obligation*〔ˌɑblə'geʃən〕n. 義務（= *duty* = *commitment*）

   (C) appliance〔ə'plaɪəns〕n. 設備；裝置（= *device*）

   (D) deficit〔'dɛfəsɪt〕n. 短缺（= *shortage* = *deficiency*）；赤字

   * accept〔ək'sɛpt〕v. 接受；承認　　*take over* 接管

8.（**A**）要減重，你必須讓自己保持<u>水分充足</u>，因為口渴有時候會以飢餓疼痛的方式呈現。

   (A) *hydrated*〔'haɪdretɪd〕adj. 水分充足的；含水的（↔ dehydrated）

   (B) paralyze〔'pærəˌlaɪz〕v. 使麻痺；使癱瘓（= *disable*）

   (C) deceive〔dɪ'siv〕v. 欺騙（= *delude*）
      deceit n.（蓄意）欺騙

   (D) testify〔'tɛstəˌfaɪ〕v. 作證；證實（= *demonstrate*）

   * *lose weight* 減重　　thirst〔θɝst〕n. 口渴
     present〔prɪ'zɛnt〕v. 表達；呈現　　pain〔pen〕n. 疼痛

9.（**B**）仲介表示，在中國，購屋人數已<u>大大地</u>減少，而且在某些地區，尤其是中國的東南部，價格甚至跌了百分之四十。

   (A) economically〔ˌikə'nɑmɪkl̩ɪ〕adv. 節儉地（↔ wastefully）

   (B) *dramatically*〔drə'mætɪkl̩ɪ〕adv. 重大地（= *significantly* = *greatly*）

   (C) objectively〔əb'dʒɛktɪvlɪ〕adv. 客觀地（↔ subjectively）

   (D) dogmatically〔dɔg'mætɪkl̩ɪ〕adv. 武斷地

   * broker〔'brokɚ〕n. 仲介；經紀人
     neighborhood〔'nebɚˌhʊd〕n. 地區　　drop〔drɑp〕v. 下跌

10. (**D**) 在課堂上做上課筆記，能使學生將注意力集中在所講授的課程，從而增加<u>專注力</u>、記憶和理解。

　　(A) delegation〔͵dɛlə'geʃən〕*n.* 代表團；授權 (= *authorization*)

　　(B) access〔'æksɛs〕*n.* 途徑；管道；接近⋯的權利　　*v.* 使用

　　(C) restriction〔rɪ'strɪkʃən〕*n.* 限制　　restrict *v.*

　　(D) *concentration*〔͵kɑnsn̩'treʃən〕*n.* 專心 (= *absorption*)

　　* *take notes* 做筆記　　lecture〔'lɛktʃɚ〕*n.* 講課

　　focus on 集中於　　thereby〔'ðɛr͵baɪ〕*adv.* 藉以；從而

　　retention〔rɪ'tɛnʃən〕*n.* 記憶力

11. (**B**) 你會延遲重要的工作嗎？這就叫作<u>拖延</u>。

　　(A) admission〔əd'mɪʃən〕*n.* 允許進入（學校、組織、場所等）；

　　　　入場費；承認

　　(B) *procrastination*〔pro͵kræstə'neʃən〕*n.* 拖延；耽擱

　　　　Procrastination is the thief of time.（【諺】拖延為時間之賊。）

　　(C) circulation〔͵sɝkjə'leʃən〕*n.* 循環；（雜誌等）發行量

　　(D) extension〔ɪk'stɛnʃən〕*n.* 擴展；延伸；分機

　　　　extend *v.* 擴大 (= *expand*)；延長 (= *stretch* = *lengthen*)

　　* *put off* 拖延；延期　　task〔tæsk〕*n.* 工作

12. (**C**) 許多人因為大雨<u>受困</u>在橋上，村民們前往營救，但由於水流，牽引車無法抵達那裡。

　　(A) acquaint〔ə'kwent〕*v.* 告知 (= *notify* = *inform*)；使熟悉

　　(B) acquire〔ə'kwaɪr〕*v.* 獲得 (= *obtain*)

　　(C) *strand*〔strænd〕*v.* 使處於困境；使擱淺

　　(D) smother〔'smʌðɚ〕*v.* 使窒息 (= *choke*)；悶熄 (= *extinguish*)

　　* *due to* 由於　　villager〔'vɪlɪdʒɚ〕*n.* 村民

　　rescue〔'rɛskju〕*n.* 援救

　　go to one's *rescue* 前去拯救某人

　　tractor〔'træktɚ〕*n.* 牽引車　　flowing〔'floɪŋ〕*adj.* 流動的

13. (**A**) 爲了趕上流行的月餅浪潮，冰淇淋鉅子哈根達斯創造了一條高檔的、包冰淇淋餡的月餅生產線，給那些負擔得起昂貴月餅的族群。

　　(A) **high-end** (ˈhaɪˈɛnd) *adj.* 高檔的 (↔ low-end)

　　(B) low-cal (ˈloˈkæl) *adj.* 低卡的 (= *low-calorie*)

　　(C) upside-down (ˈʌp,saɪdˈdaun) *adj.* 顛倒的

　　(D) out-of-date (ˈautəvˈdet) *adj.* 過期的；過時的 (= *out-of-fashion*)

　　* trendy (ˈtrɛndɪ) *adj.* 流行的　　bandwagon (ˈbænd,wægən) *n.* 浪潮

　　　jump on the bandwagon 趕時髦

　　　mooncake (ˈmunˈkek) *n.* 月餅　　giant (ˈdʒaɪənt) *n.* 鉅子

　　　Häagen Dazs　*n.* 哈根達斯　　line (laɪn) *n.* 生產線

　　　afford (əˈford) *v.* 負擔得起　　costly (ˈkɔstlɪ) *adj.* 昂貴的

14. (**B**) 藉著做課堂筆記，學生們不僅可以記錄重要的事情，也記錄了老師的重點和觀念。

　　(A) inherent (ɪnˈhɪrənt) *adj.* 固有的；天生的 (= *innate* = *inborn*)

　　(B) **significant** (sɪgˈnɪfəkənt) *adj.* 重要的；意義重大的；顯著的

　　(C) various (ˈvɛrɪəs) *adj.* 各式各樣的

　　(D) lengthy (ˈlɛŋθɪ) *adj.* 冗長的 (↔ brief)

　　* record (rɪˈkɔrd) *v.* 記錄　　point (pɔɪnt) *n.* 重點

　　　perspective (pɚˈspɛktɪv) *n.* 看法；正確的眼光　　*as well* 也

15. (**A**) 現在社交媒體確實是個大市場，很難找到一本沒在談論它的商業刊物。

　　(A) **definitively** (dɪˈfɪnə,tɪvlɪ) *adv.* 確定地；明確地

　　(B) scarcely (ˈskɛrslɪ) *adv.* 幾乎不 (= *hardly*)

　　(C) consciously (ˈkɑnʃəslɪ) *adv.* 有意識地；故意地

　　(D) ideally (aɪˈdɪəlɪ) *adv.* 理想地 (↔ pratically)

　　* media (ˈmidɪə) *n. pl.* 媒體【單數爲 medium (ˈmidɪəm)】

　　　social media 社交媒體【朋友間可以分享、討論資訊，以網路或移動

　　　　通訊作爲主要媒介的社交平台，如部落格】

　　　mass (mæs) *adj.* 大規模的　　trade (tred) *n.* 商業

　　　publication (,pʌblɪˈkeʃən) *n.* 刊物

二、綜合測驗：

第 16 至 20 題為題組

　　隨著工業城鎮的發展規模比以往更大，市郊也跟著拓展，在十九世紀的非洲，首度有人提出國家公園的提議。即使如此，從十九世紀直到二十世紀，非
16
洲的野生生物仍被嚴重捕獵。到 1920 年的時候，捕捉大型動物的獵人，幾乎將若干種野生動物族群都消滅了，殖民者也開墾大範圍的山地。

* ***national park*** 國家公園　　Africa (ˈæfrɪkə) *n.* 非洲
industrial (ɪnˈdʌstrɪəl) *adj.* 工業的
suburb (ˈsʌbɝb) *n.* 市郊　　swell (swɛl) *v.* 膨脹
wildlife (ˈwaɪldˌlaɪf) *n.* 野生生物
big-game (ˈbɪgˌgem) *adj.* 大型獵物的　　deplete (dɪˈplit) *v.* 使枯竭
population (ˌpɑpjəˈleʃən) *n.* 族群　　settler (ˈsɛtlɚ) *n.* 殖民者
deforest (dɪˈfɔrɪst) *v.* 開闢山地　　tract (trækt) *n.* 廣闊的面積

16. (**B**) (A) rehearsal (rɪˈhɝsl̩) *n.* 排演
　　　　 (B) ***proposal*** (prəˈpozl̩) *n.* 提議；計畫
　　　　 (C) dispersal (dɪˈspɝsl̩) *n.* 分散；離散
　　　　 (D) disposal (dɪˈspozl̩) *n.* 處置

　　曾經漫遊在南非東南端，東開普敦省的大批象群，數量削減到僅剩下十一頭，
17
而且斑馬也瀕臨絕種。

* vast (væst) *adj.* 廣大的　　roam (rom) *v.* 漫遊
Eastern Cape 東開普敦【南非東南方的一個省】
province (ˈprɑvɪns) *n.* 省
South Africa 南非【位於非洲南部的國家，以野生動物跟生產鑽石聞名】
zebra (ˈzibrə) *n.* 斑馬　　extinction (ɪkˈstɪŋkʃən) *n.* 滅絕

17. (**B**) (A) school (skul) *n.* (魚) 群
　　　　 (B) ***herd*** (hɝd) *n.* (牛、馬、象) 群
　　　　 (C) swarm (swɔrm) *n.* (昆蟲) 群
　　　　 (D) pack (pæk) *n.* (犬、狼) 群

　　因此，南非採取的初步措施，是創立公園和保育區，來扭轉這個情勢。阿
　　　　　　　　　　　　　18
多大象國家公園設立於 1931 年，現在園內擁有超過兩百頭大象。該公園佔地
　　　　　　　　　　　　　　　　　　　　　　　　　　　　　　　19
兩百四十一平方公里，它也是開普敦水牛、黑犀牛和一百八十多種鳥類的家。

　　　* *as a result* 因此　　*take steps* 採取措施
　　　reverse〔rɪˋvɝs〕*v.* 扭轉；徹底改變　　trend〔trɛnd〕*n.* 趨勢
　　　preserve〔prɪˋzɝv〕*n.* 保護區　　establish〔əˋstæblɪʃ〕*v.* 建立；設立
　　　border〔ˋbɔrdɚ〕*n.* 領域　　*sq* 平方（= *square*〔skwɛr〕）
　　　buffalo〔ˋbʌfḷo〕*n.* 水牛　　rhinoceros〔raɪˋnɑsərəs〕*n.* 犀牛
　　　species〔ˋspiʃɪz〕*n.*（生物）物種【單複數同形】　　*be home to* 為…的家

18.(**A**) 依句意，「藉著創立」公園以及保育區來逆轉情勢，選 (A) *by creating*。

19.(**B**) 原句為：The park, *which encompasses* 241 sq km, ...，關代 which
　　　　可省略，動詞改成現在分詞 *encompassing*，故選 (B)。
　　　　encompass〔ɪnˋkʌmpəs〕*v.* 包圍；含有
　　　　而 (C) (D) surpass〔səˋpæs〕*v.* 超越，則不合句意。

山地斑馬國家公園設立於 1937 年，保護超過兩百隻山地斑馬，好幾種羚羊，
和兩百種鳥類。在六十二平方公里的公園裡，有山脈、陡峭的峽谷、一些蘆薈
物種，和許多各式各樣的開花灌木。　　　　　　　　20

　　　* antelope〔ˋæntḷˌop〕*n.* 羚羊　　steep〔stip〕*adj.* 陡峭的
　　　ravine〔rəˋvin〕*n.* 峽谷　　aloe〔ˋælo〕*n.* 蘆薈
　　　numerous〔ˋnjumərəs〕*adj.* 眾多的　　variety〔vəˋraɪətɪ〕*n.* 各種各樣
　　　flowering〔ˋflaʊərɪŋ〕*adj.* 會開花的　　shrub〔ʃrʌb〕*n.* 灌木

20.(**A**) 「地方副詞 + be 動詞」，表「～有…」，又空格後為複數名詞，
　　　　故選 (A) *are*。

第 21 至 25 題為題組

　　癌症是一種細胞不正常的生長。儘管空間受限，必須和其他細胞共享營養
　　　　　　　　　　　　　　　　　21
素，或是從身體發出停止複製的訊息，癌細胞仍能快速繁殖。它們的形狀不同
於健康細胞，而且可能會出乎意料地蔓延到身體各處。

　　* cancer〔'kænsə〕*n.* 癌　　　abnormal〔æb'nɔrmḷ〕*adj.* 不正常的
　　cell〔sɛl〕*n.* 細胞　　　reproduce〔,riprə'djus〕*v.* 繁殖；生殖
　　restriction〔rɪ'strɪkʃən〕*n.* 限制　　　nutrient〔'njutrɪənt〕*n.* 營養
　　signal〔'sɪgnḷ〕*n.* 信號　　　reproduction〔,riprə'dʌkʃən〕*n.* 繁殖
　　shape〔ʃep〕*v.* 成⋯形狀　　　unexpectedly〔,ʌnɪk'spɛktɪdlɪ〕*adv.* 意外地

21. (**C**) 依句意，「儘管」空間受限，選 (C) ***despite***。

　　由於每個身體組織裡的細胞數量都被嚴密管控，所以新細胞的數量，會跟
取代快死掉的細胞所需的數量，加上生長和發育所需的數量相等。然而，不像
　　　　　　　　　　　　　　　　　　　　　　　22　　　　　　　　　23
正常細胞，腫瘤是能夠不受控制地生長和分裂的細胞叢，它們的成長不受控制。

　　* tissue〔'tɪʃʊ〕*n.* 組織　　　tightly〔'taɪtlɪ〕*adv.* 緊密地
　　replace〔rɪ'ples〕*v.* 取代　　　dying〔'daɪɪŋ〕*adj.* 瀕死的
　　plus〔plʌs〕*prep.* 加上　　　development〔dɪ'vɛləpmənt〕*n.* 發展
　　normal〔'nɔrmḷ〕*adj.* 正常的　　　tumor〔'tjumə〕*n.* 腫瘤
　　cluster〔'klʌstə〕*n.* 簇；群　　　***capable of + V-ing*** 能夠～
　　divide〔də'vaɪd〕*v.* 分裂
　　uncontrollably〔,ʌnkən'troləbḷɪ〕*adv.* 不能控制地
　　regulate〔'rɛgjə,let〕*v.* 限制

22. (**D**) As 引導副詞子句，而逗點後面是主要子句，其主詞為 the number of
　　　new cells made，故空格應填動詞，選 (D) ***equals***。
　　　equal〔'ikwəl〕*v.* 等於

23. (**C**) 依句意，選 (C) ***Unlike***「不像」。而 (A) within「在⋯之中」，(B) above
　　　「在⋯上面」，(D) beneath「在⋯之下」，均不合句意。

　　腫瘤可能是良性或惡性。良性腫瘤通常成長緩慢，而且不會擴散，然而
　　　　　　　　　　　　　　　　　　　　　　　　　　　　　　　　　24
惡性腫瘤生長迅速，可以侵入和破壞鄰近的正常組織，還可能會擴散遍及全
身。「癌症」一字，就是指當腫瘤為惡性時所使用的詞彙。

　　* benign〔bɪ'naɪn〕*adj.* 良性的　　　malignant〔mə'lɪgnənt〕*adj.* 惡性的
　　tend to 通常；傾向於　　　invade〔ɪn'ved〕*v.* 侵略
　　nearby〔'nɪr,baɪ〕*adj.* 附近的　　　term〔tɜm〕*n.* 詞彙

24. (**A**) 依句意，選 (A) ***whereas***「然而」。而 (B) since「自從」，(C) unless「除
　　　非」，(D) lest「以免」，均不合句意。

　　癌症也可能有分作「局部入侵性」和「轉移性」。若是局部入侵性，腫瘤會藉著放出癌細胞到正常組織中，來侵入環繞在腫瘤周圍的組織。當它是<u>移轉性</u>，
25
腫瘤會放出細胞到遠處組織。事實上，癌症不僅是一種疾病，而應是一組疾病。

> * locally〔'lokəlɪ〕adv. 局部地　　invasive〔ɪn'vesɪv〕adj. 侵入的
> metastatic〔,mɛtə'stætɪk〕adj. 轉移性的
> surround〔sə'raʊnd〕v. 圍繞　　**send out** 發出
> cancerous〔'kænsərəs〕adj. 癌症的　　**distant from** 距離…遠的
> **in fact** 事實上　　rather〔'ræðɚ〕adv. 而…；確切地說

25. (**B**) (A) immune〔ɪ'mjun〕adj. 免疫的
　　　　(B) **metastatic**〔,mɛtə'stætɪk〕adj. 轉移性的
　　　　(C) hysterical〔hɪs'tɛrɪkḷ〕adj. 歇斯底里的
　　　　(D) eligible〔'ɛlɪdʒəbḷ〕adj. 合格的

<u>第 26 至 30 題爲題組</u>

　　維克多看到一家餐廳的櫥窗裡，有著告示牌<u>寫著</u>「獨特早餐」。維克多一直
26
都是個愛嚐鮮的食客，於是他走進餐廳然後坐下。女服務生給他一壺茶，問他想要吃什麼。

> * sign〔saɪn〕n. 標誌；告示　　unusual〔ʌn'juʒʊəl〕adj. 獨特的；罕見的
> adventurous〔əd'vɛntʃərəs〕adj. 愛冒險的　　pot〔pat〕n. 壺

26. (**B**) 依句意，選 (B) **read**「(告示、書報雜誌上) 寫著」(= *said*)。而
　　　　(A) speak「說 (語言)」，(C) utter〔'ʌtɚ〕v. 說出，(D) tell「告訴；
　　　　說 (故事、謊言)」，則用法不合。

　　維克多禮貌性地問：「你們的獨特早餐包括什麼？」
　　女服務生<u>露齒笑著</u>說：「烤雞舌！」
27

> * politely〔pə'laɪtlɪ〕adv. 有禮貌地　　baked〔bekt〕adj. 烤過的
> tongue〔tʌŋ〕n. 舌頭　　reply〔rɪ'plaɪ〕v. 回答

27. (**B**) (A) grain〔gren〕n. 穀物　　　　(B) **grin**〔grɪn〕n. v. 露齒而笑
　　　　(C) grief〔grif〕n. 悲傷　　　　　(D) groan〔gron〕n. v. 呻吟

　　維克多大叫：「烤雞舌？烤雞舌！你知道那有多噁心嗎？我絕不會考慮吃
從雞的嘴裡拿出來的東西！」
<u>　　　　　　　　　　　　　　28　　　　　　　　　　29</u>

*　* disgusting〔dɪs'gʌstɪŋ〕*adj.* 令人作嘔的
　　come out of 來自於；出自於　　snap〔snæp〕*v.* 厲聲說

28. (**B**) 依句意，「多麼地」噁心，選 (B) *how*。

29. (**B**) (A) regard〔rɪ'gɑrd〕*v.* 認為　　　(B) ***consider***〔kən'sɪdə〕*v.* 考慮
　　　　　　(C) reflect〔rɪ'flɛkt〕*v.* 反省　　　(D) ponder〔'pɑndə〕*v.* 沉思

　　女服務生一點都<u>沒有被嚇到</u>，她說：「那麼你想要吃什麼？」
　　　　　　　　　　30
　　維克多回答：「好吧，那給我一些炒蛋就好。」

*　* scramble〔'skræmbḷ〕*v.* 炒（蛋）；攪亂　　***scrambled eggs*** 炒蛋

30. (**A**) 依句意，選 (A) ***Undaunted***〔ʌn'dɔntɪd〕*adj.* 無懼的。本句是由分詞構
　　　　句 Being undaunted 省略 being 而來。而 (B) unequaled〔ʌn'ikwəld〕
　　　　adj. 無與倫比的，(C) undesired〔ˌʌndɪ'zaɪrd〕*adj.* 不想要得到的，
　　　　(D) unexpired〔ˌʌnɪk'spaɪrd〕*adj.* 未到期的，則不合句意。

三、文意選填：

<u>第 31 至 40 題為題組</u>

　　慢性疲勞症候群（CFS）是一種能引發極度疲累的症狀。1980 年代首次替
這種疾病取名字。即使到現在，有 [31]**(E)** 越來越多人被診斷出罹患慢性疲勞症候
群，但許多保健 [32]**(B)** 業界內外的人士，仍懷疑它的存在，或堅持它只是一種心
理上的小毛病。

*　* chronic〔'krɑnɪk〕*adj.* 慢性的　　fatigue〔fə'tig〕*n.* 疲勞
　　syndrome〔'sɪnˌdrom〕*n.* 症候群
　　chronic fatigue syndrome 慢性疲勞症候群
　　condition〔kən'dɪʃən〕*n.* 狀況；疾病　　cause〔kɔz〕*v.* 引起
　　extreme〔ɪk'strim〕*adj.* 極度的　　tiredness〔'taɪrdnɪs〕*n.* 疲倦
　　increasing〔ɪn'krisɪŋ〕*adj.* 越來越多的　　diagnose〔ˌdaɪəg'nos〕*v.* 診斷
　　profession〔prə'fɛʃən〕*n.* 專業；同行　　doubt〔daʊt〕*v.* 懷疑
　　existence〔ɪg'zɪstəns〕*n.* 存在　　maintain〔men'ten〕*v.* 堅持
　　psychological〔ˌsaɪkə'lɑdʒɪkḷ〕*adj.* 心理的　　ailment〔'elmənt〕*n.* 疾病

原本健康且 [33] **(G)** 充滿精力的人，可能會經歷各種症狀，包含極度疲勞、虛弱、喉嚨痛、頭痛，還有很難 [34] **(C)** 專心。

    * previously〔'privɪəslɪ〕adv. 以前；事先　　**be full of** 充滿
      energy〔'ɛnədʒɪ〕n. 精力　　experience〔ɪk'spɪrɪəns〕v. 經歷
      a variety of 各種的　　symptom〔'sɪmptəm〕n. 徵兆
      weakness〔'wiknɪs〕n. 虛弱　　sore〔sor〕adj. 痛的；發炎的
      sore throat 喉嚨痛　　**difficulty (in) V-ing** 很難～
      concentrate〔'kɑnsn̩,tret〕v. 專心

患有慢性疲勞症候群的人，會有持續六個月或是更久的疲勞感。慢性疲勞症候群沒有已知的病因，但似乎是由一 [35] **(D)** 組病因所引起的。

    * last〔læst〕v. 持續　　known〔non〕adj. 已知的
      cause〔kɔz〕n. 原因；病因　　**appear to** 似乎　　**result from** 起因於
      combination〔,kɑmbə'neʃən〕n. 組合　　factor〔'fæktɚ〕n. 因素

    慢性疲勞症候群的併發症有疲勞、倦怠、精疲力盡以及疼痛，這些症狀讓該病很難被 [36] **(I)** 診斷出來，因為它很類似 [37] **(F)** 像狼瘡、多發性硬化症、纖維性肌痛症，和萊姆症等疾病。

    * non-specific〔,nɑnspɪ'sɪfɪk〕adj. 非特定的；併發的
      exhaustion〔ɪg'zɔstʃən〕n. 精疲力盡　　ache〔ek〕n. 疼痛
      similar to 類似於…　　**such as** 例如
      lupus〔'lupəs〕n. 狼瘡【一種病因尚不明的慢性免疫疾病，引起全身性
        器官發炎，症狀之一是皮膚發紅像被狼咬過的痕跡】
      multiple〔'mʌltəpl̩〕adj. 多重的　　sclerosis〔sklɪ'rosɪs〕n. 硬化
      multiple sclerosis 多發性硬化症【一種發生於中樞神經系統（腦部以及
        脊髓）的慢性疾病】
      fibromyalgia〔,faɪbromaɪ'ældʒɪə〕n. 纖維性肌痛症
      Lyme disease 萊姆症【一種由節肢動物傳染，影響皮膚、關節和神經系統
        的疾病，症狀有發燒、皮膚出現紅斑等】

患有慢性疲勞症候群的人，[38] **(J)** 由於長期疲勞和短期記憶問題，通常無法在工作和家庭中有正常的表現。慢性疲勞症候群症狀的特徵是不可抗的疲勞與衰弱，使人非常難以執行 [39] **(A)** 例行及日常的工作，例如起床、打扮和飲食。

　＊ unable〔ʌnʼeb!〕*adj.* 不能～的　　perform〔pɚʼfɔrm〕*v.* 做；執行
　　normally〔ʼnɔrml!〕*adv.* 正常地　　***because of*** 由於
　　long-term〔ʼlɔŋ,tɝm〕*adj.* 長期的　　short-term〔ʼʃɔrtʼtɝm〕*adj.* 短期的
　　memory〔ʼmɛmərı〕*n.* 記憶　　hallmark〔ʼhɔl,mark〕*n.* 特徵
　　overwhelming〔,ovɚʼhwɛlmıŋ〕*adj.* 不可抵抗的；強大的
　　extremely〔ıkʼstrimlı〕*adv.* 極度地　　routine〔ruʼtin〕*adj.* 例行的
　　daily〔ʼdelı〕*adj.* 每天的；日常的　　task〔tæsk〕*n.* 工作；任務

這種疾病會嚴重 [40]**(H)** 影響學業、工作和休閒活動，並引起身體跟情緒上的病
症，這些病症會持續幾個月，甚至好幾年。

　＊ illness〔ʼılnıs〕*n.* 疾病　　severely〔səʼvırlı〕*adv.* 嚴重地
　　affect〔əʼfɛkt〕*v.* 影響　　leisure〔ʼliʒɚ〕*adj.* 空閒的
　　activity〔ækʼtıvətı〕*n.* 活動　　physical〔ʼfızık!〕*adj.* 身體上的
　　emotional〔ıʼmoʃən!〕*adj.* 情感的

四、閱讀測驗：

第 41 至 44 題為題組

　　走進中國任何一家網路咖啡廳，你會看見很多人打開即時通訊的視窗和朋
友聊天，也同時可能在玩線上遊戲，或進行搜尋。在辦公室裡，當人們在用 Excel
試算表工作時，網路聊天如微風般，也透過開啟的即時通訊視窗流了進來。他
們可能會開著 QQ 或 MSN 的視窗，來廣泛地分享資訊。這兩種都是在中國很
受歡迎的即時通訊服務。

　＊ Internet〔ʼıntɚ,nɛt〕*n.* 網路　　***Internet cafe*** 網路咖啡廳
　　IM 即時通訊（＝ *instant messaging*）
　　window〔ʼwındo〕*n.* （電腦）視窗　　online〔,anʼlaın〕*adj.* 線上的
　　conduct〔kənʼdʌkt〕*v.* 執行　　search〔sɝtʃ〕*n.* 搜尋
　　breeze〔briz〕*n.* 微風　　flow〔flo〕*v.* 流
　　Excel〔ıkʼsɛl〕*n.* 微軟公司出的試算表軟體
　　spreadsheet〔ʼsprɛd,ʃit〕*n.* （電腦）空白格式表
　　QQ 深圳騰訊計算機通訊公司於 1999 年 2 月推出的免費即時通訊軟體
　　MSN 微軟公司所推出的免費即時通訊軟體（＝ *Microsoft Messenger*）
　　instant〔ʼınstənt〕*adj.* 即時的　　message〔ʼmɛsıdʒ〕*n.* 訊息
　　instant-messaging 即時通訊系統

　　深圳的騰訊控股公司以其 QQ 平台，掌控中國的即時通訊市場。使用中的 QQ 帳號已達到三億一千五百萬個，這數字是因為人們啟用多個帳戶而大量增加。QQ 是中國第一的即時通訊服務，有百分之七十九點六的市佔率。最接近它的對手，微軟公司的 MSN，它的主要目標是攻佔商業用戶，到了 2008 年第一季，其使用中的帳戶有大約一千六百五十萬個。

　　　* dominate〔'dɑmə,net〕v. 掌控；主宰

　　　Tencent Holdings Inc. 騰訊控股公司【中國大陸的網路公司名】

　　　Inc. 法人組織的【為 incorporated〔ɪn'kɔrpə,retɪd〕adj. 的縮寫】

　　　Shenzhen 深圳【中國廣東省的沿海城市】

　　　platform〔'plæt,fɔrm〕n. 平台

　　　active〔'æktɪv〕adj. 起作用的；活絡的

　　　account〔ə'kaʊnt〕n. 帳號　　figure〔'fɪgjɚ〕n. 數字

　　　boost〔bust〕v. 提高　　multiple〔'mʌltəpḷ〕adj. 多個的

　　　market share 市場佔有率　　rival〔'raɪvḷ〕n. 對手

　　　Microsoft〔'maɪkro,sɔft〕n. 微軟【全球最大電腦軟體供應商，總部設在
　　　　美國西雅圖，前總裁為比爾蓋茲，Micro-soft 為「微型軟體」之意】

　　　Corp. 法人團體【為 corporation〔,kɔrpə'reʃən〕n. 的縮寫】

　　　mainly〔'menlɪ〕adv. 主要地　　target〔'tɑrgɪt〕v. 目標為

　　　quarter〔'kwɔrtɚ〕n. 一季

　　在中國，數億人有 QQ 帳號，而且多數人的聯絡清單中，都有超過一百個 QQ 朋友。他們通常擁有幾個額外付費 QQ 號碼，每個號碼每個月大約要花費十塊人民幣（一點四三美元）。除了傳送訊息之外，他們也從 QQ 網站上閱讀新聞，並在 QQ 的聊天群組裡參與討論。不管在家裡還是在辦公室，他們只要連結到網際網路，就會馬上登入，很有可能每天花超過十小時在 QQ 上面，然而，卻只花十分鐘和現實中的朋友交談。

　　　* **hundreds of millions of** 數億的　　subscribe〔səb'skraɪb〕v. 訂閱＜ to ＞

　　　contact〔'kɑntækt〕n. 聯絡　　**contact list** 聯絡清單

　　　tend to 通常；傾向於　　premium〔'primɪəm〕n. 額外費用

　　　yuan〔ju'ɑn〕n. 元【人民幣單位】　　**in addition to** 除…之外（還有）

　　　.com 網路公司；網站（＝ dot-com ）

　　　participate〔pɑr'tɪsə,pet〕v. 參與　　discussion〔dɪ'skʌʃən〕n. 討論

　　　chat group 聊天群組　　**log in** 登入

　　因爲許多中國人是和這個產品一起成長的，他們通常不會詢問其他人電子郵件信箱，而是詢問 QQ 帳號。他們也發展了一種 QQ 生活型態，甚至是一種新的網路語言，「火星文」，主要用於在 QQ 上聊天，和 QQ 空間，也就是一個QQ 提供的多媒體網路日誌服務。舉例來說，「3Q」就是「謝謝」的意思。

　　* email〔'i,mel〕 n. 電子郵件（ = electronic mail ）
　　　address〔ə'drɛs〕 n. 郵件位址
　　　lifestyle〔'laɪf,staɪl〕 n. 生活方式　　　Mars〔mɑrz〕 n. 火星
　　　Qzone〔'kju'zon〕 QQ空間【騰訊公司所推出的網誌空間】
　　　multimedia〔,mʌltɪ'midɪə〕 n. pl. 多媒體
　　　blog〔blɑg〕 n. 網路日誌（ = web log ）

41.(**B**) 本文的作者最有可能是一位 ＿＿＿＿＿＿。
　　　(A) 專心致力的環保人士　　　　　　(B) 新聞通訊記者
　　　(C) 教育心理學家　　　　　　　　　(D) 高階工程師

　　* devoted〔dɪ'votɪd〕 adj. 熱中的
　　　environmentalist〔ɪn,vaɪrən'mɛntl̩ɪst〕 n. 環保人士
　　　correspondent〔,kɔrə'spɑndənt〕 n. 新聞特派員
　　　high-ranking〔'haɪ,ræŋkɪŋ〕 adj. 高職位的
　　　engineer〔,ɛndʒə'nɪr〕 n. 工程師

42.(**D**) 根據本文，哪家公司擁有中國最受歡迎的即時通訊服務？
　　　(A) 微軟公司　　(B) Google 公司　　(C) 雅虎公司　　(D) 騰訊控股公司

43.(**D**) 根據本文，下列何者爲非？
　　　(A) QQ 是中國最受歡迎的即時通訊服務，市佔率達百分之七十九點六。
　　　(B) 每個額外付費的 QQ 帳號，每個月要付一點四三美元。
　　　(C) 在 QQ 上聊天和 QQ 網誌空間中，「火星文」被廣泛使用。
　　　(D) 中國人用即時通訊服務玩網路線上遊戲。

44.(**A**) 作者對中國即時通訊服務流行的態度爲何？
　　　(A) 感興趣的　　(B) 漠不關心的　　(C) 悲觀的　　(D) 生氣的

　　* attitude〔'ætə,tjud〕 n. 態度　　popularity〔,pɑpjə'lærətɪ〕 n. 流行
　　　indifferent〔ɪn'dɪfərənt〕 adj. 漠不關心的
　　　pessimistic〔,pɛsə'mɪstɪk〕 adj. 悲觀的
　　　furious〔'fjʊrɪəs〕 adj. 狂怒的

第 45 至 48 題為題組

　　鑑識學，也就是法醫學，是將科學方法應用在法律上。它利用高度發展的科技，去揭發在各領域的科學證據。現代鑑識科學應用廣泛，不過，它最常被用在調查涉及受害者的犯罪案件上，像是施暴、搶劫、綁架、強暴或謀殺。

> * forensics〔fəˋrɛnsɪks〕*n.* 鑑識學　　medical〔ˋmɛdɪkl〕*adj.* 醫學的
> jurisprudence〔͵dʒʊrɪsˋprudn̩s〕*n.* 法理學
> ***medical jurisprudence*** 法醫學　　application〔͵æpləˋkeʃən〕*n.* 應用
> developed〔dɪˋvɛləpt〕*adj.* 發展的
> technology〔tɛkˋnɑlədʒɪ〕*n.* 科技　　uncover〔ʌnˋkʌvɚ〕*v.* 揭發
> ***a variety of*** 很多的　　field〔fild〕*n.* 領域
> forensic〔fəˋrɛnsɪk〕*adj.* 法庭的　　***forensic science*** 鑑識科學
> range〔rendʒ〕*n.* 範圍　　commonly〔ˋkɑmənlɪ〕*adv.* 通常地
> investigate〔ɪnˋvɛstə͵get〕*v.* 調查　　criminal〔ˋkrɪmənl̩〕*adj.* 犯罪的
> involve〔ɪnˋvɑlv〕*v.* 涉及　　victim〔ˋvɪktɪm〕*n.* 受害者
> assault〔əˋsɔlt〕*n.* 傷害；施暴　　robbery〔ˋrɑbərɪ〕*n.* 搶劫
> kidnapping〔ˋkɪdnæpɪŋ〕*n.* 綁架　　rape〔rep〕*n.* 強暴
> murder〔ˋmɝdɚ〕*n.* 謀殺

　　犯罪鑑識調查的核心人物是驗屍官，他的責任是要勘驗犯罪現場、主導驗屍（一種對遺體的檢查）、檢視醫學證據和實驗報告、研究受害者的病史，並將這些資訊整合成報告，呈送給州檢察官。驗屍官正確蒐集和處理鑑識樣本的能力，會影響到審理期間，檢方證明犯罪事實的能力。

> * figure〔ˋfɪgjɚ〕*n.* 人物　　investigation〔ɪn͵vɛstəˋgeʃən〕*n.* 調查
> crime〔kraɪm〕*n.* 犯罪　　examiner〔ɪgˋzæmɪnɚ〕*n.* 檢查員
> ***medical examiner*** 驗屍官　　responsibility〔rɪ͵spɑnsəˋbɪlətɪ〕*n.* 責任
> scene〔sin〕*n.* 場景　　conduct〔kənˋdʌkt〕*v.* 執行；做
> autopsy〔ˋɔtɑpsɪ〕*n.* 驗屍　　examination〔ɪg͵zæməˋneʃən〕*n.* 調查
> examine〔ɪgˋzæmɪn〕*v.* 調查　　laboratory〔ˋlæbrə͵torɪ〕*adj.* 實驗室的
> district〔ˋdɪstrɪkt〕*n.* 地區　　attorney〔əˋtɝnɪ〕*n.* 律師
> ***district attorney*** 美國的州檢察官
> properly〔ˋprɑpɚlɪ〕*adv.* 正確地；適當地　　collect〔kəˋlɛkt〕*v.* 收集
> process〔ˋprɑsɛs〕*v.* 處理；進行分析　　sample〔ˋsæmpl̩〕*n.* 樣本
> prosecution〔͵prɑsɪˋkjuʃən〕*n.* 檢方　　trial〔ˋtraɪəl〕*n.* 審判；審理

　　驗屍官通常是專攻鑑識病理學的內科醫師，也就是研究因為受到傷害，身體在構造和功能上的改變。他們的訓練和資格，多半要包含一個醫學學位，並且要在驗屍官辦公室實習。驗屍官依各個州、城市、或郡的不同要求，由美國病理委員會認定為鑑識病理學家。現在，美國沒有全國性驗屍官體制，也沒有聯邦法律，要求驗屍官必須是有執照的內科醫生。

* physician〔fəˋzɪʃən〕*n.* 內科醫師
  specialize〔ˋspɛʃəl͵aɪz〕*v.* 專攻＜ *in* ＞
  pathology〔pəˋθɑlədʒɪ〕*n.* 病理學
  structural〔ˋstrʌktʃərəl〕*adj.* 結構上的
  functional〔ˋfʌŋkʃənḷ〕*adj.* 功能上的　　*as a result of* 由於
  injury〔ˋɪndʒərɪ〕*n.* 傷害　　training〔ˋtrenɪŋ〕*n.* 訓練
  qualification〔͵kwɑləfəˋkeʃən〕*n.* 資格　　degree〔dɪˋgri〕*n.* 學位
  apprenticeship〔əˋprɛntɪs͵ʃɪp〕*n.* 實習期　　*depend on* 視…而定
  requirement〔rɪˋkwaɪrmənt〕*n.* 要求
  particular〔pəˋtɪkjələ〕*adj.* 各個的；特定的　　state〔stet〕*n.* 州
  county〔ˋkaʊntɪ〕*n.* 郡　　require〔rɪˋkwaɪr〕*v.* 要求
  certify〔ˋsɝtə͵faɪ〕*v.* 認證　　pathologist〔pəˋθɑlədʒɪst〕*n.* 病理學家
  board〔bord〕*n.* 董事會；政府部會；委員會　　*at present* 目前
  federal〔ˋfɛdərəl〕*adj.* 聯邦的　　coroner〔ˋkɔrənə〕*n.* 驗屍官
  licensed〔ˋlaɪsṇst〕*adj.* 領有執照的

45.（ **C** ）本文的標題最有可能是 ＿＿＿＿＿＿。
　　(A) 犯罪現場調查　　　　　　(B) 美國犯罪偵查學委員會
　　(C) 鑑識學和驗屍官　　　　　(D) 醫學證據及實驗室報告
　　* criminalistics〔͵krɪmənḷˋɪstɪks〕*n.* 刑事學；犯罪偵查學

46.（ **D** ）根據本文，誰在犯罪鑑識調查中扮演最重要的角色？
　　(A) 內科醫師　　(B) 法官　　　(C) 州檢察官　　(D) 驗屍官
　　* *play a…role* 扮演…的角色　　judge〔dʒʌdʒ〕*n.* 法官

47.（ **D** ）驗屍官的責任不包含 ＿＿＿＿＿＿。
　　(A) 驗屍　　　　　　　　　　(B) 研讀實驗報告
　　(C) 造訪犯罪現場　　　　　　(D) 對州檢察官做口頭報告
　　* oral〔ˋorəl〕*adj.* 口頭的

48.(**A**) 根據本文，以下何者為非？

(A) 美國政府發證照給有執照的驗屍官。

(B) 鑑識科學將科學與醫學應用到刑法和民法中。

(C) 驗屍官可以提供科學證據去證實犯罪。

(D) 驗屍官通常專攻鑑識病理學。

* issue〔ˈɪʃʊ〕*v.* 發行　　certificate〔səˈtɪfəkɪt〕*n.* 證照

apply…to～ 將…應用在～上　　***criminal law*** 刑法

civil law 民法　　provide〔prəˈvaɪd〕*v.* 提供

physical〔ˈfɪzɪkl̩〕*adj.* 自然科學的

第 49 至 52 題為題組

　　了解如何好好地按摩，就像擁有一種天賦。有能力幫自己按摩是有益的，特別是如果你很容易有身體上的痠痛或疼痛。實行中的按摩療程技術有很多種類。像是嬰兒按摩，是一種不需要太多訓練的按摩療程技術。多數父母成長課程，都提供關於這種溫柔、緩和的按摩技術資訊，來幫助安撫嬰兒，也能促進嬰兒的血液循環。

* massage〔məˈsɑʒ〕*n.* 按摩；推拿　　talent〔ˈtælənt〕*n.* 特殊才能

beneficial〔͵bɛnəˈfɪʃəl〕*adj.* 有益的　　***be prone to + V./N.*** 容易～

ache〔ek〕*n.* 痠痛；疼痛　　pain〔pen〕*n.* 疼痛

aches and pains 各種疼痛　　therapy〔ˈθɛrəpɪ〕*n.* 療程；療法

technique〔tɛkˈnik〕*n.* 技術；技巧　　practice〔ˈpræktɪs〕*v.* 實行

training〔ˈtrenɪŋ〕*n.* 訓練

parenting class 父母成長課程【教導父母照顧嬰兒的課程】

offer〔ˈɔfɚ〕*v.* 提供　　information〔͵ɪnfɚˈmeʃən〕*n.* 資訊

gentle〔ˈdʒɛntl̩〕*adj.* 溫柔的　　soothing〔ˈsuðɪŋ〕*adj.* 緩和的

calm sb. down 使某人平靜　　circulation〔͵sɝkjəˈleʃən〕*n.* 血液循環

　　某些其他的按摩療程技術則需要較正式的訓練。瑞典式按摩，是一種可以幫助人們放鬆，並帶走肌肉跟關節痠痛的按摩療程。它包含了輕撫、深層戳刺、輕微的搖晃、跟輕輕拍打的動作，來舒緩疲勞的肌肉。運動按摩療程技術，是被設計來幫助運動員在比賽前熱身，以及在比賽或競爭後恢復精力。運動醫學使用按摩作為預防性的跟治療性的醫療措施。

* formal〔ˈfɔrml̩〕*adj.* 正式的　　Swedish〔ˈswidɪʃ〕*adj.* 瑞典式的

relax〔rɪˋlæks〕v. 放鬆　　sore〔sor〕adj. 痠疼的
muscle〔ˋmʌsḷ〕n. 肌肉　　joint〔dʒɔɪnt〕n. 關節
stroke〔strok〕v. 輕撫　　prod〔prɑd〕v. 刺；戳　　tap〔tæp〕v. 輕拍
motion〔ˋmoʃən〕n. 動作　　loosen〔ˋlusṇ〕v. 鬆開；使～放鬆
design〔dɪˋzaɪn〕v. 設計　　athlete〔ˋæθlit〕n. 運動員
warm up 暖身　　***prior to*** 在…之前　　compete〔kəmˋpit〕v. 競爭
recover〔rɪˋkʌvɚ〕v. 恢復（精力、健康等）
competition〔͵kɑmpəˋtɪʃən〕n. 競爭；比賽
medicine〔ˋmɛdəsṇ〕n. 醫學　　preventive〔prɪˋvɛntɪv〕adj. 預防的
curative〔ˋkjʊrətɪv〕adj. 治療的　　treatment〔ˋtritmənt〕n. 治療；醫療

　　當你的肌肉疲累或痠痛的時候，按摩療程可以很有效地幫助減輕壓力，恢復活力。因為發現按摩有減少痛苦，以及減緩壓力跟疲倦的益處，它被廣為認可，在許多醫療計畫中，都允許按摩作為例行醫療照護。有些按摩治療技術被用來讓人放鬆，而其他的被用來治療局部的痠痛。

　　* effective〔əˋfɛktɪv〕adj. 有效的　　stress〔strɛs〕n. 壓力
rejuvenate〔rɪˋdʒuvə͵net〕v. 使人恢復活力
recognize〔ˋrɛkəg͵naɪz〕v. 認可
point〔pɔɪnt〕n. (事態發展的) 程度；地步　　allow〔əˋlaʊ〕v. 允許
routine〔ruˋtin〕adj. 例行的　　alleviate〔əˋlivɪ͵et〕v. 減輕；緩和
fatigue〔fəˋtig〕n. 疲倦　　treat〔trit〕v. 治療
specific〔spɪˋsɪfɪk〕adj. 特定的

49. (**D**) 你最可能在下列何本雜誌中找到這篇文章？
　　(A) 現代心理學　(B) 幹細胞與疾病　(C) 世界娛樂　　(D) 自然健康
　　* psychology〔saɪˋkɑlədʒɪ〕n. 心理學　　***stem cell*** 幹細胞

50. (**B**) 文章中提到幾種按摩治療的方法？
　　(A) 2 種。　　　(B) 3 種。　　　(C) 4 種。　　　(D) 5 種。

51. (**B**) 根據文章，下列何者為非？
　　(A) 按摩幫助父母安撫嬰兒，而且促進嬰兒的循環。
　　(B) 嬰兒按摩需要密集的訓練課程。
　　(C) 按摩現在可能被視為減輕疲勞的一種例行醫療照護工作。
　　(D) 運動醫療不只是把按摩用來預防傷害，同時也作為一種治療方法。

52.(**A**) 何者爲本篇文章的主旨？

(A) 按摩療程技術的益處。 (B) 按摩療程技術的效果。

(C) 按摩療程技術大受歡迎。 (D) 摩療程技術的多樣性。

* benefit〔'bɛnəfɪt〕*n.* 益處

impact〔'ɪmpækt〕*n.* 影響；效果

popularity〔ˌpɑpjə'lærətɪ〕*n.* 流行

第 53 至 56 題爲題組

迪雅哥・奇亞沛羅一出生就是法定盲人，他並非義大利有名的那種，長大了還跟父母住在一起的「媽媽的大男孩」。他二十七歲，自己一個人住在米蘭，是電台主管，喜歡潛水，夢想有一天可以跟一群視力受損的船員，一起橫渡大西洋。

* *legally blind* 法定盲人【指視力低於某標準，被判定爲盲人】

mama's boys 媽媽的大男孩【在西方國家，男孩到 20 歲左右就會搬離家庭，

這是長大成人的象徵。跟家人住的男性，會被視爲過度依賴、無法獨立】

adulthood〔ə'dʌlthʊd〕*n.* 成年期

Milan〔mɪ'læn〕*n.* 米蘭【義大利北部的時裝重鎮】

network〔'nɛt,wɝk〕*n.* 電視網；廣播網

administrator〔əd'mɪnə,stretɚ〕*n.* 主管

diving〔'daɪvɪŋ〕*n.* 潛水 *dream of* 夢想

Atlantic〔ət'læntɪk〕*adj.* 大西洋的 *the Atlantic* 大西洋

sight〔saɪt〕*n.* 視力 impair〔ɪm'pɛr〕*v.* 損害

sight-impaired〔'saɪt,ɪm'pɛrd〕*adj.* 視力受損的

crew〔kru〕*n.* 全體船員

顯然，他不是一般的身障者——在義大利尤其如此。在義大利，族群融合的障礙，幾乎比歐陸任何地方還要大：在整個歐陸國家中，就身障者的可接近程度來看，義大利排名倒數第三，只比希臘跟葡萄牙好而已。尤其是坐輪椅的人，會覺得在義大利的鵝卵石街道上使用輪椅、搭公車或上餐館、逛街、逛博物館都很困難。相較於歐洲有百分之四十七的人有工作，義大利身障者中，卻不到四分之一。

* obviously (ˈɑbvɪəslɪ) adv. 顯然　　disabled (dɪsˈebl̩d) adj. 殘障的
 the disabled 身障者　　barrier (ˈbærɪə) n. 障礙；阻礙
 integration (ˌɪntəˈgreʃən) n. 融合　　continent (ˈkɑntənənt) n. 大陸
 the Continent 歐陸　　rank (ræŋk) v. 排名；位居
 accessibility (æk,sɛsəˈbɪlətɪ) n. 可接近性　　**ahead of** 在⋯之前
 Greece (gris) n. 希臘　　Portugal (ˈportʃəgl̩) n. 葡萄牙
 wheelchair (ˈhwilˌtʃɛr) n. 輪椅　　**find it difficult to V.** 發覺做⋯有困難
 navigate (ˈnævəˌget) v. 駕駛；活動於
 cobblestone (ˈkɑbl̩ˌston) n. 鵝卵石　　museum (mjuˈziəm) n. 博物館
 quarter (ˈkwɔrtə) n. 四分之一　　**compared with** 相較於⋯

　　其實，對義大利身障者而言，最大的阻礙或許就是傳說中的義大利家庭。
由於社會認為殘疾是種恥辱，米蘭職業訓練中心，承辦身障人士業務的主管喬
凡尼·梅里出於大眾的觀點解釋：「人們還是傾向於把身障者留在家裡。」因此，
雖然該國百分之十五的家庭有身障者，但根據調查顯示，只有百分之二的義大
利人表示，在學校中有身障同學，而只有百分之四的人身邊有身障同事。

* obstacle (ˈɑbstəkl̩) n. 障礙　　physically (ˈfɪzɪkl̩ɪ) adv. 身體上
 challenged (ˈtʃælɪndʒd) adj. 殘障的　　**physically challenged** 身障者
 fabled (ˈfebld̩) adj. 傳說中的
 Italian (ɪˈtæljən) adj. 義大利（人）的　　n. 義大利人
 because of 由於　　stigma (ˈstɪgmə) n. 污名；恥辱
 attach (əˈtætʃ) v. 相連　　**attach A to B** 將 A 置於 B；將 A 歸於 B
 disability (ˌdɪsəˈbɪlətɪ) n. 殘疾；無能力
 tend to 傾向於　　view (vju) n. 觀點　　head (hɛd) n. 主管
 employment (ɪmˈplɔɪmənt) n. 就業；雇用
 cater (ˈketə) v. 迎合；滿足（需求）< to >
 handicapped (ˈhændɪˌkæpt) adj. 殘障的　　**the handicapped** 身障者
 survey (ˈsɝve) n. 調查

　　義大利人開始認知到這個問題。在過去十年間，政府通過了針對職場上被
歧視身障者，與身障者要求近用權的法律。最近歐盟做的調查發現，百分之八
十五的義大利人承認，給身障者的大眾交通工具跟基本建設不足，還有百分之
九十七的人說，應該要採取行動。但最大的障礙還是在精神方面。奇亞沛羅說：
「義大利公司很怕雇用身障者。」他說，唯一改變的方法，就是義大利的身障
者要做跟他一樣的事──走出家庭，要求改變。

* recognize﹝ˈrɛkəɡ͵naɪz﹞v. 承認；認知到　　decade﹝ˈdɛked﹞n. 十年
target﹝ˈtɑrɡɪt﹞v. 針對　　workplace﹝ˈwɜk͵ples﹞n. 職場
discrimination﹝dɪ͵skrɪməˈneʃən﹞n. 差別待遇；歧視
requirement﹝rɪˈkwaɪrmənt﹞n. 需要　　union﹝ˈjunjən﹞n. 聯盟
European Union 歐盟　　admit﹝ədˈmɪt﹞v. 容許；承認
transportation﹝͵trænspəˈteʃən﹞n. 交通工具
infrastructure﹝ˈɪnfrə͵strʌktʃɚ﹞n. 基本建設
inadequate﹝ɪnˈædəkwɪt﹞adj. 不足的；不適當的
action﹝ˈækʃən﹞n. 行動　　psychological﹝͵saɪkəˈlɑdʒɪkḷ﹞adj. 精神上的
be afraid of 害怕　　hire﹝haɪr﹞v. 雇用　　alter﹝ˈɔltɚ﹞v. 改變

53. (**C**) 下列哪個字最足以描述 "**mama's boys**" ？
　　(A) 討人喜歡的　　　　　　　　(B) 樂觀的
　　(C) 依賴的　　　　　　　　　　(D) 理想的

　　* describe﹝dɪˈskraɪb﹞v. 描述
　　　adorable﹝əˈdorəbḷ﹞adj. 討人喜歡的
　　　optimistic﹝͵ɑptəˈmɪstɪk﹞adj. 樂觀的
　　　dependent﹝dɪˈpɛndənt﹞adj. 依賴的
　　　desirable﹝dɪˈzaɪrəbḷ﹞adj. 理想的

54. (**A**) 本文中，奇亞沛羅被用來作為 ＿＿＿＿＿＿ 的楷模。
　　(A) 與眾不同的義大利殘疾者　　(B) 勇敢的盲人水手
　　(C) 典型的殘疾人士　　　　　　(D) 脆弱的歐洲身障者

　　* cite﹝saɪt﹞v. 談到；引用　　unusual﹝ʌnˈjuʒʊəl﹞adj. 不尋常的
　　　courageous﹝kəˈredʒəs﹞adj. 勇敢的　　sailor﹝ˈselɚ﹞n. 水手
　　　typical﹝ˈtɪpɪkḷ﹞adj. 典型的
　　　vulnerable﹝ˈvʌlnərəbḷ﹞adj. 易受傷害的；脆弱的

55. (**B**) 義大利民眾大多會同意 ＿＿＿＿＿＿ 。
　　(A) 殘疾者身上的缺陷是他們最大的障礙
　　(B) 應該做某些措施來去除身障者所面對的困境
　　(C) 職場中幾乎察覺不到對身障者的歧視
　　(D) 身障者應該減少想要到公共場所的需求

* inadequacy〔ɪn'ædəkwəsɪ〕*n.* 不足　　remove〔rɪ'muv〕*v.* 除去
prejudice〔'prɛdʒədɪs〕*n.* 偏見；歧視
recognizable〔'rɛkəg,naɪzəbl̩〕*adj.* 可辨別的
public place 公共場所

56. (**A**) 本文主旨爲何？

(A) 在幫助身障者這方面，義大利做得不夠多。

(B) 義大利的身障人士應該走出家門。

(C) 義大利人對身障者所面臨的困境視而不見。

(D) 義大利人幫助身障人士的方法應該受到鼓勵。

* ***be blind to*** 對…視而不見　　encourage〔ɪn'kɝɪdʒ〕*v.* 鼓勵

第貳部分：非選擇題

一、中譯英：

1. 全球暖化是有史以來最嚴重的問題之一，我們都應該關注這個議題。

Global warming is one of the $\begin{cases} \text{most important} \\ \text{most serious} \\ \text{major} \end{cases}$ problems

$\begin{cases} \text{of all time,} \\ \text{in history,} \end{cases}$ so we should all $\begin{cases} \text{pay attention to} \\ \text{keep an eye on} \\ \text{focus on} \end{cases}$ this issue.

2. 騎腳踏車已經成爲一股潮流，不僅可以節省能源，也是很好的一種運動方式。

Riding a bicycle has become a $\begin{cases} \text{fashion} \\ \text{trend} \\ \text{movement} \end{cases}$ that can not only save

energy but also be a(n) $\begin{cases} \text{wonderful} \\ \text{good} \\ \text{excellent} \end{cases}$ way of exercising.

二、英文作文：

作文範例

Dear Paul,   Jan. 28, 2013

    I know you must be feeling down in the dumps over the break-up with Sarah. I just wanted to let you know I'm really sorry things didn't work out between you two. Life certainly takes some unexpected turns, Paul. And from my experience, relationships can take the sharpest turn of all. I don't want to pry and I don't need any details you don't feel comfortable sharing. I just want you to know that I'm there for you.

    Listen, I've got a great idea! My father is taking me on a camping trip this weekend and he said it would be no problem if you came along. Spending some time out in nature might be good for you, Paul. Camping is so much fun and it might take your mind off things. What do you say? Are you up for it?

Your friend,
Stanley

down〔daʊn〕*adj.*（意志）消沈的；低落的
in the dumps 心情沮喪的；悶悶不樂的
break-up〔'brekˌʌp〕*n.* 分手　***work out*** 進行順利
unexpected〔ˌʌnɪk'spɛktɪd〕*adj.* 意外的　　turn〔tɜn〕*n.* 變化
sharp〔ʃɑrp〕*adj.* 急轉的；急遽的　　pry〔praɪ〕*v.* 刺探；打聽
detail〔'ditel〕*n.* 細節　***take one's mind off*** 暫時忘記～
What do you say? 你覺得如何？　　***be up for*** 準備好⋯

大學入學學科能力測驗英文模擬試題 ⑦

第壹部分：單選題（佔 72 分）

一、詞彙（佔 15 分）

說明： 第 1 題至第 15 題，每題 4 個選項，其中只有一個是最適當的答案，畫記在答案卡之「選擇題答案區」。各題答對得 1 分；未作答、答錯、或畫記多於一個選項者，該題以零分計算。

1. This is a _____ gesture, but at least it is a good start.
   (A) token　　　(B) legitimate　　　(C) ridge　　　(D) continent

2. _____, fungi, and small animals break down nature's wastes into ever smaller pieces.
   (A) Statistics　　(B) Bacteria　　(C) Ambassadors　(D) Mackintoshes

3. The toilets and laundry facilities are located in the common area of the _____.
   (A) conference　(B) dormitory　　(C) terminal　　　(D) alliance

4. Everyone agrees to build an _____ to burn rubbish but no one agrees to build it in their neighborhood.
   (A) occupation　(B) abbey　　　(C) incinerator　　(D) institute

5. All department stores _____ their sales by giving special discounts.
   (A) wipe　　　(B) boost　　　(C) thrill　　　(D) dismiss

6. We need a _____ to fix the toilet. There is a leak.
   (A) carpenter　(B) plumber　　(C) decorator　　(D) mason

7. If you keep idling around, you'll have to suffer the _____.
   (A) consequences　　　　　　(B) comprehension
   (C) breathtaking　　　　　　(D) prerequisites

8. Tea was the first _____ beverage. The Chinese emperor
   ShenNong introduced the drink in 2737 B.C.
   (A) brewed   (B) formatted   (C) instilled   (D) tempested

9. It has rained cats and dogs for three _____ days. No wonder
   there is now high water in the township.
   (A) rigorous   (B) consecutive   (C) recessive   (D) anonymous

10. Some women's libbers are offended by the word "_____," let
    alone words like manmade or chairman.
    (A) tsunamis   (B) superficial   (C) trauma   (D) stewardess

11. The hotel is _____ for the coming weekend. Why don't we go
    camping for a change?
    (A) build up   (B) booked up   (C) kept up   (D) fastened up

12. There has been unrest in the country _____, especially in two
    major cities.
    (A) at large   (B) by and large
    (C) as large as life   (D) in large

13. I heard the voices but I couldn't _____ what they were saying.
    (A) pull up   (B) come round
    (C) make out   (D) pay off

14. His ways of behaving are unusual and silly, but I can _____
    them.
    (A) put up with   (B) come down with
    (C) do away with   (D) run away with

15. He always _____ from difficulties. That's why he didn't get a
    promotion in 10 years.
    (A) pulls over   (B) runs into   (C) takes down   (D) backs away

二、綜合測驗 (佔 15 分)

說明：　第 16 題至第 30 題，每題一個空格，請依文意選出最適當的一個答案，
　　　　畫記在答案卡之「選擇題答案區」。各題答對得 1 分；未作答、答錯、
　　　　或畫記多於一個選項者，該題以零分計算。

第 16 至 20 題為題組

　　　16　in the haunted city of Derry, four boys stood together and did a brave thing. Certainly a good thing, perhaps even a great thing. Something that changed them in ways they could never begin to understand.

　　　Twenty-five years later, the boys are 　17　 men with separate lives and separate troubles. But the ties endure. Each hunting season the foursome reunite in the woods of Maine. This year, a stranger stumbles into their camp, 　18　, mumbling something about lights in the sky. His lunatic remarks prove to be true. 　19　, these men will be plunged into a horrifying struggle with a creature from another world. Their only chance of 　20　 is locked in a box…

16. (A) For many years　　　　　　(B) Once upon a time
　　(C) In the past decades　　　　(D) Once a while
17. (A) then　　　(B) becoming　　(C) now　　　(D) those
18. (A) bewildered　(B) perplexing　(C) disorienting　(D) approached
19. (A) Long enough　　　　　　　(B) Once and for all
　　(C) Before long　　　　　　　(D) Now and then
20. (A) leakage　　(B) insane　　(C) survival　　(D) procedure

第 21 至 25 題為題組

　　Taiwan's levels of nearsightedness are higher than those of Japan and Singapore, two countries generally considered to have more nearsighted people. As many as 85 percent of Taiwan's high school students and 90 percent of its college students are nearsighted, figures high enough to call Taiwan "the island of ___21___." And the number of young people in Taiwan who are nearsighted ___22___ more rapidly than in the past. This is the result of parents ___23___ children to read and write at too early an age. The longer a person goes without developing nearsightedness, the less severe the condition is likely to be. So it is especially important to ensure people ___24___ nearsightedness as children. ___25___ the seriousness of the problem, the government will give eye exams to children in kindergartens islandwide.

21. (A) myopia   (B) piracy   (C) casino   (D) glassware
22. (A) have increased   (B) to be increased
    (C) is increasing   (D) increasing
23. (A) to make   (B) having   (C) to allow   (D) asking
24. (A) blending with   (B) underdeveloping
    (C) not to be   (D) do not develop
25. (A) Acknowledging   (B) Abiding by
    (C) Accusing of   (D) Anticipating

第 26 至 30 題為題組

The moon is the earth's nearest neighbor ___26___ other major heavenly bodies. Unlike the earth, there's no life on the moon. Probably it is because no water exists on the moon's surface. It rotates on its own ___27___ once every time it turns around the earth. This is the reason the moon shows the same side to the earth ___28___.

___29___, the moon gets light from the sun, and does not give off light as the sun does. If you point a mirror to the sun, the mirror reflects sunlight. It is the same with the moon. Another important feature is that the pull of the moon causes the ocean tides. Finally, we can only see moonlight ___30___. The moon actually reflects the sunlight all day long, but when the sky is clear and the sun shines brightly, we cannot see moonlight.

26. (A) on behalf of　　　　　(B) in consequence of
　　(C) in comparison with　　(D) accompanied by
27. (A) cord　　　(B) axis　　　(C) agenda　　(D) paralysis
28. (A) at all time　　　　　　(B) continual
　　(C) once and for all　　　　(D) all the time
29. (A) Additionally　(B) Likewise　(C) Conversely　(D) Theoretically
30. (A) in the daytime　　　　　(B) all day long
　　(C) at night　　　　　　　(D) all night long

三、文意選填（佔 10 分）

說明：　第 31 題至第 40 題，每題一個空格，請依文意在文章後所提供的 (A) 到
　　　　(J) 選項中分別選出最適當者，並將其英文字母代號畫記在答案卡之「選
　　　　擇題答案區」。各題答對得 1 分；未作答、答錯、或畫記多於一個選項
　　　　者，該題以零分計算。

第 31 至 40 題為題組

　　Typhoon Morakot was the worst-ever typhoon to strike Taiwan.
The ___31___ of the damage was more severe than that of a 1959
typhoon that killed 667 people and left around 1,000 missing.
Morakot caused severe damage to the southern part of Taiwan with
___32___ breaking rainfall of 2,900 millimeters (114 inches) in 3 days.
The highest single day regional record was broken on August 8th, at
1,403 millimeters (55 inches). To put it in ___33___, Vancouver's
average annual rainfall is only 1,117 mm (44 inches).

　　Some buildings were flooded up to the second floor, many
towns ___34___. Military personnel were deployed to help with the
rescue and reconstruction efforts. In TaiDong County, segments of a
highway and railway were washed away, 20 houses were washed into
the sea, and a major hotel ___35___. Dozens of helicopters crisscrossed
mountains and ravines, delivering food and water, and airlifting
survivors. In central JiaYi county nearly 9,000 people were ___36___.
And in GaoXiong, the hardest-hit county, where most of the rescue
missions were concentrated, troops evacuated 2,000 more people.

Rescue workers said they had to risk their lives ___37___ through rivers to deliver relief items such as biscuits, canned food and instant noodles. In XinFa village, a hot-spring resort where bodies were found buried by mudslides, volunteer rescuers had to snake through some 18 kilometers of roads ravaged by ___38___ floods and three half-blocked tunnels. But a toppled bridge still prevented them from getting relief supplies to trapped victims. The ___39___ economic impact is 110 billion dollars. Taiwan seemed ___40___. This had never happened before.

(A) perspective   (B) wading   (C) cursed   (D) extent   (E) flash
(F) stranded   (G) record   (H) isolated   (I) collapsed   (J) estimated

四、閱讀測驗（佔 32 分）

說明： 第 41 題至第 56 題，每題 4 個選項，請分別根據各篇文章之文意選出最適當的一個答案，畫記在答案卡之「選擇題答案區」。各題答對得 2 分；未作答、答錯、或畫記多於一個選項者，該題以零分計算。

第 41 至 44 題為題組

My boss was a horrible person. He used to yell at me constantly about not doing things right. One day I came in and I was really stressed out. I just wasn't going to take anyone yelling at me on this day. He stayed away from me that morning. But after lunch in our afternoon meeting, he started.

Somehow, I held on to my **composure** until after the meeting. Then, I calmly walked out of there, walked into the lounge and screamed at the top of my lungs for relief.

On the way back to my desk I realized that I had had enough of him. So I decided to quit. But if I was going to quit, I was going to take him down with me. So I dug up all the stuff he had lied to his boss about and typed it up into a nice letter and mailed it off.

Last I heard, he got fired two days after I quit. It was great!

41. How did the narrator feel the morning he resigned?
    (A) conceited   (B) stressed   (C) terrific   (D) suspicious

42. Why do you think the narrator used the word "somehow" at the beginning of the second paragraph?
    (A) He wasn't sure if he was right.
    (B) He felt ashamed of himself.
    (C) He used to be scolded by his boss.
    (D) He doesn't know how he was able to do it.

43. Which of the following is NOT TRUE?
    (A) The narrator shouted loudly to release his emotion after the meeting.
    (B) The narrator's boss told some lies to his boss.
    (C) The narrator got fired two days before his boss got fired.
    (D) The narrator managed to take his boss down with him.

44. Which one can best replace "**composure**"?
    (A) self-concept   (B) self-control   (C) self-sacrifice   (D) self-esteem

第 45 至 48 題為題組

    Introducing others will make you seem gracious and well connected, but be sure to follow the proper **protocol**.

    In social situations the order in which you introduce two people is based on gender and age (women and older people first). In business settings the order is determined by rank.

    Think of it as a circle. Begin the introduction by addressing the higher-ranking person and presenting the lower-ranking person. Then reverse the order, so you say each person's name two times. Try to add an interesting tidbit to start the conversation.

    If you were introducing Mrs. Smith, a vice president of the company, and Mr. Jones, a junior associate, for example, you might say:

"Mrs. Smith, I would like to introduce you to Mr. Jones, a junior associate. Mr. Jones, this is Mrs. Smith. Mr. Jones just returned from Thailand."

If you're unsure who the more important person is, default to the gender and age guideline.

Don't panic if you forget a name. Most people will be happy to remind you and appreciate the introduction.

45. The best title for this passage would be _____.
    (A) Making Connections　　　(B) Presenting Yourself
    (C) Making a Presentation　　(D) Introduction Etiquette

46. We can replace "**protocol**" with _____.
    (A) default　　　　　　(B) attachment
    (C) practice　　　　　　(D) underlines

47. In social situations the order in which you introduce two people will be _____
    (A) Ms. Chang, this is Chen Meling. She is a student of mine.
        Meling, this is Ms. Chang. We're teaching at the same school.
    (B) Ms. Xue, this is Ms. Chen. We're in the same office. Ms. Chen,
        Ms. Xue, a student of mine.
    (C) Mr. Wang, this is Ms. Chao. Ms. Chao, Mr. Wang.
    (D) Mr. Tan, this is Ms. Lee. Ms. Lee just returned from the U.S.

48. While you're introducing others, if you forget a name,

    _____.
    (A) it will make you more gracious
    (B) you should stay calm
    (C) it makes you seem well-connected
    (D) happy folks will look on the bright side of it

第 49 至 52 題為題組

"I'll count to ten. If you do not surrender before I reach ten, this pleasant young woman will die."

On the lower deck, Marshall was elated and destroyed by the sound of his wife's voice. His legs felt like rubber. He sat and listened to the awful countdown.

"One…two…three…"

"…four…five…"

Marshall knew that to surrender would betray everything he believed in, and that he would very likely lose any chance to save the other hostages. But could he allow Melanie to be shot down like an animal? Nausea coursed through him…an awful sickness.

"…six…seven…"

Melanie's tears were streaming as she bit her lip and silently, desperately, prayed.

"…eight," Korshunov said.

Marshall almost screamed, "You can't do this!" His tears clouding his eyes but not his judgment, the president rose to his feet slowly.

"…nine!"

"Oh, god, no!" Marshall shut his eyes, as if it would all go away. "Ten," Korshunov said, and, with a single round of his machine pistol, the chemistry of Melanie's brain ceased to function.

49. Melanie is ＿＿＿＿＿＿.
   (A) a kidnapper　(B) a first lady　(C) a contractor　(D) a coordinator

50. What was Marshall's final attitude towards Korshunov's threat?
   (A) firm　　　(B) swaying　　(C) timid　　　(D) ironical

51. All of the following descriptions of Marshall are true EXCEPT
    (A) He failed to save his wife.
    (B) His eyes were once full of tears.
    (C) He screamed, "You can't do this!"
    (D) He was president.

52. Which of the following is true?
    (A) Melanie was shot to death.
    (B) Melanie was on the lower deck.
    (C) Marshall was in the conference room.
    (D) Korshunov held a rifle.

第 53 至 56 題為題組

Thousands of Icelanders lined up at McDonald's restaurants to order their last Big Macs before the U.S. fast-food chain abandons the crisis-hit island at midnight Saturday due to soaring costs. The world's largest fast-food company said earlier this week that all three of its restaurants in Iceland, operated by franchisee Jon Ogmundsson, would shut down, October 31, 2009.

The outlets have been packed since the announcement, with lines at one restaurant on the east side of the city backing up out the door and onto the street. At lunchtime Friday the outlet's parking lot was full and staff inside were working furiously to keep up with the soaring demand.

"It's my last chance for a while to have a real Big Mac," Siggi, a 28-year-old salesman waiting in line told Reuters. "With the economy as it is, I won't be traveling abroad any time soon," he added. "It's not that I'm a big fan of McDonald's, but a Big Mac now and then adds to variety."

Ogmundsson, who will continue running the restaurants under a different name after taking down the golden arches, said he had even run out of Big Macs for a few hours Thursday.

"Sales have not just gone up," Ogmundsson was quoted saying in the local media. "They've gone turbo." Ogmundsson said he managed to catch up with the surge in demand and had been selling about 10,000 burgers a day—more than ever before.

Iceland has been reeling from the effects of the financial crisis since October 2008, when its banks collapsed in the space of a week under the weight of billions of dollars in debt. The fall of the banks sapped confidence in Iceland's economy and sent its currency, the crown, into freefall. McDonald's said the crown's weakness was part of the reason for its withdrawal, along with the high cost of importing food from abroad. McDonald's said it would not seek to come back to Iceland.

In a nearby stationery store, Thora Sigurdardottir, a 35-year old nursing assistant, said she had no intention of going for a final McDonald's meal.

"Good riddance," she said.

53. All of the following are true EXCEPT
   (A) Ogmundsson is going out of the restaurant business by the end of 2009.
   (B) There are three McDonald's restaurants in Iceland.
   (C) Iceland is still stumbling from the effects of the 2008 financial crisis.
   (D) McDonald's decided to withdraw from Iceland partly because of the cost.

54. Which of the following statements is NOT true?
   (A) McDonald's is looking for another franchisee in Iceland.
   (B) October 31, 2009 was on a weekend.
   (C) A lot of Icelanders ate burgers on October 30, 2009.
   (D) The sales of burgers at Ogmundsson's restaurant on October 30, 2009 were record high.

55. Based on the passage, which of the following is not a side effect of the financial crisis?
   (A) The suicidal rate is still high.
   (B) Iceland is heavily in debt.
   (C) The value of Iceland's currency dropped sharply.
   (D) McDonald's has pulled out of Iceland.

56. What was Sigurdardottir's attitude toward McDonald's shutting down?
   (A) malevolent (B) moderate
   (C) uncaring (D) dejected

第貳部分：非選擇題（佔 28 分）

一、中譯英（佔 8 分）

說明： 1. 請將以下中文句子譯成正確、通順、達意的英文，並將答案寫在「答案卷」上。

   2. 請依序作答，並標明題號。每題 4 分，共 8 分。

1. 寂寞的人可以把他們的感覺散播給別人，就像把感冒傳給別人一樣。
2. 一段時間之後，這群孤單、與他人隔絕的人就會退到社會的邊緣。

二、英文作文（佔 20 分）

說明： 1. 依提示在「答案卷」上寫一篇英文作文。

   2. 文長約 100 至 120 個單詞（words）。

提示： 你的朋友剛剛出國唸書深造。你（英文名字必須假設為 Luke 或 Ellen），要寫一封信給你的朋友（英文名字必須假設為 Willow 或 Cathy），恭喜他（她）出國深造，並表達你對他（她）的支持和鼓勵。

請注意：必須使用上述的 Luke 或 Ellen 在信末署名，**不得使用自己的真實中文或英文名字**。

大學入學學科能力測驗英文模擬試題 ⑦ 詳解

第壹部分：單選題

一、詞彙：

1. (**A**) 這是個象徵性的表示，但至少是個好的開始。

    (A) ***token*** 〔'tokən〕*adj.* 象徵性的　　*n.* 象徵；代幣
        a token protest　象徵性的抗議
    (B) legitimate 〔lɪ'dʒɪtəmɪt〕*adj.* 合法的（= *legal*）
        legitimacy *n.* 合法性　　legitimately *adv.*
    (C) ridge 〔rɪdʒ〕*n.* 山脊；鼻樑；稜線　　ridged *adj.* 隆起的
    (D) continent 〔'kɑntənənt〕*n.* 大陸
        continental *adj.* 大陸的
    * gesture 〔'dʒɛstʃɚ〕*n.* 手勢；（心意等的）表示　　***at least*** 至少

2. (**B**) 細菌、眞菌、還有小型動物會分解大自然的廢物，讓它們成爲更小的分子。

    (A) statistics 〔stə'tɪstɪks〕*n. pl.* 統計數學
        statistical *adj.* 統計的
    (B) ***bacteria*** 〔bæk'tɪrɪə〕*n. pl.* 細菌【單數爲 bacterium】
    (C) ambassador 〔æm'bæsədɚ〕*n.* 大使
    (D) mackintosh 〔'mækɪn,tɑʃ〕*n.* 橡皮布；防水外套
    * fungi 〔'fʌndʒaɪ〕*n. pl.* 眞菌類【單數 fungus 〔'fʌngəs〕】
    break down 分解　　waste 〔west〕*n.* 廢棄物

3. (**B**) 洗手間跟洗衣設備，設置在宿舍中的公共區域。

    (A) conference 〔'kɑnfərəns〕*n.* 會議（= *council*）；協商
        a news/press conference　記者會
    (B) ***dormitory*** 〔'dɔrmə,torɪ〕*n.* 宿舍
    (C) terminal 〔'tɝmənḷ〕*n.* 終點站　*adj.* 末端的；（疾病）
        末期的　　terminally *adv.*　　terminate *v.*
    (D) alliance 〔ə'laɪəns〕*n.* 同盟；合作（= *partnership*）
        ally *v.* 同盟；合作　*n.* 盟友　　in alliance 聯盟

　　　　＊ toilet〔ˋtɔɪlɪt〕*n.* 廁所；馬桶　　laundry〔ˋlɔndrɪ〕*n.* 洗衣房
　　　　facilities〔fəˋsɪlətɪz〕*n.* 設施　　located〔loˋketɪd〕*adj.* 位於～的
　　　　common area 公共區域

4.(**C**) 每個人都同意建造<u>焚化爐</u>來焚化垃圾，但沒有人同意將焚化爐蓋在
　　　自家附近。

　　　(A) occupation〔͵ɑkjəˋpeʃən〕*n.* 職業（= *profession*）；居住；佔據
　　　　　occupy *v.* 佔據　　occupational *adj.* 職業的
　　　(B) abbey〔ˋæbɪ〕*n.* 大修道院；大教堂
　　　(C) **incinerator**〔ɪnˋsɪnə͵retə〕*n.* 焚化爐　　incinerate *v.* 焚化
　　　(D) institute〔ˋɪnstə͵tjut〕*n.* 協會　*v.* 制定；設立
　　　　　institution *n.* 制定；設立
　　　＊ rubbish〔ˋrʌbɪʃ〕*n.* 垃圾　　neighborhood〔ˋnebə͵hʊd〕*n.* 附近

5.(**B**) 所有百貨公司都大打折扣，來提高<u>銷售額</u>。

　　　(A) wipe〔waɪp〕*v.* 擦拭　*n.* 擦拭　　wipe out 除去；徹底消滅
　　　(B) **boost**〔bust〕*v.* 哄抬（= *lift*）；提高（= *raise*）
　　　(C) thrill〔θrɪl〕*v.* 使興奮；使顫慄　*n.* 刺激；顫慄
　　　　　thriller *n.* 恐怖小說（電影）
　　　(D) dismiss〔dɪsˋmɪs〕*v.* 解散　　dismissal *n.*
　　　＊ sales〔selz〕*n. pl.* 銷售額　　discount〔ˋdɪskaʊnt〕*n.* 折扣

6.(**B**) 廁所漏水了，我們要找個<u>水管工人</u>來修一修。

　　　(A) carpenter〔ˋkɑrpəntə〕*n.* 木匠　*v.* 做木工
　　　　　carpentry *n.* 木匠業
　　　(B) **plumber**〔ˋplʌmə〕*n.* 水管工人
　　　　　plumbing *n.* 水管工程
　　　(C) decorator〔ˋdɛkə͵retə〕*n.* 裝潢業者；裝飾者
　　　　　decorate *v.* 裝飾　　decoration *n.*
　　　(D) mason〔ˋmesn̩〕*n.* 石匠
　　　＊ leak〔lik〕*n.* 漏水

7.(**A**) 如果你再這樣無所事事下去，你一定會嚐到苦果。

(A) *consequence* (ˈkɑnsəˌkwɛns) n. 結果；後果

　　in consequence　因此；結果 (= *as a result*)

(B) comprehension (ˌkɑmprɪˈhɛnʃən) n. 理解

(C) breathtaking (ˈbrɛθˌtekɪŋ) adj. 令人驚嘆的；令人屏息的

(D) prerequisite (priˈrɛkwəzɪt) n. 先決條件　adj. 預先需要的

　　requisite adj. 必需的；必要的 (= *necessary*)

* idle (ˈaɪdl̩) v. 遊手好閒；浪費時間

idle around 無所事事

suffer (ˈsʌfɚ) v. 遭受 (苦難)；忍受 (痛苦)

8.(**A**) 茶是第一種沖泡的飲料。中國皇帝神農氏，在西元前兩千七百三十七年時，讓這種飲料問世。

(A) *brew* (bru) v. 沖泡 (茶、咖啡)；釀造 (酒)

(B) format (ˈfɔrmæt) v. 編排　n. 形式；格式

(C) instill (ɪnˈstɪl) v. 灌輸

(D) tempest (ˈtɛmpɪst) v. 起暴風雨 (或雪)　n. 大風雪；風暴

* beverage (ˈbɛvrɪdʒ) n. 飲料　　emperor (ˈɛmpərɚ) n. 皇帝

introduce (ˌɪntrəˈdus) v. 使 (產品) 問世；推出

9.(**B**) 連續下了三天的傾盆大雨。難怪這個小鎮現在快要淹水了。

(A) rigorous (ˈrɪgərəs) adj. 嚴格的 (= *rigid* = *stringent*)

(B) *consecutive* (kənˈsɛkjətɪv) adj. 連續的

　　consecutively adv.

(C) recessive (rɪˈsɛsɪv) adj. 後退的

　　recessionary adj. 景氣蕭條的　　recession n. 景氣蕭條

　　in recession　經濟蕭條

(D) anonymous (əˈnɑnəməs) adj. 匿名的

　　anonym n. 匿名者

* *it rains cats and dogs* 下傾盆大雨　　*no wonder* 難怪

high water 高水位　　township (ˈtaʊnʃɪp) n. 小鎮

10. (**D**) 有些女權運動支持者對「女空服員」這個字感到生氣，更不用說像是 "manmade" 或者 "chairman" 這些字了。

(A) tsunami〔tsu'nɑmɪ〕n. 海嘯（= *tidal wave*）

(B) superficial〔,supɚ'fɪʃəl〕adj. 膚淺的（= *shallow*）
（↔ profound）；表面的（= *exterior*） superficially adv.

(C) trauma〔'trɔmə〕n. 外傷；創傷 traumatize v. 使受創

(D) *stewardess*〔'stjuwədɪs〕n. 女空服員

* libber〔'lɪbɚ〕n. 男女平等論者
a women's libber 女權運動支持者
offend〔ə'fɛnd〕v. 觸犯；冒犯 *let alone* 更不用說
manmade〔'mæn,med〕adj. 人造的；合成的
chairman〔'tʃɛrmən〕n. 總裁；主席

11. (**B**) 下週末的飯店都被<u>預訂一空</u>了。我們何不改去露營？

(A) build up 建立；增強

(B) *book*〔buk〕v. 預訂（房間、車票）
be booked up（旅館、座位等）被預訂一空

(C) keep up 維持；持續 keep up with 趕上

(D) fasten up 固定；釘住（↔ loose up）
fasten v. 繫上；鎖住（= *lock*）

* coming〔'kʌmɪŋ〕adj. 接下來的 *go camping* 去露營
for a change 改變一下

12. (**A**) <u>整個</u>國家都動盪不安，特別是兩個主要都市。

(A) *at large* 整個的【放在名詞之後】；逍遙法外的

(B) by and large 整體來說；大致上

(C) as large as life 跟實物一樣

(D) in large 大規模地（= *in the large*）

* unrest〔ʌn'rɛst〕n. 不安；動盪

13. (**C**) 我有聽到聲音，但我<u>聽不懂</u>他們在說什麼。

　　(A) pull up　停下（馬、車子）；豎起

　　　　pull〔pʊl〕*v.* 拉扯；拉住（↔ push）　*n.* 拉力；影響力

　　(B) come round　恢復意識；順道而來

　　(C) ***make out***　理解；分辨；填寫（表格）

　　(D) pay off　還清（= *pay up*）；成功

14. (**A**) 他的行為怪異又愚蠢，不過我可以<u>忍受</u>。

　　(A) ***put up with***　忍受

　　(B) come down with　罹患（= *suffer from*）

　　(C) do away with　除去；廢除（= *abolish* = *cancel* = *put an end to*）

　　(D) run away with　帶著（物品）逃跑；與人私奔

　　　　run away　逃跑

　　* behave〔bɪˋhev〕*v.* 動作；行為　　silly〔ˋsɪlɪ〕*adj.* 愚蠢的

15. (**D**) 他面對難題總是<u>退縮</u>。這就是他十年來都沒法升遷的原因。

　　(A) pull over　將（車子）停靠路邊

　　(B) run into　偶然遇見（= *come across*）；與…相撞（= *collide with*）

　　(C) take down　（自高處）取下；拆毀

　　(D) ***back away***　退縮；躊躇不前

　　* difficulty〔ˋdɪfə͵kʌltɪ〕*n.* 困難

　　　promotion〔prəˋmoʃən〕*n.* 升遷

二、綜合測驗：

<u>第 16 至 20 題為題組</u>

　　<u>很久很久以前</u>，在德里郡一座鬧鬼的城市裡，有四個小男孩，一起做了一
　　　　16
件很勇敢的事。當然是件好事，甚至可以說是件偉大的事。他們怎樣都想不到
這件事情對他們的影響有多大。

　　* haunted〔ˋhɔntɪd〕*adj.* 鬧鬼的

　　　Derry〔ˋdɛrɪ〕*n.* 德里郡【緬因州地名】

　　　stand together　團結一致　　brave〔brev〕*adj.* 勇敢的

16. (**B**) 依句意，選 (B) *Once upon a time*「很久很久以前」。而 (A) for many years「多年來」，(C) in the past decades「在過去數十年內」，不合句意。(D) 無此說法。 *once in a while* 偶爾

二十五年後，男孩現已<u>長大成人</u>，也有各自的生活以及難題。但他們還繼
　　　　　　　　　　　17
續保持聯絡。每年的打獵季節，這四個人就重新聚在緬因州的森林裡。

* separate〔ˈsɛprɪt〕*adj.* 各自的　　tie〔taɪ〕*n.* 關係
  endure〔ɪnˈdjʊr〕*v.* 保持　　***hunting season*** 打獵季節
  foursome〔ˈforsəm〕*n.* 四人一組　　reunite〔ˌrijʊˈnaɪt〕*v.* 重聚
  woods〔wʊdz〕*n. pl.* 森林　　Maine〔men〕*n.* 緬因州

17. (**C**) 依句意，選 (C) *now*「現在」。

今年，有個陌生人跌跌撞撞地走進他們的營地，神情<u>驚慌失措</u>，嘴巴唸唸有詞，
　　　　　　　　　　　　　　　　　　18
說一些天空中亮光的事。但他這些瘋瘋癲癲的話，證明結果是真的。

* stumble〔ˈstʌmbḷ〕*v.* 搖搖晃晃地走　　mumble〔ˈmʌmbḷ〕*v.* 喃喃地說
  lunatic〔ˈlunəˌtɪk〕*adj.* 怪異的；瘋狂的
  remark〔rɪˈmɑrk〕*n.* 評論；話語　　prove〔pruv〕*v.* 證為實

18. (**A**) 依句意，選 (A) *bewildered*〔bɪˈwɪldəd〕*adj.* 感到困惑的；困惑的。
而 (B) perplexing〔pɚˈplɛksɪŋ〕*adj.* 令人困惑的，(D) approach
〔əˈprotʃ〕*v.* 接近，則不合句意。(C) disorient〔dɪsˈoriˌɛnt〕*v.* 使混
亂；使迷失方向，應改為 disoriented。

<u>不久之後</u>，這些人將與另一個世界來的生物，陷入一場可怕的鬥爭。他們唯一
　19
<u>生存</u>的機會，鎖在一只箱子裡…
　20

* plunge〔plʌndʒ〕*v.* 使陷入
  horrifying〔ˈhɔrəˌfaɪɪŋ〕*adj.* 可怕的；駭人的
  struggle〔ˈstrʌgḷ〕*n.* 掙扎；戰鬥　　creature〔ˈkritʃɚ〕*n.* 生物

19. (**C**) 依句意，選 (C) *Before long*「不久之後」。而 (A) long enough「夠
久」，(B) once and for all「斷然地」，(D) now and then「偶爾；
有時候」，均不合句意。

20. (**C**) (A) leakage〔'likɪdʒ〕*n.* 漏水；漏洞
　　　　(B) insane〔ɪn'sen〕*adj.* 瘋狂的
　　　　(C) ***survival***〔sə'vaɪvḷ〕*n.* 生存
　　　　(D) procedure〔prə'sidʒə〕*n.* 程序

第 21 至 25 題為題組

　　台灣的近視程度比日本跟新加坡還要高。一般認為，這兩個國家的近視人口比較多。台灣有高達百分之八十五的高中生，還有百分之九十的大學生，都有近視。這個數字可以讓台灣得到「近視之島」的封號。
　　　　　　　　　　　　　　　21

　　* nearsighted〔'nɪr'saɪtɪd〕*adj.* 近視的
　　　generally〔'dʒɛnərəlɪ〕*adv.* 一般；通常　　　figure〔'fɪgjə〕*n.* 數字

21. (**A**) (A) ***myopia***〔maɪ'opɪə〕*n.* 近視
　　　　(B) piracy〔'paɪrəsɪ〕*n.* 盜版
　　　　(C) casino〔kə'sino〕*n.* 賭場
　　　　(D) glassware〔'glæs,wɛr〕*n.* 玻璃製品

　　而且現在台灣年輕人近視的人數，增加的速度比以前更快。這是因為父母要求
　　　　　　　　　　　　　22　　　　　　　　　　　　　　　　　　23
小孩子，在很小的時候就開始讀書寫字的結果。沒有罹患近視的時間越長，近視的情況就可能會越輕。

　　* rapidly〔'ræpɪdlɪ〕*adv.* 迅速地　　　***be the result of*** 是…的結果
　　　develop〔dɪ'vɛləp〕*v.* 患（病）；顯現（症狀）
　　　nearsightedness〔'nɪr'saɪtɪdnɪs〕*n.* 近視
　　　severe〔sə'vɪr〕*adj.* 嚴重的；劇烈的
　　　condition〔kən'dɪʃən〕*n.* 情況　　　***be likely to*** + ***V.*** 可能~

22. (**C**) 主詞 number（人數）為單數名詞，且空格應填動詞，依句意，
　　　　選 (C) ***is increasing***「正在增加中」。

23. (**D**) 原句為：...parents ***who ask*** children to read...，關代 who 可省略，
　　　　但 ask 須改為 ***asking***，選 (D)。

因此，在幼童時期，確保孩子<u>不罹患</u>近視就顯得格外重要。<u>知道</u>這個問題
24　　　　　　　　　　　　25
的嚴重性後，政府會讓全台灣的幼稚園小孩，都接受視力檢查。

　　* especially〔ə'spɛʃəlɪ〕*adv.* 特別；尤其　　ensure〔ɪn'ʃʊr〕*v.* 確保
　　seriousness〔'sɪrɪəsnɪs〕*n.* 嚴重性　　***eye exam*** 視力檢查
　　kindergarten〔'kɪndəˌgɑrtn̩〕*n.* 幼稚園
　　islandwide〔'aɪlənd'waɪd〕*adv.* 全島

24.（**D**）依句意，確保孩子們「不罹患」近視，選 (D) ***do not develop***「不罹
　　　患」。　　develop〔dɪ'vɛləp〕*v.* 罹患（疾病）
　　　而 (A) blend with「和～混合」，(B) underdevelop「使發育不完全」，
　　　則不合句意。

25.（**A**）依句意，選 (A) ***Acknowledging***。
　　　acknowledge〔ək'nɑlɪdʒ〕*v.* 承認；注意
　　　而 (B) abide by「遵守」，(C) accuse *sb.* of「控告某人～」，
　　　(D) anticipate〔æn'tɪsəˌpet〕*v.* 期待，均不合句意。

<u>第 26 至 30 題為題組</u>

　　<u>和</u>其他大型天體<u>比起來</u>，月亮是地球最近的鄰居。和地球不同的是，月球
26　　　　　26
上沒有生命，這可能是因為月球表面上沒有水的原因。

　　* moon〔mun〕*n.* 月亮；月球　　earth〔ɝθ〕*n.* 地球
　　heavenly〔'hɛvənlɪ〕*adj.* 天空的　　***heavenly body*** 天體
　　unlike〔ʌn'laɪk〕*prep.* 與…不同　　probably〔'prɑbəblɪ〕*adv.* 可能
　　exist〔ɪg'zɪst〕*v.* 存在　　surface〔'sɝfɪs〕*n.* 表面

26.（**C**）依句意，選 (C) ***in comparison with***「和～相比」。
　　　comparison〔kəm'pærəsn̩〕*n.* 比較
　　　而 (A) on behalf of「代表」，(B) in consequence of「由於」，
　　　(D) accompanied by「有…陪伴」，均不合句意。

它繞著地球公轉的時候，也依自己的<u>軸心</u>自轉。這就是為什麼月球<u>總</u>是以同一
27　　　　　　　　　　　　　　28
面面對地球的原因。

　　* rotate〔'rotet〕*v.* 旋轉；（天體）自轉

27. (**B**)　(A) cord〔kɔrd〕*n.* 繩子
　　　　　(B) *axis*〔'æksɪs〕*n.* 軸；地軸
　　　　　(C) agenda〔ə'dʒɛndə〕*n.* 議程
　　　　　(D) paralysis〔pə'ræləsɪs〕*n.* 癱瘓

28. (**D**)　依句意，選 (D) *all the time*「總是」。而 (A) at all time 無此片語。
　　　　　(B) continual〔kən'tɪnjuəl〕*adj.* 連續不斷的，(C) once and for all「斷
　　　　　然地」，均不合句意。

此外，月球從太陽那裡得到光，但它本身並不會像太陽一樣發光。當你將鏡
　29
子對準太陽，鏡子會反射陽光。月球就跟鏡子一樣。月球另一個重要的特點就
是它的引力引發潮汐作用。

　　　* *give off* 散發；發出　　point〔pɔɪnt〕*v.* 指向
　　　　mirror〔'mɪrɚ〕*n.* 鏡子　　reflect〔rɪ'flɛkt〕*v.* 反射
　　　　sunlight〔'sʌn͵laɪt〕*n.* 陽光；日光
　　　　feature〔'fitʃɚ〕*n.* 特徵；要點　　pull〔pul〕*n.* 拉力；引力
　　　　tide〔taɪd〕*n.* 潮汐　　*ocean tide* 海潮；潮汐

29. (**A**)　(A) *additionally*〔ə'dɪʃənl̩ɪ〕*adv.* 此外
　　　　　(B) likewise〔'laɪk͵waɪz〕*adv.* 同樣地
　　　　　(C) conversely〔kən'vɜslɪ〕*adv.* 相反地
　　　　　(D) theoretically〔͵θiə'rɛtɪkl̩ɪ〕*adv.* 理論上

最後一點，我們只能在晚上看見月光。其實月球整天都會反射陽光，只是當天
　　　　　　　　　30
氣晴朗，陽光燦爛的時候，我們是看不見月光的。

　　　* finally〔'faɪnlɪ〕*adv.* 最後
　　　　moonlight〔'mun͵laɪt〕*n.* 月光
　　　　all day long 整天　　*a clear sky* 天氣晴朗
　　　　shine〔ʃaɪn〕*v.* 發光；閃耀

30. (**C**)　依句意，選 (C) *at night*「在晚上」。而 (A) in the daytime「在白天」，
　　　　　(B) all day long「一整天」，(D) all night long「一整晚」，均不合句意。

三、文意選填：

第 31 至 40 題為題組

　　莫拉克颱風是有史以來，使台灣受創最嚴重的颱風。受損的 [31] **(D)** 程度比 1959 年，讓 667 人死亡、大約一千人失蹤的颱風還要更嚴重。莫拉克颱風有破 [32] **(G)** 紀錄的降雨量，三天內下了 2,900 毫米（114 英吋）的雨，讓南台灣嚴重受創。八月八日時，地區性的最高單日雨量紀錄被打破，達到單日 1,403 毫米（55 英吋）。[33] **(A)** 全盤性地看來，溫哥華平均年雨量才 1,117 毫米（44 英吋）。

　　　　* typhoon〔taɪ'fun〕*n.* 颱風
　　　　strike〔straɪk〕*v.*（風雨）襲擊
　　　　extent〔ɪk'stɛnt〕*n.* 程度　　　damage〔'dæmɪdʒ〕*n.* 損害
　　　　severe〔sə'vɪr〕*adj.* 嚴重的　　***record breaking*** 破紀錄的
　　　　leave sth. ***V-ing*** 讓某事物保持～狀態
　　　　missing〔'mɪsɪŋ〕*adj.* 失蹤的　　cause〔kɔz〕*v.* 引起
　　　　southern〔'sʌðən〕*adj.* 南部的　　rainfall〔'ren,fɔl〕*n.* 降雨
　　　　millimeter〔'mɪlə,mitə〕*n.* 毫米
　　　　regional〔'ridʒənḷ〕*adj.* 地區性的
　　　　perspective〔pə'spɛktɪv〕*n.* 全盤性的看法；透視
　　　　Vancouver〔væn'kuvə〕*n.* 溫哥華【加拿大西部臨海的城市】
　　　　average〔'ævərɪdʒ〕*adj.* 平均的　　annual〔'ænjʊəl〕*adj.* 每年的

　　有的建築物淹水淹到二樓，還有很多市鎮 [34] **(H)** 孤立無援。軍方派人手去幫忙救援還有重建工作。在台東縣，部分公路還有鐵路被沖走，二十間房舍被沖進海裡，還有一棟大飯店 [35] **(I)** 倒塌。

　　　　* flood〔flʌd〕*v.* 淹水　　town〔taʊn〕*n.* 鎮；市
　　　　isolated〔'aɪsḷ,etɪd〕*adj.* 孤立的；被隔離的
　　　　military〔'mɪlə,tɛrɪ〕*adj.* 軍事的　　personnel〔,pɝsṇ'ɛl〕*n.* 人員
　　　　deploy〔dɪ'plɔɪ〕*v.* 部署　　rescue〔'rɛskjʊ〕*n.* 救援
　　　　reconstruction〔,rikən'strʌkʃən〕*n.* 重建
　　　　segment〔'sɛgmənt〕*n.* 部分　　highway〔'haɪ,we〕*n.* 公路
　　　　railway〔'rel,we〕*n.* 鐵路　　major〔'medʒə〕*adj.* 大的；主要的
　　　　collapse〔kə'læps〕*v.* 倒塌

許多直升機在山區還有峽谷地區交叉飛行，運送食物跟水，還有空運生還者。在嘉義縣中部，將近有九千位民衆 36 **(F)** 受困。在受創最嚴重的高雄，是救災任務最集中的地方，軍隊撤離超過兩千位民衆。救援隊員說他們必須冒著生命危險，37 **(B)** 跋涉過河流，運送救濟物資，像是餅乾、罐頭食品，還有泡麵等。

* *dozens of* 許多；數十　　helicopter (ˋhɛlɪ͵kɑptɚ) n. 直升機
crisscross (ˋkrɪs͵krɔs) v. 交叉通過　　ravine (rəˋvin) n. 峽谷
deliver (dɪˋlɪvɚ) v. 運送　　airlift (ˋɛr͵lɪft) v. 空運
survivor (səˋvaɪvɚ) n. 生還者　　central (ˋsɛntrəl) adj. 中央的
strand (strænd) v. 使擱淺；使受困
hardest-hit (ˋhɑrdɪstˋhɪt) adj. 受創最嚴重的
mission (ˋmɪʃən) n. 任務　　concentrate (ˋkɑnsn͵tret) v. 集中
troop (trup) n. 軍隊　　evacuate (ɪˋvækju͵et) v. 撤退
risk (rɪsk) v. 冒著危險　　*risk one's life* 冒生命危險
wade (wed) v. (在河、雪、水中) 跋涉　　relief (rɪˋlif) adj. 救濟的
item (ˋaɪtəm) n. 物資　　biscuit (ˋbɪskɪt) n. 餅乾
canned (kænd) adj. 罐裝的　　instant (ˋɪnstənt) adj. 立即的
instant noodles 泡麵

在溫泉勝地新發村，發現屍體被土石流埋住了，自願救難隊員必須要蜿蜒穿過大約十八公里，被 38 **(E)** 瞬間大水沖壞的道路，和三座半掩埋的隧道。但是崩塌的橋樑還是讓他們無法將救援物資送給受困的災民。39 **(J)** 估計對經濟的影響達到一千一百億台幣。台灣似乎是被 40 **(C)** 詛咒了一樣。這樣的災難從未發生過。

* hot-spring (ˋhɑtˋsprɪŋ) n. 溫泉　　resort (rɪˋzɔrt) n. 休閒勝地
body (ˋbɑdɪ) n. 屍體　　bury (ˋbɛrɪ) v. 埋葬
mudslide (ˋmʌd͵slaɪd) n. 土石流　　volunteer (͵vɑlənˋtɪr) adj. 自願的
rescuer (ˋrɛskjuɚ) n. 救難者　　snake (snek) v. 蛇行前進；蜿蜒而行
kilometer (ˋkɪlə͵mitɚ) n. 公里　　ravage (ˋrævɪdʒ) v. 破壞；踐踏
flash (flæʃ) adj. 瞬間的　　*flash flood* 瞬間洪水
half-blocked (ˋhæfˋblɑkt) adj. 半掩埋的　　tunnel (ˋtʌnḷ) n. 隧道
toppled (ˋtɑpḷd) adj. 崩塌的　　*prevent sb. from V-ing* 阻止某人~
supplies (səˋplaɪz) n. pl. 補給品　　trapped (træpt) adj. 受困的
victim (ˋvɪktɪm) n. 受難者　　estimated (ˋɛstə͵metɪd) adj. 預估的
economic (͵ikəˋnɑmɪk) adj. 經濟的　　impact (ˋɪmpækt) n. 影響
curse (kɝs) v. 詛咒

四、閱讀測驗：

第 41 至 44 題爲題組

　　我的上司是個很恐怖的人。他以前常常對我吼叫，說我事情沒做好。有一天，我進辦公室時，覺得壓力眞的好大。我今天不想忍受任何人對我吼叫。我的上司早上都沒來煩我。但是午餐後，在我們下午會議中，他又開始罵我。

> * **horrible**〔'hɔrəbḷ〕*adj.* 恐怖的；討厭的
> **used to**（過去）常常；曾經　　**yell at sb.** 對某人大吼
> **constantly**〔'kɑnstəntlɪ〕*adv.* 經常　　**stress**〔strɛs〕*v.* 使緊張；加壓
> **be stressed out** 壓力很大；緊張的　　take〔tek〕*v.* 承受
> **stay away from** 遠離…【stay away from sb. 可引申爲「少去招惹某人」】
> meeting〔'mitɪŋ〕*n.* 會議

　　不知什麼緣故，我沉住氣直到會議結束。然後我冷靜地離開那個地方。走進休息室，開始用最大的音量尖叫，藉以紓解壓力。

> * **hold on(to)** 緊抓（著）；保持　　composure〔kəm'poʒɚ〕*n.* 冷靜；沉著
> calmly〔'kɑmlɪ〕*adv.* 平靜地　　**walk out of** 走出
> lounge〔laʊndʒ〕*n.* 休息室
> scream〔skrim〕*v.* 尖叫；大叫　　lung〔lʌŋ〕*n.* 肺
> **scream at the top of** *one's* **lungs** 用最大音量尖叫
> relief〔rɪ'lif〕*n.* 減輕；放心

　　走回辦公桌的路上，我知道我已經受不了我的老闆，所以決定辭職。但如果我要走的話，也一定讓他好看。所以我挖出所有他對上司說的謊，打成一封漂漂亮亮的信，然後把信寄發出去。

　　最後我聽說我辭職兩天後，他就被開除了。這眞是太棒了！

> * **on the way to** 前往…的路上　　realize〔'riə,laɪz〕*v.* 了解
> **have enough of sb.** 受夠了某人　　quit〔kwɪt〕*v.* 辭職
> **take down**（從高處）取下【take sb. down 意爲「挫某人銳氣」，故全句
> 　　take him down with me 有作者「離職也要拖他下水」之意】
> **dig up** 發掘；發現【三態爲 dig-dug-dug】　　stuff〔stʌf〕*n.* 東西；事情
> **lie to sb. about sth.** 對某人在某件事說謊　　type〔taɪp〕*v.* 打字
> mail〔mel〕*v.* 郵寄　　**mail off** 寄出　　**get fired** 被開除

41.(**B**) 說話的人辭職當天的感覺為何？
 (A) 自負的 (B) <u>壓力很大</u> (C) 很棒 (D) 猜疑的
 * narrator〔'næretɚ〕*n.* 敘述者 resign〔rɪ'zaɪn〕*v.* 辭職
 conceited〔kən'sitɪd〕*adj.* 自負的 terrific〔tə'rɪfɪk〕*adj.* 很棒的
 suspicious〔sə'spɪʃəs〕*adj.* 猜疑的

42.(**D**) 你覺得在第二段開頭，敘述者為什麼要用 "somehow" 這個字？
 (A) 他不確定自己是對或錯。
 (B) 他感到很羞恥。 (C) 他以前常常被主管責備。
 (D) <u>他不知道自己怎麼做到的。</u>
 * ashamed〔ə'ʃemd〕*adj.* 感到羞愧的 ***be ashamed of*** 對…感到羞恥
 scold〔skold〕*v.* 責罵

43.(**C**) 下列何者為非？
 (A) 會議過後敘述者大聲叫以宣洩情緒。
 (B) 敘述者的上司對他的主管說謊。
 (C) <u>敘述者在他主管被開除的兩天前被開除了。</u>
 (D) 敘述者成功地拖他主管下水。
 * shout〔ʃaʊt〕*v.* 大叫 release〔rɪ'lis〕*v.* 釋放
 emotion〔ɪ'moʃən〕*n.* 情緒 ***manage to*** 設法（完成）

44.(**B**) 用哪個字最能代替 "**composure**"？
 (A) self-concept〔'sɛlf'kansɛpt〕*n.* 自我意識
 (B) ***self-control***〔ˌsɛlfkən'trol〕自制
 (C) self-sacrifice〔'sɛlf'sækrəˌfaɪs〕*n.* 自我犧牲
 (D) self-esteem〔ˌsɛlfə'stim〕*n.* 自尊

第 45 至 48 題為題組

 介紹別人認識，會讓你給人親切，人際關係良好的感覺。不過，請務必要遵守正確的禮節。
 * introduce〔ˌɪntrə'djus〕*v.* 介紹 gracious〔'greʃəs〕*adj.* 親切的
 well-connected〔'wɛlkəˌnɛktɪd〕*adj.* 人際關係好 ***be sure to V.*** 務必～
 follow〔'falo〕*v.* 遵守 proper〔'prapɚ〕*adj.* 正確的；適當的
 protocol〔'protəˌkɔl〕*n.* 禮節；儀式

在社交場合，介紹兩個人互相認識的順序，要視性別跟年齡而定（女性以及較年長的先介紹）。在商業場合中，介紹順序要看位階而定。

* social（'soʃəl）adj. 社會的；社交的
situation（ˌsɪtʃʊ'eʃən）n. 情況；位置
social situation 社會環境；社交場合　　order（'ɔrdɚ）n. 順序
be based on 視…而定；依據…　　gender（'dʒɛndɚ）n. 性別
setting（'sɛtɪŋ）n. 環境　　business setting 商業場合
determine（dɪ't3mɪn）v. 決定　　rank（ræŋk）n. 階級；地位

把介紹別人想成一個循環。一開始先介紹階級較高的人並引見階級較低的人。然後把順序倒過來，所以每個人的名字你都要說兩次。試著在開始對話的時候，加上一點有趣的話題。

* think of A as B 認為 A 是 B　　circle（'s3kl̩）n. 圓；循環
introduction（ˌɪntrə'dʌkʃən）n. 介紹
address（ə'drɛs）v. 向人說話
high-ranking（'haɪ'ræŋkɪŋ）adj. 高階層的
present（prɪ'zɛnt）v. 介紹
low-ranking（'lo'ræŋkɪŋ）adj. 低階的
reverse（rɪ'v3s）v. 反轉　　time（taɪm）n. 次數
interesting（'ɪntrɪstɪŋ）adj. 有趣的
tidbit（'tɪdˌbɪt）n. 一小則趣聞；少許

例如，如果你要介紹公司的副總裁史密斯小姐，給新進同事瓊斯先生認識，你可能會說：

「史密斯小姐，這位是瓊斯先生，他剛進公司服務。瓊斯先生，這位是史密斯小姐。瓊斯先生才剛從泰國回來。」

* vice（vaɪs）adj. 副的　　vice president 副總裁
junior（'dʒunjɚ）adj. 後進的；資淺的
associate（ə'soʃɪɪt）n. 同事
would like to V. 想要～（禮貌用法）
return（rɪ't3n）v. 返回　　Thailand（'taɪlənd）n. 泰國

假如你不確定誰比較重要，就用性別跟年齡作為介紹的依據。

假如你忘了別人的名字，別驚慌。大部分的人都很樂意提醒你，並感謝你的引見。

* unsure〔ʌn'ʃʊr〕adj. 不確定的
 default〔dɪ'fɔlt〕v. 不履行；怠忽　***default to*** 使用（= *use*）；參考
 guideline〔'gaɪd,laɪn〕n. 準則；指導方針
 panic〔'pænɪk〕v. 驚慌　***be happy to*** 樂意
 remind〔rɪ'maɪnd〕v. 提醒；使想起
 appreciate〔ə'priʃɪ,et〕v. 感激

45.(**D**) 本文最佳標題為 ＿＿＿＿＿＿。
 (A) 交朋友 　　　　　　　　　　(B) 介紹自己
 (C) 做簡報 　　　　　　　　　　(D) <u>介紹的禮節</u>
 * connection〔kə'nɛkʃən〕n. 連結；交情
 presentation〔,prɛzn̩'teʃən〕n. 報告
 etiquette〔'ɛtɪ,kɛt〕n. 禮節；禮儀

46.(**C**) 我們可以將 "**protocol**" 替換為 ＿＿＿＿＿＿。
 (A) 怠忽 　　　(B) 附件 　　　(C) <u>習俗</u> 　　　(D) 底線
 * attachment〔ə'tætʃmənt〕n. 附件
 practice〔'præktɪs〕n. 習俗　　underline〔,ʌndə'laɪn〕n. 底線

47.(**A**) 在社交場合中，你介紹兩個人的順序應該是 ＿＿＿＿＿＿
 (A) <u>張老師，這是陳美玲。她是我的學生。美玲，這是張老師，</u>
 　　<u>我們在同一所學校教書。</u>
 (B) 蘇小姐，這是陳小姐。我們在同個辦公室。陳小姐，這是蘇
 　　小姐，她是我的學生。
 (C) 王先生，這是趙小姐。趙小姐，這是王先生。
 (D) 譚先生，這是李小姐。李小姐才剛從美國回來。

48.(**B**) 當你在介紹其他人時，如果你忘記名字，＿＿＿＿＿＿。
 (A) 這讓你感覺更親切 　　　　　(B) <u>你應該要保持冷靜</u>
 (C) 讓你感覺跟他人的關係很好　　(D) 快樂的人會看事情的光明面
 * folks〔foks〕n. pl. 人們

第 49 至 52 題為題組

　　「我數到十。在我數到十之前如果你不投降的話，這位年輕漂亮的女士就會死。」

　　在下層甲板上，馬修聽到他妻子的聲音很高興，但又因她被挾持而要崩潰。他有點腿軟。他坐著聽可怕的倒數。

* surrender〔sə'rɛndɚ〕v. 投降
  pleasant〔'plɛznt〕adj. 令人愉快的
  deck〔dɛk〕n. 甲板　　　elate〔ɪ'let〕v. 情緒高漲
  destroy〔dɪ'strɔɪ〕v. 毀壞；打破（希望、計畫）
  rubber〔'rʌbɚ〕n. 橡膠　　awful〔'ɔfḷ〕adj. 可怕的；嚇人的
  countdown〔'kaʊnt,daʊn〕n. 倒數

　　「一…二…三…」
　　「…四…五…」

　　馬修知道，投降就會背叛他堅信的一切，而且他很可能會失去拯救其他人質的機會。但是他能讓梅蘭妮像隻動物一樣地被射殺嗎？一種反胃的感覺流竄他全身…一種不舒服的噁心感。

* betray〔bɪ'tre〕v. 背叛；出賣　　**believe in** 相信；深信
  be likely to + V. 可能～　　hostage〔'hɑstɪdʒ〕n. 人質
  allow〔ə'laʊ〕v. 允許　　**shoot down** 射殺；擊中
  nausea〔'nɔʒə〕n. 反胃；噁心　　course〔kors〕v. 流動
  sickness〔'sɪknɪs〕n. 噁心；疾病

　　「…六…七…」
　　梅蘭妮的眼淚一直流，她咬著嘴唇，安靜絕望地禱告。
　　「…八，」寇舒諾夫倒數著。

* stream〔strim〕v. 流出　　**bite** one's **lip** （因痛苦而）咬住嘴唇
  desperately〔'dɛspərɪtlɪ〕adv. 絕望地　　pray〔pre〕v. 禱告

　　馬修幾乎要大喊：「你不能這麼做！」他的眼淚遮蔽了視線，但沒有讓他失去判斷能力。這位總統慢慢地站起來。
　　「…九！」

* scream〔skrim〕v. 尖叫；大喊　　cloud〔klaʊd〕v. 遮蔽；使模糊
judgment〔'dʒʌdʒmənt〕n. 判斷力；思考
president〔'prɛzədənt〕n. 總統　　rise〔raɪz〕v. 起立
rise to** one's **feet 站起來

「噢，天吶，不要！」馬修閉上眼睛，就像這些事情會消失一樣。「十，」
寇舒諾夫數著。他的自動手槍一聲槍響，梅蘭妮的腦部停止運作。

* shut〔ʃʌt〕v. 關；閉　　***shut** one's **eyes*** 閉上眼睛　　***as if*** 就像
go away 消失　　round〔raʊnd〕n. 一發（彈藥）
pistol〔'pɪstl̩〕n. 手槍　　***machine pistol*** 機關槍；自動手槍
chemistry〔'kɛmɪstrɪ〕n. 化學作用　　cease〔sis〕v. 停止

49. (**B**) 梅蘭妮是 _____ 。
　　(A) 綁匪　　　(B) 第一夫人　　(C) 承包商　　(D) 協調者
　　* kidnapper〔'kɪdnæpɚ〕n. 綁匪　　***first lady*** 第一夫人
　　　contractor〔'kɑntræktɚ〕n. 承包商
　　　coordinator〔ko'ɔrdn̩͵etɚ〕n. 協調者

50. (**A**) 對於寇舒諾夫的威脅，馬修的最後態度為何？
　　(A) 堅定的　　(B) 搖擺不定　　(C) 膽小的　　(D) 諷刺的
　　* firm〔fɝm〕adj. 堅定的；穩定的
　　　swaying〔'sweɪŋ〕adj. 搖擺不定的
　　　timid〔'tɪmɪd〕adj. 膽小的　　ironical〔aɪ'rɑnɪkl̩〕adj. 諷刺的

51. (**C**) 下列對於馬修的描述都是正確的，除了 _____
　　(A) 他未能拯救他妻子。　　　　(B) 他的雙眼一度充滿淚水。
　　(C) 他大叫：「你不能這麼做！」　(D) 他是總統。
　　* description〔dɪ'skrɪpʃən〕n. 描述；敘述　　***be full of*** 充滿

52. (**A**) 下列何者為真？
　　(A) 梅蘭妮被射殺。　　　　　(B) 梅蘭妮在下層甲板上。
　　(C) 馬修在會議室裡。　　　　(D) 寇舒諾夫拿著來福槍。
　　* shoot〔ʃut〕v. 開槍　　***be shot to death*** 被槍殺身亡
　　　conference〔'kɑnfərəns〕n. 會議　　***conference room*** 會議室
　　　rifle〔'raɪfl̩〕n. 來福槍

第 53 至 56 題為題組

　　許多冰島人在麥當勞排隊，要在它還在的時候，點最後一份大麥克。這家美國速食連鎖店，目前遇到成本高漲的危機，預計要在這個星期六午夜退出冰島。這家全球最大的速食公司，在本週稍早的時候表示，由經銷商瓊‧歐曼德森在冰島經營的三家分店，將於二〇〇九年十月三十一日關閉。

　　* ***thousands of*** 許多　　　Icelander〔ˋaɪsləndɚ〕*n.* 冰島人
　　line up 排隊　　***Big Mac*** 大麥克餐　　chain〔tʃen〕*n.* 連鎖店
　　abandon〔əˋbændən〕*v.* 捨棄；拋棄
　　crisis-hit〔ˋkraɪsɪsˏhɪt〕*adj.* 遭遇危機的　　midnight〔ˋmɪdˏnaɪt〕*n.* 午夜
　　due to 由於　　soaring〔ˋsorɪŋ〕*adj.* 高漲的　　cost〔kɔst〕*n.* 成本
　　Iceland〔ˋaɪslənd〕*n.* 冰島　　operate〔ˋɑpəˏret〕*v.* 運轉；經營
　　franchisee〔ˏfræntʃaɪˋzi〕*n.* 經銷商　　***shut down*** 關閉

　　自從消息公布後，各家分店的東西都已經收拾好了。東城邊的一家分店前，排隊隊伍從門口一直排到大街上。星期五午餐時間，分店的停車場都客滿了。裡面的員工動作飛快，為了要滿足大排長龍的人。

　　* outlet〔ˋaʊtˏlɛt〕*n.* 零售店；出口　　pack〔pæk〕*v.* 打包；收拾
　　announcement〔əˋnaʊnsmənt〕*n.* 宣布；佈告
　　line〔laɪn〕*n.* 行列；隊伍　　***back up*** 擁塞；堵塞
　　onto〔ˋɑntə〕*prep.* 到…上面
　　lunchtime〔ˋlʌntʃˏtaɪm〕*n.* 午餐時間　　***parking lot*** 停車場
　　staff〔stæf〕*n.* 員工　　furiously〔ˋfjʊrɪəslɪ〕*adv.* 猛烈地；高速地
　　keep up with 跟上　　demand〔dɪˋmænd〕*n.* 需求

　　排隊等候的二十八歲業務員席基，告訴路透社說：「這是我這陣子最後一次可以吃到道地大麥克的機會。以我目前的經濟情況，是沒辦法隨時出國旅行的。」他又說：「我不是麥當勞的忠實顧客，但是偶爾來一個大麥克，吃的東西多了點變化。」

　　* ***for a while*** 一陣子　　real〔ˋriəl〕*adj.* 真正的；道地的
　　salesman〔ˋselzmən〕*n.* 業務員　　***wait in line*** 排隊等候
　　Reuters 路透通訊社【創設於倫敦】　　economy〔ɪˋkɑnəmɪ〕*n.* 經濟
　　abroad〔əˋbrɔd〕*adv.* 到國外　　add〔æd〕*v.* 補充說；又說
　　fan〔fæn〕*n.* 迷　　***now and then*** 偶爾；有時
　　add to 增加　　variety〔vəˋraɪətɪ〕*n.* 變化

　　不用麥當勞的黃金拱門後，歐曼德森會用不同的名字，繼續經營餐廳。他說星期四那天，有幾個小時的時間，大麥克都賣光了。

* continue〔kən'tɪnju〕v. 繼續　　run〔rʌn〕v. 經營
  under a different name 以不同的名稱　　**take down** 取下
  arch〔ɑrtʃ〕n. 拱門；拱狀物　　**run out of** 耗盡；用盡

　　當地媒體引用歐曼德森所說的話：「銷售額不單上升，簡直是一飛沖天。」他說他努力趕上急速增加的需求量，一天之內已經賣了大概有一萬個漢堡，這是前所未有的紀錄。

* sales〔selz〕n. pl. 銷售額　　**go up** 上升　　quot〔kwot〕v. 引用
  local〔'lokl〕adj. 當地的　　media〔'midɪə〕n. pl. 媒體
  turbo〔'tɝbo〕n. 渦輪　　**go turbo** 加速
  manage to 努力完成　　**catch up with** 趕上
  surge〔sɝdʒ〕n. 急速增加　　burger〔'bɝgɚ〕n. 漢堡（= *hamburger*）

　　冰島從二〇〇八年十月以來，就受到金融危機的影響而搖搖欲墜。當時冰島的銀行，因承受數十億美元債務的重擔在一週內倒閉。銀行倒閉使得對冰島經濟的信心崩盤，連帶使得冰島的貨幣克郎幣值像自由落體般狂跌。麥當勞說，克郎幣值走弱，使國外進口食物成本上揚，是他們撤出冰島的原因之一。麥當勞提到，他們不會再回到冰島。

* reel〔ril〕v. 搖晃；蹣跚　　effect〔ɪ'fɛkt〕n. 影響
  financial〔faɪ'nænʃəl〕adj. 財務的；財政的
  crisis〔'kraɪsɪs〕n. 危機　　collapse〔kə'læps〕v. 倒塌；衰退
  space〔spes〕n. （時間的）間隔
  in the space of a week 一週之內
  under the weight of 承受…的重量；承受…的壓力
  billion〔'bɪljən〕n. 十億　　debt〔dɛt〕n. 債務
  fall〔fɔl〕n. 落下；沒落　　sap〔sæp〕v. 使衰弱
  confidence〔'kɑnfədəns〕n. 信心　　currency〔'kɝənsɪ〕n. 貨幣
  crown〔kraʊn〕n. 克郎　　freefall〔'fri,fɔl〕n. 自由落體
  weakness〔'wiknɪs〕n. 虛弱；弱點　　**be part of** 是…的一部分
  withdrawal〔wɪð'drɔəl〕n. 撤回　　**along with** 伴隨…一起
  import〔ɪm'port〕v. 進口　　**seek to + V.** 尋求～；試圖～

在附近的文具店裡，三十五歲的看護助理朵拉・席古達多蒂說，她不想要去吃最後一份麥當勞餐。

「走了最好，」她說。

> * nearby〔'nɪr,baɪ〕*adj.* 附近的　　stationery〔'steʃən,ɛrɪ〕*n.* 文具
> ***stationery store*** 文具店　　nursing〔'nɜsɪŋ〕*n.* 看護
> assistant〔ə'sɪstənt〕*n.* 助理　　intention〔ɪn'tɛnʃən〕*n.* 意圖
> riddance〔'rɪdn̩s〕*n.* 除去；樂意沒有
> ***good riddance*** 走了最好

53. (**A**) 下列敘述都是正確的，除了 ＿＿＿＿＿＿
   (A) 歐曼德森到 2009 年底的時候就會退出餐飲業。
   (B) 冰島有三家麥當勞。
   (C) 冰島從 2008 年受到金融危機的影響，到現在仍搖搖欲墜。
   (D) 麥當勞決定退出冰島，部分是因為成本的緣故。

   > * stumble〔'stʌmbl̩〕*v.* 搖搖晃晃地走
   > withdraw〔wɪð'drɔ〕*v.* 退出；撤退　　***because of*** 由於

54. (**A**) 下列敘述何者「不是」真的？
   (A) 麥當勞正在冰島找其他經銷商。
   (B) 2009 年 10 月 31 日是週末。
   (C) 2009 年 10 月 30 日這天很多冰島人去吃漢堡。
   (D) 2009 年 10 月 30 日這天，歐曼德森的漢堡店業績創歷史紀錄。

   > * ***look for*** 尋找

55. (**A**) 根據本文，下列何者不是金融危機的副作用？
   (A) 自殺率還是很高。
   (B) 冰島負債很高。
   (C) 冰島的貨幣一週內大貶值。
   (D) 麥當勞撤出冰島。

   > * ***side effect*** 副作用　　***suicidal rate*** 自殺率
   > sharply〔'ʃɑrplɪ〕*adv.* 急轉地；陡地　　***pull out of*** 撤出；撤退

56. (**C**) 席古達多蒂對於麥當勞關閉的態度為何？

    (A) 惡毒的。

    (B) 溫和的。

    (C) <u>不在意的。</u>

    (D) 沮喪的。

    * malevolent (mə'lɛvələnt) *adj.* 惡毒的；壞心腸的
      moderate ('madərɪt) *adj.* 溫和的
      uncaring (ʌn'kɛrɪŋ) *adj.* 不在意的
      dejected (dɪ'dʒɛktɪd) *adj.* 沮喪的

第貳部分：非選擇題

一、中譯英：

1. 寂寞的人可以把他們的感覺散播給別人，就像把感冒傳給別人一樣。

    People who feel lonesome can $\left\{\begin{array}{l}\text{spread}\\\text{transmit}\\\text{pass on}\end{array}\right\}$ their feelings

    to others like spreading a cold.

2. 一段時間之後，這整群孤單、與他人隔絕的人就會退到社會的邊緣。

    $\left\{\begin{array}{l}\text{After a while,}\\\text{Over time,}\\\text{With time,}\end{array}\right\}$ the whole group of lonely, disconnected people

    will $\left\{\begin{array}{l}\text{move to}\\\text{end up on}\\\text{wind up on}\end{array}\right\}$ the $\left\{\begin{array}{l}\text{fringes}\\\text{edge}\end{array}\right\}$ of the society.

二、英文作文：

作文範例

Dear Willow,   Jan. 28, 2013

　　Do you know how proud of you I am? From the time we were kids, you were always saying you were going to medical school in the U.S. And look at you! You're doing it! You're living the dream. I feel like a part of me is with you, cheering you on.

　　Though it might be a little scary being in a foreign country all by yourself, if anyone is brave enough to accept the challenge, it's you. Just remember that when you are feeling down or discouraged, I am here for you 100 percent. You can call me anytime, day or night, even if it's just to say hello.

　　I know how important this is to you, Willow, so I don't want to bring you down by saying how much we all miss you back home. We are so proud of you and look forward to the day we can call you Doctor Chen!

Yours truly,

Ellen

be proud of 以…爲榮　　medical (ˈmɛdɪkḷ) *adj.* 醫學的
medical school 醫學院　　*You are doing it!* 你做到了！
live (lɪv) *v.* 實踐；經歷　　*live the dream* 實現夢想
cheer on 鼓勵　　brave (brev) *adj.* 勇敢的
down (daʊn) *adj.* (意志) 消沈的
discouraged (dɪsˈkɝɪdʒd) *adj.* 灰心的；沮喪的
100 percent 百分之百；一定
bring sb. down 使某人失望　　*look forward to* 期待

大學入學學科能力測驗英文模擬試題⑧

第壹部分：單選題（佔 72 分）

一、詞彙（佔 15 分）

說明：第 1 題至第 15 題，每題 4 個選項，其中只有一個是最適當的答案，畫記在答案卡之「選擇題答案區」。各題答對得 1 分；未作答、答錯、或畫記多於一個選項者，該題以零分計算。

1. Having failed several times, I felt such _____ when I learned I had finally passed my math exam.
   (A) relief   (B) request   (C) reform   (D) reply

2. As a Christian, Richard _____ a small amount of his salary to charity every month.
   (A) admires   (B) contributes   (C) prescribes   (D) separates

3. Sandy is on a diet, so the chocolate cake at the party was a big _____ for her.
   (A) determination   (B) collection
   (C) temptation   (D) celebration

4. Ryan isn't very _____. He's afraid to explore new places or to try new things.
   (A) promising   (B) responsible   (C) optimistic   (D) adventurous

5. The operation of the Maokung gondola has been _____ because of safety concerns.
   (A) extended   (B) suspended   (C) introduced   (D) calculated

6. After years of a state-controlled economy, China has begun to _____ a capitalist system.
   (A) benefit   (B) replace   (C) adopt   (D) reject

7. Because of the _____ heat of the midday sun, dozens of marathon runners either fainted or became dangerously dehydrated.
   (A) intense   (B) refreshing   (C) delightful   (D) tough

8. We're _____ enough to disagree on this issue but still respect each other.
   (A) generous   (B) mature   (C) aware   (D) sociable

9. _____, we all have to grow up and accept the responsibility of adulthood.
   (A) Miraculously   (B) Originally
   (C) Slightly   (D) Inevitably

10. The _____ of meeting the President will be given to the most outstanding students.
    (A) privilege   (B) facility   (C) highlight   (D) rank

11. The Clippers _____ beat the Lakers 97-96 at the last second last night, winning the championship game.
    (A) annually   (B) narrowly   (C) consequently   (D) efficiently

12. Many people visit war museums to _____ on the sufferings caused by conflicts.
    (A) witness   (B) reflect   (C) concentrate   (D) influence

13. Since there was no _____ linking the man to the crime, he was not arrested.
    (A) variety   (B) identity   (C) evidence   (D) devotion

14. Only by trying to live in _____ with nature can we leave an inhabitable environment for the future generations.
    (A) extravagance   (B) appreciation
    (C) harmony   (D) resolution

15. There was a _____ display of fireworks in the opening ceremony of the Olympic Games.

    (A) spectacular   (B) vacant   (C) various   (D) series

二、綜合測驗（佔 15 分）

說明：　第 16 題至第 30 題，每題一個空格，請依文意選出最適當的一個答案，
       畫記在答案卡之「選擇題答案區」。各題答對得 1 分；未作答、答錯、
       或畫記多於一個選項者，該題以零分計算。

第 16 至 20 題為題組

    Anytime you need to get somewhere, you can just stand at the roadside, raise your arm, and before long a bright yellow taxi will be in front of you. It's almost like having a personal driver ___16___ 24 hours a day!

    Taxis first began to operate in Paris and London in the early 17th century. Back then, they were ___17___ those we see today. Instead, they were cabriolets, or horse-drawn carriages. The era of the modern taxi really began in 1891, when German Wilhelm Bruhn invented the "taximeter," ___18___ shortened form is "taxi." It is a device that calculates how much you pay for your ride, usually based on a combination of how far you go and ___19___ it takes to get there. Besides, it contains the word "tax," which is another word for the "___20___" you pay when you ride in a taxi. In the 1940s, thanks to radio dispatching, it was even more convenient to get a taxi. Nowadays, taxis have become widespread and indispensable.

16. (A) on call   (B) in control   (C) out of work (D) in hand
17. (A) nothing but   (B) similar to
    (C) identical with   (D) nothing like
18. (A) whose   (B) which   (C) its   (D) of which
19. (A) how soon   (B) how fast   (C) how long   (D) how heavy
20. (A) rent   (B) rate   (C) tuition   (D) tip

第 21 至 25 題為題組

    For Internet users, whenever information is needed quickly, Wikipedia is a popular source. But how   21   is its information? According to an investigation, Wikipedia is almost as good as *Encyclopedia Britannica*, which is the world's oldest encyclopedia. In 42 entries tested, both made about the same number of errors. However, the editors at *Britannica*   22   with the result, arguing that the two encyclopedias are basically different in quality. Theirs is written by experts and all articles go through careful and strict editing. Wikipedia,   23 , is written by anybody, without professional editors to make sure the information is correct. Nevertheless, one thing remains true, which is that Wikipedia is a work   24 . With 3.7 million articles in over 200 languages, it uses the power of the Internet to tap into people's knowledge. All that being said, it never   25   to have a second source of information.

21. (A) reliant   (B) evident   (C) dependable   (D) influential
22. (A) angry   (B) doubt   (C) compare   (D) disagree
23. (A) on the other hand   (B) believe it or not
    (C) upside down   (D) out of the question
24. (A) in progress   (B) over the counter
    (C) on the way   (D) at rest
25. (A) matches   (B) hurts   (C) sweats   (D) covers

第 26 至 30 題為題組

    American humor is difficult to define because Americans are such a diverse people. In the early days, when the country was largely   26 , America's humor derived from stories about people in rural areas.   27 , it has been adapted and restyled to reflect the new conditions of present day life. The following is an example.

    As the airplane   28   from O'Hare Airport, a metallic voice came over the loudspeaker: "Ladies and gentlemen, Vista Airlines would like to welcome you to the first transatlantic flight that ___29___ completely by computer. The possibility of human error has been eliminated because there is no pilot and no crew aboard. All of your needs will be taken care of by ___30___ latest technology. Just relax and enjoy your flight. Every contingency has been prepared for, and nothing can possibly go wrong…go wrong…go wrong…"

26. (A) agricultural　(B) adventurous　(C) sophisticated (D) delicate
27. (A) Generally　(B) Otherwise　(C) However　(D) Likewise
28. (A) ran out　(B) took off　(C) piled up　(D) put away
29. (A) has controlled　　　　(B) has been controlling
　　(C) is being controlled　　(D) was controlled
30. (A) the most　(B) the very　(C) the ever　(D) the same

三、文意選填（佔 10 分）

說明：　第 31 題至第 40 題，每題一個空格，請依文意在文章後所提供的 (A) 到
　　　　(J) 選項中分別選出最適當者，並將其英文字母代號畫記在答案卡之「選
　　　　擇題答案區」。各題答對得 1 分；未作答、答錯、或畫記多於一個選項
　　　　者，該題以零分計算。

第 31 至 40 題為題組

　　The French have always been proud of their culture and language. However, with words like "le mail" and "l' internet" ___31___ French, they complain that the spread of English is pushing the French language ___32___. Some even view the English language "___33___" as nothing less than modern imperialism.

　　The French actually have taken measures ___34___ it by passing laws which limit the amount of time ___35___ to English pop songs on the radio. However, English is still ___36___ into almost every aspect of life in France. A recent study concludes that seven percent of French businesses use English as their ___37___ language.

This has also ___38___ concern that both efficiency and safety may be ___39___ when, for example, French employees receive ___40___ in English. "They might not want to confess that they don't understand what they are reading, and that could be very dangerous," says a trade union leader.

(A) against　　　　(B) aroused　　　(C) creeping　　　(D) devoted
(E) in question　　(F) infiltrating　(G) instructions　(H) invasion
(I) primary　　　　(J) into a corner

四、閱讀測驗（佔 32 分）

說明： 第 41 題至第 56 題，每題 4 個選項，請分別根據各篇文章之文意選出最適當的一個答案，畫記在答案卡之「選擇題答案區」。各題答對得 2 分；未作答、答錯、或畫記多於一個選項者，該題以零分計算。

第 41 至 44 題爲題組

Lighthouses possess an undeniable charm. By their very nature, they are visually striking structures. They stand like guardians, marking harbor entrances or warning ships not to stray too close to the shore because of dangerous rocks. Lighthouses are often surrounded by dramatic and beautiful coastal scenery, making them favorite subjects for tourists' souvenir photos.

One world-famous lighthouse is the Peggy's Point Lighthouse in Peggy's Cove, Nova Scotia, Canada. This white and red tower has appeared on countless postcards and works of art. Despite warnings, tourists are swept into the sea each year because they want to stand next to the lighthouse for pictures.

Because they are typically found in remote locations and must endure **intense** weather, lighthouses are symbols of independence and perseverance. They're symbolic of safety and hope, too. Once widely used, the number of operational lighthouses has declined due to the expense of maintenance and replacement by modern electronic navigational aids. Still, they are links to a disappearing past. Wherever they are found, lighthouses are automatically historical landmarks.

41. Which is NOT one of the functions of lighthouses?
   (A) As a warning of dangerous coastlines.
   (B) As a landmark for ships at sea.
   (C) As a shelter for fishermen and sailors.
   (D) As a tourist attraction.

42. What sign is most likely to be set up next to the Peggy's Point
   Lighthouse?
   (A) No Trespassing Allowed   (B) No Photographing
   (C) Watch Your Step   (D) Beware of Huge Waves

43. What does "**intense**" mean in this passage?
   (A) mild   (B) extreme   (C) fair   (D) pleasant

44. Which statement is true about lighthouses?
   (A) Some no longer serve practical purposes.
   (B) They are of no use in the daytime.
   (C) Every harbor must have one just in case.
   (D) They are always veiled in mystery.

第 45 至 48 題爲題組

    The world is **on the brink of** a major global food crisis. Even
people living in developed nations, who once thought that food
shortages and hunger only occurred in poor or developing countries,
are starting to feel the effects through ever increasing food prices.
Natural calamities and population growth have always affected the
supply and demand for foodstuffs. However, in today's world, other
factors are contributing to this dilemma, such as global warming,
which is causing more crop failures. The energy shortage, a crisis in
itself, is also worsening the food crisis as a large proportion of land
available for growing food is being used to grow crops to produce
bio-fuels. In addition, limited exports from food-producing nations and
investors gambling that food prices will continue to rise are adding to
shortages and driving prices sky high.

So, what does this all mean? To the developing world it means more hunger and food riots as even food staples such as corn, wheat and rice are in short supply. To the rest of the world it means higher and higher prices due to the shortages and the increasing cost of transporting the food. There is no need to worry about a global famine right now, but it is time to start doing something to prevent one. Unfortunately, there is no easy solution. But what we can do is be even more thankful for what we have and try not to waste it.

45. What's the main purpose of this passage?
    (A) To conceal how serious the food shortage is.
    (B) To discuss what has caused the food crisis.
    (C) To come up with solutions to a global famine.
    (D) To urge us to cope with the food crisis.

46. Which is NOT mentioned as one of the factors that caused the food shortage?
    (A) Global warming.　　　　　(B) Natural disasters.
    (C) Financial storms.　　　　(D) Population growth.

47. According to this passage, how does the energy crisis affect food supply problems?
    (A) It causes an increase in the cost of transporting food.
    (B) Developed countries refuse to exchange energy for food.
    (C) Crops grown for bio-fuel production fail to grow as well as expected.
    (D) Farmland is transformed into wasteland so as to save energy.

48. The phrase "__on the brink of__" can best be replaced by "_____."
    (A) breaking away from　　　(B) headed for
    (C) focusing on　　　　　　(D) accustomed to

第 49 至 52 題爲題組

　　E-mail spam, the electronic version of junk mail, is generally messages sent in bulk by advertisers as a cost-effective way of contacting consumers. For most recipients the practice is both unwanted and annoying. But why is it called *spam*?

　　In the first place, the word *spam* is best known as SPAM, the brand name of a canned pork product that is either loved or hated depending on who you ask. The British Monty Python comedy troupe made the word even more familiar with their classic "SPAM sketch," which takes place in a diner. The sketch involves the waiter reading off a menu of the various dishes, such as "SPAM, eggs, SPAM, SPAM, bacon and SPAM," to a couple of patrons and leads to a chorus in the background singing the SPAM song until one of the characters gets annoyed and screams for everyone to shut up. It is generally believed that in the pre-Internet days, early users of BBSs, mostly computer geeks who typically have a peculiar liking for quoting from Monty Python sketches, would type SPAM repeatedly on message boards or over other people's messages as a joke to **tie up** the services. Over time the term became associated with unwanted garbage over the Internet.

　　So, it seems quite fitting that junk e-mail is called spam as checking your inbox these days may seem like you're reading the menu from that diner. While there are other types of Internet spam, e-mail spam is the most common and probably the most hated.

49. What's the topic of this passage?
　　(A) The origin of the word "spam."
　　(B) How annoying junk e-mail is.
　　(C) A comparison between a menu and e-mail spam.
　　(D) Who created unwanted garbage on the Internet.

50. According to the passage, SPAM is _____.
    (A) a popular breakfast food
    (B) a meat product which became part of a funny sketch
    (C) a word that refers to early users of BBSs
    (D) a comic strip produced by Monty Python

51. We may infer that the SPAM song is annoying most probably because _____.
    (A) it is noisy   (B) it is out of tune
    (C) it is not harmonious
    (D) it repeats "SPAM" over and over

52. The phrase "**tie up**" in Paragraph 2 is close to "_____" in meaning.
    (A) speed up   (B) set up
    (C) keep occupied   (D) hook up to

第 53 至 56 題為題組

　　Almost all animals shed tears, but many believe that only humans shed tears under emotional duress. Although some claim other animals, like elephants and seals, cry when they feel pain, there is little scientific proof that these tears are caused by emotions. They are most likely basal tears or reflex tears. Basal tears are tears that keep the eyes from drying up, and they fight bacterial infections. Reflex tears are created when eyes are bothered by irritants, like pollen or dust. While humans, of course, have these kinds of tears, we also have the unique ability to create emotional tears.

　　Emotional tears differ from basal or reflex tears in their chemical composition. This fact has led scientists to believe that crying emotional tears provides a cleansing and curative effect, as well as an emotional outlet, much as Aristotle believed 2,500 years ago.

By crying, we vent our anguish and grief. This, combined with the fact that the tears themselves are carrying poisons and toxins out of our bodies, makes crying an important part of dealing with stress. It's important to realize that holding back valid tears may be damaging to mental health.

With more public figures forgoing the "**stiff upper lip**" of the past and a growing sensitivity to people's emotional needs, society is beginning to recognize that crying is a natural way of coping with pain, stress, and sorrow. Nowadays, "putting on a brave face" may not always be the best or healthiest response.

53. Which statement is true about emotional tears?
    (A) All animals shed emotional tears.
    (B) They expel poisons and toxins out of our body.
    (C) They have the same chemicals in them as other kinds of tears.
    (D) They are shed only when people are under stress.

54. When it comes to crying, what did Aristotle believe?
    (A) Heroes were not supposed to cry.
    (B) Tears were a sign of weakness.
    (C) Crying led to emotional cleansing.
    (D) People used to be more emotional.

55. It can be inferred that if an eyelash falls into your eye the tears you shed are _____.
    (A) emotional tears   (B) basal tears
    (C) reflex tears   (D) crocodile tears

56. What does the phrase "**stiff upper lip**" represent?
    (A) Holding back one's feelings.
    (B) Remaining silent about one's secret.
    (C) Being sensitive to others' emotional needs.
    (D) Being unable to control one's anger and grief.

第貳部分：非選擇題（佔 28 分）

一、中譯英（佔 8 分）

說明： 1. 請將以下中文句子譯成正確、通順、達意的英文，並將答案寫在「答案卷」上。

2. 請依序作答，並標明題號。每題 4 分，共 8 分。

1. 緋聞，是否真或假，都能為藝人和運動員帶來更多知名度。

2. 但在某個程度上，一個受損的名譽也會影響他們的職業生涯。

二、英文作文（佔 20 分）

說明： 1. 依提示在「答案卷」上寫一篇英文作文。

2. 文長約 100 至 120 個單詞（words）。

提示：你有一位正要進入高中就讀的朋友。你（英文名字必須假設為 Oscar 或 Eva），要寫一封信給你的朋友（英文名字必須假設為 Travis 或 Jennifer），告訴他（她）一些建議，說明如何應付高中的生活。

請注意：必須使用上述的 Oscar 或 Eva 在信末署名，**不得使用自己的真實中文或英文名字**。

大學入學學科能力測驗英文模擬試題 ⑧ 詳解

第壹部分：單選題

一、詞彙：

1. (**A**) 多次不及格後，當我得知終於通過數學考試時，我感到好<u>放心</u>。
   - (A) ***relief*** 〔rɪ'lif〕 *n.* 放心；救濟（物資）　　relieve *v.*
   - (B) request 〔rɪ'kwɛst〕 *n. v.* 要求
   - (C) reform 〔rɪ'fɔrm〕 *n.* 改革　*v.* 改善（= *improve*）
   - (D) reply 〔rɪ'plaɪ〕 *n.* 回答；回覆（= *response*）
   - * fail 〔fel〕 *v.* 失敗；不及格　　time 〔taɪm〕 *n.* 次數
     learn 〔lɜn〕 *v.* 得知　　pass 〔pæs〕 *v.* 通過

2. (**B**) 身為一位基督徒，理查每個月都會<u>捐出</u>他一點薪水來少量做善事。
   - (A) admire 〔əd'maɪr〕 *v.* 讚賞　　admiration *n.* 讚賞；欽佩
     admirable 〔'ædmərəbl̩〕 *adj.* 極佳的
   - (B) ***contribute*** 〔kən'trɪbjut〕 *v.* 捐贈；貢獻 < *to* >
   - (C) prescribe 〔prɪ'skraɪb〕 *v.* 規定；開藥方　　prescription *n.*
   - (D) separate 〔'sɛpə,ret〕 *v.* 分開；分隔　〔'sɛprɪt〕 *adj.*
   - * Christian 〔'krɪstʃən〕 *n.* 基督徒　　amount 〔ə'maʊnt〕 *n.* 數量
     salary 〔'sælərɪ〕 *n.* 薪水　　charity 〔'tʃærətɪ〕 *n.* 慈善

3. (**C**) 珊蒂正在節食，所以派對上的巧克力蛋糕對她而言是個巨大的<u>誘惑</u>。
   - (A) determination 〔dɪ,tɜmə'neʃən〕 *n.* 決心（= *resolution*）
     determine *v.* 決心；決定　　determined *adj.* 堅決的
   - (B) collection 〔kə'lɛkʃən〕 *n.* 蒐集　　collect *v.*
   - (C) ***temptation*** 〔tɛmp'teʃən〕 *n.* 誘惑　　tempt *v.*
   - (D) celebration 〔,sɛlə'breʃən〕 *n.* 慶祝；慶典　　celebrate *v.*
   - * ***on a diet*** 節食　　chocolate 〔'tʃɔklɪt〕 *adj.* 巧克力的

4. (**D**) 萊恩並不是非常<u>愛冒險的</u>人。他害怕探索新地方，或嘗試新事物。
   - (A) promising 〔'prɑmɪsɪŋ〕 *adj.* 有希望的（= *hopeful*）；有前途的
     promise *v. n.* 承諾

(B) responsible〔rɪˋspɑnsəbḷ〕adj. 負責任的；可靠的

(C) optimistic〔͵ɑptəˋmɪstɪk〕adj. 樂觀的（↔ pessimistic）

(D) **adventurous**〔ədˋvɛntʃərəs〕adj. 愛冒險的；大膽的

* **be afraid to V.** 害怕～　　　explore〔ɪkˋsplor〕v. 探索

5. (**B**) 貓空纜車的營運，因為安全的顧慮，已經暫時停止了。

(A) extend〔ɪkˋstɛnd〕v. 延伸；擴大　　extended adj. 長期的
　　　extensive adj. 廣泛的　　extension n. 延長

(B) **suspend**〔səˋspɛnd〕v.（暫時）中止；使停學（職、賽）

(C) introduce〔͵ɪntrəˋdjus〕v. 介紹（= present）；引進
　　　introduction n.　　introductory adj. 入門的

(D) calculate〔ˋkælkjə͵let〕v. 計算　　calculation n.

* operation〔͵ɑpəˋreʃən〕n. 營運　　Maokung n. 貓空
　　gondola〔ˋgɑndələ〕n. 纜車；威尼斯平底船
　　concern〔kənˋsɝn〕n. 關心的事

6. (**C**) 在這麼多年國家掌控經濟之後，中國已經開始採用資本主義制度了。

(A) benefit〔ˋbɛnəfɪt〕v. 有利於　n. 利益　　beneficial adj. 有益的

(B) replace〔rɪˋples〕v. 代替；取代；放回
　　　replace A with B 用 B 取代 A

(C) **adopt**〔əˋdɑpt〕v. 採用；領養

(D) reject〔rɪˋdʒɛkt〕v. 拒絕（= refuse = decline）

* state〔stet〕n. 國家　　control〔kənˋtrol〕v. 控制
　　state-controlled adj. 國家掌控的　　economy〔ɪˋkɑnəmɪ〕n. 經濟
　　capitalist〔ˋkæpətḷɪst〕adj. 資本主義的（= capitalistic）

7. (**A**) 因為中午太陽強烈的熱度，許多馬拉松選手不是昏倒，就是嚴重脫水。

(A) **intense**〔ɪnˋtɛns〕adj.（光、熱度、感情）強烈的；（比賽）激烈的
　　　intensify v. 加強　　intense heat/cold 酷熱/酷寒

(B) refreshing〔rɪˋfrɛʃɪŋ〕adj. 使人神清氣爽的；提神的　　refresh v.

(C) delightful〔dɪˋlaɪtfəl〕adj. 令人愉快的　　delight v. n.

(D) tough〔tʌf〕adj. 堅硬的；固執的；艱難的

* heat〔hit〕n. 熱度　　midday〔'mɪd,de〕adj. 正午的
  dozens of 許多　　marathon〔'mærə,θɑn〕adj. 馬拉松的
  runner〔'rʌnɚ〕n. 跑者　　***either…or~*** 若不是…就是~
  faint〔fent〕v. 昏倒　　dehydrate〔di'haɪdret〕v. 脫水

8.(**B**) 我們夠<u>成熟</u>，能對這個議題持不同意見，但雙方仍互相尊重。

(A) generous〔'dʒɛnərəs〕adj. 慷慨的；豐富的　　generosity n.

(B) ***mature***〔mə'tʃur〕adj.（人）成熟的（↔ immature ）　　v. 變成熟
  maturity n. 成熟（期）

(C) aware〔ə'wɛr〕adj. 注意到的　　awareness n. 意識；察覺

(D) sociable〔'soʃəbl̩〕adj. 善交際的；有人緣的
  socialize v. 交際＜ *with* ＞

* disagree〔,dɪsə'gri〕v. 不同意　　issue〔'ɪʃu〕n. 議題
  respect〔rɪ'spɛkt〕v. 尊重

9.(**D**) <u>必然地</u>，我們每個人都必須長大，並接受成年的責任。

(A) miraculously〔mə'rækjələslɪ〕adv. 不可思議地（= *incredibly* ）
  miraculous adj.　　miracle n. 奇蹟

(B) originally〔ə'rɪdʒən̩lɪ〕adv. 原來；最初地（= *initially* = *at first* ）
  original adj.　　origin n. 起源　　originate v. 起源於

(C) slightly〔'slaɪtlɪ〕adv. 輕微地　　slight adj.

(D) ***inevitably***〔ɪn'ɛvətəblɪ〕adv. 必然地　　inevitable adj.

* accept〔ək'sɛpt〕v. 接受　　responsibility〔rɪ,spɑnsə'bɪlətɪ〕n. 責任
  adulthood〔ə'dʌlt,hud〕n. 成年時期

10.(**A**) 與總統會面的<u>殊榮</u>，將會給那些最優秀的學生。

(A) ***privilege***〔'prɪvl̩ɪdʒ〕n. 特權；殊榮

(B) facility〔fə'sɪlətɪ〕n. 設備；設施；便利
  public facilities 公共設施

(C) highlight〔'haɪ,laɪt〕n. 最精彩的部分　　v. 強調（= *emphasize* ）

(D) rank〔ræŋk〕n. 階級；排、列　　v. 排名；位居…
  ranking adj. 一流的

* outstanding〔'aut'stændɪŋ〕adj. 傑出的

11.（**B**）快艇隊昨晚在最後一秒，<u>勉強</u>以 97 比 96 的比數擊敗了湖人隊，在總
　　　　冠軍賽中獲得勝利。

　　　(A) annually〔'ænjʊəlɪ〕adv. 每年一次地　　　annual adj.
　　　(B) ***narrowly***〔'nærolɪ〕adv. 勉強地　　　narrow adj.
　　　(C) consequently〔'kɑnsə,kwɛntlɪ〕adv. 因此（= hence = accordingly）
　　　　　consequent adj. 隨之發生的　　consequence n. 結果
　　　(D) efficiently〔ə'fɪʃəntlɪ〕adv. 有效率地　　efficient adj.
　　　　　efficiency n. 效率

　　　* clipper〔'klɪpɚ〕n. 快艇　　***the Clippers*** 快艇隊
　　　 beat〔bit〕v. 擊敗　　***the Lakers*** 湖人隊
　　　 championship〔'tʃæmpɪən,ʃɪp〕n. 冠軍賽

12.（**B**）許多人參觀戰爭博物館，<u>反省</u>由衝突所引起的苦難。

　　　(A) witness〔'wɪtnɪs〕v. 目擊　　n. 目擊者
　　　(B) ***reflect***〔rɪ'flɛkt〕v. 反射；反省 < on >
　　　　　reflection n.　　reflective adj.
　　　(C) concentrate〔'kɑnsn̩,tret〕v. 專心
　　　　　concentration n.
　　　(D) influence〔'ɪnflʊəns〕v. 影響（= affect）　　n. 影響
　　　　　influential〔,ɪnflʊ'ɛnʃəl〕adj. 有影響力的

　　　* museum〔mju'ziəm〕n. 博物館　　suffering〔'sʌfərɪŋ〕n. 苦難
　　　 conflict〔'kɑnflɪkt〕n. 衝突

13.（**C**）因為沒有<u>證據</u>證明那個男人與那場犯罪有關，所以他並沒有被逮捕。

　　　(A) variety〔və'raɪətɪ〕n. 多樣性（= diversity）；種類　　various adj.
　　　(B) identity〔aɪ'dɛntətɪ〕n. 身分
　　　　　identical adj. 完全相同的　　identify v. 辨認；證明
　　　(C) ***evidence***〔'ɛvədəns〕n. 證據（= proof）；跡象（= indication）
　　　　　v. 證明（= prove）　　evident adj. 明顯的
　　　(D) devotion〔dɪ'voʃən〕n. 奉獻（= dedication）；摯愛 < to >
　　　　　devote oneself to 致力於（= be devoted to）

　　　* link〔lɪŋk〕v. 連結　　crime〔kraɪm〕n. 犯罪
　　　 arrest〔ə'rɛst〕v. 逮捕

14. (**C**) 唯有試著跟大自然<u>和諧</u>共處，我們才能留給下一代適合居住的環境。

 (A) extravagance〔ɪkˈstrævəgəns〕*n.* 奢侈　extravagant *adj.*

 (B) appreciation〔əˌpriʃɪˈeʃən〕*n.* 感激；欣賞　appreciate *v.*
 appreciative *adj.* 感激的

 (C) ***harmony***〔ˈharmənɪ〕*n.* 和諧　harmonious *adj.*
 be in harmony with 與…和諧共處

 (D) resolution〔ˌrɛzəˈluʃən〕*n.* 決心　resolute *adj.* 堅決的
 resolve *v.* 決心

 * nature〔ˈnetʃɚ〕*n.* 大自然
 inhabitable〔ɪnˈhæbɪtəbḷ〕*adj.* 適合居住的
 generation〔ˌdʒɛnəˈreʃən〕*n.* 世代

15. (**A**) 在奧運開幕典禮上，有一場<u>壯麗的</u>煙火表演。

 (A) ***spectacular***〔spɛkˈtækjələ〕*adj.* 壯觀的（= *impressive*）

 (B) vacant〔ˈvekənt〕*adj.* 空的（↔ occupied）
 vacancy *n.* 空缺；空房

 (C) various〔ˈvɛrɪəs〕*adj.* 各種不同的

 (D) series〔ˈsɪrɪz〕*n.* 一連串；一系列
 a series of 一連串的

 * display〔dɪˈsple〕*n.* 展示　ceremony〔ˈsɛrəˌmonɪ〕*n.* 典禮
 opening ceremony 開幕典禮　***the Olympic Games*** 奧運

二、綜合測驗：

<u>第 16 至 20 題為題組</u>

 每當你需要去某個地方的時候，你只要站在路邊，舉起手臂，不久之後，一台鮮黃色的計程車就會停在你面前。這幾乎就像有個二十四小時<u>隨時待命的</u>私人司機！

 * roadside〔ˈrodˌsaɪd〕*n.* 路邊　raise〔rez〕*v.* 舉起
 arm〔arm〕*n.* 手臂　***before long*** 不久（= *soon*）
 bright〔braɪt〕*adj.* 鮮明的　***in front of*** 在…的面前
 personal〔ˈpɜsṇḷ〕*adj.* 私人的

16. (**A**) 依句意，選 (A) ***on call*** 「隨時待命的」。而 (B) in control 「掌控中」，
 (C) out of work 「失業」，(D) in hand 「在手中；在控制下」，不合句意。

16

　　計程車首先是在十七世紀初期，在巴黎跟倫敦開始營運的。在當時，它們一點也不像我們現在看到的計程車，而是敞篷馬車，或是四輪馬車。
　　　　17

> * operate〔ˈɑpəˌret〕v. 營運　　Paris〔ˈpærɪs〕n. 巴黎
> London〔ˈlʌndən〕n. 倫敦　　***back then*** 當時
> instead〔ɪnˈstɛd〕adv. 反而
> cabriolet〔ˌkæbrɪəˈle, -ˈlɛt〕n. 敞篷馬（汽）車
> horse-drawn〔ˈhɔrsˈdrɔn〕adj. 用馬拉的
> carriage〔ˈkærɪdʒ〕n. 四輪馬車

17.（**D**）依句意，選 (D) ***nothing like***「一點也不像」。而 (A) nothing but「只不過」(= *only*)，(B) similar to「和…相似」，(C) identical with「和…完全相同」，則不合句意。

　　現代計程車的時代，其實是始於 1891 年，當時德國的威廉‧布魯恩（Wilhelm Bruhn）發明了計程表，它的縮寫是 "taxi"。它是一種計算你要為你的車程
　　　　　　　　　　　　　　18
付多少錢的裝置，通常根據走了多遠，和花多久時間到目的地一起合併計算。
　　　　　　　　　　　　　　　　　　　　19

> * era〔ˈɪrə〕n. 年代；時代　　modern〔ˈmɑdən〕adj. 現代的
> German〔ˈdʒɝmən〕adj. 德國的
> Wilhelm Bruhn n. 威廉‧布魯恩【計程車表發明者】
> invent〔ɪnˈvɛnt〕v. 發明　　taximeter〔ˈtæksɪˌmitɚ〕n. 計程表
> shorten〔ˈʃɔrtn̩〕v. 縮短　　form〔fɔrm〕n. 形式
> device〔dɪˈvaɪs〕n. 裝置；發明　　calculate〔ˈkælkjəˌlet〕v. 計算
> ride〔raɪd〕n. 行程；路程　　***be based on*** 根據…
> combination〔ˌkɑmbəˈneʃən〕n. 組合　　take〔tek〕v. 花（時間）

18.（**A**）依句意，空格應填入關係代名詞的所有格形式，選 (A) ***whose***。而 (B) which 是主格而非所有格，用 (C) its 的話應在逗點後加上連接詞，(D) of which 所修飾的名詞應有定冠詞 the，故不合。

19.（**C**）依句意，看計程車花「多久」時間到目的地，動詞 take 表示花費時間，故選 (C) ***how long***「多久」。而 (A) how soon「還要多久」，(B) how fast「多快」，(D) how heavy「多重」，與 take 的用法不合。

此外，它包含了「稅」這個字，也是另一個指你搭計程車時，所付的「費用」
　　　　　　　　　　　　　　　　　　　　　　　　　　　　　　　20
的字。在 1940 年代，因為有無線電派遣系統，叫計程車方便得多了。現在，計
程車已經變得很普及，也是不可或缺的。

* contain〔kənˈten〕*v.* 包含　　tax〔tæks〕*n.* 稅金（動詞有「負擔」之意）
thanks to 由於；多虧　　radio〔ˈredɪ͵o〕*n.* 無線電廣播
dispatch〔dɪˈspætʃ〕*v.* 派遣　　nowadays〔ˈnauə͵dez〕*adv.* 現今
widespread〔ˈwaɪd͵sprɛd〕*adj.* 普及的
indispensable〔͵ɪndɪˈspɛnsəbl〕*adj.* 不可或缺的

20. (**B**) 依句意，選 (B) **rate**〔ret〕*n.* （按照一定收費標準的）費用；費率。
　　　　而 (A) rent〔rɛnt〕*n.* 租金，(C) tuition〔tuˈɪʃən〕*n.* 學費，(D) tip〔tɪp〕*n.*
　　　　小費，則不合句意。

第 21 至 25 題為題組

　　對網路族來說，每當要快速得到資訊的時候，維基百科是一個很普遍的資
訊來源。但這些資訊有多可靠呢？根據一項調查，維基百科幾乎就跟大英百
　　　　　　　　　　　21
科全書，也就是全世界最古老的百科全書一樣好。

* Internet〔ˈɪntɚ͵nɛt〕*n.* 網際網路　　information〔͵ɪnfɚˈmeʃən〕*n.* 資訊
Wikipedia〔ˈwɪkɪˈpidɪə〕*n.* 維基百科【一個由網路使用者共同創作、編纂
　　的線上知識共享系統】
popular〔ˈpɑpjəlɚ〕*adj.* 普及的　　source〔sors〕*n.* 來源
according to 根據　　investigation〔ɪn͵vɛstəˈgeʃən〕*n.* 調查
encyclopedia〔ɪn͵saɪkləˈpidɪə〕*n.* 百科全書
Britannica〔brɪˈtænɪkə〕*adj.* 英國的；大不列顛的
Encyclopedia Britannica 大英百科全書【1768 年首次出版，經過兩百多年
　　再版與修訂，是當今世界上最知名、最具權威的百科全書】

21. (**C**) (A) reliant〔rɪˈlaɪənt〕*adj.* 依賴的
　　　　(B) evident〔ˈɛvədənt〕*adj.* 明顯的
　　　　(C) **dependable**〔dɪˈpɛndəbl〕*adj.* 可靠的
　　　　(D) influential〔͵ɪnfluˈɛnʃəl〕*adj.* 有影響力的

測試過四十二項條目之後，兩者犯的錯誤數量大約相同。然而，大英百科全書的編輯群卻<u>不同意</u>此結果，他們主張，基本上，兩種百科全書的品質差很多。
22

    * entry〔ˈɛntrɪ〕*n.* 條目；項目   test〔tɛst〕*v.* 測試
    error〔ˈɛrə〕*n.* 錯誤   editor〔ˈɛdɪtə〕*n.* 編輯者
    argue〔ˈɑrgju〕*v.* 爭論；主張   basically〔ˈbesɪklɪ〕*adv.* 基本上

22.(**D**) 依句意，選 (D) *disagree*〔ˌdɪsəˈgri〕*v.* 與…意見不合；不同意＜*with*＞。
    而 (A) be angry with「對…生氣」，(B) doubt〔daʊt〕*v.* 懷疑，(C)
    compare〔kəmˈpɛr〕*v.* 比較，均不合句意。

他們的大英百科全書是由專家所寫，而且所有的文章都經過審慎跟嚴格的校對。
<u>另一方面</u>，維基百科不知道是誰寫的，沒有專業的編輯群來確認這些資訊是否
23
正確。儘管如此，有一件事卻是真的，那就是，維基百科是個<u>進行中</u>的著作。
24

    * expert〔ˈɛkspɝt〕*n.* 專家   article〔ˈɑrtɪkḷ〕*n.* 文章
    go through 經過；通過   strict〔strɪkt〕*adj.* 嚴格的
    edit〔ˈɛdɪt〕*v.* 編輯；校對   professional〔prəˈfɛʃənḷ〕*adj.* 專業的
    make sure 確定；確認   correct〔kəˈrɛkt〕*adj.* 正確的
    nevertheless〔ˌnɛvəðəˈlɛs〕*adv.* 儘管如此   remain〔rɪˈmen〕*v.* 仍舊

23.(**A**) 依句意，選 (A) *on the other hand*「另一方面」。而 (B) believe it or
    not「信不信由你」，(C) upside down「上下顛倒地」，(D) out of the
    question「不可能」，則不合句意。

24.(**A**) 依句意，選 (A) *in progress*「進行中；未完的」。
    progress〔ˈprɑgrɛs〕*n.* 進行；發展
    而 (B) over the counter「(買藥)不需處方籤的」，(C) on the way
    「在路上」，(D) at rest「安靜地」，皆不合句意。

它有三百七十萬篇文章，使用的語言超過兩百種，維基百科利用網路的力量，
擷取民眾的智慧。綜合以上，多一個資料來源也不會有什麼<u>損失</u>。
25

    * tap〔tæp〕*v.* 開發；擷取

25.(**B**)　依句意，選 (B) *hurt*〔hɝt〕*v.* 妨礙；對…不方便。
　　　　　It never hurts 或 It does not hurt + to V. 表「做～又不會有什麼損失」。
　　　　　而 (A) match〔mætʃ〕*v.* 配合, (C) sweat〔swɛt〕*v.* 流汗, (D) cover
　　　　　〔'kʌvɚ〕*v.* 覆蓋，均不合句意。

第 26 至 30 題為題組

　　美式幽默很難去定義，因為美國人是如此多樣化的民族。在早期，當美國
人大多過著農業生活的時候，美式幽默是源自於鄉間居民的故事。然而，這些
　　　　　　　　　　26　　　　　　　　　　　　　　　　　　　27
鄉間的幽默，都已被改寫，風格也已改變，以反映現代日常生活的情況。以下
是一則例子。

　　　* humor〔'hjumɚ〕*n.* 幽默　　　define〔dɪ'faɪn〕*v.* 下定義
　　　diverse〔də'vɝs〕*adj.* 多種的　　people〔'pipl̩〕*n.* 民族
　　　derive from 源自於…　　　rural〔'rʊrəl〕*adj.* 鄉村的
　　　adapt〔ə'dæpt〕*v.* 改寫；使適應　　restyle〔rɪ'staɪl〕*v.* 重新設計
　　　reflect〔rɪ'flɛkt〕*v.* 反映　　condition〔kən'dɪʃən〕*n.* 情況；狀況
　　　present〔'prɛznt̩〕*adj.* 現在的　　following〔'faloɪŋ〕*adj.* 下面的

26.(**A**)　(A) ***agricultural***〔͵ægrɪ'kʌltʃərəl〕*adj.* 農業的
　　　　　(B) adventurous〔əd'vɛntʃərəs〕*adj.* 愛冒險的
　　　　　(C) sophisticated〔sə'fɪstɪ͵ketɪd〕*adj.* 老練的
　　　　　(D) delicate〔'dɛləkət , -kɪt〕*adj.* 精緻的

27.(**C**)　依句意，選 (C) ***However***「然而」。而(A) generally〔'dʒɛnərəlɪ〕*adv.*
　　　　　一般地, (B) otherwise〔'ʌðɚ͵waɪz〕*adv.* 否則, (D) likewise〔'laɪk͵waɪz〕
　　　　　adv. 同樣地，均不合句意。

　　一架從奧黑爾國際機場起飛的飛機上，一種金屬般的聲音從擴音器中傳出：
　　　　　　　　　　　　　　　　28
「各位先生女士，遠景航空歡迎您搭乘第一班全程由電腦控制，橫越大西洋的
　　　　　　　　　　　　　　　　　　　　　　　29
班機。人為疏失的可能性已完全排除，因為機上沒有機長和組員。

　　　* ***O'Hare Airport*** 奧黑爾國際機場【位於美國伊利諾州芝加哥市的主要機場】
　　　metallic〔mə'tælɪk〕*adj.* 金屬般的　　***come over*** 從…傳出來
　　　loudspeaker〔'laʊd'spikɚ〕*n.* 擴音器　　vista〔'vɪstə〕*n.* 遠景；景色

airlines〔'ɛr,laɪnz〕n. 航空公司
transatlantic〔,trænsət'læntɪk〕adj. 橫越大西洋的
flight〔flaɪt〕n. 班機　　completely〔kəm'plitlɪ〕adv. 完全地
possibility〔,pɑsə'bɪlətɪ〕n. 可能性　　error〔'ɛrɚ〕n. 錯誤
human error 人爲疏失　　eliminate〔ɪ'lɪmə,net〕v. 剔除
crew〔kru〕n. 全體機務人員　　aboard〔ə'bord〕adv. 在飛機上

28.(**B**) 依句意，選 (B) **took off**「起飛」。
而 (A) run out「耗盡」，(C) pile up「堆積」，(D) put away「收拾」，
均不合句意。

29.(**C**) 關係代名詞 that 引導形容詞子句，子句中的時態表示飛機「全程都在
電腦掌控之下」，故用被動的現在進行式，選 (C) **is being controlled**。

最新的科技將滿足您所有的需求。請放輕鬆，並享受您的航程。我們已爲每種
30
突發事件做好準備，而且不可能有任何事情會出錯…出錯…出錯…」

　　* need〔nid〕n. 需求　　**take care of** 照顧
latest〔'letɪst〕adj. 最新的　　technology〔tɛk'nɑlədʒɪ〕n. 科技
relax〔rɪ'læks〕v. 放鬆　　contingency〔kən'tɪndʒənsɪ〕n. 偶發事件
prepare for 爲…做好準備　　possibly〔'pɑsəblɪ〕adv. 可能地

30.(**B**) **the very** + adj. 表「最～的」，故選 (B)。

三、文意選填：

第 31 至 40 題爲題組

　　法國人一直以自己的文化跟語言自豪。然而，隨著像是「le mail」，還有
「l' Internet」 [31] **(F)** 滲透到法語中，他們抱怨英語的普及將法語逼 [32] **(J)** 入困境。
有些人甚至把英語的 [33] **(H)** 「入侵」，視爲簡直就像是現代版帝國主義。

　　* **be proud of** 對～感到自豪　　le mail n. 電子郵件（= the mail）【法】
l' internet n. 網路（= the Internet）【法】
infiltrate〔ɪn'fɪltret〕v. 滲透；滲入　　spread〔sprɛd〕n. 普及
push sb. into a corner 將某人逼入困境　　**view** A **as** B 把 A 視爲 B
invasion〔ɪn'veʒən〕n. 入侵　　**nothing less than** + N. 簡直是～
imperialism〔ɪm'pɪrɪəl,ɪzəm〕n. 帝國主義；領土擴張主義

　　法國人其實已經 34 **(A)** 對這件事採取措施，通過法律限制電台 35 **(D)** 用在播放英文流行歌曲的時間。然而，英語還是 36 **(C)** 悄悄地溜進法國的生活中，幾乎每個層面。最近有項研究指出，法國有百分之七的商業行為，是用英語作為它們的 37 **(I)** 主要語言。

* actually〔'æktʃʊəlɪ〕adv. 實際上　　***take measures*** 採取措施
  pass〔pæs〕v. 通過（法律）　　　limit〔'lɪmɪt〕v. 限制
  amount〔ə'maʊnt〕n. 總額　　　devote〔dɪ'vot〕v. 將（時間）奉獻給…
  pop〔pɑp〕adj. 流行的　　radio〔'redɪo〕n. 廣播電台
  creep〔krip〕v. 悄悄接近　　aspect〔'æspɛkt〕n. 層面
  conclude〔kən'klud〕v. 總結　　business〔'bɪznɪs〕n. 商業；業務
  primary〔'praɪmərɪ〕adj. 主要的

　　這也 38 **(B)** 引發對於效率跟安全性可能會 39 **(E)** 有問題的疑慮，例如，當法國員工接到英文的 40 **(G)** 指示。「他們可能不想承認自己讀不懂的東西，而這可能會非常危險，」工會的領袖說到。

* arouse〔ə'raʊz〕v. 喚起；激起　　concern〔kən'sɝn〕n. 擔憂
  efficiency〔ə'fɪʃənsɪ〕n. 效率　　safety〔'seftɪ〕n. 安全性
  be in question 有問題　　employee〔ͺɛmplɔɪ'i〕n. 員工
  receive〔rɪ'siv〕v. 接到　　instruction〔ɪn'strʌkʃən〕n. 教育；指示
  in English 用英語寫（說）的　　confess〔kən'fɛs〕v. 坦白
  trade〔tred〕n. 商業　　***trade union*** 工會　　leader〔'lidɚ〕n. 領導者

四、閱讀測驗：

第 41 至 44 題為題組

　　燈塔具有一種無可否認的魅力。本質上，它們是視覺上相當醒目的建築物。它們像守護者一樣矗立，標示著港灣的入口，或是警告船隻，不要漂流到靠海岸太近的地方，因為會有危險的岩礁。燈塔常被引人注目的美麗海岸風景所環繞，也因此成為遊客紀念照裡的最佳景物。

* lighthouse〔'laɪtͺhaʊs〕n. 燈塔　　possess〔pə'zɛs〕v. 擁有
  undeniable〔ͺʌndɪ'naɪəbḷ〕adj. 無可否認的　　charm〔tʃɑrm〕n. 魅力
  nature〔'netʃɚ〕n. 本質　　visually〔'vɪʒʊəlɪ〕adv. 視覺上
  striking〔'straɪkɪŋ〕adj. 醒目的　　structure〔'strʌktʃɚ〕n. 建築物；結構
  guardian〔'gɑrdɪən〕n. 守護者　　mark〔mɑrk〕v. 標示

harbor〔'hɑrbɚ〕*n.* 港灣　　entrance〔'ɛntrəns〕*n.* 入口

warn〔wɔrn〕*v.* 警告　　stray〔stre〕*v.* 迷路；漂泊

shore〔ʃor〕*n.* 海岸　　rock〔rɑk〕*n.* 岩礁；暗礁

surround〔sə'raʊnd〕*v.* 圍繞　　dramatic〔drə'mætɪk〕*adj.* 引人注目的

coastal〔'kostl̩〕*adj.* 沿岸的　　subject〔'sʌbdʒɪkt〕*n.* 題材；物體

souvenir〔ˌsuvə'nɪr〕*n.* 紀念品

　　世界有名的燈塔之一，就是在加拿大新斯科細亞省，佩姬灣的佩姬岬燈塔。這座紅白相間的高塔，出現在無數的明信片跟藝術作品上。每年都有不顧警告的遊客們被捲入海裡，因為他們希望能站在燈塔旁邊拍照。

* point〔pɔɪnt〕*n.* 海角；岬

Peggy's Point 佩姬岬【加拿大景點之一，位於佩姬灣內】

Peggy's Point Lighthouse 佩姬岬燈塔　　cove〔kov〕*n.* 小海灣

Peggy's Cove 佩姬灣【位於加拿大的新斯科細亞省，面對北極海，峽灣地形
　　獨特，以眾多燈塔聞名】

Nova Scotia 新斯科細亞省【位於加拿大東部的一省】

Canada〔'kænədə〕*n.* 加拿大　　tower〔'taʊɚ〕*n.* 高塔

appear〔ə'pɪr〕*v.* 出現　　countless〔'kaʊntlɪs〕*adj.* 數不盡的

postcard〔'postˌkɑrd〕*n.* 明信片　　despite〔dɪ'spaɪt〕*prep.* 儘管

sweep〔swip〕*v.* 清掃；橫掃；風靡【三態變化為：sweep-swept-swept】

　　因為燈塔大多是在偏遠地區，而且都必須忍受強烈的氣候，所以燈塔成為獨立與堅忍的象徵。它們也象徵安全與希望。它們曾被廣泛使用，但因維護的費用，以及被現代電子輔助航運儀器所取代，運作中的燈塔數量已經減少。但它們依舊是與消失過往的連結。不管燈塔在何處，它們總是成為歷史地標。

* typically〔'tɪpɪkl̩ɪ〕*adv.* 一般地　　remote〔rɪ'mot〕*adj.* 偏遠的

location〔lo'keʃən〕*n.* 地點；位置　　endure〔ɪn'djur〕*v.* 忍受

intense〔ɪn'tɛns〕*adj.* 強烈的　　symbol〔'sɪmbl̩〕*n.* 象徵

independence〔ˌɪndɪ'pɛndəns〕*n.* 獨立

perseverance〔ˌpɝsə'vɪrəns〕*n.* 堅忍

symbolic〔sɪm'bɑlɪk〕*adj.* 象徵的　　**be symbolic of** 象徵

operational〔ˌɑpə'reʃənl̩〕*adj.* 使用中的

decline〔dɪ'klaɪn〕*v.* 下降；衰退　　**due to** 由於

expense〔ɪk'spɛns〕*n.* 花費　　maintenance〔'mentənəns〕*n.* 維持

replacement〔rɪˈplesmənt〕*n.* 替換
electronic〔ɪˌlɛkˈtrɑnɪk〕*adj.* 電子的
navigational〔ˌnævəˈgeʃənəl〕*adj.* 航運的　　aid〔ed〕*n.* 幫助
link〔lɪŋk〕*n.* 連結　　disappear〔ˌdɪsəˈpɪr〕*v.* 消失
automatically〔ˌɔtəˈmætɪklɪ〕*adv.* 自動地
historical〔hɪsˈtɔrɪkl̩〕*adj.* 歷史的　　landmark〔ˈlændˌmɑrk〕*n.* 地標

41. (**C**) 何者不是燈塔的功能？

(A) 作為海岸線的危險警示。　　(B) 作為海上船隻的地標。
(C) <u>作為漁民和水手的避難所。</u>　　(D) 作為觀光景點。

* function〔ˈfʌŋkʃən〕*n.* 功能　　coastline〔ˈkostˌlaɪn〕*n.* 海岸線
shelter〔ˈʃɛltə〕*n.* 避難所　　attraction〔əˈtrækʃən〕*n.* 吸引人的事物
tourist attraction 觀光景點

42. (**D**) 在佩姬岬燈塔旁邊，最有可能設置什麼標誌？

(A) 禁止進入　　(B) 不准拍照　　(C) 注意腳步　　(D) <u>注意大浪</u>

* ***be likely to*** + *V.* 可能～　　***no V-ing*** 不准做～
trespass〔ˈtrɛspəs〕*v.* 入侵（私人土地）
photograph〔ˈfotəˌgræf〕*v.* 拍照　　watch〔wɑtʃ〕*v.* 注意
beware of 提防；注意　　***huge waves*** 大浪

43. (**B**) 本文中的 "**intense**" 是什麼意思？

(A) 溫和的　　(B) <u>極端的</u>　　(C) 公平的　　(D) 令人愉悅的

* mild〔maɪld〕*adj.* 溫和的　　extreme〔ɪkˈstrim〕*adj.* 極端的
fair〔fɛr〕*adj.* 公平的　　pleasant〔ˈplɛznt〕*adj.* 令人愉悅的

44. (**A**) 關於燈塔的敘述何者為真？

(A) <u>有些燈塔不再具有實際用途。</u>
(B) 燈塔在白天是沒有用的。
(C) 為了以防萬一，每個港口都要有一座燈塔。
(D) 燈塔總是蒙著神秘的面紗。

* ***no longer*** 不再　　serve〔sɝv〕*v.* 合於（用途、目的）
practical〔ˈpræktɪkl̩〕*adj.* 實際的；實用的
purpose〔ˈpɝpəs〕*n.* 目的；用途　　***of no use*** 沒有用的
in case 以防萬一　　veil〔vel〕*v.* 以面紗罩住

第 45 至 48 題為題組

　　這世界瀕臨全球重大糧食危機。即使是住在已開發國家的民眾，他們曾經以為食物短缺跟飢荒，只會發生在貧窮或開發中國家，現在也開始感受到食品價格不斷攀升的影響。大型天災跟人口成長，一直都影響著糧食的供給跟需求。然而，在現今的世界裡，其他因素也促成了這個困境，像是全球暖化造成越來越多農作物歉收。

> ＊ brink〔brɪŋk〕n. 邊緣　　**on the brink of** 在…的緊要關頭
> major〔'medʒɚ〕adj. 重大的　　global〔'globḷ〕adj. 全球的
> crisis〔'kraɪsɪs〕n. 危機【複數為 crises】
> **developed nation** 已開發國家　　shortage〔'ʃɔrtɪdʒ〕n. 短缺
> hunger〔'hʌŋgɚ〕n. 飢荒　　occur〔ə'kɝ〕v. 發生
> **developing country** 開發中國家　　effect〔ɪ'fɛkt〕n. 影響
> increasing〔ɪn'krisɪŋ〕adj. 日益增多的
> natural〔'nætʃərəl〕adj. 自然的　　calamity〔kə'læmətɪ〕n. 大災難
> **natural calamity** 大型天災　　population〔ˌpɑpjə'leʃən〕n. 人口
> affect〔ə'fɛkt〕v. 影響　　supply〔sə'plaɪ〕n. 供給
> demand〔dɪ'mænd〕n. 需求　　foodstuff〔'fud,stʌf〕n. 糧食
> factor〔'fæktɚ〕n. 因素　　**contribute to** 促成
> dilemma〔də'lɛmə〕n. 兩難的局面；窘境
> **global warming** 全球暖化　　cause〔kɔz〕v. 引起
> crop〔krɑp〕n. 農作物　　failure〔'feljɚ〕n. 缺乏；不足

　　能源短缺本身就是一種危機，而且也惡化了糧食危機的情況，因為大部分可用來耕作糧食的農地，現在都被用來種植製造生物燃料的農作物。此外，食品製造國的出口限制，和指望食物價格持續上揚的投資者，都使糧食短缺問題更加嚴重，也驅使食物價格有如天價。

> ＊ energy〔'ɛnɚdʒɪ〕n. 能源　　worsen〔'wɝsṇ〕v. 惡化
> proportion〔prə'porʃən〕n. 比例　　available〔ə'veləbḷ〕adj. 可取得的
> bio-fuel〔'baɪo'fjuəl〕n. 生物燃料【又稱綠色燃料，主要從油菜籽、玉米、
> 　　小麥或甘蔗等作物提煉。製造時需消耗大量作物，間接導致穀物價格上漲】
> **in addition** 此外　　limited〔'lɪmɪtɪd〕adj. 受限制的
> export〔'ɛksport〕n. 出口　　investor〔ɪn'vɛstɚ〕n. 投資者
> gamble〔'gæmbḷ〕v. 打賭；指望　　rise〔raɪz〕v. 上升
> **add to** 增加　　drive〔draɪv〕v. 驅使　　**sky high** 如天一般高

　　所以這全部代表了什麼呢？對開發中世界而言，這代表更嚴重的飢荒，與因食物而起的暴動，因為甚至是玉米、小麥、稻米等主食的供應量都不足。

* riot〔'raɪət〕n. 暴動　　staple〔'stepl〕n. 重要產品；主食
corn〔kɔrn〕n. 玉米；穀類　　wheat〔hwit〕n. 小麥

　　對世界其他地區而言，這代表由於食物短缺跟運送食物的費用增加，食品價格會越來越高。現在沒有必要擔心會有全球性的飢荒，但該是開始做些事情，來預防飢荒的時候了。不幸的是，解決方法並不容易。我們能做的，是對於我們所擁有的感到更加感激，並試著不要浪費食物。

* *the rest of* 剩下的　　*due to* 由於　　transport〔træns'port〕v. 運輸
famine〔'fæmɪn〕n. 飢荒　　*it's time to + V.* 該是做～的時候了
prevent〔prɪ'vɛnt〕v. 防止　　unfortunately〔ʌn'fɔrtʃənɪtlɪ〕adv. 不幸地
solution〔sə'luʃən〕n. 解答　　thankful〔'θæŋkfəl〕adj. 感激的

45.(**D**) 本文的主要目的為何？
(A) 隱瞞糧食短缺的問題有多嚴重。
(B) 討論引發糧食危機的原因。
(C) 想出解決全球飢荒的方法。　　(D) 催促人們處理糧食危機。

* conceal〔kən'sil〕v. 隱藏　　discuss〔dɪ'skʌs〕v. 討論
come up with 想出（點子）　　urge〔ɝdʒ〕v. 催促；促使
cope with 處理

46.(**C**) 下列何者沒有被提到是引起糧食短缺的因素之一？
(A) 全球暖化。　(B) 自然災害。　　(C) 金融風暴。　(D) 人口成長。

* financial〔fə'nænʃəl〕adj. 金融的　　storm〔stɔrm〕n. 暴風雨

47.(**A**) 根據本文，能源危機如何影響糧食供給問題？
(A) 它導致運輸食物的成本增加。
(B) 已開發國家拒絕用能源來交換食物。
(C) 種來生產生物燃料的作物，長得沒有預期的好。
(D) 耕地被轉變成荒地以節省能源。

* increase〔'ɪnkris〕n. 增加　　*exchange* A *for* B 用 A 交換 B
production〔prə'dʌkʃən〕n. 生產　　*fail to + V.* 未能～
as well as 與…一樣好　　expect〔ɪk'spɛkt〕v. 預期
be transformed into 被轉變成
wasteland〔'west,lænd〕n. 荒地　　*so as to* 以便

48.(**B**) 最能用來替換片語 "**on the brink of**" 的是 ＿＿＿＿＿＿。

    (A) break away from 逃離　　　(B) *head for* 前往

    (C) focus on 專注於　　　　　　(D) be accustomed to 習慣於

第 49 至 52 題為題組

　　豬肉罐頭電子郵件，一種電子版的垃圾郵件，通常是由廣告商大量發送的訊息，作為一種低成本又有效能接觸消費大眾的方式。對於大多數的收件者而言，這種手法不僅不受歡迎，而且很煩人。但為什麼要將垃圾信件稱為「豬肉罐頭」呢？

    * e-mail（'i,mel）*n.* 電子郵件（= *electronic mail*）

    spam（spæm）*n.* 豬肉罐頭品牌名稱【1937 年，美國人發明了一種由香料

      （spice）加上火腿（ham）所製成的豬肉罐頭，現在則作為垃圾郵件的代稱】

    electronic（ɪ,lɛk'trɑnɪk）*adj.* 電子的

    version（'vɝʒən）*n.* 版本　　junk（dʒʌŋk）*n.* 垃圾

    in bulk 大量地　　advertiser（'ædvɚ,taɪzɚ）*n.* 廣告商

    cost-effective（'kɑstə'fɛktɪv）*adj.* 有成本效益的

    contact（'kɑntækt）*v.* 接觸　　consumer（kən'sumɚ）*n.* 消費者

    recipient（rɪ'sɪpɪənt）*n.* 接收者　　practice（'præktɪs）*n.* 做法

    unwanted（ʌn'wɑntɪd）*adj.* 不受歡迎的

    annoying（ə'nɔɪɪŋ）*adj.* 擾人的

　　一開始「豬肉罐頭」這個字，是因豬肉罐頭品牌 SPAM 而廣為人知，每個人對這種產品的好惡都不同。英國的蒙提・派森喜劇團，將這個字結合在他們經典的「豬肉罐頭短劇」中，讓大家對它更為熟悉。短劇發生地點是在一個餐廳。內容是服務生對一些老主顧逐一念著菜單上的菜色，像是「豬肉罐頭、雞蛋、豬肉罐頭、豬肉罐頭、培根、還有豬肉罐頭」，並帶動背景音樂大合唱，重複地唱著這首豬肉罐頭歌曲，直到其中一個角色被激怒，並大叫著要每個人住口。

    * *in the first place* 首先　　*be known as* 以（身分）而聞名

    brand（brænd）*n.* 品牌　　canned（kænd）*adj.* 罐裝的

    pork（pork）*n.* 豬肉　　product（'prɑdəkt）*n.* 產品

    depend on 視…而定　　British（'brɪtɪʃ）*adj.* 英國的

    comedy（'kɑmədɪ）*n.* 喜劇　　troupe（trup）*n.*（一團）歌手

    Monty Python comedy troupe 蒙提・派森喜劇團【英國的六人喜劇團體】

familiar〔fəˋmɪljə〕adj. 熟悉的　　sketch〔skɛtʃ〕n. 短劇

take place 發生　　diner〔ˋdaɪnə〕n. 餐廳　　bacon〔ˋbekən〕n. 培根

a couple of 一些　　patron〔ˋpetrən〕n. 老顧客　　***lead to*** 導致

chorus〔ˋkorəs〕n. 合唱；歌曲重複的部分

background〔ˋbæk͵graʊnd〕n. 背景（音樂）

character〔ˋkærɪktə〕n. 角色　　annoy〔əˋnɔɪ〕v. 使…惱怒

scream〔skrim〕v. 尖叫　　***shut up*** 閉嘴

一般認為，在有網路之前，早期電子佈告欄使用者，也就是大部分的電腦阿宅，特別喜歡引用蒙提·派森短劇，他們會反覆地在留言板，或是其他人的訊息裡面輸入「豬肉罐頭」，當作一種玩笑，要讓服務系統變慢。時間久了，人們就把這個詞彙跟網路上不受歡迎的垃圾連結起來。

* pre-Internet〔priˋɪntə͵nɛt〕adj. 有網路之前的

BBS 電子佈告欄系統（= *Bulletin Board System*）

geek〔gik〕n. 怪胎；電腦迷　　typically〔ˋtɪpɪkl̩ɪ〕adv. 一般地

peculiar〔pɪˋkjuljə〕adj. 獨特的　　liking〔ˋlaɪkɪŋ〕n. 喜好；嗜好

quote〔kwot〕v. 引用　　type〔taɪp〕v. 輸入；打字

repeatedly〔rɪˋpitɪdlɪ〕adv. 反覆地　　***message board*** 留言板

tie up 使忙碌　　***over time*** 隨時間過去　　term〔tɝm〕n. 詞彙；說法

become associated with 和…連結；和…有關

　　這樣看來，把垃圾郵件稱為「豬肉罐頭」似乎挺合適的，現在當你看電子信箱的時候，就像是在閱讀那間餐廳的菜單。雖然網路上有其他種類的垃圾資訊，垃圾郵件是最常見，或許也是最令人痛恨的一種。

* fitting〔ˋfɪtɪŋ〕adj. 適當的　　check〔tʃɛk〕v. 檢查

inbox〔ˋɪnbɑks〕n. 電子收件匣　　***these days*** 現在；近來

common〔ˋkɑmən〕adj. 普遍的

49.(**A**) 本文的標題是？

(A) "Spam" 這個字的起源。　　(B) 垃圾電子郵件有多麼惱人。

(C) 比較菜單和電子垃圾郵件。

(D) 誰創造了網路上不受歡迎的垃圾。

* origin〔ˋɔrədʒɪn〕n. 起源

comparison〔kəmˋpærəsn̩〕n. 比較；對照

50. (**B**) 根據本文，SPAM 是 _____。
    (A) 受歡迎的早餐食品
    (B) 一種肉類產品，後來成為有趣短劇的一部分
    (C) 指稱早期電子佈告欄使用者的單字
    (D) 蒙提・派森喜劇團創作的漫畫專欄

    * ***refer to*** 涉及；有關　　strip〔strɪp〕*n.* 長條；（報上的）連環漫畫

51. (**D**) 我們可以知道，SPAM 歌曲這麼令人厭煩可能是因為 _____。
    (A) 它很吵　　　　　　　　　　(B) 音不準
    (C) 曲調不合諧　　　　　　　　(D) 它一直重複唱著 SPAM

    * tune〔tjun〕*n.* 曲調　　***out of tune*** 不合調子；走音
    harmonious〔hɑr'monɪəs〕*adj.* 合諧的
    repeat〔rɪ'pit〕*v.* 重複　　***over and over*** 一再地

52. (**C**) 第二段的片語 "**tie up**" 的意思最接近 _____。
    (A) 加速　　(B) 設立　　(C) 一直佔用　　(D) 接上（電源）

    * ***speed up*** 加速　　***set up*** 設立
    occupied〔'ɑkjə,paɪd〕*adj.* 被佔領的　　***hook up to*** 接上（電源）

第 53 至 56 題為題組

　　幾乎所有的動物都會流淚，但很多人相信，只有人類才會因為情緒的壓迫而流淚。雖然有些人宣稱其他動物，像是大象跟海豹，感覺到痛的時候也會哭，但很少科學證據顯示，這些眼淚是因情緒而引發的。這些眼淚最有可能是基礎淚液，或是反射性眼淚。基礎淚液是為了防止眼睛乾燥，它們會擊退細菌性感染。反射性眼淚，是當眼睛受到像花粉或灰塵等刺激物侵入時所引起的。當然人類也有這樣的眼淚，但我們還有一個與眾不同的能力，就是製造情緒性眼淚。

    * shed〔ʃɛd〕*v.* 流（淚）【三態變化為：shed-shed-shed】
    tear〔tɪr〕*n.* 眼淚　　emotional〔ɪ'moʃənḷ〕*adj.* 情感的；善感的
    duress〔'djurɪs〕*n.* 脅迫；壓迫　　claim〔klem〕*v.* 宣稱
    seal〔sil〕*n.* 海豹　　scientific〔,saɪən'tɪfɪk〕*adj.* 科學的
    proof〔pruf〕*n.* 證明　　basal〔'besḷ〕*adj.* 基本的；基礎的
    reflex〔'riflɛks〕*adj.* 反射作用的　　***dry up*** 完全變乾；枯竭
    fight〔faɪt〕*v.* 抵抗　　bacterial〔bæk'tɪrɪəl〕*adj.* 細菌的

infection〔ɪnˈfɛkʃən〕n. 感染　　create〔krɪˈet〕v. 製造

bother〔ˈbɑðɚ〕v. 困擾　　irritant〔ˈɪrətənt〕n. 刺激物

pollen〔ˈpɑlən〕n. 花粉　　unique〔juˈnik〕adj. 特殊的

　　情緒性眼淚，在化學成分上，有別於基礎淚液或反射性眼淚。此事實讓科學家相信，流情緒性眼淚，可以提供一種淨化、治癒的效果，以及作爲一種情緒宣洩，這就像是亞里斯多德在兩千五百年前所認爲的。

* ***differ from*** 不同於　　chemical〔ˈkɛmɪkḷ〕adj. 化學的

　composition〔͵kɑmpəˈzɪʃən〕n. 組成　　***lead to*** 導致

　scientist〔ˈsaɪəntɪst〕n. 科學家　　provide〔prəˈvaɪd〕v. 提供

　cleansing〔ˈklɛnzɪŋ〕adj. 淨化的　　curative〔ˈkjʊrətɪv〕adj. 有療效的

　effect〔ɪˈfɛkt〕n. 效果　　***as well as*** 以及　　outlet〔ˈaʊt͵lɛt〕n. 宣洩

　Aristotle〔ˈærə͵stɑtḷ〕n. 亞里斯多德【384-322 B.C.，古希臘三哲人之一】

　　藉由哭泣，我們宣洩痛苦跟傷悲。再加上眼淚本身會將身體裡的有毒物質帶出我們的身體，這使得哭泣變成處理壓力的一個重要環節。知道壓抑妥當的眼淚會對心理健康有害是很重要的。

* vent〔vɛnt〕v. 發洩（情緒）　　anguish〔ˈæŋgwɪʃ〕n. 極度痛苦

　grief〔grif〕n. 悲傷　　***be combined with*** 與…結合

　poison〔ˈpɔɪsṇ〕n. 有毒物質　　toxin〔ˈtɑksɪn〕n. 毒素

　deal with 處理　　stress〔strɛs〕n. 壓力　　realize〔ˈriə͵laɪz〕v. 了解

　hold back 壓抑（情感）　　valid〔ˈvælɪd〕adj. 妥當的；有效的

　be damaging to 對…有害　　mental〔ˈmɛntḷ〕adj. 心理的

　　隨著越來越多的公眾人物都拋棄過去那種緊閉雙唇的倔強形象，並且大家更能體恤人們需要表現情緒，因此社會開始認可哭泣是一種處理痛苦、壓力、跟悲傷自然的方法。現在，「故作堅強」或許已經不是最好，或最健康的反應了。

* public〔ˈpʌblɪk〕adj. 公眾的　　figure〔ˈfɪgjɚ〕n. 人物

　forgo〔fɔrˈgo〕v. 拋棄　　stiff〔stɪf〕adj. 倔強的

　upper〔ˈʌpɚ〕adj. 上面的　　lip〔lɪp〕n. 嘴唇

　stiff upper lip 咬緊牙關；倔強　　sensitivity〔͵sɛnsəˈtɪvətɪ〕n. 體恤

　recognize〔ˈrɛkəg͵naɪz〕v. 認同　　natural〔ˈnætʃərəl〕adj. 自然的

　cope with 對待；處理　　sorrow〔ˈsɑro〕n. 哀傷

　brave〔brev〕adj. 勇敢的　　response〔rɪˈspɑns〕n. 回應

53.(**B**) 關於情緒性的眼淚，哪個敘述為眞？

(A) 所有動物都會流下情緒性的眼淚。

(B) 它們會將有毒物質跟毒素排出我們的身體。

(C) 它跟其他種眼淚所含有的化學物質相同。

(D) 只有人們有壓力時才流出情緒性的眼淚。

* expel〔ɪk'spɛl〕*v.* 排出

54.(**C**) 談到哭泣的時候，亞里斯多德怎麼想？

(A) 英雄不應該哭。　　　　(B) 眼淚是脆弱的象徵。

(C) 哭泣可以淨化情緒。　　(D) 以前的人比較情緒化。

* *when it comes to* 一提到

be supposed to + *V.* 應該要～

cleansing〔'klɛnzɪŋ〕*n.* 淨化　　*used to* 以前～

55.(**C**) 從文章中可推測，如果一根眼睫毛掉到眼睛裡，你流的眼淚是

_____。

(A) 情緒性眼淚　　　　　　(B) 基礎淚液

(C) 反射性眼淚　　　　　　(D) 鱷魚的眼淚（假慈悲）

* infer〔ɪn'fɝ〕*v.* 推測　　eyelash〔'aɪˌlæʃ〕*n.* 眼睫毛

(*shed*) *crocodile tears* 假慈悲

56.(**A**) 片語 "**stiff upper lip**" 代表的意思爲何？

(A) 壓抑個人感受。

(B) 不洩露他人的秘密。

(C) 對他人的情感需求很敏銳。

(D) 無法控制個人的憤怒與悲傷。

* remain〔rɪ'men〕*v.* 依舊是；保持

silent〔'saɪlənt〕*adj.* 沈默的

sensitive〔'sɛnsətɪv〕*adj.* 敏感的

be sensitive to 對…很敏感

第貳部分：非選擇題

一、中譯英：

1. 緋聞，是否眞或假，都能爲藝人和運動員帶來更多的知名度。

$$
\left\{\begin{array}{l} \text{(Sex) Scandals,} \\ \text{Love affairs,} \end{array}\right\}
\text{whether (they are)}
\left\{\begin{array}{l} \text{true or false / not} \\ \text{real or unreal / not} \end{array}\right\}
\text{can bring}
$$

$$
\left\{\begin{array}{l} \text{more} \\ \text{greater} \end{array}\right\}
\left\{\begin{array}{l} \text{popularity / notice} \\ \text{publicity / fame} \\ \text{prominence} \\ \text{attention} \end{array}\right\}
\text{to artists / entertainers and athletes.}
$$

2. 但在某種程度上，一個受損的名譽也會影響他們的職業生涯。

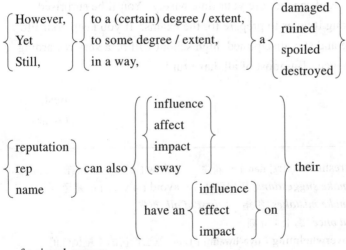

$$
\left\{\begin{array}{l} \text{However,} \\ \text{Yet} \\ \text{Still,} \end{array}\right\}
\left\{\begin{array}{l} \text{to a (certain) degree / extent,} \\ \text{to some degree / extent,} \\ \text{in a way,} \end{array}\right\}
a
\left\{\begin{array}{l} \text{damaged} \\ \text{ruined} \\ \text{spoiled} \\ \text{destroyed} \end{array}\right\}
$$

$$
\left\{\begin{array}{l} \text{reputation} \\ \text{rep} \\ \text{name} \end{array}\right\}
\text{can also}
\left\{\begin{array}{l} \left\{\begin{array}{l} \text{influence} \\ \text{affect} \\ \text{impact} \\ \text{sway} \end{array}\right\} \\ \text{have an} \left\{\begin{array}{l} \text{influence} \\ \text{effect} \\ \text{impact} \end{array}\right\} \text{on} \end{array}\right\}
\text{their}
$$

professional careers.

二、英文作文：

作文範例

Dear Travis,   Jan. 28, 2013

　　It wasn't so long ago I was a high school freshman, so I remember it well. Allow me to share some of my knowledge and perhaps make a few suggestions. Maybe you can avoid making some of the mistakes I made.

　　First of all, don't try to do everything and meet everyone at once. The first few weeks can be overwhelming. Just keep it in the back of your mind that you're not going anywhere for a while. There will be plenty of time to do all the things you want to do. And second, use your time wisely. You'll be surprised how long it takes to prepare for the exams. If you keep your life simple and stay disciplined, high school will be a very rewarding experience. But most of all, have fun!

                                                Best,
                                                Oscar

freshman ('frɛʃmən) *n.* 新生　　allow (ə'laʊ) *v.* 允許
make suggestions 提出建議　　avoid (ə'vɔɪd) *v.* 避免
make mistakes 犯錯　　*first of all* 首先
at once 馬上；立刻
overwhelming (,ovə'hwɛlmɪŋ) *adj.* 無法抵抗的；壓倒性的
keep sth. in the back of one's mind 對…稍加注意；別忘記
for a while 一陣子　　*plenty of* 很多的
wisely ('waɪzlɪ) *adv.* 明智地
disciplined ('dɪsəplɪnd) *adj.* 守紀律的
rewarding (rɪ'wɔrdɪŋ) *adj.* 有益的
most of all 最重要的是　　*have fun* 玩得愉快

大學入學學科能力測驗英文模擬試題 ⑨

第壹部分：單選題（佔 72 分）

一、詞彙（佔 15 分）

說明： 第 1 題至第 15 題，每題 4 個選項，其中只有一個是最適當的答案，畫記在答案卡之「選擇題答案區」。各題答對得 1 分；未作答、答錯、或畫記多於一個選項者，該題以零分計算。

1. Mark Twain is famous for his quick wit and _____. He surely had no fear of speaking in public.
   (A) ornament　(B) eloquence　(C) panorama　(D) esteem

2. I didn't realize we were on the same flight to Taipei until I met Jenny; our encounter was _____.
   (A) periodical　(B) sentimental　(C) accidental　(D) recital

3. The patient was admitted to hospital for _____ so that the doctors could check what happened to him.
   (A) imprisonment　　(B) observation
   (C) surgeon　　(D) comment

4. Confidence _____ from Jason; those who saw him said he was well-prepared for the interview.
   (A) unwinds　(B) wraps　(C) mends　(D) radiates

5. With the approach of the winter, more and more snow has _____ at the top of the mountain.
   (A) spared　(B) absorbed　(C) unpacked　(D) accumulated

6. Bill is very _____ and he would never show any hesitation to die for his country.
   (A) energetic　(B) patriotic　(C) artistic　(D) allergic

7. _____ for this championship should go to every player in the team. It was the team spirit that led to their victory.
(A) Title (B) Labor (C) Credit (D) Defeat

8. Taipei County has decided to fine those caught littering by _____ their cigarette butts on the street between NT$1,200 and NT$6,000.
(A) tossing (B) sniffing (C) immigrating (D) smuggling

9. Cell phones have become a(n) _____ part of modern people's lives. You can see people talking on their phones everywhere.
(A) extravagant (B) supplementary
(C) indispensable (D) dazzling

10. The girl had an _____ that the boy loved her, but actually he didn't.
(A) illusion (B) upbringing
(C) enchantment (D) impact

11. The people could not help _____ at the president's funeral; they felt terribly sad about the sudden loss to the whole country.
(A) memorizing (B) ridiculing (C) weeping (D) depressing

12. _____, if you are willing to offer higher pay, more people will come to work for you.
(A) Ironically (B) Unexpectedly
(C) Amazingly (D) Predictably

13. Diane's _____ with gorillas can be traced back to her childhood; she had been friends with them since she was born in Africa.
(A) craze (B) resentment (C) fascination (D) talent

14. The little girl jumped up and down _____ when informed that she had won the first prize.
(A) fairly (B) gleefully (C) gently (D) skillfully

15. Rebecca is always looking herself in the mirror; she is such a
    _____ girl that her appearance means the world to her.
    (A) practical　　(B) vain　　　(C) loyal　　　(D) plain

二、綜合測驗（佔 15 分）

說明： 第 16 題至第 30 題，每題一個空格，請依文意選出最適當的一個答案，
　　　畫記在答案卡之「選擇題答案區」。各題答對得 1 分；未作答、答錯、
　　　或畫記多於一個選項者，該題以零分計算。

第 16 至 20 題為題組

　　According to official figures, the musical film *Mamma Mia!* has
become the UK's biggest-selling DVD of all time. ___16___ twenty-two
Abba songs including *The Winner Takes It All* and *Dancing Queen*,
Mamma Mia! is the first disc to sell more than five million copies,
___17___ it in one in four UK households. Yet some may not realize the
musical actually has a storyline and is not about the Swedish pop group.
It tells the tale of Sophie, a young bride-to-be who invites three men,
one of ___18___ she believes to be her father, to her wedding in Greece.
As musical adaptations go, the film stays pretty ___19___ to the stage
production from the script to the choreography. Since its release in the
UK in mid-November, 2008, the Abba-themed movie has become the
number one DVD of 2008, and other releases linked to the film have
proved successful as well, ___20___ its soundtrack becoming the
biggest-selling compilation of 2008.

16. (A) To feature　　　　　　　　(B) Featuring
    (C) Being featured　　　　　　(D) Featured
17. (A) grading　　(B) scoring　　(C) ranking　　(D) placing
18. (A) them　　　(B) whom　　　(C) those　　　(D) which
19. (A) irrelevant　(B) distracted　(C) faithful　　(D) conditional
20. (A) with　　　(B) and　　　　(C) while　　　(D) yet

第 21 至 25 題爲題組

　　US President Barrack Obama's Nobel Prize win has got mixed reviews worldwide. As for the President himself, he accepted his surprising Nobel Peace Prize ___21___ a challenge to make good on his bold goals, including peace in the Middle East and Persian Gulf, climate change, nuclear disarmament and a renewed U.S. ___22___ with the world. As foreign policy experts questioned the wisdom of the Nobel committee's decision, Obama said that he didn't ___23___ the win as a recognition of his own accomplishments, but rather as an affirmation of American leadership ___24___ aspirations held by people in all nations. He has yet to achieve any major breakthroughs on the many international efforts he has undertaken. Obama, a president less than nine months into his first ___25___, becomes the fourth current or former U.S. president to win the prize, after Theodore Roosevelt in 1906, Woodrow Wilson in 1919 and Jimmy Carter in 2002, long after his presidency had ended.

21. (A) to　　　　　　(B) of　　　　　　(C) for　　　　　(D) as
22. (A) championship (B) scholarship　(C) membership (D) partnership
23. (A) look　　　　　(B) think　　　　 (C) view　　　　(D) consider
24. (A) in terms of　　(B) as a result of　(C) on behalf of (D) in spite of
25. (A) candidate　　　(B) term　　　　 (C) election　　(D) vote

第 26 至 30 題爲題組

　　If you are a coaster lover, you will not want to miss the king of all coaster theme parks, Cedar Point in Sandusky, Ohio. ___26___ seventeen roller coasters in one amusement park, Cedar Point has become a coaster mecca with thrill-ride ___27___. As the self-proclaimed roller coaster capital of the world, Cedar Point is able to give a thrill ride to everyone. One ___28___ coaster at Cedar Point is the 215-foot-high Wicked Twister, the world's tallest and fastest double twisting impulse coaster, which combines two vertical drops with a twist on each end. Reaching a top speed of 72 miles per hour, Wicked Twister is not a(n)　29　coaster. The train rides on backwards and forwards on one U-shaped twisted track, increasing in speed as well as in height. For Wicked Twister riders, every seat is a good seat. When the ride moves forward, the front seat goes the highest and when the ride moves backwards the last seat goes the highest, but　30　you're in the middle, you get height on both sides.

26.　(A) With　　　(B) For　　　　　(C) As　　　　　(D) On
27.　(A) donors　　(B) interviewees　(C) examinees　(D) devotees
28.　(A) break-record　　　　　　(B) record-breaking
　　(C) record-broken　　　　　　(D) breaking-record
29.　(A) typical　　(B) extraordinary　(C) stimulating　(D) unusual
30.　(A) since　　　(B) because　　　(C) if　　　　　(D) though

三、文意選填（佔 10 分）

說明：　第 31 題至第 40 題，每題一個空格，請依文意在文章後所提供的 (A) 到
　　　　(J) 選項中分別選出最適當者，並將其英文字母代號畫記在答案卡之「選
　　　　擇題答案區」。各題答對得 1 分；未作答、答錯、或畫記多於一個選項
　　　　者，該題以零分計算。

第 31 至 40 題爲題組

　　The death of Yoshito Usui, 51, creator of manga and anime Crayon Shin-chan, has left a lot of people shocked. A long-time friend, commenting on his　31　death, said, "He was a man of few words but a good listener, always observant and looking for ideas to use in his work." Usui's body was found a week after he was reported　32　, under the cliff of a mountain bordering Gumma and Nagano. The publisher of the manga series said that Usui must have accidentally fallen based on the digital camera found　33　, the last image of which was the bottom of the cliff.

However, it remains questionable if the tragedy was indeed an accident. Some people had noticed a change in Usui's behavior just before the accident. On the very same day, Usui's wife had gone to the police to state that family and relatives were concerned that his disappearance was no accident but ___34___ indicated suicide. A source said that the writer, who used to go scuba diving and fishing with work-related friends, had stopped all such ___35___ in recent years. Another acquaintance also noted how Usui had become introverted over the last few years, ___36___ worried many who knew him. His colleague Sumishi Alan commented that the comedic nature of Usui's manga had changed since 2007, incorporating more serious ___37___ such as terrorism, alcoholism and death wishes. Referring to some Crayon Shin-chan episodes, Alan said he felt Usui was under a great deal of ___38___ stress. A psychotherapist said that the writer must have been experiencing depression. That was ___39___ he deliberately chose to go to a dangerous place, whether or not he had any intention of killing himself. With Usui's sudden death, what thoughts had actually crossed his mind ___40___ he stood at the top of the cliff will never be known.

(A) at the scene   (B) emotional   (C) recreation   (D) unexpected
(E) possibly   (F) as   (G) why   (H) themes
(I) which   (J) missing

四、閱讀測驗（佔 32 分）

說明： 第 41 題至第 56 題，每題 4 個選項，請分別根據各篇文章之文意選出最適當的一個答案，畫記在答案卡之「選擇題答案區」。各題答對得 2 分；未作答、答錯、或畫記多於一個選項者，該題以零分計算。

第 41 至 44 題為題組

Kite flying is more than a pastime in Afghanistan; it is a national obsession. The streets of the capital, Kabul, are filled with shops selling kite-flying equipment, and the skies above the city are decorated each day with hundreds of colorful kites fluttering in the wind. To the first-time visitor, the skies above Kabul appear to be filled with fluttering birds or pieces of paper caught in the wind. A closer look reveals hundreds of brightly colored kites soaring high into the air.

Kite flying is a two-person affair. One person holds the wooden spool around which the wire is wound, and the second person, or kite flyer, actually controls the movement of the kite in the air. Afghans have elevated kite flying to an art form, and one of its chief tourist attractions is kite fighting. During the fight, two kites are flown close to one another, often at great heights. The object is to use the wire of your kite to cut the wire of your opponent's kite and set it free. Everything in Afghan kite fighting depends on the quality of the wire and how it is prepared. First, glass is finely ground and combined with an **adhesive** to make a thick paste. The wire is then coated with this paste to make it strong and sharp. After it is dry, the wire is wound around the spool. Kite fighters often wrap a piece of leather around their fingers to protect themselves from the tight wire, which can cut them without their noticing. When an opponent's kite is cut free, it flutters like a colorful, dying bird into the far reaches of the city. Such kites are said to be "free and legal," and can be retrieved by neighborhood children to fly another day. Winter is the most popular time for kite fighting in Afghanistan. The winds are strong, and schools are closed because of the cold weather. While it brings mostly smiles, it is also dangerous. Many people are injured when they fall from roofs chasing free kites or when they lose concentration during a heated battle. Come what may, there will be, for Afghans, many battles to be won.

41. Which of the following is the most important for one who wants to win a kite fight?
    (A) The spool.　(B) The wire.　(C) The paste.　(D) The kite.

42. What happens to a kite that was cut free in a kite fight?

    (A) The kite fighter has to find it.

    (B) Those who find it can keep it.

    (C) It flies high and then disappears.

    (D) The loser will keep it as a reminder.

43. What does "**adhesive**" refer to in the passage?

    (A) A substance that sticks things together.

    (B) A tool which looks like scissors.

    (C) A paint used to color the kite.

    (D) A wire that tightens the kite.

44. Which of the following is true about kite fighting?

    (A) Two kites start fighting when they meet at low heights.

    (B) Winners usually get some money as a prize.

    (C) It is a safe recreational activity.

    (D) It attracts many people to Afghanistan.

第 45 至 48 題爲題組

    Most of our planet is covered with water. There is so much of it that if all the mountains of the world were leveled and their debris dumped into the oceans, the surface of the globe would be entirely beneath water to a depth of several thousand meters. Regarding the physical features of land, the great basins between the continents, in which all this water lies, are more varied than the surface of the land. The highest mountain, Mount Everest, would fit into the deepest part of the ocean, the Mariana Trench, with its peak a kilometer beneath the surface.

    The sea first formed when the Earth began to cool soon after its birth and hot water vapor condensed on its surface. The water of these young seas was not pure, like rainwater, but contained significant quantities of chlorine, bromine, iodine, boron, and nitrogen, as well as traces of many rarer substances. Since then, other ingredients have been added. As continental rocks erode with time, they produce salts that are carried down to the sea by rivers. So, over thousands of years, the sea has been getting saltier and saltier.

Life first appeared in this chemically rich water some 3.5 billion years ago. We know from fossils that the first organisms were simple single-celled bacteria and algae. Organisms which are very like them still exist in the sea today. They are the basis of all marine life; indeed, were it not for these algae, the seas would still be completely dead and the land uninhabited.

45. What is this article mainly about?
    (A) The reasons why the sea gets salty.
    (B) The different life forms in the sea.
    (C) The origin of the bacteria and algae.
    (D) The water on the Earth.

46. From where can one get the information on the earliest life forms in the sea water?
    (A) Fossils.   (B) Continental rocks.
    (C) Chemicals.   (D) Mountain debris.

47. What is true about the sea water?
    (A) Salts in the sea partly come from the rainwater.
    (B) Rare chemicals can be found in it.
    (C) It was pure at the early stage of its formation.
    (D) It gets less salty with time passing.

48. Which of the following is not mentioned in the passage?
    (A) Algae are what life forms in the sea mainly depend on.
    (B) The Earth contains a lot of water.
    (C) The sea water can be recycled to produce energy.
    (D) The Earth would be covered with water if there were no mountains.

第 49 至 52 題為題組

Glaciers produce some of the most beautiful caves in the world. Streams of melting ice flow through the glaciers just as water from a faucet melts its way through an ice cube. Water from the surface drips down through cracks, hollowing out the snow tunnels and decorating the caves with crystal icicles. The smooth walls and floors are so glasslike that pebbles frozen six feet deep can easily be seen. Crystal-clear icicles hanging down from the ceilings flash blue-green, as though they were carved from precious jewels instead of ice.

Although most of the cave ice in the United States is found in volcanic caves, there are a number of limestone ice caves as well. Some people believe that the ice was formed thousands of years ago, when temperatures were much colder than they are today. Others think that the cave ice broke off from the ancient glaciers as they spread over the country.

Today many cave scientists have another idea. They believe that cold water sinks down through cracks into these caves until the temperature is chilly enough to freeze the water that seeps in. The ice keeps the cave cool, and helps build up still more ice. Many caves become covered with so much ice that no one knows just how thick it is. In some, such as Crystal Falls Cave in Idaho, there are frozen rivers and even frozen waterfalls. Native Americans and early settlers used to store food in these underground refrigerators and chip out blocks of ice to melt for drinking water.

49. What is the article mainly about?

    (A) The beauty of the glaciers.

    (B) The formation of ice caves.

    (C) The history of the early Native Americans.

    (D) The functions of cave ice.

50. Which of the following is not used in the passage to describe icicles?

    (A) Crystal-clear.　　　　　　(B) Blue-green.

    (C) Jewel-like.　　　　　　　(D) Sharply-pointed.

51. What theory do many cave scientists hold according to the passage?

    (A) In the United States, most cave ice is found in the volcanoes.

    (B) With the temperature getting higher, water is hard to freeze now.

    (C) The cave ice might have come from the ancient glaciers.

    (D) Cold water seeps through cracks first and then freezes into ice.

52. What did the early settlers in America do with ice?

    (A) Make iced food.　　　　　(B) Produce wine.

    (C) Make drinking water.　　　(D) Do the laundry.

第 53 至 56 題爲題組

Orchids are unique, for they have the most highly developed of all blossoms, in which the usual male and female reproductive organs are **fused** in a single structure called the column. The column is designed so that a single pollination will fertilize hundreds of thousands, and in some cases millions of seeds, so microscopic and light they are easily carried by the breeze. Surrounding the column are three petals and three sepals, a leaf-like part that supports the petal. They are easily recognizable, and often distorted into gorgeous, weird, but always functional shapes. The most noticeable of the petals is called the lip, which is often dramatically marked as an unmistakable part to attract the specific insect the orchid has chosen as its pollinator. To attract their pollinators from afar, orchids use unusually interesting shapes, colors, and scents. At least 50 different aromatic compounds have been analyzed in the orchid family, each blended to attract one, or at most a few species of insects or birds. Some orchids even change their scents to interest different insects at different times. Once the right insect has been attracted, some orchids do all they can do to make sure it does not leave until pollen has been accurately placed or removed. By such ingenious adaptations to specific pollinators, orchids have avoided the risks of rampant crossbreeding in the wild. At the same time, they can assure the survival of each species as different.

53. Why is the orchid unique among all of the flowers?
    (A) Because the habitat in which it lives is warm and humid.
    (B) Because the most products can be made from it.
    (C) Because the structure of its blossom is special.
    (D) Because it lives longest among all flowers.

54. What does the word "**fused**" mean in the passage?
    (A) combined　　(B) produced　　(C) hidden　　(D) attracted

55. Which one of the following is NOT mentioned as a means by which an orchid attracts insects?
    (A) Size　　(B) Shape　　(C) Color　　(D) Perfume

56. Which of the following is true about the smells of the orchids?
    (A) They are effective only when an insect is near the blossom.
    (B) Harmful insects may stay away from them.
    (C) Different species of orchids smell quite alike.
    (D) They may change.

第貳部分：非選擇題 (佔 28 分)

一、中譯英 (佔 8 分)

說明：1. 請將以下中文句子譯成正確、通順、達意的英文，並將答案寫在「答
案卷」上。

2. 請依序作答，並標明題號。每題 4 分，共 8 分。

1. 因為 H1N1 的爆發，有越來越多的人寧可自己開車而不坐飛機。

2. 儘管航空公司的一再保證，大部分的乘客是不願冒著感染病毒的危險。

二、英文作文 (佔 20 分)

說明：1. 依提示在「答案卷」上寫一篇英文作文。

2. 文長約 100 至 120 個單詞 (words)。

提示：你剛從高中畢業。你 (英文名字必須假設為 Rick Nielsen 或 Mariah
Carey)，要寫一封信給你的老師 (英文名字必須假設為 Mr. Grant)，
表達你對老師的感謝，以及你如何從老師的教導上受益。

請注意：必須使用上述的 Rick Nielsen 或 Mariah Carey 在信末署名，**不得
使用自己的真實中文或英文名字**。

大學入學學科能力測驗英文模擬試題 ⑨ 詳解

第壹部分：單選題

一、詞彙：

1. (**B**) 馬克・吐溫以機智和<u>口才</u>而聞名。他不怕在公衆前演說。

    (A) ornament〔'ɔrnəmənt〕 n. 裝飾品（ = decoration ）
    ornamental adj. 裝飾用的

    (B) **eloquence**〔'ɛləkwəns〕 n. 雄辯；口才　　eloquent adj.

    (C) panorama〔,pænə'ræmə〕 n. 全景；概觀（ = overview ）
    panoramic adj.

    (D) esteem〔ə'stim〕 n. 尊敬　 v. 敬重；認爲

    * Mark Twain〔'mɑrk'twen〕 n. 馬克・吐溫【1835-1910，美國知名作家】
    be famous for 因…而著名
    wit〔wɪt〕 n. 智慧；機智　　surely〔'ʃʊrlɪ〕 adv. 無疑地
    fear〔fɪr〕 n. 害怕　　**in public** 公開地

2. (**C**) 直到我遇見珍妮之前，我都不知道我跟她搭同一班飛機到台北；我們的相遇是<u>偶然</u>。

    (A) periodical〔,pɪrɪ'ɑdɪk!〕 adj. 定期的（ = periodic ）
    n. 期刊　　period n. 期間

    (B) sentimental〔,sɛntə'mɛnt!〕 adj. 多愁善感的
    sentiment n. 感情；情緒

    (C) **accidental**〔,æksə'dɛnt!〕 adj. 偶然的　　accident n.
    accidentally adv. 偶然地（ = by accident = by chance ）

    (D) recital〔rɪ'saɪt!〕 n. 獨奏會　　recite v. 背誦

    * encounter〔ɪn'kaʊntɚ〕 n. 邂逅；遭遇

3. (**B**) 病人獲准進入醫院<u>觀察</u>，讓醫生檢查他發生什麼事。

    (A) imprisonment〔ɪm'prɪzn̩mənt〕 n. 坐牢；監禁　　imprison v.

    (B) **observation**〔,ɑbzɚ'veʃən〕 n. 觀察　　observe v.
    observatory n. 天文觀測台

(C) surgeon〔'sɝdʒən〕*n.* 外科醫生　　surgery *n.* 外科手術
　　surgical *adj.* 外科的

(D) comment〔'kɑmɛnt〕*n. v.* 評論

* patient〔'peʃənt〕*n.* 病人　　admit〔əd'mɪt〕*v.* 允許進入
　so that 以便

4.(**D**) 傑森全身<u>散發</u>自信；看到他的人說，他面試準備得很充分。

(A) unwind〔ʌn'waɪnd〕*v.* 鬆開；放鬆 (= *relax*)

(B) wrap〔ræp〕*v.* 包裝；包裹

(C) mend〔mɛnd〕*v.* 改正

(D) ***radiate***〔'redɪ,et〕*v.* 散發；射出 (光、熱)
　　radiant *adj.* 光輝燦爛的　　radiation *n.* 發光；輻射

* confidence〔'kɑnfədəns〕*n.* 自信
　well-prepared〔'wɛl,prɪ'pɛrd〕*adj.* 準備完善的 < *for* >
　interview〔'ɪntɚ,vju〕*n.* 面試

5.(**D**) 隨著冬天腳步接近，越來越多雪<u>堆積</u>在山頂上。

(A) spare〔spɛr〕*v.* 節省　*n.* 備用物
　　adj. 備用的；多餘的

(B) absorb〔əb'sɔrb〕*v.* 吸收；使專心 (= *engross*)
　　absorption *n.*　　be absorbed in 專心於

(C) unpack〔ʌn'pæk〕*v.* 打開 (包裹、行李等) (↔ pack)

(D) ***accumulate***〔ə'kjumjə,let〕*v.* 累積　　accumulation *n.*

* approach〔ə'protʃ〕*n.* 接近

6.(**B**) 比爾非常<u>愛國</u>，若要爲國捐軀，他絕不會顯得猶豫。

(A) energetic〔,ɛnɚ'dʒɛtɪk〕*adj.* 有活力的 (= *vigorous*)
　　energy *n.*

(B) ***patriotic***〔,petrɪ'ɑtɪk〕*adj.* 愛國的　　patriot *n.* 愛國者

(C) artistic〔ɑr'tɪstɪk〕*adj.* 藝術的

(D) allergic〔ə'lɝdʒɪk〕*adj.* 過敏的 < *to* >　　allergy *n.* 過敏症

* hesitation〔,hɛzə'teʃən〕*n.* 猶豫

7. (**C**) 冠軍的榮耀屬於每位隊員。是團隊精神讓他們得到勝利。

    (A) title〔'taɪtḷ〕*n.* 頭銜；標題

    (B) labor〔'lebɚ〕*n.* 勞動（力）　　laborer *n.* 勞工

    laborious　*adj.* 辛苦的；吃力的

    (C) *credit*〔'krɛdɪt〕*n.* 榮譽；信用　*v.* 歸功

    credit A to B　將 A 歸功於 B

    (D) defeat〔dɪ'fit〕*v.* 打敗　*n.* 挫敗

    * championship〔'tʃæmpɪənˌʃɪp〕*n.* 冠軍（資格）　*go to* 給予；歸屬

    spirit〔'spɪrɪt〕*n.* 精神　*team spirit* 團隊精神　*lead to* 導致

8. (**A**) 台北縣決定要對在街上丟擲煙蒂的人，處以新台幣一千兩百元到六千元的罰款。

    (A) *toss*〔tɔs〕*v.* 投；擲（= *fling* = *throw*）

    (B) sniff〔snɪf〕*v. n.* 嗅；聞（= *smell*）

    (C) immigrate〔'ɪməˌgret〕*v.*（自國外）移入（↔ emigrate）

    immigration *n.* 移居　immigrant *n.* 移民

    (D) smuggle〔'smʌgḷ〕*v.* 走私　smuggler *n.* 走私者

    * fine〔faɪn〕*v.* 罰款　litter〔'lɪtɚ〕*v.* 亂丟；使凌亂

    cigarette〔'sɪgəˌrɛt〕*n.* 香煙　butt〔bʌt〕*n.* 煙蒂

    cigarette butt 煙蒂

9. (**C**) 手機已經成為現代人生活中，不可或缺的一部分。你到處都可以看到有人用手機在講電話。

    (A) extravagant〔ɪk'strævəgənt〕*adj.* 奢侈的

    extravagance *n.* 奢侈

    (B) supplementary〔ˌsʌplə'mɛntərɪ〕*adj.* 補充的

    supplement *n.* 補充（= *complement*）　*v.* 補充

    (C) *indispensable*〔ˌɪndɪ'spɛnsəbḷ〕*adj.* 不可或缺的（↔ dispensable）

    (D) dazzling〔'dæzḷɪŋ〕*adj.* 耀眼的；燦爛的

    dazzle *v.* 使目眩（= *daze*）

    * *cell phone* 手機

10. (**A**) 那女孩幻想那男孩愛她，但其實他沒有。

　　(A) ***illusion*** 〔ɪˋluʒən〕 *n.* (看似眞實的) 幻覺；錯覺　　illusory *adj.*

　　(B) upbringing 〔ˋʌpˏbrɪŋɪŋ〕 *n.* 敎養；養育

　　(C) enchantment 〔ɪnˋtʃæntmənt〕 *n.* 魅力；迷人之物　　enchant *v.*
　　　　enchanted *adj.* 著了魔的　　enchanting *adj.* 迷人的

　　(D) impact 〔ˋɪmpækt〕 *n.* 影響

11. (**C**) 民眾忍不住在總統的葬禮上哭泣，國家突然失去元首，人民覺得非常難過。

　　(A) memorize 〔ˋmɛməˏraɪz〕 *v.* 記憶；背誦 (= *learn by heart*)
　　　　memory *n.* 記憶 (力)　　memorization *n.* 記憶；背誦

　　(B) ridicule 〔ˋrɪdɪˏkjul〕 *v.* 嘲笑 (= *laugh at* = *make fun of*)
　　　　ridiculous *adj.* 可笑的

　　(C) ***weep*** 〔wip〕 *v.* 哭泣　　weep over 爲⋯哭泣

　　(D) depress 〔dɪˋprɛs〕 *v.* 使沮喪；使蕭條
　　　　depressed *adj.* 憂鬱的；不景氣的
　　　　depression *n.* 蕭條；憂鬱症

　　*** cannot help + V-ing*** 忍不住～
　　funeral 〔ˋfjunərəl〕 *n.* 葬禮
　　terribly 〔ˋtɛrəblɪ〕 *adv.* 非常

12. (**D**) 可以預期地，如果你願意出高一點的薪水，就有更多人會來替你工作。

　　(A) ironically 〔aɪˋrɑnɪkḷɪ〕 *adv.* 諷刺地
　　　　irony *n.* 諷刺　　ironic *adj.*

　　(B) unexpectedly 〔ˏʌnɪkˋspɛktɪdlɪ〕 *adv.* 出乎意料地
　　　　unexpected *adj.*

　　(C) amazingly 〔əˋmezɪŋlɪ〕 *adv.* 驚人地　　amazing *adj.*

　　(D) ***predictably*** 〔prɪˋdɪktəblɪ〕 *adv.* 可預料地
　　　　predict *v.* 預測 (= *forecast*)　　prediction *n.*
　　　　predictable *adj.* 可預測的

　　*** be willing to + V.*** 願意～　　offer 〔ˋɔfɚ〕 *v.* 提供
　　pay 〔pe〕 *n.* 薪水

13. (**C**) 黛安娜對大猩猩的著迷，可追溯至她的童年，她在非洲出生後，
就一直都跟大猩猩是朋友。

　　(A) craze〔krez〕*n.* （一時的）熱潮（= *fashion* = *fad* = *vogue*）；
　　　　熱衷 < *for* >　　crazy *adj.*

　　(B) resentment〔rɪ'zɛntmənt〕*n.* 憎恨　　resent *v.*
　　　　resentful *adj.*

　　(C) *fascination*〔ˌfæsn̩'eʃən〕*n.* 著迷；有魅力的人或物
　　　　fascinate *v.*　　fascinating *adj.* 迷人的

　　(D) talent〔'tælənt〕*n.* 天份
　　　　talented *adj.* 多才多藝的

　　* gorilla〔gə'rɪlə〕*n.* 大猩猩　　*be traced back to* 追溯至

14. (**B**) 那位小女孩被告知她贏得第一名時，興高采烈地跳上跳下。

　　(A) fairly〔'fɛrlɪ〕*adv.* 公平地；相當地
　　　　fair *adj.* 公平的；晴朗的

　　(B) *gleefully*〔'glifəlɪ〕*adv.* 興高采烈地　　glee *n.*　　gleeful *adj.*

　　(C) gently〔'dʒɛntlɪ〕*adv.* 溫和地　　gentle *adj.*

　　(D) skillfully〔'skɪlfəlɪ〕*adv.* 巧妙地　　skill *n.* 技巧
　　　　skilled *adj.* 熟練的

　　* inform〔ɪn'fɔrm〕*v.* 通知　　*the first prize* 第一名

15. (**B**) 蕾貝卡永遠都在照鏡子，她是這麼虛榮的一個女孩，對她而言，
外貌就代表一切。

　　(A) practical〔'præktɪkl̩〕*adj.* 實際的

　　(B) *vain*〔ven〕*adj.* 虛榮的；徒勞的（= *useless* = *fruitless*）
　　　　vanity *n.* 空虛；自負　　vainly *adv.* 徒勞地（= *in vain*）

　　(C) loyal〔'lɔɪəl〕*adj.* 忠實的　　loyalty *n.*

　　(D) plain〔plen〕*adj.* 清楚的；明白的；樸素的；平凡的

　　* mirror〔'mɪrɚ〕*n.* 鏡子
　　　appearance〔ə'pɪrəns〕*n.* 外表
　　　mean the world to sb. 對某人很重要；對某人而言是一切

二、綜合測驗：

第 16 至 20 題為題組

　　根據官方數據，音樂劇電影「媽媽咪呀！」已成為英國史上最賣座的 DVD。以二十二首「阿巴合唱團」的歌曲，包括「勝者為王」以及「舞后」等為特色
16　　　　　　　　　　　　　　　　　　　　　　　　　　　　　　　　　16
的音樂劇「媽媽咪呀！」，是第一張銷售超過五百萬張的光碟，每四個英國家庭中就有一張。
　　17

* ***according to*** 根據　　official〔əˈfɪʃəl〕*adj.* 官方的
　　figure〔ˈfɪgjɚ〕*n.* 數字　　musical〔ˈmjuzɪkḷ〕*n.* 音樂劇　*adj.* 音樂的
　　film〔fɪlm〕*n.* 電影；影片
　　Mamma Mia! 媽媽咪呀！【英國劇作家 Catherine Johnson 所創作的音樂
　　　　劇，由知名的瑞典 ABBA 合唱團所演唱的多首成名曲串連而成】
　　biggest-selling〔ˈbɪgɪstˈsɛlɪŋ〕*adj.* 賣最好的（＝ *best-selling*）
　　of all time 有史以來
　　Abba〔ˈɑbɑ〕*n.* 阿巴合唱團【瑞典合唱團，1970 年成軍，1982 年解散】
　　The Winner Takes It All 勝者為王　　disc〔dɪsk〕*n.* 唱片（＝ *disk*）
　　copy〔ˈkɑpɪ〕*n.*（書籍、雜誌的）本；份
　　household〔ˈhaʊsˌhold〕*n.* 家庭；家族

16.（ **B** ）原句為：***Mamma Mia! features*** twenty-two Abba songs..., ***and*** is
　　　　the first..., 對等子句可改成分詞構句，但須放在主詞前，轉化為：
　　　　Featuring twenty-two Abba songs..., ***Mamma Mia!*** is the first...,
　　　　故選 (B) ***Featuring***。　　feature〔ˈfitʃɚ〕*v.* 以…為特色

17.（ **D** ）依句意，選 (D) ***placing***。　　place〔ples〕*v.* 放置
　　　　而 (A) grade〔gred〕*v.* 分等級，(B) score〔skor〕*v.* 得分，(C) rank
　　　　〔ræŋk〕*v.* 位居；名列，則不合句意。

但有些人可能不知道，這齣音樂劇是有故事情節的，而且跟瑞典的流行合唱團無關。它是講一位年輕的準新娘蘇菲的故事，她邀請三個男人，到希臘參加她的婚禮，她認為其中一個男人是她的父親。雖然這是改編的音樂劇，但電影從
　　　　　　　　　18
腳本到編舞，都相當忠實呈現了原來的戲劇作品。
　　19

　　　* yet〔jɛt〕adv. 然而；但是（= however）
　　　　actually〔'æktʃʊəlɪ〕adv. 實際上
　　　　storyline〔'storɪ,laɪn〕n. 故事情節
　　　　Swedish〔'swidɪʃ〕adj. 瑞典的　　　pop〔pɑp〕adj. 流行的
　　　　tale〔tel〕n. 故事　　　bride-to-be〔'braɪdtəbi〕n. 準新娘
　　　　wedding〔'wɛdɪŋ〕n. 婚禮　　　Greece〔gris〕n. 希臘
　　　　adaptation〔,ædəp'teʃən〕n. 改編；改寫
　　　　stay〔ste〕v. 停留；保持　　　stage〔stedʒ〕n. 舞台
　　　　production〔prə'dʌkʃən〕n. 演出；上演的作品
　　　　script〔skrɪpt〕n. 腳本
　　　　choreography〔,korɪ'ɑgrəfɪ〕n. 編舞

18.(**B**) 兩個逗點中間的形容詞子句修飾 three men，空格應填關代，而且
　　　　先行詞爲人，又是受格形式，故選 (B) **whom**。

19.(**C**) (A) irrelevant〔ɪ'rɛləvənt〕adj. 不相關的 < to >
　　　　　(B) distracted〔dɪ'stræktɪd〕adj. 分心的
　　　　　(C) **faithful**〔'feθfəl〕adj. 忠實的 < to >
　　　　　(D) conditional〔kən'dɪʃənḷ〕adj. 有條件限制的

　自從二〇〇八年十一月中旬，DVD 在英國發行以來，這部以阿巴合唱團爲主題
的電影，就成爲二〇〇八年銷售第一的 DVD，其他跟電影有關的發行物，也證
實相當賣座，而它的原聲帶也是二〇〇八年最暢銷的專輯。
　　　　　　　20

　　　　* release〔rɪ'lis〕n. 發行；發行的事物
　　　　UK 英國　　　**mid-November** 十一月中
　　　　Abba-themed〔'ɑbɑ'θimd〕adj. 以阿巴合唱團爲主題的
　　　　be linked to 和…有關　　　prove〔pruv〕v. 證明爲
　　　　as well 也　　　soundtrack〔'saʊnd,træk〕n. 電影配樂
　　　　compilation〔,kɑmpɪ'leʃən〕n. 編輯物；編纂

20.(**A**) 表「附帶狀態」，須用「with + 受詞 + $\begin{cases} \text{V-ing} \\ \text{p.p.} \end{cases}$」，故選 (A)。

第 21 至 25 題爲題組

　　美國總統巴拉克・歐巴馬獲得諾貝爾獎一事，在全世界引起不同評論。至
於總統本人，他將這個意外的諾貝爾和平獎，視爲一項挑戰，來實踐他各項大
　　　　　　　　　　　　　　　　　　21
膽的目標，包括中東以及波斯灣的和平、氣候變遷、裁減核子軍備，以及美國
與世界的新合夥關係。
　　　　22

* Barrack Obama〔'bʌrək,o'bamɑ〕*n.* 巴拉克・歐巴馬【1961-，美國第 44

　　任總統，2009 年獲頒諾貝爾和平獎】

Nobel Prize 諾貝爾獎　　　win〔wɪn〕*n.* 贏；勝利

mixed〔mɪkst〕*adj.* 混合的　　review〔rɪ'vju〕*n.* 評論；批評

worldwide〔'wɜld'waɪd〕*adv.* 在全世界　　*as for* 至於

accept〔ək'sɛpt〕*v.* 接受　　surprising〔sə'praɪzɪŋ〕*adj.* 意外的

Nobel Peace Prize 諾貝爾和平獎　　challenge〔'tʃælɪndʒ〕*n.* 挑戰

make good on 履行；成功　　bold〔bold〕*adj.* 大膽的

including〔ɪn'kludɪŋ〕*prep.* 包括　　*the Middle East* 中東

Persian〔'pɜʒən, 'pɜʃən〕*adj.* 波斯的　　gulf〔gʌlf〕*n.* 海灣

the Persian Gulf 波斯灣　　*climate change* 氣候變遷

nuclear〔'njuklɪɚ〕*adj.* 核子的

disarmament〔dɪs'ɑrməmənt〕*n.* 解除武裝；裁軍

nuclear disarmament 裁減核子軍備　　renewed〔rɪ'njud〕*adj.* 更新的

21. (**D**) 依句意，歐巴馬「認爲」諾貝爾和平獎「是」一項挑戰，選 (D) *as*。

　　accept A *as* B　認爲 A 是 B

22. (**D**) (A) championship〔'tʃæmpɪən,ʃɪp〕*n.* 冠軍（資格）

　　　　(B) scholarship〔'skɑlɚ,ʃɪp〕*n.* 獎學金

　　　　(C) membership〔'mɛmbɚ,ʃɪp〕*n.* 會員資格

　　　　(D) *partnership*〔'pɑrtnɚ,ʃɪp〕*n.* 合夥關係

正如同外交政策專家質疑，諾貝爾委員會的決定是否明智，歐巴馬說他並沒有
把贏得諾貝爾和平獎，看成是對自我成就的認同，而是將勝利視爲對美國領導
　　　　　　　　　　　　　　　　23
能力的認定，就是代表了全世界民衆都懷有的渴望。
　　　　24

> * **_foreign policy_** 外交政策 　　expert〔'ɛkspɜt〕 n. 專家
> question〔'kwɛstʃən〕 v. 質疑
> wisdom〔'wɪzdəm〕 n. 智慧；(做…的) 明智之舉
> committee〔kə'mɪtɪ〕 n. 委員會
> recognition〔,rɛkəg'nɪʃən〕 n. 承認；認可
> accomplishment〔ə'kamplɪʃmənt〕 n. 成就；實現
> rather〔'ræðɚ〕 adv. 更確切地說 　　affirmation〔,æfɚ'meʃən〕 n. 確定
> leadership〔'lidɚ,ʃɪp〕 n. 領導能力
> aspiration〔,æspə'reʃən〕 n. 渴望；願望 　　hold〔hold〕 v. 持有；懷著

23. (**C**) **_view_** A **_as_** B 視 A 為 B；認為 A 是 B
    = regard A as B
    = look upon A as B
    = think of A as B
    = consider A (to be) B

24. (**C**) 依句意，選 (C) **_on behalf of_**「代表」。而 (A) in terms of「以…的觀點」，(B) as a result of「由於」，(D) in spite of「儘管」，均不合句意。

　　歐巴馬在國際上所付出的努力，尚未達成任何重大突破。他的第一屆總統任期還不滿九個月，卻成為繼一九〇六年的迪奧多·羅斯福、一九一九年的伍德羅·威爾遜、跟二〇〇二年的吉米·卡特後，第四位現任或卸任後獲得諾貝爾和平獎的美國總統，而他離任期屆滿還有一段很長的時間呢。

> * **_have yet to_** + V. 尚未~；有待~
> achieve〔ə'tʃiv〕 v. 達成；完成 　　major〔'medʒɚ〕 adj. 重大的
> breakthrough〔'brek,θru〕 n. 突破；重大成就
> international〔,ɪntɚ'næʃənḷ〕 adj. 國際的 　　effort〔'ɛfɚt〕 n. 努力；奮鬥
> undertake〔,ʌndɚ'tek〕 v. 著手；從事；保證
> current〔'kɜənt〕 adj. 現在的；現任的 　　former〔'fɔrmɚ〕 adj. 先前的
> Theodore Roosevelt〔'θiə,dor'rozə,vɛlt〕 n. 迪奧多·羅斯福【1858-1919，美國第 26 任總統，因調解日俄戰爭，在 1906 年獲頒諾貝爾和平獎】
> Woodrow Wilson〔'wudro'wɪlsṇ〕 n. 伍德羅·威爾遜【1856-1924，美國第 28 任總統，一次大戰後提倡國際聯盟，在 1919 年獲頒諾貝爾和平獎】
> Jimmy Carter〔'dʒɪmɪ'kartɚ〕 n. 吉米·卡特【1924-，美國第 39 任總統，全名 James Earl Carter, Jr.，因為堅持不懈地找尋國際衝突的解決方案、致力於增進民主及改善人權、以及促進經濟和社會發展的努力，在 2002 年獲頒諾貝爾和平獎】 　　presidency〔'prɛzədənsɪ〕 n. 總統任期；總統職位

25. (**B**) 依句意，選 (B) *term* 〔tɜm〕*n.* 任期；期間。而 (A) candidate
〔'kændə,det〕*n.* 候選人，(C) election〔ɪ'lɛkʃən〕*n.* 選舉，(D) vote
〔vot〕*n.* 投票；選票，均不合句意。

第 26 至 30 題為題組

　　如果你是雲霄飛車的愛好者，你絕對不想錯過所有雲霄飛車主題公園中的
王者——俄亥俄州，桑達斯基的雲杉角主題樂園。雲杉角主題樂園<u>有</u>十七座雲霄
　　　　　　　　　　　　　　　　　　　　　　　　　　　　26
飛車，它已經成為刺激雲霄飛車<u>狂熱者</u>的聖地。它自稱為世界雲霄飛車的首都，
　　　　　　　　　　　　　　27
而且絕對能帶給每個人一趟刺激的旅程。

* coaster〔'kostɚ〕*n.* 雲霄飛車 (= *roller coaster = switchback*)
  lover〔'lʌvɚ〕*n.* 愛人；愛好者　　theme〔θim〕*n.* 主題
  theme park 主題樂園　　cedar〔'sidɚ〕*n.* 西洋杉
  point〔pɔɪnt〕*n.* 點；尖端；角　　***Cedar Point*** 雲杉角主題遊樂公園
  Sandusky〔sən'dʌskɪ〕*n.* 桑達斯基【美國俄亥俄州東北部的一個城市】
  Ohio〔o'haɪo〕*n.* 俄亥俄州　　***roller coaster*** 雲霄飛車
  amusement〔ə'mjuzmənt〕*n.* 娛樂；樂趣
  amusement park 遊樂場；遊樂園　　mecca〔'mɛkə〕*n.* 聖地；麥加
  thrill〔θrɪl〕*n.* 刺激；興奮　　ride〔raɪd〕*n.* 騎乘；遊樂設施
  self-proclaimed〔,sɛlfprə'klemd〕*adj.* 自我宣稱的
  capital〔'kæpətl〕*n.* 首都；中心

26. (**A**) 表「有」，介系詞用 *with*，選 (A)。

27. (**D**) (A) donor〔'donɚ〕*n.* 捐贈者
    (B) interviewee〔,ɪntɚvju'i〕*n.* 被採訪者
    (C) examinee〔ɪg,zæmə'ni〕*n.* 應試者
    (D) *devotee*〔,dɛvə'ti〕*n.* 狂熱者

　　雲杉角裡面有個<u>破紀錄的</u>雲霄飛車，就是兩百一十五英呎高的「邪惡旋風」，它
　　　　　　　　　　28
是全世界最高，也是速度最快的兩段推進式雲霄飛車，它結合了兩段垂直落體，
每一段最後都有一個大旋轉。最高速是每小時七十二英哩，它可不是<u>一般的</u>雲
　　　　　　　　　　　　　　　　　　　　　　　　　　　　　　29
霄飛車。

* 215-foot-high *adj.* 兩百一十五英尺高的
  wicked〔'wɪkɪd〕*adj.* 邪惡的　　twister〔'twɪstɚ〕*n.* 龍捲風；旋風
  double〔'dʌbl̩〕*adj.* 兩倍的；雙重的　　twist〔twɪst〕*v.* 扭曲；旋轉
  impulse〔'ɪmpʌls〕*n.* 衝擊；推進力　　combine〔kəm'baɪn〕*v.* 結合
  vertical〔'vɝtɪkl̩〕*adj.* 垂直的　　drop〔drɑp〕*n.* 下降

28. (**B**) 這裡用「名詞＋分詞」形式的複合形容詞，主動用現在分詞，被動用
　　　 過去分詞，主詞是雲霄飛車，雲霄飛車是主動打破紀錄，故用現在分
　　　 詞，選 (B) *record-breaking*「破紀錄的」。

29. (**A**) (A) *typical*〔'tɪpɪkl̩〕*adj.* 典型的；一般的
　　　 (B) extraordinary〔ɪk'strɔdn̩,ɛrɪ〕*adj.* 特別的
　　　 (C) stimulating〔'stɪmjə,letɪŋ〕*adj.* 激勵人心的
　　　 (D) unusual〔ʌn'juʒʊəl〕*adj.* 不尋常的

在 U 型扭曲的軌道上，列車會往後以及往前移動，同時增加速度跟高度。對乘
坐「邪惡旋風」的人而言，每個座位都是好位子。當列車往前開時，前面座位
的高度最高，當列車往後開時，後面座位的高度最高，但是如果你坐在中間時，
不管往前或往後開，你的高度都很高。 30

* U-shaped *adj.* U 型的　　track〔træk〕*n.* 軌道
  backwards〔'bækwədz〕*adv.* 往後　　forwards〔'fɔrwədz〕*adv.* 往前
  as well as 以及　　height〔haɪt〕*n.* 高度

30. (**C**) 依句意，選 (C) *if*「如果」。

三、文意選填：

第 31 至 40 題為題組

　　「蠟筆小新」漫畫跟卡通的作者，臼井儀人的去世，讓很多人感到震驚。
他的老友說到他 31 **(D)** 意外死亡時，說：「他這個人話不多，但是個很好的傾聽
者，觀察力很好，找尋可以用在作品中的點子。」在他被通報 32 **(J)** 失蹤一個星
期後，他的屍體在長野縣跟群馬縣臨界的一處懸崖下被發現。根據 33 **(A)** 現場找
到的數位相機裡，最後一張照片是懸崖底部，所以蠟筆小新系列漫畫的出版商
說，他一定是不小心摔下去了。

* Yoshito Usui n. 臼井儀人【1958-2009，日本漫畫家，成名作品《蠟筆小新》】
  creator (krɪˋetɚ) n. 創作者　　manga (ˋmæŋɡə) n. 漫畫【日文】
  anime (ˋænɪˏme) n. 動畫【日文】　　crayon (ˋkreən) n. 蠟筆
  leave sb. + adj. 讓某人～　　shocked (ʃɑkt) adj. 受打擊的
  long-time (ˋlɔŋˏtaɪm) adj. 長期的　　comment (ˋkɑmɛnt) v. 評論
  unexpected (ˏʌnɪkˋspɛktɪd) adj. 意外的
  observant (əbˋzɝvənt) adj. 善於觀察的　　**look for** 尋找
  body (ˋbɑdɪ) n. 身體；屍體　　report (rɪˋport) v. 報告
  missing (ˋmɪsɪŋ) adj. 失蹤的　　cliff (klɪf) n. 懸崖
  border (ˋbɔrdɚ) v. 接鄰　　Gumma n. 群馬縣【日本地名】
  Nagano n. 長野縣【日本地名】　　publisher (ˋpʌblɪʃɚ) n. 出版商
  series (ˋsɪrɪz) n. 系列　　**must have** + p.p. 過去一定是～
  accidentally (ˏæksəˋdɛntl̩ɪ) adv. 意外地　　**be based on** 根據～
  digital (ˋdɪdʒɪtl̩) adj. 數位的　　camera (ˋkæmərə) n. 相機
  at the scene 在現場　　image (ˋɪmɪdʒ) n. 影像
  bottom (ˋbɑtəm) n. 底部

　　然而，這起悲劇是否眞爲意外還有爭議。有的人發現，意外前臼井儀人的行爲舉止變了。而且在那天，臼井儀人的妻子也跟警方說，家人與親戚都擔心他失蹤並非意外，而 [34] **(E)** 可能爲自殺的徵兆。

* remain (rɪˋmen) v. 依然是　　questionable (ˋkwɛstʃənəbl̩) adj. 可疑的
  tragedy (ˋtrædʒədɪ) n. 悲劇　　indeed (ɪnˋdid) adv. 的確
  notice (ˋnotɪs) v. 注意　　behavior (bɪˋhevjɚ) n. 行爲
  state (stet) v. 說明　　relative (ˋrɛlətɪv) n. 親戚
  concern (kənˋsɝn) v. 擔心　　disappearance (ˏdɪsəˋpɪrəns) n. 失蹤
  possibly (ˋpɑsəblɪ) adv. 或許　　indicated (ˋɪndəˏketɪd) adj. 徵兆的
  suicide (ˋsuəˏsaɪd) n. 自殺

消息來源指出，該作者以前常跟工作上有往來的朋友，去玩水肺潛水還有釣魚，近幾年來都不再做這些 [35] **(C)** 休閒活動。另一個友人也說近幾年他變得很內向，[36] **(I)** 這讓很多認識他的人感到憂心。

* source (sors) n. 來源　　**used to** + V. 以前
  scuba (ˋskubə) n. 水肺　　diving (ˋdaɪvɪŋ) n. 潛水

go scuba diving　用水肺潛水
work-related〔'wɜk,rɪ'letɪd〕*adj.* 工作上有關係的
recreation〔,rɛkrɪ'eʃən〕*n.* 休閒活動
acquaintance〔ə'kwentəns〕*n.* 認識的人　　note〔not〕*v.* 注意到
introverted〔'ɪntrə,vɜtɪd〕*adj.* 內向的

他的同事 Sumishi Alan（阿蘭）說臼井儀人的漫畫從二〇〇七年起就不一樣了，結合更多嚴肅的 [37](H) 主題，像是恐怖主義、酗酒，還有想死的念頭。看了幾集的蠟筆小新之後，阿蘭說他覺得臼井儀人承受很多 [38](B) 情緒上的壓力。

　　* colleague〔'kɑlig〕*n.* 同事　　comedic〔kə'midɪk〕*adj.* 喜劇的
　　nature〔'netʃɚ〕*n.* 天性　　incorporate〔ɪn'kɔrpə,ret〕*v.* 與…結合
　　serious〔'sɪrɪəs〕*adj.* 嚴肅的　　theme〔θim〕*n.* 主題
　　terrorism〔'tɛrə,rɪzəm〕*n.* 恐怖主義
　　alcoholism〔'ælkəhɔl,ɪzəm〕*n.* 酗酒　　**death wish** 死亡願望
　　refer to 參照　　episode〔'ɛpə,sod〕*n.* 一集；插曲
　　emotional〔ɪ'moʃən!〕*adj.* 情緒的

有位精神治療師說，臼井儀人一定患有憂鬱症。這就是 [39](G) 為什麼他故意選擇去危險的地方，不管他是不是有自殺的意圖。隨著臼井儀人的驟然去世，他在崖頂 [40](F) 時，心中閃過的最後一個念頭已經不得而知了。

　　* psychotherapist〔,saɪkə'θɛrəpɪst〕*n.* 心理治療師
　　experience〔ɪk'spɪrɪəns〕*v.* 經歷　　depression〔dɪ'prɛʃən〕*n.* 憂鬱
　　deliberately〔dɪ'lɪbərɪtlɪ〕*adv.* 故意地　　intention〔ɪn'tɛnʃən〕*n.* 意圖
　　sudden〔'sʌdn̩〕*adj.* 突然的　　**cross one's mind**（想法）浮現；掠過

四、閱讀測驗：

第 41 至 44 題為題組

　　在阿富汗，放風箏不只是一種消遣，而是全國都為之著迷的運動。首都喀布爾的街道上，滿是販售風箏器材的店家，而且喀布爾市的天空，每天都點綴著上百只五顏六色，在風中飄動的風箏。對於第一次來到這裡的訪客而言，喀布爾的天空，就像被振翅而飛的鳥兒，或是風中飛舞的紙花所填滿。近一點看就會發現，其實是許許多多色彩明亮的風箏，在空中翱翔。

* kite〔kaɪt〕n. 風箏
fly〔flaɪ〕v. 放（風箏）【三態變化為：fly-flew-flown】
kite flying 放風箏　　　pastime〔'pæs,taɪm〕n. 娛樂；消遣
Afghanistan〔æf'gænə,stæn〕n. 阿富汗【西亞國家，首都喀布爾。放風箏是
　　阿富汗的全民運動，每年冬天會舉辦鬥風箏比賽，除了看風箏互相纏鬥，將
　　對手風箏切斷之外，比賽的另一個焦點就是「追風箏」，撿到風箏的人可以
　　擁有那只風箏，這項傳統被寫在 2005 年全球暢銷小說「追風箏的孩子」中】
national〔'næʃənḷ〕adj. 全國的　　　obsession〔əb'sɛʃən〕n. 著迷；惦念
capital〔'kæpətḷ〕n. 首都　　　Kabul〔'kɑbul〕n. 喀布爾
be filled with 充滿…；滿是…　　　kite-flying adj. 放風箏的
equipment〔ɪ'kwɪpmənt〕n. 設備；器材
decorate〔'dɛkə,ret〕v. 裝飾　　***be decorated with*** 以…裝飾
hundreds of 數以百計的　　　colorful〔'kʌləfəl〕adj. 五顏六色的
flutter〔'flʌtə〕v.（鳥）拍動翅膀；（旗幟）飄動；振翅而飛
first-time〔'fɝst'taɪm〕adj. 第一次的
visitor〔'vɪzɪtə〕n. 訪客；觀光客　　***appear to*** 似乎（= seem to）
be filled with 充滿　　　reveal〔rɪ'vil〕v. 揭露；顯示
brightly〔'braɪtlɪ〕adv. 明亮地
colored〔'kʌləd〕adj. 有顏色的　　　soar〔sor〕v. 翱翔；飛

　　放風箏是兩個人的活動。其中一人拿著纏有鐵線的木製線軸，另一個人，
或說是放風箏者，實際上控制風箏在空中的動作。不過，阿富汗人已經將放風
箏提升到一種藝術形式，而且阿富汗最主要的觀光吸引力之一，就是鬥風箏。
在鬥風箏的過程中，兩只風箏通常會在很高的地方，接近彼此，目的是要用自
己的風箏線，去切斷對手的風箏線，讓對手的風箏飛走。

* two-person〔'tu'pɝsn̩〕adj. 兩個人的　　　affair〔ə'fɛr〕n. 事情
wooden〔'wudn̩〕adj. 木製的　　spool〔spul〕n. 線軸；捲軸
wire〔waɪr〕n. 鐵絲；鐵線
wind〔waɪnd〕v. 纏繞；繞住【三態變化為：wind-wound-wound】
flyer〔'flaɪə〕n. 放風箏的人　　　movement〔'muvmənt〕n. 運動；動作
Afghan〔'æfgən〕n. 阿富汗人　　elevate〔'ɛlə,vet〕v. 提升
art form 藝術形式　　chief〔tʃif〕adj. 主要的
attraction〔ə'trækʃən〕n. 魅力；受歡迎之物
tourist attraction 觀光勝地　　fight〔faɪt〕v. 打仗；戰鬥
kite fighting 鬥風箏　　object〔'ɑbdʒɪkt〕n. 目標
opponent〔ə'ponənt〕n. 對手　　***set free*** 釋放

鬥風箏完全仰賴風箏線的品質，以及如何準備風箏線。首先把玻璃細細地磨碎，然後跟接合劑拌在一起，做成濃稠的漿糊。然後，將風箏線裹上漿糊，讓它既堅固又銳利。當外層乾了之後，線就被纏到捲軸上。風箏鬥士通常會在手指頭上綁一塊皮革來保護手指頭，以免緊繃的繩線，稍不留意就割傷他們的手指。

　　* *depend on* 依賴；視…而定　　quality〔'kwɑlətɪ〕*n.* 品質
　　finely〔'faɪnlɪ〕*adv.* 微細地
　　grind〔graɪnd〕*v.* 磨碎【三態變化為：grind-ground-ground】
　　combine〔kəm'baɪn〕*v.* 結合
　　adhesive〔əd'hisɪv〕*n.* 接合劑；有黏性的東西　　thick〔θɪk〕*adj.* 濃稠的
　　paste〔pest〕*n.* 糊狀物；漿糊　　coat〔kot〕*v.* 塗於…上；覆以…
　　fighter〔'faɪtɚ〕*n.* 鬥士　　wrap〔ræp〕*v.* 包裹；包覆
　　leather〔'lɛðɚ〕*n.* 皮革　　tight〔taɪt〕*adj.* 緊密的；(繩索)緊繃的

當對手的風箏被切斷的時候，它會像一隻色彩繽紛，但瀕死的鳥兒，飛向城市遠端。這樣的風箏被稱為「免費且合法」的風箏，附近的孩童可以拿回去，改天再拿來放。冬天是阿富汗鬥風箏最受歡迎的季節，風勢很強，而且因為天氣寒冷不必上學。雖然鬥風箏經常帶來笑容，但也很危險。很多人在追免費風箏時，從屋頂掉下來，或是在激烈的風箏比賽中失神而受傷。對阿富汗人來說，不管有什麼困難，有許多的戰役是要贏的。

　　* dying〔'daɪɪŋ〕*adj.* 垂死的；瀕死的　　reach〔ritʃ〕*n.* 所及的範圍
　　legal〔'ligḷ〕*adj.* 合法的　　retrieve〔rɪ'triv〕*v.* 取回；取得
　　neighborhood〔'nebɚ͵hʊd〕*n.* 附近地區　　*because of* 因為
　　injure〔'ɪndʒɚ〕*v.* 受傷　　roof〔ruf〕*n.* 屋頂
　　chase〔tʃes〕*v.* 追逐　　concentration〔͵kɑnsṇ'treʃən〕*n.* 注意力
　　heated〔'hitɪd〕*adj.* 激烈的　　battle〔'bætḷ〕*n.* 戰鬥
　　come what may 不論發生什麼事情；不管出現什麼困難

41.(**B**) 如果有人想要贏得鬥風箏比賽，下列何者最為重要？
　　(A) 線軸。　　(B) 風箏線。　　(C) 漿糊。　　(D) 風箏。

42.(**B**) 在鬥風箏中被切斷的風箏會怎樣？
　　(A) 鬥風箏的人必須找到它。　　(B) 找到的人就可以擁有它。
　　(C) 它會飛得很高然後消失。
　　(D) 失敗者留下它作為提醒失敗之物。
　　* reminder〔rɪ'maɪndɚ〕*n.* 提醒人的東西

43.（**A**）"**adhesive**" 這個字的意思爲何？

(A) 把東西黏在一起的物質。　　(B) 看起來像剪刀的東西。
(C) 用來彩繪風箏的顏料。　　(D) 用來拉緊風箏的線。

* ***refer to*** 指稱　　substance (ˈsʌbstəns) *n.* 物質
stick (stɪk) *v.* 黏　　scissors (ˈsɪzəz) *n. pl.* 剪刀
color (ˈkʌlə) *v.* 彩繪　　tighten (ˈtaɪtṇ) *v.* 拉緊；使變緊

44.（**D**）關於鬥風箏，下列何者爲眞？

(A) 兩只風箏在低空相遇時開始打鬥。
(B) 贏家通常得到一些錢作爲獎勵。
(C) 它是很安全的休閒活動。　　(D) 它吸引很多人來到阿富汗。

* recreational (ˌrɛkrɪˈeʃənḷ) *adj.* 休閒的

第 45 至 48 題爲題組

我們的星球大部分被水所覆蓋。水量是如此的多，如果世界上所有山脈被剷平，而把剷下的部分倒到海裡，地表就會完全在水底下，深達數千公尺的地方。關於陸地的地表特質，大陸與大陸之間有水存在的海盆地，其變化比地表還要多。如果把地表最高峰埃佛勒斯峰的山頂，放到海底最深的馬里亞納海溝中，山峰會低於水面一公里。

* planet (ˈplænɪt) *n.* 星球；行星　　***be covered with*** 被…所覆蓋
level (ˈlɛvḷ) *v.* 剷平　　debris (dəˈbri) *n.* 碎片；瓦礫
dump (dʌmp) *v.* 傾倒　　surface (ˈsɝfɪs) *n.* 表面；水面
entirely (ɪnˈtaɪrlɪ) *adv.* 完全地　　beneath (bɪˈniθ) *prep.* 在…之下
depth (dɛpθ) *n.* 深度　　meter (ˈmitə) *n.* 公尺
regarding (rɪˈgɑrdɪŋ) *prep.* 關於；至於
physical (ˈfɪzɪkḷ) *adj.* 自然界的；物質的　　feature (ˈfitʃə) *n.* 特徵
basin (ˈbesṇ) *n.* 盆；海盆地　　continent (ˈkɑntənənt) *n.* 大陸
lie (laɪ) *v.* 躺；位於　　varied (ˈvɛrɪd) *adj.* 不同的；各式各樣的
Mount Everest (ˈmaʊntˈɛvrɪst) *n.* 埃佛勒斯峰【即聖母峰，爲世界最高峰，
　　高度爲 8,848 公尺】　　trench (trɛntʃ) *n.* 深溝
the Mariana Trench 馬里亞納海溝【世界最深的海溝，位於北太平洋的馬
　　里亞納群島，深度爲海平面下 10,911 公尺，是太平洋板塊與菲律賓板塊的交
　　接處，也是距離地心最近的地方】　　peak (pik) *n.* 山頂；高峰

　　在地球剛形成並開始冷卻的時候，熱的水蒸氣立刻在地表凝結而形成海洋。年輕海洋裡的水就像雨水一樣並不純淨，而是包含許多氯、溴、碘、硼、氮，以及許多微量的罕見物質。從那時候起，許多其他成分陸續被加進來。當大陸岩塊隨時間而受到侵蝕，它們會產生鹽分，這些鹽分被河流帶進海中。因此，過了數千年，海洋的鹹度就越來越高。

* form〔fɔrm〕*v.* 形成　　cool〔kul〕*v.* 冷卻　　***soon after*** 緊接在…之後
  birth〔bɝθ〕*n.* 誕生　　vapor〔'vepə〕*n.* 蒸氣
  condense〔kən'dɛns〕*v.* 濃縮；凝結　　pure〔pjur〕*adj.* 純的
  rainwater〔'ren,wɔtə〕*n.* 雨水　　contain〔kən'ten〕*v.* 包含；含有
  significant〔sɪg'nɪfəkənt〕*adj.* 重要的；顯著的
  quantity〔'kwɑntətɪ〕*n.* 數量　　chlorine〔'klorin〕*n.* 氯
  bromine〔'bromin〕*n.* 溴　　iodine〔'aɪə,din〕*n.* 碘
  boron〔'borɑn〕*n.* 硼　　nitrogen〔'naɪtrədʒən〕*n.* 氮
  as well as 以及　　trace〔tres〕*n.* 極微量　　rare〔rɛr〕*adj.* 罕見的
  substance〔'sʌbstəns〕*n.* 物質　　ingredient〔ɪn'gridɪənt〕*n.* 原料；成分
  continental〔,kɑntə'nɛntl̩〕*adj.* 大陸的　　rock〔rɑk〕*n.* 岩石
  erode〔ɪ'rod〕*v.* 侵蝕；腐蝕　　salt〔sɔlt〕*n.* 鹽
  thousands of 數以千計的　　salty〔'sɔltɪ〕*adj.* 含鹽分的；鹹的

　　生命最早就是在大約三十五億年前，從這樣有著豐富化學物質的水中誕生。我們可以從化石中知道，最早的有機體是單細胞的細菌跟藻類。跟它們很像的有機體，仍存在現今的海洋中。它們是所有海洋生命的源頭；的確，如果沒有這些藻類，海洋到現在還是一片死寂，陸地上也不會有生物居住。

* chemically〔'kɛmɪklɪ〕*adv.* 在化學方面　　some〔səm〕*adv.* 大約
  billion〔'bɪljən〕*n.* 十億　　fossil〔'fɑsl̩〕*n.* 化石
  organism〔'ɔrgən,ɪzəm〕*n.* 有機體；生物　　cell〔sɛl〕*n.* 細胞
  single-celled〔'sɪŋgl̩'sɛld〕*adj.* 單細胞的
  bacteria〔bæk'tɪrɪə〕*n. pl.* 細菌
  algae〔'ældʒi〕*n. pl.* 海藻【單數為 alga〔'ælgə〕】　　exist〔ɪg'zɪst〕*v.* 存在
  basis〔'besɪs〕*n.* 基礎；主要成分　　marine〔mə'rin〕*adj.* 海洋的
  indeed〔ɪn'did〕*adv.* 的確　　***were it not for*** 若非…的話
  completely〔kəm'plitlɪ〕*adv.* 完全地　　dead〔dɛd〕*adj.* 無生命的
  uninhabited〔,ʌnɪn'hæbɪtɪd〕*adj.* 無人居住的

45. (**D**) 本文主要關於什麼？
　　(A) 為什麼海水是鹹的。　　　　(B) 海中不同的生命型態。
　　(C) 細菌跟海藻的起源。　　　　(D) <u>地球上的水。</u>

46. (**A**) 我們可以從何處得到有關海中最早生命形式的資訊？
　　(A) <u>化石。</u>　　　　　　　　　(B) 大陸岩塊。
　　(C) 化學物質。　　　　　　　　(D) 山脈碎片。

47. (**B**) 關於海水，下列何者為真？
　　(A) 海裡的鹽分部分來自於雨水。
　　(B) <u>海水中可以找到稀有的化學元素。</u>
　　(C) 它跟早期形成時一樣純淨。
　　(D) 隨時間過去，鹽分越來越少。

　　* formation〔fɔr'meʃən〕*n.* 形成；構造

48. (**C**) 文章中沒有提到下列何者？
　　(A) 海中生命形成是仰賴海藻。
　　(B) 地球上有非常多水。
　　(C) <u>海水可以被回收來生產能源。</u>
　　(D) 如果地球上沒有山脈的話，就會被水掩蓋。

　　* recycle〔ri'saɪkl〕*v.* 回收　　energy〔'ɛnədʒɪ〕*n.* 能源

<u>第 49 至 52 題為題組</u>

　　冰河會產出一些世界上最美麗的洞穴。溶化的冰流過冰河，就像水龍頭裡流出來的水，一路溶化所流經的冰塊。表面的水從縫隙中滴落，鑿穿雪的通道，並且用水晶冰柱裝飾洞穴。光滑的牆面與地面就像是玻璃一樣，凍結在六呎深的小鵝卵石都清晰可見。清澈的冰柱從洞穴頂部垂掛而下，閃耀著藍綠色，就像它們是用最珍貴的寶石所雕刻而來，而不是冰塊。

　　* glacier〔'gleʃɚ〕*n.* 冰河　　cave〔kev〕*n.* 洞穴
　　stream〔strim〕*n.* 溪流
　　melting〔'mɛltɪŋ〕*adj.* 溶化中的
　　flow〔flo〕*v.* 流；流動【三態變化為：flow-flew-flown】
　　just as 就如同　　faucet〔'fɔsɪt〕*n.* 水龍頭　　melt〔mɛlt〕*v.* 溶化
　　cube〔kjub〕*n.* 立方體　　surface〔'sɝfɪs〕*n.* 表面；水面

drip〔drɪp〕v. 滴落　　crack〔kræk〕n. 裂縫

hollow〔'halo〕v. 使凹陷；使中空　　***hollow out*** 鑿穿

tunnel〔'tʌnḷ〕n. 隧道　　decorate〔'dɛkəˌret〕v. 裝飾

crystal〔'krɪstḷ〕n. 水晶　　adj. 水晶似的；清澈的

icicle〔'aɪˌsɪkḷ〕n. 冰柱　　smooth〔smuð〕adj. 光滑的；平滑的

glasslike〔'glæsˌlaɪk〕adj. 玻璃般的　　pebble〔'pɛbḷ〕n. 鵝卵石

freeze〔friz〕v. 結凍；結冰【三態變化為：freeze-froze-frozen】

crystal-clear〔'krɪstḷ'klɪr〕adj. 清澈透明的

hang down 懸掛；垂吊　　ceiling〔'silɪŋ〕n. 頂部；天花板

flash〔flæʃ〕v. 閃亮　　blue-green〔'blu'grin〕n. 藍綠色

as though 似乎；好像（= *as if*）　　carve〔karv〕v. 雕刻

precious〔'prɛʃəs〕adj. 珍貴的；寶貴的

jewel〔'dʒuəl〕n. 珠寶　　***instead of*** 而不是

　　雖然在美國，大部分穴冰都是在火山洞穴中被發現，也有一些是石灰岩冰穴。有的人認為這些冰塊是幾千年前形成的，那時候的溫度比現在還要低多了。還有一些人認為，穴冰是古代冰河散佈到整個美國時，從中斷裂而來。

＊volcanic〔val'kænɪk〕adj. 火山的　　***a number of*** 一些

limestone〔'laɪmˌston〕n. 石灰石　　***as well*** 也（= *too*）

form〔fɔrm〕v. 形成　　***thousands of*** 數以千計的

break off 斷裂　　ancient〔'enʃənt〕adj. 古代的

spread over 散佈；攤開

　　今日，很多洞穴科學家有另一種想法。他們認為冰冷的水，透過細縫而滲入到洞穴中，一直到溫度低得能讓滲進來的水結冰。而冰層又能保持洞穴中的低溫，並且製造出更多冰塊。許多洞穴因此被厚厚的冰層所覆蓋，沒有人知道這些冰層到底有多厚。有些洞穴，像是愛達荷州的水晶瀑布洞穴，有結凍的河流，甚至是結冰的瀑布。美國原住民跟早期的開墾者，曾經把食物貯存在這樣的地下冰庫中，並削下小塊的冰，溶化作為飲用水。

＊sink〔sɪŋk〕v. 下沉　　***sink down*** 沈沒；陷入

chilly〔'tʃɪlɪ〕adj. 寒冷的　　seep〔sip〕v. 滲；漏

build up 建立；增進　　***such as*** 例如

falls〔fɔlz〕*n.* 瀑布　　***Crystal Falls Cave*** 水晶瀑布洞穴

Idaho〔'aɪdə,ho〕*n.* 愛達荷州【美國西北部的一州，境內有許多冰河鑿穿的峽谷地形】　　waterfall〔'wɔtə,fɔl〕*n.* 瀑布

Native American 美國原住民　　settler〔'sɛtlə〕*n.* 開墾者

used to 以前　　store〔stor〕*v.* 儲存

underground〔'ʌndə'graʊnd〕*adj.* 地下的

refrigerator〔rɪ'frɪdʒə,retə〕*n.* 冰箱（= *fridge* = *icebox*）

chip〔tʃɪp〕*v.* 削去　　block〔blɑk〕*n.* 一塊

drinking water 飲用水

49. (**B**) 本文主要關於什麼？
    (A) 冰河之美。　　　　　　　(B) 冰穴的形成。
    (C) 早期美洲原住民的歷史。　(D) 穴冰的功用。

    * formation〔fɔr'meʃən〕*n.* 形成
      function〔'fʌŋkʃən〕*n.* 功能

50. (**D**) 下列何者沒有用來描述冰柱？
    (A) 清澈透明。　　　　　　　(B) 藍綠色。
    (C) 像珠寶一樣。　　　　　　(D) 尖銳鋒利。

    * describe〔dɪ'skraɪb〕*v.* 描述
      sharply-pointed〔'ʃɑrplɪ'pɔɪntɪd〕*adj.* 尖銳鋒利的

51. (**D**) 根據本文，很多洞穴科學家抱持什麼理論？
    (A) 在美國，多數穴冰都在火山中發現。
    (B) 隨著氣溫越來越高，水現在很難結成冰。
    (C) 穴冰可能來自於古代冰河。
    (D) 冰水先滲入裂縫中然後才結成冰。

52. (**C**) 美國早期的殖民者拿冰塊來做什麼？
    (A) 做冷凍食品。　　　　　　(B) 製造酒。
    (C) 做成飲用水。　　　　　　(D) 用來洗衣服。

    * ***iced food*** 冷凍食品　　wine〔waɪn〕*n.* 葡萄酒
      laundry〔'lɔndrɪ〕*n.* 待洗的衣物　　***do the laundry*** 洗衣服

第 53 至 56 題為題組

　　蘭花很特殊，因為它擁有最高度進化的花朵，通常它雄性跟雌性的生殖器官會結合成一種單一的結構，稱為蕊柱。蕊柱的功能是為了方便一次的授粉，就能使幾十萬顆，在某些情況中，甚至是上百萬顆種子，都能受精，這些種子既小又輕，可以輕易地被風帶走。

* orchid (ˋɔrkɪd) *n.* 蘭花【蘭科植物被認為是植物進化的頂點，對昆蟲授粉有
　高度適應性，並且跟真菌建立起共生關係，它也是目前開花植物中最具多樣
　性的科別，主要特徵是雄蕊跟雌蕊共生於同一花柱上，方便昆蟲授粉，授粉
　後的種子會隨風散佈，因此蘭花也是分佈最廣的開花植物之一】

unique (juˋnik) *adj.* 唯一的；特殊的

develop (dɪˋvɛləp) *v.* 進化；發展　　***highly developed*** 高度進化的

blossom (ˋblɑsəm) *n.* 花；開花　　male (mel) *adj.* 雄的

female (ˋfimel) *adj.* 雌的　　　reproductive (͵riprəˋdʌktɪv) *adj.* 生殖的

organ (ˋɔrgən) *n.* 器官　　fuse (fjuz) *v.* 融合；結合

single (ˋsɪŋgl) *adj.* 單一的；一個的　　structure (ˋstrʌktʃɚ) *n.* 結構

column (ˋkɑləm) *n.* 圓柱狀體；【植物】蕊柱

so that 以便於　　pollination (͵pɑləˋneʃən) *n.* 授粉（作用）

fertilize (ˋfɝtl͵aɪz) *v.* 使授精；使肥沃

hundreds of thousands 數十萬

case (kes) *n.* 情況　　seed (sid) *n.* 種子

microscopic (͵maɪkrəˋskɑpɪk) *adj.* 極小的；顯微鏡的

breeze (briz) *n.* 微風

　　在蕊柱周圍有三片花瓣跟三片萼片，萼片就是像葉子般保護花瓣的部分。它們很容易被辨識，而且經常扭曲成非常美麗、奇妙，但總是非常實用的形狀。最引人注目的花瓣稱為唇瓣，唇瓣非常地明顯，吸引蘭花選擇作為授粉者的特定昆蟲，絕不可能錯看它。

* surround (səˋraʊnd) *v.* 圍繞　　petal (ˋpɛtl) *n.* 花瓣

sepal (ˋsipl) *n.* 萼片　　leaf-like (ˋlif͵laɪk) *adj.* 葉子般的

support (səˋport) *v.* 支撐

recognizable (ˋrɛkəg͵naɪzəbl) *adj.* 可辨識的

distort (dɪsˋtɔrt) *v.* 扭曲

gorgeous (ˋgɔrdʒəs) *adj.* 華麗的；極美的

weird〔wɪrd〕*adj.* 奇妙的；怪異的

functional〔ˈfʌŋkʃənḷ〕*adj.* 實用的；功能的

noticeable〔ˈnotɪsəbḷ〕*adj.* 引人注意的　　lip〔lɪp〕*n.* 唇；【植物】唇瓣

dramatically〔drəˈmætɪklɪ〕*adv.* 大大地；戲劇性地

mark〔mɑrk〕*v.* 標示；標明

unmistakable〔ˌʌnməˈstekəbḷ〕*adj.* 不會弄錯的；明顯的

attract〔əˈtrækt〕*v.* 吸引　　specific〔spɪˈsɪfɪk〕*adj.* 特殊的

pollinator〔ˈpɑlɪˌnetɚ〕*n.* 授粉媒介；授粉昆蟲

蘭花通常會用特別有趣的形狀、顏色、跟香氣，來吸引遠處的授粉者。在蘭花科中，已經分析出至少有五十種以上的香氣成分，各個成分混合後，會吸引一種，或最多數種昆蟲或鳥類。有些蘭花甚至會改變香氣，以便在不同的時間，吸引不同的昆蟲。

　　* afar〔əˈfɑr〕*adv.* 在遠處　　***from afar*** 從遠處

　　unusually〔ʌnˈjuʒʊəlɪ〕*adv.* 特別地

　　interesting〔ˈɪntrɪstɪŋ〕*adj.* 有趣的　　shape〔ʃep〕*n.* 形狀

　　scent〔sɛnt〕*n.* 氣味；香氣　　***at least*** 至少

　　aromatic〔ˌærəˈmætɪk〕*adj.* 芳香的；香氣濃的

　　compound〔ˈkɑmpaʊnd〕*n.* 合成物　　analyze〔ˈænḷˌaɪz〕*v.* 分析

　　family〔ˈfæməlɪ〕*n.* (動植物分類上的) 科

　　blend〔blɛnd〕*v.* 混合；調和　　***at most*** 最多

　　species〔ˈspiʃɪz〕*n.* 種類【單複數同形】

　　interest〔ˈɪntrɪst〕*v.* 使感興趣

一旦吸引了合適的昆蟲，有些蘭花會盡一切努力，確保昆蟲在離開前，將花粉正確地安置，或被帶走。對特定的授粉者而言，如此巧妙的適應能力，讓蘭花避免在野外，有過多異種交配的風險。同時，也確保每個種類的差異性得以保存下來。

　　* once〔wʌns〕*conj.* 一旦　　***do all*** one ***can*** 盡某人最大的努力

　　make sure 確認　　pollen〔ˈpɑlən〕*n.* 花粉

　　accurately〔ˈækjərɪtlɪ〕*adv.* 正確地

　　place〔ples〕*v.* 放置　　remove〔rɪˈmuv〕*v.* 移除；移開

　　ingenious〔ɪnˈdʒinjəs〕*adj.* 聰明靈巧的；巧妙的

adaptation〔͵ædəp'teʃən〕*n.* 適應；適合
avoid〔ə'vɔɪd〕*v.* 避免
rampant〔'ræmpənt〕*adj.* 猖獗的
crossbreed〔'krɔs͵brid〕*v.* 異種交配　　*at the same time* 同時
assure〔ə'ʃur〕*v.* 確保　　survival〔sə'vaɪvl̩〕*n.* 生存

53. (**C**) 為什麼在所有植物中，蘭花是獨一無二的？

(A) 因為它的棲息地又溫暖又潮濕。

(B) 因為它可以用來做成最多產品。

(C) 因為它花朵的構造很特別。

(D) 因為它是最長壽的植物。

* habitat〔'hæbə͵tæt〕*n.* 棲息地；繁殖地
　humid〔'hjumɪd〕*adj.* 潮濕的
　A *be made from* B　A 是由 B 做成的

54. (**A**) 本文中 "**fused**" 這個字是什麼意思？

(A) 結合的

(B) 生產出來的

(C) 隱藏的

(D) 被吸引的

* combined〔kəm'baɪnd〕*adj.* 結合的
　hidden〔'hɪdn̩〕*adj.* 隱藏的
　attracted〔ə'træktɪd〕*adj.* 有吸引力的

55. (**A**) 下列何者在文中沒有被提到是蘭花用來吸引昆蟲的工具？

(A) 尺寸　　　　　　　(B) 形狀

(C) 顏色　　　　　　　(D) 香味

* perfume〔'pɝfjum〕*n.* 香水；芳香

56. (**D**) 關於蘭花的香味，下列何者為眞？

(A) 只有在昆蟲接近花朵時才會發揮效果。

(B) 有害的昆蟲可能會遠離蘭花。

(C) 不同種類的蘭花聞起來都差不多。

(D) <u>香味可能會改變。</u>

* smell〔smɛl〕*n.* 味道（香氣跟臭味）

effective〔ɪˈfɛktɪv〕*adj.* 有效的　　***stay away from*** 遠離

alike〔əˈlaɪk〕*adv.* 同樣地

第貳部分：非選擇題

一、中譯英：

1. 因為 H1N1 的爆發，有越來越多的人寧可自己開車而不坐飛機。

$$\left\{\begin{array}{l}\text{Due to}\\\text{Owing to}\\\text{Because of}\end{array}\right\}$$ the outbreak of H1N1, more and more people

would rather drive themselves than take an airplane.

2. 儘管航空公司的一再保證，大部分的乘客是不願冒著感染病毒的危險。

$$\left\{\begin{array}{l}\text{In spite of}\\\text{Despite} \quad \text{(the)}\\\text{Regardless of}\end{array}\right\}$$ repeated guarantee from the airlines, most passengers

are unwilling to $$\left\{\begin{array}{l}\text{run}\\\text{take}\end{array}\right\}$$ the risk of $$\left\{\begin{array}{l}\text{catching}\\\text{getting infected with}\end{array}\right\}$$ the virus.

二、英文作文：

作文範例

Dear Mr. Grant,　　　　　　　　　　　　　　Jan. 28, 2013

　　I wanted to formally thank you and let you know how much I appreciate all the words of support and encouragement during my high school years. As both my teacher and counselor, your guidance paved my way to success.

　　I know I'm still young but high school was the most difficult and yet rewarding time of my life. I can't thank you enough for giving me perspective on my academics and interests. Your input about joining the science club was totally on target—you said, "Do what you love, love what you do." I will keep that advice in mind as I enter the next phase of my education.

　　Please know that I owe you a huge debt of gratitude for my achievements and perhaps some day I can return the favor.

Sincerely,

Rick Nielsen

formally〔'fɔrmlɪ〕*adv.* 正式地　　appreciate〔ə'priʃɪ,et〕*v.* 感謝
counselor〔'kaʊnsl̩ɚ〕*n.* 建議者；顧問
guidance〔'gaɪdn̩s〕*n.* 指導；教導　　***pave one's way*** 鋪路；做準備
rewarding〔rɪ'wɔrdɪŋ〕*adj.* 有益的
can't thank sb. enough 再怎麼感謝某人也不為過；對某人感激不盡
perspective〔pɚ'spɛktɪv〕*n.* 正確的眼光；洞察力
academics〔,æk'dɛmɪks〕*n.* 學業（= *studies*）　　input〔'ɪn,pʊt〕*n.* 投入
target〔'tɑrgɪt〕*n.* 靶；目標　　***on target*** 擊中要害；準確的
keep…in mind 牢記…　　phase〔fez〕*n.* 階段　　owe〔o〕*v.* 欠（債）
debt〔dɛt〕*n.* 債；恩惠　　gratitude〔'grætə,tud〕*n.* 感激
achievement〔ə'tʃivmənt〕*n.* 成就　　return〔rɪ'tɝn〕*v.* 回報
favor〔'fevɚ〕*n.* 好意　　***some day*** （將來）有一天
return the favor 回報；報答

大學入學學科能力測驗英文模擬試題 ⑩

第壹部分：單選題（佔72分）

一、詞彙（佔15分）

說明： 第1題至第15題，每題4個選項，其中只有一個是最適當的答案，畫記在答案卡之「選擇題答案區」。各題答對得1分；未作答、答錯、或畫記多於一個選項者，該題以零分計算。

1. I used to go to GaoXiong from QiJin by _____, but now there's a tunnel.
   (A) crash   (B) ferry   (C) escort   (D) diversion

2. She was too _____ to hear me coming in.
   (A) consolidated (B) acquainted   (C) preoccupied   (D) executed

3. The mayor used illegal documents as _____ to throw mud at her rival.
   (A) alienation   (B) aluminum   (C) ammunition   (D) acceleration

4. It would be _____ to say that Mary was his girlfriend.
   (A) overruling   (B) penetrating   (C) circulating   (D) misleading

5. I have a cool _____ in summer, but I don't have time to enjoy it.
   (A) isolation   (B) retreat   (C) cemetery   (D) compartment

6. Driving while _____ is not only dangerous. It is also against the law.
   (A) intoxicated   (B) pathetic   (C) sober   (D) hazardous

7. The former governments placed a _____ upon cross-strait trade. But it will all be history soon.
   (A) tattoo   (B) reel   (C) curb   (D) trophy

8. I really want to know his _____ in arranging such a meeting.
   (A) intention　　(B) potential　　(C) proficiency　　(D) treaty

9. The street is _____ deserted late at the night.
   (A) virtually　　(B) solely　　(C) shortly　　(D) liberally

10. Your goal is _____ as long as you continue to work as hard as you do now.
    (A) attainable　　(B) critical　　(C) superficial　　(D) vacant

11. Sue didn't study at all. She passed the exam on her first _____, though.
    (A) orientation　　(B) consistency　　(C) promotion　　(D) attempt

12. A careful driver is _____ of the traffic conditions.
    (A) productive　　(B) observant　　(C) moderate　　(D) loyal

13. The cheapest apartment costs the _____ of 10 years' wages for a factory worker.
    (A) equivalent　　(B) discipline　　(C) condemnation　　(D) suspicion

14. I sent my boss my _____ while I was on vacation in Kenting National Park.
    (A) invoice　　(B) resignation　　(C) ratio　　(D) therapy

15. I work for a research agency that tests the _____ of foot deodorant. I smell people's feet all day.
    (A) effectiveness　　　　　　(B) presumption
    (C) variation　　　　　　　(D) congregation

二、綜合測驗（佔 15 分）

說明： 第 16 題至第 30 題，每題一個空格，請依文意選出最適當的一個答案，畫記在答案卡之「選擇題答案區」。各題答對得 1 分；未作答、答錯、或畫記多於一個選項者，該題以零分計算。

第 16 至 20 題為題組

Malaysian legislators in the poor conservative Muslim northeastern state of Kelantan ___16___ single mothers to help care for their children, a state representative ___17___. The state's family and health committee chairwoman Wan Ubaidah Omar said that legislators should be awarded prizes for increasing their "quota" of wives. "What I mean ___18___ quota is adding to the number of wives," Wan Ubaidah, a female legislator said, according to Thursday's Star newspaper.

___19___ is legal in Malaysia for Muslims, who ___20___ 55 percent of the 28 million population. According to the Star there are 16,500 single mothers under 60 years of age.

16. (A) must be married with　　(B) should marry
　　(C) could be able to marry　　(D) would have married to
17. (A) launched　(B) trespassed　(C) suggested　(D) victimized
18. (A) by　(B) in　(C) with　(D) at
19. (A) Adultery　(B) Buggery　(C) Polygamy　(D) Solicitation
20. (A) attribute to　(B) respond to　(C) appeal to　(D) account for

第 21 至 25 題為題組

Police arrested a gang of teenagers that tortured and repeatedly raped a teenage girl over a period of several days. A 14-year-old girl was battered and ___21___ to death by a couple of teenagers of both sexes. Several teenagers stabbed passersby in broad daylight on a crowded street. News like this often appears in the newspaper. Violent crimes among young people have become a national ___22___.

There are a lot of things schools can do to help ___23___ the problem. If teachers put emphasis on students' good grades, a large ___24___ of students are likely to give up hope. The exam-oriented school system has to be changed. Textbooks should be easier. The ___25___ service for students has to be strengthened. Things like these can change the pressure-filled school system for the better.

21.	(A) beaten	(B) retorted	(C) pondered	(D) sketched
22.	(A) question	(B) target	(C) concern	(D) wardrobe
23.	(A) highlighted	(B) smooth out	(C) reckon	(D) focusing on
24.	(A) quotation	(B) proportion	(C) presumption	(D) quality
25.	(A) counseling	(B) overwhelming	(C) conciliating	(D) mediation

第 26 至 30 題為題組

A man may be known by the books he reads as well as by the company he keeps, ___26___ there is a companionship of books as well as of humans. A good book may be among the best of friends. It is the same today that it always was, and it will never change. It is the most patient and cheerful of companions. It does not turn its back upon us ___27___ adversity. It always receives us with the same kindness; instructing us in youth and ___28___ us in age. In a word, a good book is our everlasting friend.

One of the best books I've ___29___ read is the sacred book of Christians, the Bible. It tells the story of God's dealings with men, beginning with the creation of the world. I've read it time and again ___30___ I was six years old. To me it teaches wisdom and gives advice.

26.	(A) because of	(B) while	(C) for	(D) whereas
27.	(A) in terms of		(B) in times of	
	(C) as consequence of		(D) in the cause of	
28.	(A) moaning	(B) lamenting	(C) suffocating	(D) consoling
29.	(A) ever	(B) once	(C) miraculously	(D) used to
30.	(A) when	(B) right after	(C) since	(D) as soon as

三、文意選填（佔 10 分）

說明： 第 31 題至第 40 題，每題一個空格，請依文意在文章後所提供的 (A) 到 (J) 選項中分別選出最適當者，並將其英文字母代號畫記在答案卡之「選擇題答案區」。各題答對得 1 分；未作答、答錯、或畫記多於一個選項者，該題以零分計算。

第 31 至 40 題為題組

The Taipei City Government fined the Apple Daily NT$500,000 and NT$600,000 on December 1 and 2 ___31___ over its animated news content.

The Apple Daily is being investigated for violating the Child and Youth Sexual Exploitation Act, inciting people to commit crimes and damaging society's mores. The investigation ___32___ from the Apple Daily's ___33___ animated news content. It's being handled by the Women and Children's Special Division of the Taipei District Prosecutors Office. Women's groups, media reform ___34___, teachers' associations and other civil groups ___35___ at Apple Daily's headquarters on Thursday morning. One of the protestors, secretary-general of the Awakening Foundation, argues that the animated news content is a violation of human rights. She says sexual assault, sexual ___36___, and ___37___ violence shouldn't be portrayed using animation to offer details of the crime because that's a violation of the victims' human rights.

After speaking with the ___38___, the Apple Daily made a public apology in regard to the animated news content. In the future, such realistic rendering ___39___ will not be used for animated stories that deal with news that does harm to society as a whole, says Apple Daily Editor-in-Chief.

But the two sides didn't reach an agreement on exactly what types of violent and sexual news won't be made into animated news in the future. The lack of ___40___ led women's groups to say that they'll talk about the possibility of more protests by next week at the earliest.

(A) advocates　　(B) respectively　　(C) consensus　　(D) controversial

(E) stems　　(F) protestors　　(G) techniques　　(H) domestic

(I) assembled　　(J) harassment

四、閱讀測驗（佔 32 分）

說明： 第 41 題至第 56 題，每題 4 個選項，請分別根據各篇文章之文意選出最
適當的一個答案，畫記在答案卡之「選擇題答案區」。各題答對得 2 分；
未作答、答錯、或畫記多於一個選項者，該題以零分計算。

第 41 至 44 題為題組

British physicist Alan Calverd thinks that giving up pork chops, lamb cutlets and chicken burgers would do more for the environment than burning less oil and gas. Calverd calculates that the animals we eat emit 21% of all the carbon dioxide that can be attributed to human activity. We could therefore slash man-made emissions of carbon dioxide simply by abolishing all livestock. Moreover, there would be no adverse effects to health and it would be an experiment that we could abandon at any stage. "Worldwide reduction of meat production in the pursuit of the targets set in the Kyoto treaty seems to carry fewer political unknowns than cutting our consumption of fossil fuels," he says.

The 2006 United Nations Food and Agriculture Organization (FAO) report "Livestock's Long Shadow" concluded that the livestock industry is responsible for 18 percent of greenhouse gas emissions. This figure is significant considering that global emissions from the transportation sector, the focus of many current government reduction programs, accounts for only 13 percent of greenhouse gases released worldwide.

Livestock's Long Shadow examined the end-to-end emissions attributable to the livestock industry, including those from producing fertilizer, growing food crops for livestock and raising, killing, processing, refrigerating and transporting animal products. The report found that livestock produce nine percent of human-caused carbon dioxide, 37 percent of methane and 67 percent of nitrous oxide emissions. The study also stated that over a hundred-year period methane has 23 times the global warming potential of carbon dioxide, while nitrous oxide has 296 times the global warming potential.

41. What is the main idea this passage is trying to convey?
    (A) Livestock and transportation emissions overlap.
    (B) Livestock does no harm to the environment.
    (C) We can cut global warming by becoming vegetarians.
    (D) Human gas emissions are destroying the earth.

42. Which of the following statements is implied?
    (A) According to the Livestock's Long Shadow report, the transportation of animals emits more greenhouse gases worldwide than livestock.
    (B) Many countries have not ratified the Kyoto treaty because of political concerns.
    (C) The Livestock's Long Shadow report concluded that livestock produce 18 percent of human-caused carbon dioxide.
    (D) Many countries are launching programs to reduce their livestock.

43. Based on the passage, which of the following statements is NOT true?
    (A) Raising livestock makes a lot of methane and nitrous oxide gas.
    (B) The production of livestock causes serious environmental problems.
    (C) One way to save the planet is to stop animal breeding.
    (D) Carbon dioxide emissions are the number one factor of global warming.

44. All of the following statements are true EXCEPT
    (A) Methane is far more destructive than CO2 as far as the process of global warming is concerned.
    (B) A diet without meat would have undesirable effects on health.
    (C) A plant-based diet would be more effective than reducing the consumption of oil in reducing the amount of pollutants in the atmosphere.
    (D) Emissions of nitrous oxide and methane are closely-related to global warming.

第 45 至 48 題為題組

Have you ever wondered what ancient books were like? The first books were stories, poems, histories, prayers, and law records. Writers made them by scratching words on cakes of moist clay. When the clay was baked, it formed hard tablets that lasted a long time.

Egyptians made books of two kinds. Record books, which people used and handled over and over, were written on leather. For ordinary reading a more fragile material called papyrus was used instead. Writers used brushes and ink to paint words on long strips of papyrus. Then the strips were rolled up and stored in containers.

The Greeks and Romans used a material called parchment. Parchment was made either from goatskin or calfskin, which was scraped with a special knife until it was very thin. The finished product was white and so strong that the Romans used it for permanent record scrolls.

The Maya Indians wrote their books on paper made of bark that they pulled in long strips from wild fig trees. After the bark had been soaked and washed, it was beaten with paddles to stretch it out thin and wide.

Early Chinese books were handwritten in a kind of varnish on slabs of wood or strips of bamboo. Later, perhaps about A.D. 100, a Chinese inventor made paper from bark and rags. Books in China were soon being written on paper—a millennium before the idea finally reached Europe.

45. Where was papyrus made?
    (A) Egypt　　(B) Greece　　(C) China　　(D) Central America

46. Egyptians made their record books with leather because leather was _____.
    (A) durable　　(B) valuable　　(C) fragile　　(D) white

47. Maya Indians obtained material for their paper from _____.
    (A) goats　　　　　(B) trees　　　　(C) clay　　　　　(D) canines

48. How long were the Chinese writing on paper before the idea finally reached Europe?
    (A) 100 years　　　(B) 200 years　　(C) 1,000 years　　(D) 2,000 years

第 49 至 52 題為題組

　　A treaty that tries to tackle cybercrime has been adopted by the 43-nation Council of Europe. The treaty outlaws some online activities such as fraud and child pornography, clarifies some jurisdictional issues and outlines what police forces can do when pursuing computer criminals.

　　The treaty tries to standardize just what constitutes cybercrime and allows national police forces to ask their overseas counterparts to help with investigations or even detain suspects wanted in connection with the crimes they commit overseas. The treaty comes into force once five nations, including at least three Council of Europe members, have **ratified** it. Already the US, Japan and Canada have been invited to adopt the treaty.

　　Critics of the treaty have few complaints about what it categorizes as criminal, but they do worry that the powers it grants to police forces could erode online privacy. Many nations, such as the UK, already have in place legislation that lets police forces monitor online life, and some experts fear that these powers will be extended by nations adopting the treaty.

49. The cybercrime treaty is _____.
    (A) democratic　　　　　　　　(B) ethical
    (C) snooping　　　　　　　　　(D) controversial

50. What kind of photo is outlawed according to the treaty?

    (A) criminal scenes　　　　　(B) corpses

    (C) nude children　　　　　　(D) sexy women

51. The purpose of the treaty is ＿＿＿＿＿＿＿.

    (A) to protect privacy

    (B) to get computer criminals

    (C) to terminate international cooperation

    (D) to condemn Internet liberty

52. The word "**ratified**" can best be replaced with ＿＿＿＿＿＿.

    (A) affirmed　　　　　　　　(B) dehumidified

    (C) penetrated　　　　　　　　(D) certificated

第 53 至 56 題為題組

　　Rosalyn Yalow has studied the role of hormones in the human body for forty years. Hormones are substances that control the activities of various parts of the body. You know that your body needs the sugar from carbohydrates in order to get energy. The hormone insulin helps your body to use and store sugar. Too much or too little of any hormone can mean that the body is not healthy.

　　In 1977, Yalow won a Nobel Prize in medicine for a test she developed together with Solomon Berson. This test, known as RIA, can identify traces of different substances in the blood. For example, it can measure the amount of insulin that is in a person's blood. Doctors can then see if there is a normal amount of that hormone in the body. This is especially helpful for people with diabetes who need to control their levels of insulin.

　　The RIA test can be used in many other ways. It is used by blood banks to make sure that the blood used for transfusions is not contaminated by certain viruses.

Rosalyn Yalow grew up in New York City. Throughout her schooling, she had a special interest in mathematics. In high school and college, she became interested in chemistry and in physics. Yalow was the first woman to graduate from Hunter College in New York City with a degree in physics. Happily for her, Rosalyn Yalow is able to combine all three of her interests—mathematics, chemistry, and physics—in her work on the role of hormones in the human body!

53. Which description of the hormone insulin is TRUE?
    (A) It was first discovered by Rosalyn Yalow.
    (B) It helps store sugar.
    (C) It controls the activities of various parts of the body.
    (D) It helps sugar transform into carbohydrates.

54. Why is RIA useful for people with diabetes?
    (A) It can measure the amount of insulin in blood.
    (B) It can help them get energy.
    (C) It can identify traces of different substances in blood.
    (D) It can control the levels of insulin in blood.

55. The RIA test is mainly used to _____.
    (A) cure diabetes
    (B) control the levels of insulin
    (C) help transfuse blood
    (D) analyze blood

56. All of the following are true of Rosalyn Yalow EXCEPT
    (A) She was interested in math in college.
    (B) She graduated from college with a degree in physics.
    (C) She won a Nobel Prize alone.
    (D) What she did was of great help to blood banks.

第貳部分：非選擇題（佔 28 分）

一、中譯英（佔 8 分）

說明： 1. 請將以下中文句子譯成正確、通順、達意的英文，並將答案寫在「答案卷」上。

2. 請依序作答，並標明題號。每題 4 分，共 8 分。

1. 二〇〇九年十二月七日這天，來自全世界一百二十九國的代表，聚集在哥本哈根（Copenhagen）尋求限制溫室氣體排放的方法。

2. 不過，期望在幾天之內，就有可以抑制全球暖化的國際協議，是不切實際的。

二、英文作文（佔 20 分）

說明： 1. 依提示在「答案卷」上寫一篇英文作文。

2. 文長約 100 至 120 個單詞（words）。

提示：你妹妹（英文名字必須假設為 Jessica Williams）的生日快到了。你（英文名字必須假設為 Josh Williams 或 Helen Williams），要寫一封信給你妹妹的朋友（英文名字必須假設為 Donald, Susan, Reggie），邀請他們來參加你妹妹的生日派對，並說明生日派對的時間、地點和活動，以及其他可能的要求。

請注意：必須使用上述的 Josh Williams 或 Helen Williams 在信末署名，**不得使用自己的真實中文或英文名字**。

大學入學學科能力測驗英文模擬試題 ⑩ 詳解

第壹部分：單選題

一、詞彙：

1. (**B**) 我以前都從旗津搭<u>渡船</u>去高雄，但現在有了隧道。

    (A) crash〔kræʃ〕*n.* 隆隆聲；<u>墜毀</u>

        v. 發出巨響；撞上

    (B) *ferry*〔'fɛrɪ〕*n.* 渡船；渡口　　ferryboat *n.* 渡輪

    (C) escort〔'ɛskɔrt〕*n.* 護衛；護送；護花使者　〔ɪ'skɔrt〕*v.*

    (D) diversion〔də'vɝʒən〕*n.* 消遣；娛樂

    * *used to* 以前　　　tunnel〔'tʌnḷ〕*n.* 隧道；通道

2. (**C**) 她太<u>專心</u>了而沒有聽到我進來。

    (A) consolidated〔kən'sɑlə,detɪd〕*adj.* 合併的；鞏固的

        consolidate *v.* 團結；合併　　consolidation *n.* 合併；統一

    (B) acquainted〔ə'kwentɪd〕*adj.* 精通的；熟識的 < *with* >

        acquaint *v.* 告知 (= *inform*)；使熟悉 < *with* >

    (C) *preoccupied*〔pri'ɑkjə,paɪd〕*adj.* 全神貫注的

        preoccupation *n.*

    (D) execute〔'ɛksɪ,kjut〕*v.* 實施；執行；處死刑　　execution *n.*

        executive〔ɪg'zɛkjutɪv〕*adj.* 有執行力的　*n.* 經營者；高階主管

3. (**C**) 市長把非法文件作為<u>武器</u>拿來中傷她的對手。

    (A) alienation〔,eljən'eʃən〕*n.* 孤獨感；疏離　　alienate *v.*

        alien *adj.* 外國的；不相容的　*n.* 外國人；外星人

    (B) aluminum〔ə'lumɪnəm〕*n.* 鋁

    (C) *ammunition*〔,æmjə'nɪʃən〕*n.* 軍火；攻擊手段

    (D) acceleration〔æk,sɛlə'reʃən〕*n.* 加速；促進　　accelerate *v.*

    * mayor〔'meɚ〕*n.* 市長　　illegal〔ɪ'ligḷ〕*adj.* 違法的

      document〔'dɑkjəmənt〕*n.* 文件　　mud〔mʌd〕*n.* 泥巴

      throw mud at 中傷；拿泥巴丟…的臉　　rival〔'raɪvḷ〕*n.* 對手

4. (**D**) 說瑪莉是他的女朋友是一種<u>誤傳</u>。
  (A) overrule〔͵ovɚ'rul〕*v.* 推翻；駁回
  (B) penetrating〔'pɛnə͵tretɪŋ〕*adj.* 有洞察力的；尖銳的
    penetrate *v.* 滲透；看穿 penetration *n.*
  (C) circulating〔'sɝkjə͵letɪŋ〕*adj.* 循環的；巡迴的
    circulate *v.* 循環；流通 circulation *n.* 循環；發行量；流通
  (D) *misleading*〔mɪs'lidɪŋ〕*adj.* 引起誤解的 mislead *v.*

5. (**B**) 在夏天我有個避暑<u>住所</u>，但我卻沒有時間享受。
  (A) isolation〔͵aɪsḷ'eʃən〕*n.* 隔離；孤立 isolated *adj.* 孤立的
    isolate *v.* 孤立；隔離（= *segregate* ）
  (B) *retreat*〔rɪ'trit〕*n.* 撤退；避難所（= *shelter* = *sanctuary* ）
  (C) cemetery〔'sɛmə͵tɛrɪ〕*n.* 公墓
  (D) compartment〔kəm'pɑrtmənt〕*n.* 隔間
    compartmentalize〔͵kəmpɑrt'mɛntḷaɪz〕*v.* 區分；劃分
  * *have time to* + *V.* 有時間去做～

6. (**A**) <u>酒醉</u>駕車不僅危險，而且也違法。
  (A) *intoxicated*〔ɪn'tɑksə͵ketɪd〕*adj.* 酒醉的（= *drunken* ）；陶醉的
    intoxicating *adj.*
  (B) pathetic〔pə'θɛtɪk〕*adj.* 可悲的（= *pitiful* ）
  (C) sober〔'sobɚ〕*adj.* 清醒的；冷靜的（= *composed* = *calm* ）
    soberness *n.*
  (D) hazardous〔'hæzɚdəs〕*adj.* 危險的 hazardously *adv.*
    hazard *n.* 危險 *v.* 冒風險 be hazardous to 對⋯有害
  * *against the law* 違法

7. (**C**) 前政府<u>控制</u>海峽兩岸的貿易。但這很快就會是過去式了。
  (A) tattoo〔tæ'tu〕*n.* 刺青 *v.* 刺青於⋯之上
  (B) reel〔ril〕*n.* 捲軸；一卷 *v.* 用捲軸捲線
  (C) *curb*〔kɝb〕*n.* 抑制；約束 *v.* 克制
  (D) trophy〔'trofɪ〕*n.* 戰利品；獎品（= *prize* ）
  * strait〔stret〕*n.* 海峽 cross-strait〔'krɔs'stret〕*adj.* 海峽兩岸的
   trade〔tred〕*n.* 交易；貿易 history〔'hɪstrɪ〕*n.* 過去的事；往事

8. (**A**) 我真的很想知道，他安排這場會議的<u>用意</u>是什麼。

    (A) ***intention*** 〔ɪnˈtɛnʃən〕*n.* 意圖　　intentional *adj.* 有意的

        intentionally *adv.* 有意地 (= *on purpose* = *deliberately*)

    (B) potential 〔pəˈtɛnʃəl〕*n.* 潛力　*adj.* 可能的；潛在的

        potentiality *n.* 可能性；潛力

    (C) proficiency 〔prəˈfɪʃənsɪ〕*n.* 精通　　proficient *adj.* 擅長的

    (D) treaty 〔ˈtritɪ〕*n.* 條約；盟約

    * arrange 〔əˈrendʒ〕*v.* 安排；籌備

9. (**A**) 深夜的街道<u>幾乎</u>像是被棄置了一般。

    (A) ***virtually*** 〔ˈvɝtʃʊəlɪ〕*adv.* 實際上；幾乎　　virtual *adj.*

    (B) solely 〔ˈsollɪ〕*adv.* 單獨；僅　　sole *adj.* 唯一的；僅有的

    (C) shortly 〔ˈʃɔrtlɪ〕*adv.* 很快地 (= *soon*)；簡略地

    (D) liberally 〔ˈlɪbərəlɪ〕*adv.* 大方地；充分地

        liberalize *v.* 使自由；放寬

        liberal *adj.* 大方的；充分的；自由主義的

    * deserted 〔dɪˈzɝtɪd〕*adj.* 荒涼的；被遺棄的

10. (**A**) 只要你能像現在一樣繼續認真下去，你的目標是<u>可以達成的</u>。

    (A) ***attainable*** 〔əˈtenəbḷ〕*adj.* 可達成的　　　attain *v.*

    (B) critical 〔ˈkrɪtɪkḷ〕*adj.* 批評的；危急的；重大的

        criticize *v.* 批評；苛求　　critic *n.* 評論家

        criticism *n.* 評語；評論

    (C) superficial 〔͵supɚˈfɪʃəl〕*adj.* 表面的；膚淺的　　superficiality *n.*

    (D) vacant 〔ˈvekənt〕*adj.* 空虛的；空著的 (↔ occupied)

        vacancy *n.* 空間；空房；空缺

    * goal 〔gol〕*n.* 目標　　***as long as*** 只要

11. (**D**) 蘇完全沒唸書。不過，她第一次<u>嘗試</u>就通過考試。

    (A) orientation 〔͵orɪɛnˈteʃən〕*n.* 適應；新生訓練；定方向

        orient *v.* 使了解方位；使適應環境　　the Orient 東方

    (B) consistency 〔kənˈsɪstənsɪ〕*n.* 一貫性　　consistent *adj.*

(C) promotion〔prəˈmoʃən〕*n.* 升遷；促銷　　promote *v.*

(D) **attempt**〔əˈtɛmpt〕*n. v.* 嘗試；企圖

attempted *adj.* 未遂的　　attempted murder 謀殺未遂

* **not…at all** 一點不…　　pass〔pæs〕*v.* 通過

12.（**B**）小心的駕駛會<u>留意</u>交通狀況。

(A) productive〔prəˈdʌktɪv〕*adj.* 有生產力的

productivity *n.* 生產（力）　　production *n.* 生產；製造

(B) **observant**〔əbˈzɝvənt〕*adj.* 留心的；善於觀察的；遵守的

observe *v.* 觀察；遵守

observation *n.* 觀察　　observance *n.* 遵守

(C) moderate〔ˈmɑdərɪt〕*adj.* 適度的

moderation *n.* 適度；中庸

(D) loyal〔ˈlɔɪəl〕*adj.* 忠實的　　loyalty *n.*

* condition〔kənˈdɪʃən〕*n.* 情況

13.（**A**）最便宜的公寓，價值<u>相當</u>於工廠工人十年的薪水。

(A) **equivalent**〔ɪˈkwɪvələnt〕*n.* 等值之物（= *parallel*）

adj. 相等的（= *equal*）< *to* >

(B) discipline〔ˈdɪsəplɪn〕*n.* 紀律；訓練

(C) condemnation〔ˌkɑndɛmˈneʃən〕*n.* 譴責　　condemn *v.*

(D) suspicion〔səˈspɪʃən〕*n.* 懷疑　　suspicious *adj.*

* wage〔wedʒ〕*n.* 工資

14.（**B**）我在<u>墾丁國家公園</u>度假的時候，把<u>辭呈</u>寄給我老闆。

(A) invoice〔ˈɪnvɔɪs〕*n.* 發票　*v.* 開發票

(B) **resignation**〔ˌrɛzɪgˈneʃən〕*n.* 辭職

resign *v.* 辭職　　hand in *one's* resignation 遞出辭呈

(C) ratio〔ˈreʃo〕*n.* 比例；比率

in direct/reciprocal ratio 成正/反比

(D) therapy〔ˈθɛrəpɪ〕*n.* 治療法

* **on vacation** 度假中

Kenting National Park 墾丁國家公園

15. (**A**) 我在研究腳部除臭劑功效的機構工作。我整天都要聞別人的腳。

      (A) ***effectiveness*** (ə'fɛktɪvnɪs) *n.* 有效

         effect *n.* 效果　　effective *adj.* 有效的

      (B) presumption (prɪ'zʌmpʃən) *n.* 假定 (= *assumption*)；猜測

         presume *v.* 假定；猜測

      (C) variation (ˏvɛrɪ'eʃən) *n.* 變化

         vary *v.* 變化　　variable *adj.* 易變的

      (D) congregation (ˏkɑŋgrɪ'geʃən) *n.* 集合

         congregate *v.* 聚集

      * agency ('edʒənsɪ) *n.* 機構；仲介

        deodorant (di'odərənt) *n.* 防臭劑

二、綜合測驗：

<u>第 16 至 20 題爲題組</u>

    吉蘭丹位於馬來西亞東北部，是一個貧困又保守的回敎州，州裡的一位立法委員<u>建議</u>，吉蘭丹的議員<u>應該要娶</u>單親媽媽，幫助照顧她們的孩子。

          17   16

    * Malaysian (mə'leʃən) *adj.* 馬來西亞的

      legislator ('lɛdʒɪsˏletə) *n.* 立法者 (= *law maker*)

      conservative (kən'zɝvətɪv) *adj.* 保守的

      Muslim ('mʊslɪm) *n.* 回敎徒

      northeastern (ˏnɔrθ'istən) *adj.* 東北方的　　state (stet) *n.* 州

      Kelantan (kɛ'læntən) *n.* 吉蘭丹　　***single mother*** 單親媽媽

      care for 關心；關懷

      representative (ˏrɛprɪ'zɛntətɪv) *n.* 民意代表；議員

16. (**B**) 依句意，選 (B) ***should marry*** 「應該和～結婚」(= *should be married to*)。

17. (**C**) 依句意，選 (C) ***suggest*** (səg'dʒɛst) *v.* 建議。而 (A) launch (lɔntʃ) *v.* 發售 (新產品)，(B) trespass ('trɛspəs) *v.* 入侵，(D) victimize ('vɪktɪmˏaɪz) *v.* 使 (人) 受苦，則不合句意。

該州的家庭與健康委員會女會長，婉·烏拜達·歐馬爾表示，立法委員增加了自己妻子的「額度」，應該被頒發獎章。根據星期四的星報報導，這位女性立法委員說：「我說額度的意思，是指增加妻子的數字。」
      18

> * committee〔kə'mɪtɪ〕*n.* 委員會
> chairwoman〔'tʃɛr͵wʊmən〕*n.* 女主席；女會長
> award〔ə'wɔrd〕*v.* 頒發（獎賞） prize〔praɪz〕*n.* 獎；獎品
> quota〔'kwotə〕*n.* 分配；配額 ***add to*** 加上；增加
> female〔'fimel〕*adj.* 女性的 ***according to*** 根據
> ***the Star*** 星報【馬來西亞發行量最大的娛樂小報】

18.（**A**）表「意味著；有⋯的意思」，介系詞用 *by*，選 (A)。

重婚對馬來西亞的回教徒而言是合法的，在該國兩千八百萬人口中，回教
 19
徒佔了百分之五十五。而根據星報報導，年齡在六十歲以下的單親媽媽，共有
 20
一萬六千五百位。

> * legal〔'ligḷ〕*adj.* 合法的 population〔͵pɑpjə'leʃən〕*n.* 人口

19.（**C**）(A) adultery〔ə'dʌltərɪ〕*n.* 通姦
   (B) buggery〔'bʌgərɪ〕*n.*（男性間的）性行為
   (C) ***polygamy***〔pə'lɪgəmɪ〕*n.* 重婚
   (D) solicitation〔sə͵lɪsə'teʃən〕*n.* 懇求

20.（**D**）依句意，選 (D) ***account for***「佔～」。而 (A) attribute to「歸因於」，
   (B) respond to「對～做出回應」，(C) appeal to「吸引」，均不合句意。

第 21 至 25 題為題組

  警方逮捕了一群青少年，他們在過去幾天之中，不斷地折磨，強姦一位少女。有一位十四歲的少女，被一群才十多歲的少男少女毆打致死。
               21

> * arrest〔ə'rɛst〕*v.* 逮捕 gang〔gæŋ〕*n.* 一群；幫派
> ***a gang of*** 一群 teenager〔'tin͵edʒə〕*n.* 青少年
> torture〔'tɔrtʃə〕*v.* 折磨；拷問
> repeatedly〔rɪ'pitɪdlɪ〕*adv.* 再三地 rape〔rep〕*v.* 強姦
> teenage〔'tin͵edʒ〕*adj.* 十幾歲的 batter〔'bætə〕*v.* 猛打

21.(**A**) 依句意，選 (A) *beaten*。　　beat〔bit〕*v.* 打
　　　　而 (B) retort〔rɪˋtɔrt〕*v.* 反駁，(C) ponder〔ˋpɑndɚ〕*v.* 仔細考慮，
　　　　(D) sketch〔skɛtʃ〕*v.* 素描；畫草圖，均不合句意。

有幾個青少年，光天化日之下，在擁擠街道上刺傷行人。像這樣的新聞常常在
報紙上出現。青少年之間的暴力犯罪已經成為全國<u>關切</u>的問題。
　　　　　　　　　　　　　　　　　　　22

* stab〔stæb〕*v.* 刺；戳　　passerby〔ˋpæsɚˏbaɪ〕*n.* 路人
broad〔brɔd〕*adj.* 寬的；光明的　　daylight〔ˋdeˏlaɪt〕*n.* 日光；白天
in broad daylight 光天化日之下　　crowded〔ˋkraʊdɪd〕*adj.* 擁擠的
appear in 出現在⋯上　violent〔ˋvaɪələnt〕*adj.* 暴力的
crime〔kraɪm〕*n.* 犯罪　　national〔ˋnæʃənḷ〕*adj.* 全國的

22.(**C**) (A) question〔ˋkwɛstʃən〕*n.* 問題
　　　　(B) target〔ˋtɑrgɪt〕*n.* 目標
　　　　(C) *concern*〔kənˋsɝn〕*n.* 關心的事
　　　　(D) wardrobe〔ˋwɔrdˏrob〕*n.* 衣櫥

　　學校可以做很多事情，來幫助<u>解決</u>這個問題。老師如果強調學生要有好成
　　　　　　　　　　　　　　　　23
績，<u>很多</u>學生就可能會放棄希望。
　24

* *put emphasis on* 強調⋯；注重⋯
be likely to + V. 有可能～　　*give up* 放棄

23.(**B**) 依句意，選 (B) *smooth out*「除去（困難）」。
　　　　smooth〔smuð〕*v.* 撫平
　　　　而 (A) highlight〔ˋhaɪˏlaɪt〕*v.* 強調，(C) reckon〔ˋrɛkən〕*v.* 以為，
　　　　(D) focus on「專注於」，則不合句意。

24.(**B**) 依句意，選 (B) *proportion*〔prəˋporʃən〕*n.* 比例；部分。
　　　　a large proportion of 很多的～
　　　　而 (A) quotation〔kwoˋteʃən〕*n.* 引用，(C) presumption〔prɪˋsʌmpʃən〕
　　　　n. 假定，(D) quality〔ˋkwɑlətɪ〕*n.* 品質，皆不合句意。

以考試爲導向的學校體制應該要改變。教科書內容應該要簡單一點。而給學生的**輔導**服務應該要更加強。諸如此類的事情，可以讓充滿壓力的學校體制變得
　　　25
更好。

> * oriented (ˈorɪˌɛntɪd) *adj.* 以…爲取向的
> exam-oriented (ɪgˈzæmˈorɪˌɛntɪd) *adj.* 以考試爲取向的
> textbook (ˈtɛkstˌbʊk) *n.* 教科書；課本
> service (ˈsɝvɪs) *n.* 服務　　strengthen (ˈstrɛŋθən) *v.* 加強
> pressure-filled (ˈprɛʃɚˈfɪld) *adj.* 充滿壓力的
> ***change for the better*** 變得更好

25. (**A**) (A) ***counseling*** (ˈkaʊnslɪŋ) *n.* 指導；商議
　　　　　(B) overwhelming (ˌovɚˈhwɛlmɪŋ) *adj.* 壓倒性的
　　　　　(C) conciliate (kənˈsɪlɪˌet) *v.* 安撫；調停
　　　　　(D) mediation (ˌmidɪˈeʃən) *n.* 調停；仲裁

第 26 至 30 題爲題組

　　你可以從一個人看的書，也可以從他交的朋友，來了解一個人。因爲書可
　　　　　　　　　　　　　　　　　　　　　　　　　　　　　26
以跟人一樣成爲人的朋友。一本好書可能是你最好的朋友。這道理從古到今都
不變，以後也永不會改變。書本是最有耐心，也是最讓人愉快的同伴。

> * ***as well as*** 以及　　***keep company*** 交朋友
> companionship (kəmˈpænɪənˌʃɪp) *n.* 友誼；交往
> patient (ˈpeʃənt) *adj.* 有耐心的
> cheerful (ˈtʃɪrfəl) *adj.* 快樂的；令人愉快的
> companion (kəmˈpænɪən) *n.* 夥伴

26. (**C**) 依句意，選 (C) ***for*** 「因爲」(= *because*)。而 (A) because of 爲介系詞，
　　　　　須接名詞或動名詞，在此用法不合；(B) while 「當…時候；雖然；然
　　　　　而」，(D) whereas 「然而」，則不合句意。

書本不會**在**我們遇到逆境的**時候**拋棄我們。它永遠都會用相同的慈愛迎接我
　　　　27　　　　　　　27
們，在我們年少時指導我們方向，在我們年老時**撫慰**我們。簡言之，一本好
　　　　　　　　　　　　　　　　　　　　　　28
書是我們永遠的朋友。

* ***turn** one's **back upon*** 忽視；拋棄
  adversity〔əd'vɝsətɪ〕*n.* 逆境；不幸
  kindness〔'kaɪndnɪs〕*n.* 仁慈　　instruct〔ɪn'strʌkt〕*v.* 指導
  in age 年老時　　***in a word*** 簡言之
  everlasting〔͵ɛvə'læstɪŋ〕*adj.* 永遠的

27. (**B**) 依句意，選 (B) ***in times of*** 「在…的時刻」。而 (A) in terms of「就…而言」，(C) as consequence of「由於」，consequence〔'kɑnsə͵kwɛns〕*n.* 結果，(D) in the cause of「為了」，均不合句意。

28. (**D**) 依句意，選 (D) ***consoling***。　　console〔kən'sol〕*v.* 安慰 而 (A) moan〔mon〕*v.* 呻吟，(B) lament〔lə'mɛnt〕*v.* 哀悼，(C) suffocate〔'sʌfə͵ket〕*v.* 使窒息而死，均不合句意。

　　我唸過最好的一本書就是基督徒的聖書－聖經。書裡的內容是神跟人之間
　　　　　　29
的故事，從創世紀開始。自我六歲以來，聖經已經讀過好多次了。對我來說，
　　　　　　　　　　30　　　　30
它教人智慧或給予忠告。

　　* sacred〔'sekrɪd〕*adj.* 神聖的　　Christian〔'krɪstʃən〕*n.* 基督徒
　　Bible〔'baɪbḷ〕*n.* 聖經　　dealings〔'dilɪŋz〕*n. pl.* 關係
　　begin with 以…為開頭；以…為開始
　　creation〔krɪ'eʃən〕*n.* 創造　　***time and again*** 多次
　　wisdom〔'wɪzdəm〕*n.* 智慧　　advice〔əd'vaɪs〕*n.* 忠告

29. (**A**) 依句意，選 (A)。the best book I've ***ever*** read「我曾經讀過最好的書」。而 (B) once〔wʌns〕*adv.* 曾經；一次，用法不合；(C) miraculously〔mə'rækjələslɪ〕*adv.* 奇蹟似地，(D) used to + V.「以前～」，則不合句意。

30. (**C**) 因主要子句是「現在完成式」，空格後又是「過去式」，故選 (C) ***since*** 「自從～以來」。而 (A) when「當…時候」，(B) right after「就在…之後」，(D) as soon as「一…就～」，則不合句意。

三、文意選填：

第 31 至 40 題為題組

　　蘋果日報因為動新聞的內容，在十二月一日跟二日，[31](**B**) 分別被台北市政府罰款五十萬台幣和六十萬台幣。

> * ***Taipei City Government*** 台北市政府　　　fine〔faɪn〕*v.* 罰款
> daily〔'delɪ〕*n.* 日報　　***Apple Daily*** 蘋果日報
> respectively〔rɪ'spɛktɪvlɪ〕*adv.* 分別地
> animated〔'ænə,metɪd〕*adj.* 動態的　　***animated news*** 動新聞
> content〔'kɑntɛnt〕*n.* 內容

　　蘋果日報因為違反兒童與少年性交易防治法，煽動人們犯罪，以及傷害社會的道德風俗，而正在接受調查。調查是 [32](**E**) 起因於蘋果日報 [33](**D**) 具爭議性的動新聞內容。這次調查是由台北地方檢察署的婦女暨兒童特殊部門所負責的。婦女團體、媒體改革 [34](**A**) 支持者、教師協會、還有其他公民團體，星期四上午 [35](**I**) 聚集在蘋果日報的總部。

> * investigate〔ɪn'vɛstə,get〕*v.* 調查　　violate〔'vaɪə,let〕*v.* 違反
> sexual〔'sɛkʃʊəl〕*adj.* 性的
> exploitation〔,ɛksplɔɪ'teʃən〕*n.* 利用；剝削　　act〔ækt〕*n.* 法案
> ***Child and Youth Sexual Exploitation Act*** 兒童及少年性交易防治法
> incite〔ɪn'saɪt〕*v.* 激起；煽動　　commit〔kə'mɪt〕*v.* 犯（罪）
> damage〔'dæmɪdʒ〕*v.* 傷害　　mores〔'moriz〕*n. pl.* 社會傳統道德
> investigation〔ɪn,vɛstə'geʃən〕*n.* 調查　　***stem from*** 起因於；來自
> controversial〔,kɑntrə'vɝʃəl〕*adj.* 具爭議性的
> handle〔'hændḷ〕*v.* 處理　　division〔də'vɪʒən〕*n.* 部門；局
> ***Women and Children's Special Division*** 婦女暨兒童特殊部門
> district〔'dɪstrɪkt〕*n.* 地區；地方
> prosecutor〔'prɑsɪ,kjutɚ〕*n.* 檢察官
> ***Taipei District Prosecutors Office*** 台北地方檢察署
> media〔'midɪə〕*n. pl.* 媒體　　reform〔rɪ'fɔrm〕*n.* 改革
> advocate〔'ædvəkɪt〕*n.* 倡導者　　association〔ə,soʃɪ'eʃən〕*n.* 協會
> civil〔'sɪvḷ〕*adj.* 公民的　　assemble〔ə'sɛmbḷ〕*v.* 聚集
> headquarters〔'hɛd'kwɔrtɚz〕*n. pl.* 總部

其中一位抗議者是婦女新知基金會的秘書長，她主張動新聞的內容危害了人權。她說性侵害、性 [36] **(J)** 騷擾、還有 [37] **(H)** 家庭暴力不應該用動態表現出來，提供犯罪的細節，因為這樣會違害被害人的人權。

* protestor〔prə'tɛstə〕*n.* 抗議者
  secretary-general〔'sɛkrə,tɛrɪ'dʒɛnərəl〕*n.* 秘書長
  awaken〔ə'wekən〕*v.* 喚醒　foundation〔faʊn'deʃən〕*n.* 基金會
  Awakening Foundation 婦女新知基金會
  argue〔'ɑrgjʊ〕*v.* 主張　violation〔,vaɪə'leʃən〕*n.* 侵犯；侵害
  human rights 人權　assault〔ə'sɔlt〕*n.* 毆打；攻擊
  harassment〔'hærəsmənt, hə'ræsmənt〕*n.* 騷擾
  domestic〔də'mɛstɪk〕*adj.* 家庭的　violence〔'vaɪələns〕*n.* 暴力
  portray〔por'tre〕*v.* 描繪　animation〔,ænə'meʃən〕*n.* 動畫
  detail〔'ditel〕*n.* 細節　victim〔'vɪktɪm〕*n.* 受害者

　　跟 [38] **(F)** 抗議者談過之後，蘋果日報對於動新聞的內容公開道歉。蘋果日報的主編說，未來，如此寫實的描繪 [39] **(G)** 手法，將不會用於對社會整體造成傷害的動態報導上。

* apology〔ə'pɑlədʒɪ〕*n.* 道歉　***public apology*** 公開道歉
  in regard to 關於　realistic〔,riə'lɪstɪk〕*adj.* 實際的
  rendering〔'rɛndərɪŋ〕*n.* 演出；表現
  technique〔tɛk'nik〕*n.* 技巧；手法　story〔'storɪ〕*n.* 報導
  deal with 處理　***do harm to*** 對…造成傷害
  as a whole 整個的　editor〔'ɛdɪtə〕*n.* 編輯
  chief〔tʃif〕*adj.* 主要的　editor-in-chief *n.* 主編

　　對於以後到底哪種形式的暴力或性新聞，不會做成動態新聞，雙方還沒有達成協議。因為缺乏 [40] **(C)** 共識，婦女團體說她們會討論，最快下週會有更多抗議行動的可能。

* agreement〔ə'grimənt〕*n.* 協議　***reach an agreement*** 達成協議
  exactly〔ɪg'zæktlɪ〕*adv.* 正確地　A ***be made into*** B　A 被做成 B
  lack〔læk〕*n.* 缺乏　consensus〔kən'sɛnsəs〕*n.* 共識
  lead to 導致　possibility〔,pɑsə'bɪlətɪ〕*n.* 可能性
  protest〔'protɛst〕*n.* 抗議　***at the earliest*** 最早

四、閱讀測驗：

第 41 至 44 題爲題組

　　英國物理學家，亞倫·卡博德認爲，不吃豬排、羊排、雞肉漢堡給環境帶來的好處，超過燃燒較少的石油跟天然氣。卡博德計算出我們吃的動物所釋放的二氧化碳，佔了人類活動所製造二氧化碳的百分之二十一。因此，只要我們不再養家畜，就可以大幅減少人類製造的二氧化碳排放量。

* British〔'brɪtɪʃ〕*adj.* 英國的
  physicist〔'fɪzəsɪst〕*n.* 物理學家　　***give up*** 放棄
  chop〔tʃɑp〕*n.* 小肉片　　***pork chop*** 豬排
  lamb〔læm〕*n.* 小羊；羔羊　　cutlet〔'kʌtlɪt〕*n.* 薄肉片
  burger〔'bɝgɚ〕*n.* 漢堡（= *hamburger*）
  oil〔ɔɪl〕*n.* 油；石油　　gas〔gæs〕*n.* 氣體；瓦斯
  calculate〔'kælkjəˌlet〕*v.* 計算；估計
  emit〔ɪ'mɪt〕*v.* 發射；發出　　carbon〔'kɑrbən〕*n.* 碳
  dioxide〔daɪ'ɑksaɪd〕*n.* 二氧化物
  carbon dioxide 二氧化碳　　attribute〔ə'trɪbjut〕*v.* 歸因於
  attribute…to 將…歸因於　　***human activity*** 人類活動
  slash〔slæʃ〕*v.* 大幅減少
  man-made〔'mænˌmed〕*adj.* 人造的
  emission〔ɪ'mɪʃən〕*n.* 排放（量）；放射
  abolish〔ə'bɑlɪʃ〕*v.* 廢除；廢止　　livestock〔'laɪvˌstɑk〕*n.* 家畜

　　此外，這對健康不會有任何負面影響，而且這是我們無論在哪個階段，都可以終止的實驗。卡博德說：「爲了追求京都議定書中所設立的目標，減少全球肉品產量在政治上的不確定性，似乎比減少石化燃料消耗量來得更少。」

* moreover〔mor'ovɚ〕*adv.* 此外；再者
  adverse〔əd'vɝs〕*adj.* 不利的；相反的　　***adverse effects*** 負面影響
  experiment〔ɪk'spɛrəmənt〕*n.* 實驗
  abandon〔ə'bændən〕*v.* 放棄；拋棄　　stage〔stedʒ〕*n.* 時期；程度
  reduction〔rɪ'dʌkʃən〕*n.* 減少；下降
  production〔prə'dʌkʃən〕*n.* 生產；製造　　***in the pursuit of*** 追求
  target〔'tɑrgɪt〕*n.* 目標　　treaty〔'tritɪ〕*n.* 條約

Kyoto treaty 京都議定書【1997 年,「聯合國氣候變化綱要公約（UNFCCC）
　諦約國」,於日本京都召開第三次大會時擬定,要求溫室氣體總排放量佔全球
　百分之五十五的工業國家,簽署控制造成全球暖化及溫室效應的氣體排放量
　之協議,又叫作 Kyoto Protocol】

unknown〔ʌn'nɑn〕*n.* 未知數

consumption〔kən'sʌmpʃən〕*n.* 消費；消耗（↔ *production*）

fossil〔'fɑsḷ〕*adj.* 化石的　　fuel〔'fjuəl〕*n.* 燃料

fossil fuel 石化燃料

　　根據二〇〇六年,聯合國糧食及農業組織的「畜牧業的巨大陰影」報告做
出的結論,畜牧業佔總溫室氣體排放量的百分之十八。這個數字很可觀,因為
全球交通運輸的排放量,也就是許多政府現在減量計畫的要點,只佔全世界溫
室氣體釋放量的百分之十三。

* ***the United Nations*** 聯合國（= *the U.N.*）

agriculture〔'ægrɪ͵kʌltʃɚ〕*n.* 農業

organization〔͵ɔrgənə'zeʃən〕*n.* 組織

United Nations Food and Agriculture Organization 聯合國糧食及
　農業組織（= *U.N. FAO*）

report〔rɪ'port〕*n.* 報告　　shadow〔'ʃædo〕*n.* 陰影；影子

Livestock's Long Shadow 畜牧業的巨大陰影【聯合國糧食及農業組織在
　2006 年所做的一項調查報告,其中指出畜牧業所產生的溫室氣體,佔總溫室
　氣體排放量的 18%,而更新的報告指出,真實數據可能高達 51%】

conclude〔kən'klud〕*v.* 結束；下結論

industry〔'ɪndəstrɪ〕*n.* 工業；產業

be responsible for 應為…負責；造成…

greenhouse〔'grin͵haʊs〕*n.* 溫室　　***greenhouse gas*** 溫室氣體

figure〔'fɪgjɚ〕*n.* 數字

significant〔sɪg'nɪfəkənt〕*adj.* 顯著的；有意義的

considering that 鑒於…；就…而論

transportation〔͵trænspɚ'teʃən〕*n.* 運送；運輸工具；運輸系統

sector〔'sɛktɚ〕*n.* 部門；領域　　focus〔'fokəs〕*n.* 焦點

current〔'kɝənt〕*adj.* 現在的　　program〔'progræm〕*n.* 計畫

account for 佔…的比例；為…負責　　release〔rɪ'lis〕*v.* 釋放

　　檢視畜牧業中，包括製造肥料、種植給牲畜的糧食作物、飼養、宰殺、加工、冷藏以及運送動物產品等，每個環節所製造的排放量。

　　* examine〔ɪgˈzæmɪn〕v. 檢查；檢視
　　end-to-end〔ˈɛndtuˈɛnd〕adj. 點對點的；頭尾相連的
　　attributable〔əˈtrɪbjʊtəbl〕adj. 可歸因的；由⋯所引起的
　　fertilizer〔ˈfɝtlˌaɪzɚ〕n. 肥料　　crop〔krap〕n. 農作物
　　raise〔rez〕v. 撫養；舉起　　process〔ˈprasɛs〕v. 加工
　　refrigerate〔rɪˈfrɪdʒəˌret〕v. 冷藏　　transport〔trænsˈport〕v. 運送

報告發現，畜牧業製造的二氧化碳，佔人類製造二氧化碳的百分之九，還有百分之三十七的甲烷、跟百分之六十七的一氧化二氮排放量。這項研究也說到在一百年內，甲烷對全球暖化造成的影響，是二氧化碳的二十三倍，而一氧化二氮對全球暖化的影響是兩百九十六倍。

　　* human-caused〔ˈhjumənˈkɔzd〕adj. 因人類而起的
　　methane〔ˈmɛθen〕n. 甲烷　　nitrous〔ˈnaɪtrəs〕adj. 含氮的
　　oxide〔ˈaksaɪd〕n. 氧化物　　*nitrous oxide* 一氧化二氮；笑氣
　　state〔stet〕v. 陳述；說明　　time〔taɪm〕n. 倍
　　global warming 全球暖化　　potential〔pəˈtɛnʃəl〕n. 潛力；可能性

41.（**C**）本文試圖傳達的主要理念是什麼？
　　(A) 畜牧業跟運輸排放量交互重疊。
　　(B) 畜牧業不會傷害環境。
　　(C) 我們可以藉由當素食者來減緩全球暖化。
　　(D) 人們排放的氣體正在摧毀地球。
　　* convey〔kənˈve〕v. 傳達　　overlap〔ˌovɚˈlæp〕v. 部分重疊
　　do no harm to 對⋯不會造成傷害　　destroy〔dɪˈstrɔɪ〕v. 破壞

42.（**B**）本文中暗示下列何者？
　　(A) 根據畜牧業的巨大陰影報告，運輸動物在全球所排放的溫室氣體，比家畜排放的溫室氣體還多。
　　(B) 很多國家因為政治上的考量而沒有簽署京都議定書。
　　(C) 畜牧業的巨大陰影報告的結論是，家畜所產生的二氧化碳，佔人類製造的二氧化碳的百分之十八。
　　(D) 很多國家正著手計畫要減少家畜。
　　* imply〔ɪmˈplaɪ〕v. 暗示　　launch〔lɔntʃ〕v. 著手做
　　ratify〔ˈrætəˌfaɪ〕v. 批准；承認

43. (**D**) 根據本文，下列敘述何者爲非？
    (A) 飼養家畜會製造很多甲烷還有一氧化二氮氣體。
    (B) 生產家畜會引起嚴重的環境問題。
    (C) 拯救地球的一種方法就是不再飼養動物。
    (D) 二氧化碳排放量是全球暖化最主要的因素。

    * breed〔brid〕*v.* 飼養　　factor〔'fæktɚ〕*n.* 因素

44. (**B**) 下列敘述除了何者之外都是正確的？
    (A) 就全球暖化的進程而言，甲烷的破壞力比二氧化碳要大得多。
    (B) 不包含肉類的飲食方式，會對健康造成不良影響。
    (C) 要減少大氣中的汙染物，以植物爲主的飲食方式，會比減少油料消耗還要更有效。
    (D) 一氧化二氮與甲烷的排放量與全球暖化息息相關。

    * destructive〔dɪ'strʌktɪv〕*adj.* 有破壞性的
    as far as*‧‧‧*be concerned 就‧‧‧而言
    undesirable〔ˌʌndɪ'zaɪrəbļ〕*adj.* 不宜的
    pollutant〔pə'lutn̩t〕*n.* 污染物
    closely-related〔'kloslɪˌrɪ'letɪd〕*adj.* 密切相關的

第 45 至 48 題爲題組

　　你曾經對於古代書本長什麼樣子感到好奇嗎？最早的書本是故事、詩集、史書、禱文還有法典。作者將字草草地刻在一塊潮濕的黏土上做成書。等黏土變硬之後，變成一塊可以流傳很久的硬寫字板。

　　* wonder〔'wʌndɚ〕*v.* 好奇；懷疑　　ancient〔'enʃənt〕*adj.* 古代的
    poem〔'po‧ɪm〕*n.* 詩　　history〔'hɪstrɪ〕*n.* 史學；史書
    prayer〔'prɛɚ〕*n.* 祈禱；禱告文　　***law record*** 法典
    scratch〔skrætʃ〕*v.* 刮；潦草書寫　　cake〔kek〕*n.* 塊狀物
    moist〔mɔɪst〕*adj.* 潮濕的　　clay〔kle〕*n.* 黏土；泥土
    bake〔bek〕*v.* 烘烤；曬乾變硬
    tablet〔'tæblɪt〕*n.* 平板；寫字板　　last〔læst〕*v.* 持續

　　埃及人會做兩種書。人們會將重複使用的資料紀錄書寫在皮革上。而一般的讀本則會用一種較脆弱的材料，稱爲草紙。書寫者用毛筆和墨水把字畫在一張細長的草紙上，然後將草紙捲起來，存放在容器裡。

* Egyptian〔ɪ'dʒɪpʃən〕n. 埃及人　　handle〔'hændḷ〕v. 處理；觸摸
over and over 一再地　　leather〔'lɛðə〕n. 皮革
ordinary〔'ɔrdn,ɛrɪ〕adj. 普通的　　reading〔'ridɪŋ〕n. 閱讀；讀本
fragile〔'frædʒəl〕adj. 脆弱的　　material〔mə'tɪrɪəl〕n. 材料
instead〔ɪn'stɛd〕adv. 更換；代替　　brush〔brʌʃ〕n. 刷子；毛筆
ink〔ɪŋk〕n. 墨水　　paint〔pent〕v. 畫；上漆
strip〔strɪp〕n.（細長的）一條　　papyrus〔pə'paɪrəs〕n. 草紙
roll up 捲起　　store〔stor〕v. 貯藏　　container〔kən'tenə〕n. 容器

　　希臘人跟羅馬人會用一種叫作羊皮紙的材料。羊皮紙是用山羊皮或小牛皮做成的，用特別的刀片一直刮到它變成薄薄一片。成品會是白色的，而且非常強韌，羅馬人會把它拿來作為永久的紀錄紙卷。

* Greek〔grik〕n. 希臘人　　Roman〔'romən〕n. 羅馬人
parchment〔'partʃmənt〕n. 羊皮紙　　***either…or~*** 若非…就是~
goatskin〔'got,skɪn〕n. 山羊皮　　calfskin〔'kæf,skɪn〕n. 小牛皮
scrape〔skrep〕v. 刮掉；摩擦　　knife〔naɪf〕n. 小刀
thin〔θɪn〕adj. 薄的　　finished〔'fɪnɪʃt〕adj. 完工的
permanent〔'pɜmənənt〕adj. 永久的　　scroll〔skrol〕n. 紙卷；捲軸

　　馬雅印地安人用樹皮當紙來寫書，他們將野生無花果樹的樹皮撕開成長條狀，然後把樹皮浸泡、清洗，用扁平的工具拍打樹皮，把它拉得又薄又寬。

* Maya〔'majə〕n. 馬雅人　　Indian〔'ɪndɪən〕n. 印地安人
bark〔bɑrk〕n. 樹皮　　pull〔pʊl〕v. 拉；拖　　fig〔fɪg〕n. 無花果
soak〔sok〕v. 浸泡　　beat〔bit〕v. 擊；打
paddle〔'pædḷ〕n. 槳；扁平工具　　stretch〔strɛtʃ〕v. 拉長；延伸

　　古代中國的書籍，是手寫在一種光滑的厚木板或是長條竹片上。其後，大約西元一百年時，一位中國發明家用樹皮跟碎布造紙。很快地，中國的書就寫在紙上了——這個發明一千年後才傳到歐洲。

* handwritten〔'hænd'rɪtṇ〕adj. 手寫的　　varnish〔'vɑrnɪʃ〕n. 光澤面
slab〔slæb〕n. 厚板　　bamboo〔bæm'bu〕n. 竹子　　***A.D.*** 西元後
inventor〔ɪn'vɛntə〕n. 發明者　　rag〔ræg〕n. 破布
millennium〔mə'lɛnɪəm〕n. 一千年

45.(**A**) 草紙是哪個地方做的？

(A) 埃及　　　(B) 希臘　　　(C) 中國　　　(D) 中美洲

46.(**A**) 埃及人用皮革來做資料紀錄書，因爲皮革是 ＿＿＿＿＿＿。

(A) 堅固的　　(B) 珍貴的　　(C) 脆弱的　　(D) 白色的

* durable〔'djʊrəbḷ〕 *adj.* 堅固的；耐久的

fragile〔'frædʒəl〕 *adj.* 脆弱的

47.(**B**) 馬雅印地安人從 ＿＿＿＿＿＿ 得到造紙的材料。

(A) 山羊　　　(B) 樹木　　　(C) 黏土　　　(D) 狗

* canine〔'kenaɪn〕 *n.* 犬科動物

48.(**C**) 中國人在紙上寫字的知識，多久之後才傳到歐洲？

(A) 一百年　　(B) 兩百年　　(C) 一千年　　(D) 兩千年

第 49 至 52 題爲題組

　　有四十三個會員國的歐洲執委會，已經通過一項處理網路犯罪的條約。這項條約明令禁止某些網路活動，像是詐騙以及兒童情色文學等，裡頭清楚說明一些司法管轄權的議題，並重點說明警方在追蹤電腦罪犯時可以採取的措施。

* treaty〔'tritɪ〕 *n.* 條約；協議　　tackle〔'tækḷ〕 *v.* 處理

cybercrime〔'saɪbə,kraɪm〕 *n.* 網路犯罪　　adopt〔ə'dɑpt〕 *v.* 採納

43-nation *adj.* 四十三個國家的　　council〔'kaʊnsḷ〕 *n.* 議會

Council of Europe 歐盟執委會【又稱歐洲委員會，由愛爾蘭、比利時、丹

麥、法國、荷蘭、盧森堡、挪威、瑞典、義大利和英國於 1949 年 5 月 5 日，

在倫敦簽訂《歐洲委員會法規》後成立，是歐洲整合進程中最早成立的機構。

總部位於法國史特拉斯堡】　　outlaw〔'aʊt,lɔ〕 *v.* 宣布…爲非法；禁止

online〔,ɑn'laɪn〕 *adj.* 線上的　　fraud〔frɔd〕 *n.* 詐欺

pornography〔pɔr'nɑgrəfɪ〕 *n.* 色情文學

clarify〔'klærə,faɪ〕 *v.* 澄清；清晰說明

jurisdictional〔,dʒʊrɪs'dɪkʃənḷ〕 *adj.* 司法權的；管轄的

issue〔'ɪʃu〕 *n.* 議題　　outline〔'aʊt,laɪn〕 *v.* 使清晰；略述重點

police force 警方　　pursue〔pə'su〕 *v.* 追求；追蹤（犯人）

criminal〔'krɪmənḷ〕 *n.* 犯人

　　這項協議裡頭說明構成網路犯罪的標準，並且讓國家警力能要求國外警力協助調查犯罪，甚至拘留在國外犯下相關罪行的通緝犯。這項協議只要有五個國家，其中至少要有三個歐盟執委會成員的承認即可生效。而且美國、日本跟加拿大也早已受邀採行這項協議。

* standardize〔'stændə,daɪz〕v. 使標準化
　constitute〔'kɑnstə,tjut〕v. 組成；構成
　overseas〔'ovə'siz〕adj. 海外的　adv. 在海外
　counterpart〔'kaʊntə,pɑrt〕n. 對應的人或物；配對物
　investigation〔ɪn,vɛstə'geʃən〕n. 調查；研究
　detain〔dɪ'ten〕v. 拘留；扣押　　suspect〔'sʌspɛkt〕n. 嫌疑犯
　wanted〔'wɑntɪd〕adj. 被通緝的　　connection〔kə'nɛkʃən〕n. 結合
　in connection with 與…有關　　commit〔kə'mɪt〕v. 犯（罪）
　come into force 實施；生效　　*at least* 至少
　ratify〔'rætə,faɪ〕v. 批准；承認

　　批評家對於該協議如何分類犯罪者沒有太多意見，但他們確實很擔心，這項協議給警方太多權力，可能會侵害網路隱私權。像英國等某些國家已經有適當的法律，讓警方監控網路生活，有些專家害怕諸如此類的權力，會被那些採行該協議的國家擴大。

* critic〔'krɪtɪk〕n. 評論家；批評者　　complaint〔kəm'plent〕n. 抱怨
　categorize〔'kætəgə,raɪz〕v. 分類　　grant〔grænt〕v. 允許；答應
　erode〔ɪ'rod〕v. 侵蝕　　privacy〔'praɪvəsɪ〕n. 侵蝕
　in place 適當的　　legislation〔,lɛdʒɪs'leʃən〕n. 立法
　monitor〔'mɑnətə〕v. 監視　　expert〔'ɛkspɜt〕n. 專家
　extend〔ɪk'stɛnd〕v. 擴大；擴張

49.（ **D** ）網路犯罪條約是 ＿＿＿＿＿＿＿。
　　(A) 民主的　　　　　　　　　(B) 道德的
　　(C) 窺探秘密的　　　　　　　(D) 具爭議性的
　　* democratic〔,dɛmə'krætɪk〕adj. 民主的
　　　ethical〔'ɛθɪkl̩〕adj. 合乎道德的
　　　snooping〔'snupɪŋ〕adj. 窺探秘密的
　　　controversial〔,kɑntrə'vɜʃəl〕adj. 具爭議性的

50. (**C**) 根據本文，哪種圖片會被禁止？
　　(A) 犯罪現場　　　　　　　　(B) 屍體
　　(C) 沒穿衣服的小孩　　　　　(D) 性感的女人
　　* scene〔sin〕*n.* 現場　　　corpse〔kɔrps〕*n.* 屍體
　　　nude〔njud〕*adj.* 赤裸的

51. (**B**) 本條約的目的在於 ＿＿＿＿＿＿。
　　(A) 保護隱私　　　　　　　　(B) 抓到電腦罪犯
　　(C) 終止國際合作　　　　　　(D) 譴責網路自由
　　* terminate〔ˈtɝməˌnet〕*v.* 終止　　cooperation〔koˌɑpəˈreʃən〕*n.* 合作
　　　condemn〔kənˈdɛm〕*v.* 責難　　　liberty〔ˈlɪbətɪ〕*n.* 自由

52. (**A**) 最能被用來取代 "**ratified**" 的字是 ＿＿＿＿＿＿。
　　(A) 證實的　　(B) 除去濕氣的　　(C) 被滲透的　　(D) 有執照的
　　* affirm〔əˈfɝm〕*v.* 斷言；批准
　　　dehumidify〔ˌdihjuˈmɪdəˌfaɪ〕*v.* 除濕
　　　penetrate〔ˈpɛnəˌtret〕*v.* 滲透
　　　certificated〔səˈtɪfəˌketɪd〕*adj.* 有執照的

第 53 至 56 題為題組

　　羅莎琳・雅洛研究人體內的荷爾蒙超過四十年了。荷爾蒙是控制身體許多部分活動的物質。你知道身體需要碳水化合物中的糖分，以獲得能量。胰島素會幫助身體使用跟儲存糖分。不管何種荷爾蒙，過多或過少都表示身體不健康。

　　* Rosalyn Yalow〔ˈrazəlɪnˈjɑlo〕*n.* 羅莎琳・雅洛【1921-，美國醫學物理學家，全名羅莎琳・薩斯曼・雅洛（Rosalyn Sussman Yalow），1950 年代她與所羅門・柏森開發「放射性免疫分析法（Radioimmunoassay 或稱 RIA）」，與後續開發的胰島素的放射性免疫分析法，在 1977 年獲得諾貝爾醫學獎。他們利用放射線元素，研究糖尿病患者體內胰島素被分解的速度，再將這方法延伸到研究體內特定荷爾蒙或物質的濃度，對內分泌研究及治療產生相當深遠的影響】　　hormone〔ˈhɔrmon〕*n.* 荷爾蒙
　　carbohydrate〔ˌkɑrboˈhaɪdret〕*n.* 碳水化合物；醣
　　in order to + *V.* 為了～　　energy〔ˈɛnədʒɪ〕*n.* 能量；精力
　　insulin〔ˈɪnsəlɪn〕*n.* 胰島素【由胰臟分泌的荷爾蒙，可用來治療糖尿病】

在 1977 年，雅洛因為與所羅門・柏森共同開發的實驗，而贏得諾貝爾醫學獎。這項實驗被稱為放射性免疫分析法，能辨識血液中極微量的不同物質。例如它能測量人體中胰島素的量。因此，醫生能看出體內荷爾蒙的量是否足夠。這方法對於罹患糖尿病，需要控制胰島素濃度的人來說尤其有用。

* ***Nobel Prize*** 諾貝爾獎
  RIA 放射性免疫分析法（ = *Radioimmunoassay* ）
  identify〔aɪˈdɛntəˌfaɪ〕*v.* 認明；辨識　　trace〔tres〕*n.* 痕跡；微量
  substance〔ˈsʌbstəns〕*n.* 物質　　diabetes〔ˌdaɪəˈbitɪs〕*n.* 糖尿病
  level〔ˈlɛvḷ〕*n.* 濃度；程度

放射性免疫分析法能用在其他許多方面。它能讓血庫確認用來輸血的血液，沒有被某些病毒污染。

* ***blood bank*** 血庫　　transfusion〔trænsˈfjuʒən〕*n.* 輸血
  contaminate〔kənˈtæməˌnet〕*v.* 污染　　virus〔ˈvaɪrəs〕*n.* 病毒

羅莎琳・雅洛在紐約長大。她求學的過程中一直都對數學特別感興趣。在高中跟大學時，她開始對物理學跟化學感興趣。雅洛是第一個以物理學的學位，從紐約市立杭特學院畢業的女生。她很快樂，因為能夠在研究人體荷爾蒙角色的研究中，將自己對數學、物理學跟化學的興趣做結合！

* ***grow up*** 生長；成長　　***New York City*** 紐約市
  throughout〔θruˈaʊt〕*prep.* 遍及　　schooling〔ˈskulɪŋ〕*n.* 學校教育
  interest〔ˈɪntrɪst〕*n.* 興趣　*v.* 使…感興趣
  mathematics〔ˌmæθəˈmætɪks〕*n.* 數學（ = *math* ）
  be/become interested in 對…有興趣
  chemistry〔ˈkɛmɪstrɪ〕*n.* 化學
  physics〔ˈfɪzɪks〕*n.* 物理學　　graduate〔ˈgrædʒʊˌet〕*v.* 畢業
  degree〔dɪˈgri〕*n.* 學位　　combine〔kəmˈbaɪn〕*v.* 結合

53. (**B**) 下列關於胰島素荷爾蒙的敘述何者為眞？
    (A) 最早是由羅莎琳・雅洛發現的。
    (B) 它會幫助儲存糖分。
    (C) 它控制身體許多部分的活動。
    (D) 它會幫助糖分轉化為碳水化合物。

* description〔dɪ'skrɪpʃən〕*n.* 描述　　store〔stor〕*v.* 儲存
  transform〔træns'fɔrm〕*v.* 使轉變

54.（**A**）為什麼放射性免疫分析法對於患有糖尿病的人很有幫助？
　　(A) 它可以測量血液中的胰島素含量。
　　(B) 它可以讓人們有活力。
　　(C) 它可以辨識血液中不同的微量物質。
　　(D) 它可以控制血液中的胰島素濃度。

55.（**D**）放射性免疫分析測試法主要是用來 ＿＿＿＿＿＿＿＿。
　　(A) 治療糖尿病　　　　　　　(B) 控制胰島素的濃度
　　(C) 幫助輸血　　　　　　　　(D) 分析血液
　　* transfuse〔træns'fjuz〕*v.* 輸血

56.（**C**）下列關於羅莎琳・雅洛的敘述都是正確的，除了 ＿＿＿＿＿＿＿＿
　　(A) 她在大學時對數學有興趣。
　　(B) 她大學畢業時拿的是物理學學位。
　　(C) 她一個人獲得諾貝爾獎。
　　(D) 她的工作對血庫有很大的貢獻。

第貳部分：非選擇題

一、中譯英：

1. 二〇〇九年十二月七日這天，來自全世界一百二十九國的代表聚集在哥本哈根（Copenhagen）尋求限制溫室氣體排放的方法。

On December 7, 2009,
$\left\{\begin{array}{l}\text{representatives} \\ \text{delegates}\end{array}\right\}$
from 129 countries

$\left\{\begin{array}{l}\text{gathered} \\ \text{met}\end{array}\right\}$
in Copenhagen
$\left\{\begin{array}{l}\text{, seeking ways to} \\ \text{to find ways to /, looking for ways to} \\ \text{to look for ways to}\end{array}\right\}$

$\left\{\begin{array}{l}\text{control} \\ \text{limit} \\ \text{reduce}\end{array}\right\}$
the emission of greenhouse gases.

2. 不過，期望在幾天之內就有可以抑制全球暖化的國際協議，是不切實際的。

However, it's $\left\{\begin{array}{l}\text{unrealistic} \\ \text{impractical} \\ \text{idealistic}\end{array}\right\}$ to expect that there will be an international

$\left\{\begin{array}{l}\text{agreement} \\ \text{treaty}\end{array}\right\}$ capable of $\left\{\begin{array}{l}\text{curbing} \\ \text{slowing} \\ \text{reducing}\end{array}\right\}$ global warming in a couple

of days.

或：But it's unrealistic to expect an international agreement that

$\left\{\begin{array}{l}\text{will curb} \\ \text{is capable of curbing}\end{array}\right\}$ global warming to be reached in only

a couple of days.

二、英文作文：

作文範例

Dear Donald, Susan, and Reggie,　　　　　　　　　Jan. 28, 2013

　　You are invited to a Sweet Sixteen party for Jessica Williams!
Saturday, February 11 from 7:00 p.m. to midnight, please join us
for a fun-filled evening of music and dancing at the Mandarin
Entertainment Complex. The party will be hosted by local
celebrity DJ Marx.

　　Jessica has requested that guests not bring gifts. Instead,
if you wish to make a donation to her favorite charity, Pets Are
People Too, there will be a collection box at the party. Also,

please note that the Mandarin has a strict dress code, so please dress appropriately. Please RSVP to Helen Williams before January 4. Hope to see you at the party!

Sincerely,

Helen Williams

midnight（'mɪd,naɪt）*n.* 半夜

fun-filled *adj.* 充滿歡樂的

complex（'kɑmplɛks）*n.*（建築物）綜合體；集合設施

host（host）*v.* 主辦；主持　　　local（'lokḷ）*adj.* 當地的；本地的

celebrity（sə'lɛbrətɪ）*n.* 名人

DJ 流行音樂播音員；流行音樂節目主持人（= *disc jockey*）

request（rɪ'kwɛst）*v.* 要求；請求

instead（ɪn'stɛd）*adv.* 反而

donation（do'neʃən）*n.* 捐贈

charity（'tʃærətɪ）*n.* 慈善團體　　pet（pɛt）*n.* 寵物

collection（kə'lɛkʃən）*n.* 募集

collection box 募捐箱　　note（not）*v.* 注意；留意

strict（strɪkt）*adj.* 嚴格的　　code（kod）*n.* 制度；規則

dress code 服裝規定

appropriately（ə'proprɪɪtlɪ）*adv.* 適當地

RSVP 請回應（= *Please respond.*）【源自法文 répondez s'il vous plait，用於需要確定人數時】

劉毅英文「*101年學科能力測驗*」15級分名單

姓 名	學 校	班級	姓 名	學 校	班級	姓 名	學 校	班級
白善尹	建國中學	319	王文洲	建國中學	319	王欣維	台中一中	316
徐大鈞	建國中學	326	蔡睿庭	成功高中	314	李重甫	台中一中	320
張嘉仂	中崙高中	301	黃珮瑄	中山女中	3博	楊啓蘭	台中一中	324
施宇哲	建國中學	302	黃昭維	板橋高中	320	廖城武	台中一中	316
王奕婷	北一女中	3讓	黃懷萱	北一女中	3忠	沙志軒	台中一中	308
鄭育安	建國中學	319	陶俊成	成功高中	302	陳浩天	台中一中	314
吳萬泰	建國中學	323	陳羿愷	建國中學	312	李元裕	台中二中	314
陳琦翰	建國中學	329	曾昱豪	師大附中	1237	劉欣明	台中女中	318
詹士賢	建國中學	311	隋 毅	成功高中	305	吳芝宜	台中女中	309
張喬雅	延平高中	308	王 薇	中山女中	3群	陳慧齡	台中女中	312
陳昱達	建國中學	303	余欣珊	中正高中	306	賴妤欣	台中女中	312
林述君	松山高中	319	李思嫻	市大同高中	304	徐毓襌	台中女中	314
李孟璇	景美女中	3平	戴晏寧	建國中學	321	陳綺婷	台中女中	310
廖子瑩	北一女中	3數	兪乙立	建國中學	319	姚凱瑜	台中女中	304
林耕熏	北一女中	3良	吳承恩	成功高中	322	李靖淳	台中女中	314
楊華偉	大同高中	313	蔡昀唐	建國中學	304	陳奕均	台中女中	304
薛羽彤	北一女中	3良	陳聖寶	中正高中	305	蔡孟涵	明道中學	308
吳冠廷	延平高中	310	關育姍	板橋高中	303	陳沐道	明道中學	304
龔柏儒	國立竹東	310	蔡宜潔	北一女中	3儉	徐子庭	長億高中	602
洪懿亨	建國中學	319	許維帆	建國中學	304	林晏如	國立大里高中	301
林芳寧	市大同高中	301	簡上祐	成淵高中	310	洪妮端	國立大里高中	304
高晟軒	成功高中	302	葉思芃	師大附中	1246	陳佳穎	國立大里高中	303
林上竣	建國中學	325	黃雅萱	北一女中	3御	王 嵐	華盛頓高中	301
黃莉晴	板橋高中	308	鄭之琳	中山女中	3忠	莊婷雅	曉明高中部	3乙
寇 軒	師大附中	1259	劉子銘	建國中學	329	詹宜穎	僑泰高中	307
陳俊達	板橋高中	317	林筱儒	中山女中	3群	王彥中	台南一中	319
吳昌蓉	延平高中	311	葉 蘋	板橋高中	305	林奕辰	台南一中	319
賴又華	北一女中	3毅	劉弘煒	師大附中	1257	汪廷翰	台南一中	319
林懿莩	中山女中	3業	樂 正	建國中學	325	王子誠	台南一中	317
陳仕軒	成功高中	321	何冠蓁	北一女中	3儉	林德軒	台南一中	302
李承芳	中山女中	3義	溫彥彰	建國中學	328	陳亮圻	台南一中	315
楊劭楷	建國中學	303	賴冠儒	永春高中	301	程冠連	台南一中	307
黃韻帆	板橋高中	320	廖唯翔	建國中學	328	涂昀明	台南一中	307
李承翰	建國中學	325	蔡必婕	景美女中	3讓	郭品顯	台南一中	314
賈孟衡	建國中學	325	鄧鈺如	基隆女中	301	蔡昀知	台南一中	302
呂柔霏	松山高中	302	夏定安	北一女中	3毅	吳譽皇	台南一中	303
林柏鑫	延平高中	308	林裕騏	松山高中	310	蔡東哲	台南一中	312
吳柏萱	建國中學	307	鄭惟仁	建國中學	307	楊承煒	台南一中	301
鄭雅之	中山女中	3樂	望開怡	文華高中	302	周德峻	港明中學	3智
陳瑞邦	成功高中	313	王勻圻	文華高中	308	林姿伶	台南女中	310
魏宏旻	中和高中	311	陳映融	台中一中	310	林芝萱	台南女中	308
林育正	師大附中	1243	李淳懷	台中一中	302	林思妤	台南女中	312
高偉瀚	建國中學	313	游梁田	台中一中	319	陳廼婷	台南女中	311
陳信霖	建國中學	329	王勝輝	台中一中	324	黃涵纖	台南女中	319
陳俊霖	板橋高中	316	王奕閔	台中一中	318	陳琮翰	進修生	進修生
吳雨宸	北一女中	3儉	林宇勛	台中一中	317	黃偉綸	進 修 生	進修生
黃昱菱	市大同高中	313	羅笙維	台中一中	309	韓雅蓁	進修生	進修生
張軒羽	市大同高中	303	郭宇鈞	台中一中	317			

※ 尚未前來登記的同學，請回班登記。

www.learnschool.com.tw
劉毅英文教育機構
學費最低・效果最佳

高 中 部：台北市許昌街17號6F（捷運M8出口對面・學勤補習班） TEL：（02）2389-5212
國 中 部：台北市重慶南路一段10號7F（火車站前・學林補習班） TEL：（02）2361-6101
台中總部：台中市三民路三段125號7F（世界健身中心樓上） TEL：（04）2221-8861